The Cambridge Introduction to
Theatre Historiography

This *Introduction* – an indispensable "how to" guide for students
and teachers alike – investigates the methods and aims of historical
study in the performing arts, from archival research to historical
writing. Beginning with case studies on Shakespearean theatre and
avant-garde theatre, this study examines fundamental procedures
and problems in documentary history and cultural history. It
demonstrates how historians not only construct various kinds of
performance events but also place them in relation to the historical
agents, the political and social conditions, artistic traditions,
audience responses, and historical periods. Drawing upon
scholarship in classics, literary studies, art history, performance
studies, and general history, Postlewait shows how to ask
appropriate historical questions, construct evidence, use plays as
historical documents, eliminate faulty sources, challenge unreliable
witnesses, and develop historical arguments and narratives. The
book concludes with a survey of the "twelve cruxes" of research,
analysis, and writing in theatre history.

THOMAS POSTLEWAIT is Professor in the School of Drama,
University of Washington.

The Cambridge Introduction to
Theatre Historiography

THOMAS POSTLEWAIT

CAMBRIDGE
UNIVERSITY PRESS

CAMBRIDGE UNIVERSITY PRESS
Cambridge, New York, Melbourne, Madrid, Cape Town, Singapore, São Paulo, Delhi

Cambridge University Press
The Edinburgh Building, Cambridge CB2 8RU, UK

Published in the United States of America by Cambridge University Press, New York

www.cambridge.org
Information on this title: www.cambridge.org/9780521499170

First published 2009

Printed in the United Kingdom at the University Press, Cambridge

A catalogue record for this publication is available from the British Library

Library of Congress Cataloguing in Publication data
Postlewait, Thomas.
  The Cambridge introduction to theatre historiography / Thomas Postlewait.
    p.   cm.
  Includes bibliographical references and index.
  ISBN 978-0-521-49570-7 (hardback)
  1. Theatre–Historiography.   I. Title.   II. Title:
  Cambridge introduction to theatre historiography.
  PN2101.P67 2009
  792.09–dc22   2009000049

ISBN 978-0-521-49570-7 hardback
ISBN 978-0-521-49917-0 paperback

Contents

Illustrations

Acknowledgements

This book, which unites several aspects of my scholarship in theatre history, began two decades ago with an appointment at the Institute for Advanced Study in the Humanities at Edinburgh University. During those months in Scotland I was able to launch my studies on the problem of periodization. Three years later, when I received a Research Fellowship from the National Endowment for the Humanities, I continued my readings in historiography and wrote some initial sections of this book, including two published essays. Over several years, while working on this study – and taking on a number of other writing, editing, and administrative projects – I had to learn, rather slowly, that the task of composing an introduction to one's field of study is always a preliminary, not a final, project. After writing and rewriting various sections and publishing several articles, I completed a full draft of this book in 2004 during my sabbatical leave at Ohio State University. Then during a research leave in London in autumn 2006, thanks to an award I received from OSU, I was able to revise the manuscript (on the basis of the reader's report and suggestions from a few colleagues). Needless to say, I am deeply grateful for the research leaves and awards I have received over these years.

I published versions of my developing ideas in several journals: *Theatre Journal* (40.3: 299–318 and 43.2: 157–78), *Contemporary Theatre Review* (12.3: 9–35), *Nordic Theatre Studies* (Special Issue: 52–55), and *Assaph* (12: 1–31). I also published some ideas on theatre historiography in *Theatrical Events – Borders, Dynamics, Frames*, edited by Vicki Cremona, Willman Sauter, John Tulloch, and Hans van Maanen (Rodoophi, 2004: 33–52) and in the two editions of *Critical Theory and Performance*, edited by Janelle Reinelt and Joseph Roach (University of Michigan, 1992: 356–68 and 2007: 198–222). I thank the editors for their support and guidance. I am grateful to the publishers for permission to draw upon and reprint parts of these essays, which in revised form have contributed to this book.

I also appreciate the invitations to deliver talks at various locations, including University of Washington, University of Pittsburgh, University of Maryland, University of Texas, Arizona State University, Northwestern University, University of California at Santa Barbara, University of Illinois, Brown University, Helsinki University, Trinity College in Dublin, Tel Aviv University (both the Porter Institute and the Department of Theatre), Stockholm University, and Warwick University. It is a pleasure to thank faculty members and students at these universities for their invitations, conversations, and challenges. I am also beholden to several archives and research libraries, including the British Theatre Association (no longer in existence), the Theatre Museum at Covent

Garden, the British Library (in its old and new locations), and the Huntington Museum and Library. I also carried out research in the Victoria and Albert Museum, the National Library of Scotland, Harvard Theatre Collection, the Harry Ransom Center at the University of Texas, the Theatre Research Institute at Ohio State University, the Fales Collection at New York University, and the Billy Rose Collection at the New York Public Library at Lincoln Center. As well, I have spent many productive hours in the main libraries at Edinburgh University, MIT, Harvard University, University of Georgia, Indiana University, Ohio State University, and the University of Washington. I thank the staffs of all of these archives and libraries.

In the penultimate stage of this project I received a detailed reader's report from Don Wilmeth, who read the manuscript for Cambridge University Press. He has my sincere regard for his support, suggestions, and corrections. I also happily acknowledge the people at the press who have encouraged me throughout the process. Sarah Stanton commissioned the project. Vicki Cooper patiently encouraged me to define the study as an introductory text. Both Rebecca Jones and Elizabeth Davey, as accomplished editors, have guided me through the last stages of preparations for the text and illustrations. And a special note of gratitude for Audrey Cotterell, my sharp-eyed copy-editor. My appreciation goes to everyone at Cambridge University Press.

In both the early and later stages of this book project, I have received valuable commentary from colleagues in the American Society for Theatre Research and the International Federation for Theatre Research. For the last two decades, these two societies have been my professional homes away from home. I want to give special thanks to the members of the Theatre Historiography Working Group in IFTR. At meetings in many locations, including Stockholm, Helsinki, Dublin, Tel Aviv, Amsterdam, Worcester, Canterbury, College Park, Maryland, and St. Petersburg, I was able to share ideas with scholars from many countries. One does not write alone, but as part of a community of scholars whose research and ideas help to define the parameters of one's own thoughts and intellectual development. I therefore offer a special tribute to the members of the Working Group.

Over the years, as I developed my teaching and scholarship, my colleagues and departmental chairs at University of Georgia, Indiana University, and Ohio State University provided a supportive community. I thank them all. In turn, I am very pleased to join my new colleagues in the School of Drama, University of Washington. In particular, this book benefits from professional engagements with a number of the leading scholars in the field of theatre history, including Dennis Kennedy for his early support and continual nudging. Greatly appreciated. In addition, I offer a special word of thanks to Ed Pechter, who graciously read and commented upon several sections of this book-in-progress. Likewise, Gary Jay Williams, as editor of *Theatre Survey*, encouraged me to pull together my thoughts on historiography for a review essay, "Writing History Today," on a dozen books (*Theatre Survey* 41.2: 83–106). I also owe special thanks to Nean Couch, Curator of the Theatre Research Institute at Ohio State University, and Mechele Leon, Department of Theatre and Film at the University of Kansas, for their timely help in procuring some of the illustrations.

To Bruce McConachie I offer, yet again, my thanks and praise. Ever since we worked together on our co-edited book, *Interpreting the Theatrical Past* (University of Iowa Press, 1989), Bruce has read my work and raised crucial questions, doubts, and alternative perspectives. I also appreciate the comments he passed on to me from his doctoral students at University of Pittsburgh who read several sections (in various draft stages). I am equally indebted to Tracy C. Davis, who last year assigned the full typescript to her doctoral students at Northwestern University. Tracy's summary of her students' responses and her astute comments on my ideas and organization proved invaluable in the final revision. As I know from working with both Tracy and Bruce on several projects, they are the best of scholarly colleagues, for they demand of others what they demand of themselves: the highest standards of scholarship.

Many colleagues have engaged me on historiographical issues and procedures, but I want to give a special nod of respect and gratitude to John Astington, Christopher Balme, Rose Bank, Herb Blau, Michael Booth, Jacky Bratton, Sarah Bryant-Bertail, Marvin Carlson, Sue-Ellen Case, Gay Gibson Cima, Claire Cochrane, Jim Davis, Peter Davis, Joseph Donohue, Richard Dutton, Jody Enders, Jon Erickson, Peter Eversmann, Buck Favorini, Lesley Ferris, Erika Fischer-Lichte, Spencer Golub, Frank Hildy, Peter Holland, Robert D. Hume, Odai Johnson, Peggy Knapp, Michal Kobialka, Pirkko Koski, Kim Marra, David Mayer, Cary Mazer, Judith Milhous, Janelle Reinelt, Joseph Roach, Freddie Rokem, Eli Rozek, Willmar Sauter, Virginia Scott, Laurence Senelick, Brian Singleton, Ron Vince, David Wiles, Simon Williams, Steve Wilmer, Barry Witham, Bill Worthen, and Yael Zahry-Levo. No doubt I have failed to credit some colleagues, but the Works cited section of this book provides a fuller register of my obligations and appreciations.

There are, of course, many different ways to write theatre history. No one has the final word. The continuing vitality of the field is most evident for me in my editorial work. Since 1991 I have edited a book series, "Studies in Theatre History and Culture," at the University of Iowa Press. I have been amazingly fortunate to have the support and guidance of the two Directors of the press – the wry Paul Zimmer, followed by the sagacious Holly Carver. Besides the invaluable opportunity to work closely with scholars from around the world, the editing has taught me much about not only the diversity and complexity of theatre history as a discipline but also the many possible methods and approaches that historians can apply successfully. This understanding has guided my editorial work at Iowa, beginning with *Interpreting the Theatrical Past* (1989), which I edited with Bruce McConachie. Two decades later the same commitment to multiple viewpoints has led to yet another Iowa book on theatre historiography, *Representing the Past* (2009), which I co-edited with Charlotte Canning. In between these two collections of essays on the historiography of performance, I have been able to publish thirty-five books in my series, written on an amazingly wide range of topics by theatre scholars from ten different countries. My debt to the Iowa writers, one and all, is profound. Many of their methods and ideas are woven into the texture of this introductory book.

In addition to the many benefits I have received during the last two decades from friends, colleagues, journals, presses, institutions, and even strangers, I owe my deepest gratitude to my wife, Marilyn L. Brownstein. I do not need to name and praise her special qualities; nor is it necessary to catalogue my abiding appreciation for her many contributions as partner and scholar (and editor of this editor). She knows. It is sufficient to say that together we have been able to shape and serve our mutual interests, commitments, careers, and goals. Thank you; you're the perfect postmodernist for my antiquarian personality. What a great adventure it has been – from Boston to Athens, Georgia, from Columbus, Ohio to Whidbey Island.

Finally, I offer my heartfelt appreciation to my graduate students, including those who took seminars with me on theatre history and historiography at Georgia, Indiana, Ohio State University, and now Washington. I extend my special regard (but no more marginal comments and demands for revision) to the two dozen students who wrote their theses and dissertations with me. This book is for all of you.

Introduction

The active pursuit of truth is our proper business. We have no excuse for
conducting it badly or unfittingly. But failure to capture our prey is another
matter. For we are born to quest after it; to possess it belongs to a greater
power ... The world is but a school of inquiry.

> Michel de Montaigne, *Essays*, Book Three, Chapter 8 (1580)

I adore the true, the possible.

> Vincent Van Gogh, letter to Émile Bernard (1889)

On some preliminary matters

Historical inquiry – the pursuit of truths about the past within the conditions and
constraints of possible knowledge – is the subject of this study. Throughout this book,
I examine the procedures and principles that historians, including theatre historians,
follow in their research, analysis, interpretation, and writing. All historians, in the
process of reconstructing past events, need to determine the authenticity of sources
and the reliability of eyewitnesses. In turn, they must transform the artifacts into facts,
develop supporting evidence for their hypotheses, place historical events in appropriate contexts, confront their own organizing assumptions and categorical ideas, and
construct arguments based upon principles of possibility and plausibility. Certainty is
often attained in matters of *who*, *what*, *where*, and *when*. But the answers for *how* and
why usually remain open to debate among historians.

In the spirit of historical inquiry, I raise many questions, and, where appropriate,
I attempt to provide some answers. Three key words in the title – *introduction, theatre,*
and *historiography* – signal my primary aims and set the organizational parameters for
meeting those aims. This book provides an *introduction* to the basic methods of
historical scholarship. Introductory knowledge is primary; primary knowledge is
essential. All historians, be they novices or old masters, should understand and be able
to apply the basic procedures of historical inquiry. With each new research project,
the fundamental requirements of these procedures reassert themselves.

All historians need to follow reliable research methods, which are the primary
building blocks of historical description and interpretation. Unfortunately, some
historians produce sloppy, flawed scholarship, either because they never learned the
basic procedures of historical methodology or because they ignore or misapply the
primary guidelines for research and analysis, as the historian A. M. Momigliano

complained in 1954: "Too much historical research is being done by people who do not know why they are doing it and without regard to the limits imposed by the evidence. An improvement in this respect is both possible and desirable" (1966: 111). A half-century later the need for improvement remains paramount.

By *theatre* I mean the comprehensive field of the performing arts, including theatre, dance, opera, folk theatre, puppetry, parades, processions, spectacles, festivals, circuses, public conventions, and related performance events.[1] All kinds of theatrical activities in the past – no matter what their mode of delivery: stage performance, public arena, radio, television, film – may require historical investigation and understanding. This is the case for events that occurred three millennia ago, three centuries ago, or three days ago. For the purposes of this book, I will draw most of my examples and case studies from my own specific areas of historical research and classroom teaching in theatre history. Yet throughout this study I have attempted to identify research procedures and interpretive strategies that apply across all areas and types of performance history.

And by *historiography* I mean not only the methods that define and guide the practice of historical study and writing but also the self-reflexive mindset that leads us to investigate the processes and aims of historical understanding. Etymologically, the word *historiography* means *the writing of history*. In this sense, it usually refers to the study of how history has been written across the centuries, from Herodotus to Carlo Ginzburg. Sometimes we study history (i.e., what happened in the past), sometimes we study the historians and what they wrote (i.e., the methods and aims of the reports about what happened in the past). In the process of examining what historians do and how they do it, we can also consider some of the fundamental traits of historical thinking. In doing so, we are entering the realm of epistemology. I take up these basic matters of historical inquiry throughout this book because the traits of the inquiring mind, so crucial to historical understanding, underlie the procedural traits of effective research and good writing. The processes of inquiry serve both the historian and the historiographer. The quality of the historian's scholarship depends directly upon the quality of the questions being asked.

Although the word *historiography* evokes the writing methods of historians, it has come to mean much more, including the theory and philosophy of history. We thus need to keep in mind this warning provided by Peter Novick:

> The word *historiography* can be confusing. Running through the English language there is a distinction between "logys" and "graphys": *biology* (the science of life) and *biography* (the description of life); *geology* (the science of the earth) and *geography* (the description of the earth), etc. The once respectable word *historiology* has dropped out of just about everybody's vocabulary, and *historiography* has had to do double duty for both *historical science* and descriptive accounts of historical writing.[2]

So, like the word *history*, the word *historiography* takes its meanings from the way a writer uses it. Writers are not always clear.

Besides these three organizing concepts for this book, there is one other very familiar and crucial yet often ambiguous word, *history*, which needs clarification. The attentive reader has probably noticed already that I have used this word in several different ways. In its dozen or more meanings and applications, the word *history* can refer to or designate

(1) whatever happened in the past; the actual events that occurred; this aspect of history is sometimes called "history-as-actuality" or "history-as-event";

(2) the records we have for whatever happened in the past; these documents are usually located in some kind of archive, though they also exist in people's memories, stories, songs, and cultural practices; the familiar documents or sources that historians usually investigate are often called "history-as-record" or "archival documents";

(3) the process of carrying out research; the act of investigating the records of what happened; in this sense, one is researching history or, as some people say, "doing history";

(4) the report that a historian prepares; it is usually written but it can also be oral; and today it can also be delivered as a video, film, tape, disk, photo-montage, or web document; this report, which draws upon "history-as-record" in order to describe "history-as-event," attempts to be true to both of them; when historians present a report, they are providing an understanding – that is, a version – of what happened; this finished product is often called "history-as-written" or "history-as-account";

(5) the kind of historical report that attempts to list only the basic information for a specific time period; it may, in the manner of an account book, offer some names, dates, purchases, payments, and similar kinds of recordkeeping and transactions; it may even offer some descriptive information as part of the documentary record, but it does not provide a fully developed survey or causal narrative; because its interpretive aspects are brief or seemingly nonexistent, it is usually called an "annals," an "account," a "record," or a "chronicle";

(6) the kind of historical report that not only places events in a descriptive sequence but also explains and interprets them; that is, besides providing who, what, where, and when, the report covers how and why; it may attempt to explain the significance of the events and analyze their developmental causes; it is called an "interpretive history";

(7) an approach to historical study that focuses primarily on the sources; this approach gives priority to the gathering and maintaining of historical data and objects, which are valued for themselves; all libraries depend upon and benefit from the dedication and discipline of antiquarians; the collecting of manuscripts and material objects and the building of archives has no specific origin (for the attempts to compile and collect records can be traced from the earliest clay tablets and stone carvings), but systems of collecting – from cabinets of curiosities to national archives – gained momentum from the Renaissance forward as personal, then public, libraries multiplied; this impulse to gather historical data and objects is sometimes called "antiquarianism";

(8) a genre, type, or kind of writing that is distinct from other kinds of prose writing, such as narrative fiction or the literary essay; today in libraries and bookstores this genre of prose writing usually has its own section, apart from the "fiction" section;

(9) a genre, type, or kind of writing that *is not* distinct from narrative or story; so understood, all forms of narrative are joined or collapsed together; for example, the same word, such as *histoire* in French, can mean both "history" and "story"; this double meaning also occurs in various languages, including English (e.g., Henry Fielding's most famous novel is titled *The History of Tom Jones*); in this sense both history and fiction are understood as narrative or storytelling forms; adding to this confusion over the meanings of *history* and *fiction*, some people argue that all historical writings partake of narrative techniques; a few people even go so far as to claim that history and fiction cannot be distinguished from one another;

(10) an academic discipline, which in modern times is usually located in departments of history within universities; during the eighteenth and nineteenth centuries, especially at German and French universities and institutes, historians developed "positivist," "scientific," or "objective" research procedures and source criticism for the historical discipline; in the process antiquarianism developed into a professional method of historical study; this discipline today attempts to deal systematically with the past; it is sometimes called a "branch of knowledge"; within the modern university system this discipline is usually located in either the humanities or the social sciences; the lack of agreement on the institutional home of the discipline is yet another sign of the confusion over not only how historical study should be constituted (e.g., is it an art or a science?) but also what kind(s) of methods it should use;

(11) a "discourse," one among several that operate in human society at any period; the discourse defines, articulates, and shapes knowledge; in recent years the concept of discourse, variously defined and applied, has been used in linguistics, cultural history, philosophy, and social theory to characterize the epistemological codes, rules, and conditions of language that organize and classify various fields of knowledge, including both *the practices* of the discipline and institution of history and *the meanings* of history that the discipline produces;

(12) the various branches of knowledge that apply a historical perspective to the study of human existence, culture, and thought; in this sense, the concept of history provides a foundational definition and method for a number of disciplines, including archeology, classics, paleography, architecture, numismatics, linguistics, language studies, religious studies, racial and gender studies, speech and rhetoric, psychology, sociology, political science, law, education, philosophy, art, music, and theatre; all of these disciplines organize their subject matter historically, though there are additional ways of organizing and pursuing knowledge in these fields; because each of these disciplines charts an aspect of human history (e.g., use of coins, etymology of words, political systems, philosophical concepts, etc.), it is possible to study the history of knowledge in many

fields or disciplines; this expansive meaning of *history* guided R. G. Collingwood's argument in *The Idea of History*, where he claims that "history is what the science of human nature professed to be" because "historical knowledge is the knowledge of what mind has done in the past;"[3] from this perspective, history encompasses all of the disciplines of human activity and knowledge in the arts, humanities, and social sciences;

(13) the various branches of knowledge that study some aspect of science from a historical perspective; whatever their subject matter – biology, microbiology, genetics, botany, zoology, geology, ecology, astronomy, neuroscience, geography – all of these disciplines use history as one of the major ways to organize the subject matter; consequently, the sciences, excepting the abstract, logical, or "pure" fields such as mathematics, are historical in their basic procedures (and even mathematics is wedded to history when the development of the discipline is considered); and

(14) a comprehensive understanding that applies to all fields of knowledge, from archeology to zoology; each discipline has its own history. In this expansive meaning, history serves as both the mode and method of knowledge for all of these branches of knowledge; this grand claim for history is based upon the epistemological understanding that human knowledge depends upon "the discovery of time," as Stephen Toulmin and June Goodfield insist.[4]

Because of our temporal consciousness, our historical understanding has become as crucial to the study of the natural world as to the study of the human world. Accordingly, numbers 12 and 13, and probably number 11 as well, collapse into number 14. Or, more ambitiously, history, in its application to all areas of human endeavor, "could sweep all other disciplines into its intellectual orbit and, from a certain point of view, subsume them," as Donald R. Kelley points out in his study of the idea and disciplines of history since the Enlightenment.[5] No doubt this grand perspective is quite satisfying to historians, who can then proudly assume that their field is the fundamental basis of all knowledge. From this perspective, historians are the keepers of the keys to the kingdom of knowledge.[6] History is the queen of all disciplines.

> Historiography (that is, *history* and *writing*) bears within its own name the paradox – almost an oxymoron – of a relation established between two antinomic terms, between the real and discourse. Its task is one of connecting them and, at the point where the link cannot be imagined, of working as if the two were being joined.
> Michel de Certeau, *The Writing of History* (1988: xxvii)

Although these various meanings of *history* are relevant, either explicitly or implicitly, to any study in historiography, including theatre historiography, I must insist that I have no intention of writing a study of all of these ideas and their possible implications. For the most part, I am interested in the basic procedures of historical scholarship, which means I will focus on numbers 1, 2, 3, and 4, with some attention also given to the problem of narrative (as both a trope and a genre) in the writing of history. Throughout this study I attempt to specify how I am using the word *history*. Often I will refer to number 1 as *history* (or just "the past" or "past events") whereas I will refer to number 2 as "historical records," "documents," "sources," or "the archive." I will refer to number 3 as "historical research" and to number 4 as "historical writing." I have also tried to avoid using the word *history* by itself to imply or signal any of the other possible meanings of the word. If, for example, I refer to the narrative genre, the disciplinary field, or the discourse of history, I will use these additional phrases in order to clarify what I am trying to say.[7]

Primarily, then, this book offers an introductory study of the operating procedures and shaping aims of theatre historians, as they practice their discipline today. In order to do justice to my task, I have imposed some serious restrictions and exclusions on the historiographical issues that will be considered. For example, this book does not present a survey or analysis of the major historians, from Herodotus and Thucydides to modern times. For the interested reader, there are already several worthy surveys that should be consulted.[8]

Although I draw upon the ideas of specific historians, especially Marc Bloch, Louis Gottschalk, M. I. Finley, and Carlo Ginzburg, I am not offering a survey of their historical methods. Also, I am not investigating historical theories and practices within specific eras, such as the Enlightenment. Nor do I consider historical ideas within intellectual movements, such as Romanticism. Here, too, there are several excellent studies to consult.[9] As for the wide range of approaches to historical study in modern times, such as the Annales history, Marxist history, women's history, intellectual history, cultural history, racial and ethnic history, and postmodernist history, both Georg G. Iggers and Michael Bentley have offered succinct interpretations of these various developments in historiography.[10] In addition, there are some excellent overviews and critiques of one or more of the modern approaches to historical study.[11]

Moreover, I am not writing a philosophy of history, though I have benefited from the writings of a number of philosophers, especially Raymond Aron and Paul Ricoeur.[12] Aron's measured critique of positivism and objectivity in *Introduction to the Philosophy of History* provides a solid foundation for my approach to historical methodology. While maintaining that the "proof of facts" and the "criticism of sources" are preliminary steps in historical research, Aron argues that historical inquiry is necessarily an interpretive procedure that limits the positivist principles of objectivity. "Thus we must admit the basic distinctions between *the establishment of historical facts* and *the explanation of changes*" (his italics).[13] These distinctions are necessary, Aron insists, not only because "any interpretation is a reconstruction" of the past events and their causes but also because "the plurality of interpretations is an incontestable fact, which the historian must accept."[14] Aron's analysis of several different interpretive approaches in historical scholarship anchors this argument. In the process of examining these approaches, he provides a basic consideration of the idea of historical change, one of the most important yet evasive concepts in historical study. He also provides a valuable analysis of the concepts of historical causality and historical determinism. Then, having assembled the results of this analysis, he navigates a course between the "limits of historical objectivity" and "the limits of relativism in history."[15] Like Aron, I am committed to this middle course between positivism and relativism. Though I will not recapitulate his philosophical analysis, which I cannot begin to match, I will attempt to demonstrate throughout this book how historical study may go forward within the limits that Aron designates. I intend to present issues and problems in methodology as clearly as possible, without recourse to philosophical terminology and debates. I do not assume that the reader has studied Aron's writings (or those of any other philosopher of history).

No such thing as a *historical reality* exists ready made, so that science merely has to reproduce it faithfully. The historical reality, because it is human, is *ambiguous* and *inexhaustible*.
Raymond Aron, *Introduction to the Philosophy of History* (1961: 118)

Paul Riceour's philosophical writings have been even more valuable for me. Riceour, who praised Aron's assessment of the problem of historical objectivity, presented his own critique of the ideas of objectivity and subjectivity in historical knowledge in his early book *History and Truth* (1965). Over a decade later, he returned to historiography in *Hermeneutics and the Human Sciences* (1981). His reflections on key issues in epistemology and hermeneutics, including the concepts of event and context in relation to "the question of the subject" and systems of discourse, have informed my own consideration of how to construct historical events. I have also benefited from his studies of the "narrative function" in historical interpretation that he presents in *Time and Narrative* (1984, 1985, 1988). Because all historians must represent people and events from the past, the representative methods and assumptions that guide this task are a central concern in all phases of historical study, from initial research to concluding narrative.

Both Aron and Riceour provide an epistemological foundation and justification for historical practice, especially in terms of their analyses of *event, representation, objectivity, narrative, time, change,* and *causality*. I will feature these concepts when I take up the practical matters of historical scholarship: the construction of an event, the criteria for evidence, the narrative aspects of historical writing, the plurality of interpretive models in history, and the nature of the historian's judgements. Because historical practice, not philosophy, is my concern, I do not need to retrace the epistemological arguments of Aron and Riceour.[16] My usage of certain controversial terms and concepts should be clear within the practical context of my investigation of historical procedures. I am not writing a study in hermeneutics or epistemology, though I necessarily take up key issues in human understanding and knowledge as I probe the nature of theatre historiography.

> Given the intermediate position in which hermeneutics operates, it follows that its work is not to develop a procedure of understanding, but to clarify the conditions in which understanding takes place.
> Hans-Georg Gadamer, *Truth and Method* (1997: 295)

In theatre historiography there are several foundational studies that contributed to this book, including the one that Bruce McConachie and I compiled in 1989.[17] During the last couple of decades a number of important studies in theatre and performance studies have refined and expanded historical methods in the broad field of study.[18] Throughout this book, I draw upon the work of my colleagues. R. W. Vince, for example, has provided valuable surveys of the development of the field of theatre history.[19] He has also described the emergence of the academic discipline of theatre history in the universities since the nineteenth century.[20] In recent years the field of theatre studies has been greatly expanded and transformed by valuable studies on women's lives and careers, gender construction, feminist methodologies, ethnic and racial studies, and the concepts of diversity and difference.[21] This work informs my own ideas on historical issues and problems, but I have not tried to summarize these studies and related issues. Likewise, because major work has emerged on historiography and dance studies, I do not need to introduce this topic and work.[22] Nor do I need to offer a study of the various critical theories that get applied to theatre history and performance studies today (e.g., theatre semiotics, media studies, postcolonial studies, race theory, cultural studies, gender and sexualities, psychoanalysis). Janelle G. Reinelt and Joseph Roach have done this admirably in *Critical Theory and Performance*.[23] Although I insist that the basic procedures of historical research are foundational for any and all of these specific critical approaches, I do not offer an evaluation of the historical strengths and weaknesses of the various critical methodologies in the study of cultural history. Likewise, I do not need to struggle with the meanings of certain widely used concepts in theatre studies, such as "performance." Marvin Carlson, for example, has done this task with his typical thoroughness and brilliance.[24] And the concept of "theatricality" has been investigated by several people, including Tracy C. Davis and myself.[25]

What, then, is there to consider in historical study? Despite these various exclusions, this introductory study still has a full agenda in the field of historical research and writing. My intention, accordingly, is to map out and analyze these fundamental features, as they operate in theatre history and performance studies. I will be concerned with various methodological matters, including the uses of primary and secondary evidence, the techniques for applying both internal and external criticism to evidence, the standards of credibility and authenticity that are applied in the examination of documents, the distinction between a source and a fact as well as the distinction between a fact and a piece of evidence, the nature of circumstantial evidence in historical argument, the problem of assigning motives to human actions that occurred in the past, and the relationship between historical events and their possible contexts.

Given my focus on practical matters, this is a "how to" book. And, in some measure, it is also a "how not to" book. For example, the two case studies in Part One – on Shakespearean theatre and avant-garde theatre – provide an opportunity to examine the kinds of methodological procedures and problems that theatre historians confront on a regular basis. By means of these two case studies I illustrate some of the drawbacks that derive from our tendency to separate documentary scholarship from cultural history. Throughout the book I offer suggestions about historical practices and warnings about misapplied procedures, but I provide no single model for theatre historians to follow. Instead, I am interested in the basic methods and challenges in historical study that we all share, the fundamental features of historical inquiry. In this endeavor I share the aims expressed by Stephen E. Toulmin in his book *The Uses of Argument*: "to raise problems, not to solve them; to draw attention to a field of inquiry, rather than to survey it fully; and to provoke discussion rather than to serve as a systematic treatise."[26] This focus on the fundamental factors and questions of historical study serves as a sufficient and worthy aim, befitting the complexity of the issues. In this spirit, I also subscribe to the principle that Richard Kostelanetz voiced in an introductory book that he wrote on the avant-garde arts: "Every 'introduction,' I believe, has an obligation to direct its readers elsewhere."[27] Throughout this book I will refer readers to various resources that might be of interest and value, including the writings of other historians, theatre historians, and philosophers who have helped me to think about this enterprise. And in various notes I will identify publications on specific areas of study and on particular aspects of historical methodology and theory (e.g., recent scholarship on classical Greek theatre, the uses and problems of visual evidence, parallel developments in methods of art history). In this way, I offer a guide to further readings in historiographical scholarship, but each reader may decide what is useful.[28]

In order to launch this investigation into theatre historiography, I want to begin with a preliminary overview that will suggest the range of topics and issues that I take up in the following chapters. For heuristic purposes, let's consider some simple diagrams that suggest the basic categories that guide our historical assumptions:

| EVENT | | CONTEXT |

This two-part separation illustrates our starting point for describing the historical task. Some historians, such as microhistorians, place primary emphasis upon individual events, which they investigate in great detail before moving outward to the conditions that may be contributing factors in the individual lives and actions. Other historians, such as those associated with the Annales group, place primary emphasis upon the large, abiding conditions and structures that direct historical conditions and development. Individual events – and individual lives – are described as consequences of the shaping context. In self-defining ways, then, the microhistorians *narrate* specific historical actions or events; the Annales historians *describe* the conditions that frame and explain the events. Both, however, are committed to cultural and social interpretation. Yet this division between microhistorians and structuralist historians seems to reinforce a basis and widespread understanding in historical scholarship: we study events by placing them within some kind of narrative; then we identify the large social, economic, religious, or political institutions, forces, or ideologies that contain and determine the meaning of the narrative. Throughout this book I address this fundamental division and understanding, which, I believe, hinders our historical research and methods of interpretation.

> . . . events can only be narrated, while structures can only be described.
> Reinhart Koselleck, *Futures Past: On the Semantics of Historical Time* (1985: 105)

Of course, there will always be some scholars, including a number of theatre historians, who attend almost exclusively to individual events. They describe the details of the event, then quickly conclude their investigation. They often fail to place events in relation to one another, either synchronically or diachronically. At best, the context is evoked as a familiar generalization (e.g., categories of racial, sexual, or national identity, a standard period concept). By contrast, there are other scholars who champion a reigning idea, derived from this or that theory. All events are illustrations of the theory, which defines the context and controls the interpretation.

Both types of scholars, the isolationist and the universalist, perpetuate a simplified idea of event and context because they are committed to a dualistic model of thinking. The isolationist gives us events that supposedly explain themselves; the universalist gives us events as formulaic illustrations of a system or theory. These two types of historians, though separated by their opposing ideas of historical procedure, are quite equal in their reductive approach to historical study. Because of their limitations, we are wise to distance ourselves from them. Yet despite our rejection of these overly neat polarities, we still tend to perceive the ideas of *event* and *context* in dualistic ways. We may refuse to isolate an event from its context, but our methods of joining them still may depend upon our own two-part formulas. Typically, instead of defining the relationship as an opposition (i.e., event versus context), we take up the idea of mimesis or representation, which suggests some kind of correspondence or interrelationship. The one equals the other.

Usually, this relational idea suggests that the event presents, portrays, reflects, or contains aspects of a representational world. The characters on stage bear comparison to people in the world. The Aristotelian principle of mimesis yokes the event to its context. This relationship suggests the mirror metaphor, which has often been tied to the idea of imitation, though the idea of representation is more appropriate. As we will see, various scholars, including Raymond Williams, prefer the metaphor of "embodying" for the relationship between theatrical events and the conditioning contexts. Because of the idea of structural enclosure, this relationship could be represented in this manner:

EVENT = CONTEXT

Or, if we wish to insist upon the determining condition of the enclosure, we might surround the event with the context. In this manner, we highlight the totality of the context, which frames or surrounds the event:

```
                    C O N T E X T
        C                                      C
        O                                      O
        N                                      N
        T            ┌─────────┐               T
        E            │  EVENT  │               E
        X            └─────────┘               X
        T                                      T
                    C O N T E X T
```

According to this historical mandate, all evidence for the event is derived from the context. In general terms, this model may satisfy our need to place historical events within framing structures and systems (e.g., geographical and economic conditions in the Annales model, the Marxist idea of base and superstructure). But what do we actually mean by the general concept of "context" when it is understood, at least potentially, as the source of all possible factors within the full circuit, frame, structure, circumference, or periphery of experience?

The problem with this idea of context (and, thus, this model) is that it tends to make the context both a singular and a total condition that completely controls the event. Like the universalist method, which imposes a theoretical idea onto the historical event, this idea of a determining context makes the event a mere effect of whatever external factors the historian identifies. Human motives, intentions, and acts become negligible (a strange position to take for explaining the history of creative endeavors and accomplishments in the arts).

Each of these models of event and context – along with the language we typically use to describe the relationship (e.g., to reflect, encompass, frame, control) – depend upon a two-part division, one that is usually too reductive in its explanatory potential. Also, the ideas of connection and correspondence – imitation, mirroring, equaling, embodying, enclosing – all seem too simple. In the process, the event and context become interchangeable images of one another, a tautological circle if we are not careful. Whatever the systematic explanation, we are usually caught within a binary that reduces historical study to inappropriate formulas.

If we want to reconceive the basic binary, we need a better model of the relationship between event and context. The solution is to rethink the nature of the binarism. That is, the categorical division is part of the problem. By changing the category, we change the organizational procedures and questions. Although each event may have a singular identity (though its contributing parts can be very complex, such as the hundreds of semiotic codes in a performance event), there is no reason to define the context in the singular. Let me suggest, as the next step in reconfiguration, that we consider a four-part model for the context. Of course all visual diagrams and models, though of pedagogical value, are simplified propositions. If taken up as systematic procedures, they are counterproductive. But my hope is that some clarity may be achieved with these models, which, in turn, may help us to assess the analytical models we use historically when we attempt to place events within their possible contexts.

I begin with yet another familiar polarity, but one that will be transformed into multiple identities. This two-part relationship posits some kind of correspondence between art works and the world they represent:

$$\boxed{\text{EVENT} - \text{WORLD}}$$

Initially, this model implies that theatrical events provide a perspective *on* and *of* the world. And the world, correspondingly, provides a basis and meanings for the event. (Note that the troubling equal sign (=) used earlier has now been replaced by a dash, which could have arrow heads on both ends; influence runs in both directions.) Every human event articulates and mediates a series of relations with the world of which it is a part. Our actions and reactions occur as continual negotiations, back and forth, with the surrounding conditions.[29] The world, though, is not really one thing, but in fact many factors, including the material and immaterial conditions of human existence. This idea of *world*, which implies everything in the global environment that human beings participate in and that art is capable of representing, includes the human and natural world, the semantic fields of language, the semiotic codes of communication, the psychological conditions of human life, the economic, political, and geographical orders that operate in human culture, the many social institutions, and the animal and material worlds. All of the codes, norms, systems, institutions, values, and conditions of a person's world are in play. The representational process of the theatrical event, though partial and often distorting, reveals aspects of the world while also drawing upon that world for the signifying content. This is equally the case for a realistic or an expressionist production, an actor's face in a film or an elaborate mask in Noh theatre, a puppet show or Mardi Gras costume. Aspects of the formal design, the formal cause, result from – not just represent – the world. The relationship is a two-way street, an exchange program. Theatre events are capable of representing and being influenced by any aspect of the world, in a multitude of modes, means, and manners. They also engage with alternative and possible worlds, the "as if" versions of existence. The theatrical arts have always been an important arena for representing the full imaginative realms of possibility (and even impossibility), as we fill the stage or the film with gods, demons, aliens, creatures, and a wild range of human beings.

Then, in addition to the exchanges between event and world, the theatrical event can be understood in terms of agency, specifically the relationship that operates between the event and those who created it: the playwright, the director, the performers, the designers. These people who plan, organize, and realize the event are all agents. This process of agency can be visualized as:

$$\boxed{\text{AGENTS} - \text{EVENT}}$$

The idea of *agents* includes the various meanings of author and authoring, both actual and implied, both direct and indirect. Each agent, carrying out an intentional program, is to be understood, in Aristotelian terms of the four causes, as an effective cause that results in the material and formal features or causes of the full action. The event also embodies aspects of the agents' final cause: the purposes and aims. Some events have a single agent, but theatre events have various agents who contribute to the making of the event. If all goes well, the event reveals a combined purpose. The ideas of agent and agency also imply the various strands of creativity: inspiration, imagination, originality, genius, and the muses. Agency taps those inspirational forces that the romantic writers celebrated with the metaphors of lamp and fire, active energy in contradistinction to the mirror metaphor derived from the concept of mimesis.[30]

In turn, the event takes part of its meaning – its contextual significance – from how it is received and understood by spectators, critics, the general public, and society at large. Reception and audience are always part of the context for theatrical events.

EVENT – RECEPTIONS

The idea of *reception* includes the conditions of perception and evaluation, the processes of comprehension by various people – their horizon of expectations and their methods of interpreting (and misinterpreting) the event at the time. The reception reveals the consequences of the event, its completion. Theatrical events obviously influence those who perceive the artistic endeavors. The reception is recorded by eyewitnesses, especially in modern times by theatre reviewers and critics. Their reception is part of the event, the final action in the sequence of making a theatrical event. The meaning of the event is achieved in the reception of the various spectators. But their reception is not the full significance of the event, even though theatre reviews often serve as our sources for the meaning of the theatrical event. We quote the critics as if they are the arbitrators: London critics said this, New York critics said that. Their assessments are major sources for reconstructing a theatrical event, but surely this is too easy, too reductive. The reviews tell us what the event meant for a handful of influential people, but they are only one part of the contextual meanings. The *reception*, though often given a singular identity, engages a range of possible responses from spectators, emotional as well as intellectual, psychological as well as ethical, social as well as political. The receptions may engender pathos, compassion, identification, approval, disapproval, judgement, understanding, misunderstanding, and many other possible perceptions and evaluations. The reception culminates (and sometimes fulfills) the purposes of the agents (the final cause). Or in some cases the reception disrupts or rejects those aims. In various ways, then, the reception may tell us things about not only the actual audience but also the implied audience (which the event and its conceivers attempted to evoke, reach, influence, satisfy, provoke, etc.). The reception may entail both those who attend the event and the community factors and conditions (e.g., governmental powers, the law, the beliefs and values of the society, the aesthetic tastes and expectations of the era). Aspects of the reception may be passive, while other aspects may be active. The etymology of the word reception implies *receptive*, but the reaction can be anything but. Sometimes the manner of reception influences the event, which undergoes adaptation, even transformation. And responses can influence subsequent artistic works, as happened when Ibsen, angry over the response to *Ghosts*, wrote his next play, *An Enemy of the People*, as an individual statement and challenge.[31] Whatever the case, the reception is a significant part of the meaning of the event.

There is, besides the contextual factors of agents, world, and receptions, a fourth and equally important contributor to the event: the artistic heritage.

EVENT – ARTISTIC HERITAGE

Each and every artistic event occurs in relation to certain aspects of its heritage. The idea of *artistic heritage* includes the artistic traditions, conventions, norms, and codes of not only drama and theatre but all of the arts. Every artistic event has a relation to the artistic tradition or heritage in which it operates, to which it refers, and out of which it shapes its own separate identity – sometimes in homage, sometimes in revolt. The heritage encompasses the artistic milieu of the event, the kinds or genres of drama, the canons, the aesthetic ideas and institutions, the artistic ideologies that may influence the work, the crafts of playwriting and theatre production, the mentors and models, the rhetorical codes and styles, the rules and regulations, the available poetics, and the cultural systems. The artistic heritage is the full *musée imaginaire* that artists draw upon, consciously and unconsciously. This heritage contributes to the intertextuality of artistic works, the processes that T. S. Eliot called "tradition and the individual talent."[32] Each artistic work is in dialogue with the heritage, yet another two-way street. This dialogue pertains equally to those who create and those who respond to the performance event.

All artistic works, no matter how innovative they may be, exist in relation to an artistic heritage of conventions and models. The voices of the ancestors echo in works, even when an artist may reject or trash the tradition. Jarry's *Ubu Roi*, no less than Racine's *Phèdre*, evokes many codes of the artistic heritage. These formal codes, styles, and conventions are part of the signifying systems that impart identity and meaning to the works, to the event. A tradition may be specific to the type of artwork, such as genre conventions for the writing of tragedy. Or a tradition may be quite expansive, such as the concepts of mimesis, verisimilitude, or realism in the arts. Whatever the case, the traditions provide a major historical context for understanding not only the formal identities of artworks but also the potential meanings that get identified in the reception processes.

These four basic aspects of the context for a theatrical event may help us break out of the two-part division of event and context. Even though we are still thinking in dualistic terms by relating each of the four factors to the event, we have created more clarity by breaking the general idea of context into its several component parts.

Within each of these four basic conditions, a plurality of factors can be identified. Various aspects of the world may contribute to the identifying traits and meanings of a specific theatrical event. Various agents participate in the making of the event. Many traits of the artistic heritage are in play. And the reception engages many people and conditions. Thus, each of these four factors – world, agents, receptions, and artistic heritage – *need to be understood as part of the event as well as part of the context.*

Moreover, we want to integrate these four definitive parts of the context. Our heuristic model, therefore, might take this visual design:

	WORLD	
AGENTS	EVENT	RECEPTIONS
	ARTISTIC HERITAGE	

The event is situated in relation to each of the four contributing factors. It is also in tension with each of them, a series of dialogues and exchanges that the historian may chart. As Elin Diamond notes, "Every performance, if it is intelligible as such, embeds features of previous performances: gender conventions, racial histories, aesthetic traditions – political and cultural pressures that are consciously and unconsciously acknowledged."[33] This is right on target, though of course we can name additional factors, such as class, ethnicity, religion, and geography that contribute to the actions and reactions of agents and audiences. And we always have to ask: "intelligible" to whom, "acknowledged" by whom?

The aesthetic factors, which Marvin Carlson calls "ghosts" in his valuable study *The Haunted Stage*, are always in play. Carlson charts how the "memory machine" of theatre and reception defines the spirit of theatre. He would fully agree with Diamond that the theatrical event is haunted also by political conditions, racial histories, and gender conventions – all of the many aspects of the world (for agents and audiences) that performance draws upon, represents, and recapitulates. Most obviously, though, he points out that these ghostly conditions are true for any play, performer, or production in relation to the traditions of theatre. No one writes, acts, designs, directs, produces, or observes in a vacuum, as if for the first time. So the ghosts of the past, as Carlson describes them, appear in many different guises:

(1) the retelling of stories, proverbs, folk tales, legends, myths, and historical events;
(2) direct and indirect quotation of passages from previous plays;
(3) intertextual references, tropes, and structural elements;
(4) the generic traditions and their rules;
(5) the functions of parody, irony, and burlesque in drama;
(6) the training of actors in types of characters, specific roles, and particular gestures and modes of delivery;

(7) the reenactment of certain roles and plays;
(8) the revival of plays, musicals, operas, pantomimes, and all other kinds of works in any repertory process;
(9) the recycling of costumes, properties, and scenery in production;
(10) the shared codes that define period styles and our ability to recognize them;
(11) the recurring patterns and conditions that determine the history of theatre spaces and buildings; and
(12) our return to any of these works, players, productions, spaces, buildings, and festivals for the experience of theatre.

In all of these cases, each theatrical work, event, and experience carries a ghostly presence of what went before. Historians thus need to be quite skilled in their spectral knowledge in order to recognize the incorporeal traces of the past in any theatrical event. Critics and literary scholars want to determine how the play itself incorporates the many aspects of the artistic heritage, not only as support and supplement but also as burden and anxiety.[34] Theatre historians also need to be aware of these matters, in all of their complexities. But in addition historians need to figure out how to read these ghostly codes as they contribute to the definitive features of the performance event. How did the various participants draw upon the available traditions? How did the audiences, in turn, recognize and interpret (and misinterpret) these many codes? Martin Meisel, for example, shows in *Shaw and the Nineteenth-century Theater* (1963) how the playwright used and reformulated the many features of the popular theatre in the writing and staging of his plays. He wrote with and against the conventions. Then in *Realizations* (1983) Meisel reveals how novels, visual arts, and theatre shared a rich artistic heritage of representational codes and meanings throughout the arts in nineteenth-century England. The challenge for all theatre historians is to recognize how the many traditions functioned for all of the agents and audiences in the making of performance events.

> Everything in the theatre, the bodies, the materials utilized, the language, the space itself, is now and has always been haunted, and that haunting has been an essential part of the theatre's meaning to and reception by its audiences in all times and all places.
> Marvin Carlson, *The Haunted Stage: The Theatre as Memory Machine* (2001: 15)

Have I, with this heuristic model of the event and its several contributing conditions, provided a systematic method for how to carry out historical constructions of events? Of course not. These diagrams and their implications are merely a reminder of the many questions a historian should consider; no system emerges for delivering formulated answers. Also, there are some vital aspects of performance events that extend across the apparent borders of the four areas. As David Wiles demonstrates in *A Short History of Western Performance Space* (2003), the idea of *performance space* is one of the primary factors in defining, describing, and interpreting a theatrical event. Where should we locate space in this model? Everywhere. Space and time provide the basic condition of all events. Historical inquiry attempts to place or locate an event within its temporal coordinate; place or location provides the spatial coordinate. Both time and space are specific. Yet for the trained eye, each kind of performance event also achieves its spatial and temporal meanings from the recurring historical practices and patterns of theatre – culture to culture, age to age.[35] The performance event also derives its significance from the geographical, societal, and political uses and purposes of spatial order (and disorder) in each community throughout history. Wiles insists that all of the attributes of performance, such as masks, costumes, stage properties, scenic design elements, dramatic texts, permanent and impermanent buildings, performers, and audiences, depend upon the foundational features of the performance space, which has achieved several distinct historical manifestations across the centuries.[36]

Yet despite the limitations of this working model, it does identify some of the recurring attributes of events – the areas of concern that theatre historians need to consider as they carry out research, formulate questions, and construct events. This model is useful for historical analysis because it alerts us to some abiding conditions of artistic events. At the very least, it moves us beyond a singular idea of context. Perhaps most tellingly, it slows us down and reminds us that we need to reflect upon the attributes of each of the four factors – agents, world, audiences, and artistic heritage – as we construct any theatrical event.

Necessarily, an event interacts collectively with all four factors, but we may still decide to focus on only a few key factors – not only because the available documentation is partial but also because few research projects call for a comprehensive analysis of every conceivable factor. Yet even though we may be rather exclusive in our historical concerns (e.g., the role of the director or a key actor in the production), we are more likely to do an effective job if we appreciate how these specific topics and factors are in dialogue with many other ones.

This model would benefit, however, from an additional configuration that signals another level of analysis. The four binaries need to be turned into triads. Four triangles should be imposed upon each diagram, linking (1) agent, world, event; (2) agent, artistic heritage, event; (3) audience, world, event; and (4) audience, artistic heritage, event. The 90 degree angles of the four triangles should meet at the central event, with open avenues existing in between the four basic binaries: (1) agents and event; (2) world and events: (3) audiences and events; and (4) artistic heritage and event. Historical influences flow both ways on these avenues. At the same time, moving along the triangles, we can chart the triadic dynamics of the relationships. Each triangle sets up a process of mediation that depends upon the three poles of articulation.

Thus, for instance, if we are attempting to understand an artist's contribution to the event, we need to consider both hermeneutical triangles that shape his or her relation to the event. On the one hand, the artist is necessarily situated in the world, so part of what we find in the event is the artist's personal relation to the world: biographical factors, linguistic codes, sociopolitical conditions, values, beliefs, and views, national experiences and identities, ideologies, and possible understanding. We also need to construct not only the interrelationship between the agent and the world but also the ways that relationship is delivered into (or arrives at) the event itself. By moving along the three sides of the triangle – in both directions – the agent and world join at the event. The event should be understood as a consequence of all of these operating conditions, as they influence or determine the experiences of the artist, which are realized in the formal features of the event.

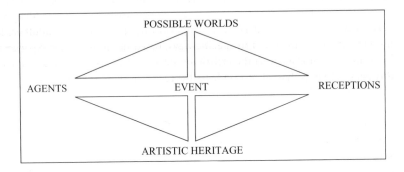

Likewise, just as artist and world interact and join at the event, so too does each artist, when creating any artistic work, operate within and against the artistic heritage – the aesthetic traditions, influences, canons, stylistic codes, mentors, institutions, and cultural semiotics. These "formal" codes are, at least potentially, just as significant as the material and immaterial codes of the world experience. For instance, we may investigate the artist in terms of his or her biological parents (aspects of the world); just as importantly, we may investigate the artist in terms of his or her artistic mentors who shaped identity and purpose. For instance, Eugene O'Neill was greatly influenced by August Strindberg. This year's Kabuki performance recapitulates a heritage stretching back across the centuries.

Thus, the theatrical event, from the perspective of the artist, develops out of both of these hermeneutical triangles, which provide the conditions of understanding, articulation, and action. The triads, as heuristic diagrams, urge us to see that playwrights, producers, directors, designers, or players (in the process of creating the event) draw upon not only their experiences with and ideas about the world but also their experiences with and ideas about the artistic heritage. Both the world and the heritage contribute to their artistic endeavors. A dynamic process of engagement with world and tradition operates in the making of play and production.

On the same principle, spectators, in the process of viewing a production, draw upon not only their experiences with and ideas about the world but also their experiences with and ideas about the artistic heritage. We construct theatrical events based upon the reception, not just conception. The action requires or produces a reaction. The reception network completes the event – sometimes in accord with the motives and aims of the agents, but sometimes in accord with the quite different agendas of the spectators. If some spectators, viewing the London productions of Ibsen's *A Doll's House* (1889) or Elizabeth Robins' *Votes for Women* (1907), had a paternalistic idea of the place of women in society, they may well have rejected the world represented on stage. Other spectators, supporting the rights of women and the suffrage movement, might have approved of the dramatic action. Both types of receptions are part of the event, part of its meaning. And in terms of the artistic heritage, some spectators may have known and enjoyed the well-made plays and melodramas of Victorian theatre, while other spectators may have been supporters of the new realism in the theatre. Clearly, the spectators' knowledge of the artistic heritage, which they bring into the theatre, contributes to their understanding and their judgement. We therefore need to distinguish one spectator from another, for each of them constructs the event in specific ways, based upon his or her experiences with the world and knowledge of the artistic heritage. The important thing to realize, from this perspective, is that all respondents bring to the event their experiences and knowledge that get charted on the third and fourth hermeneutical triangles. The responses of the audience members need to be placed within the context of both triads, as much as possible.

This model of the four hermeneutical triangles may imply that there is a system of analysis that can be applied to historical inquiry. But this model provides no system; it has no set mode of investigation, no preconceived meaning. It is, instead, a model for how to ask questions. The answers will be all over the map, from project to project. I therefore want to insist that no theory or unifying idea guides this model, which is a preliminary outline for how to avoid systematic or formulaic thinking. The model suggests many places to search, many questions to ask. By attending to these four triads, as each historical event allows, we are capable of enriching our methods of research, analysis, and interpretation. Each of the four triangles sets up the potential for a three-point investigation and analysis.

Another warning: as some readers may have noted, the model is primarily a rough synchronic representation of the theatrical event and its connecting contexts. It suggests ways to investigate the potential conditions that contribute to the full identity of the event, at a specific time and place. There is one crucial aspect of the event that such a chart fails to take into sufficient consideration: the diachronic factor. The model does not guide us to the ways that events in time, one after another, may be connected in a sequence of possible developments and causes. And of major concern, the model does not close the distance between the event and the historian. The event thus occurs at one moment, but the historian, in a different time and place, is a displaced "observer." Sitting in Plato's cave, the historian attempts to understand and describe the past event on the basis of sources, the carriers of coded versions of what apparently happened elsewhere, beyond the enclosure of the present perspective.

A point of view is chronotopic, that is, it includes both the spatial and temporal aspects.
M. M. Bahktin, "Notes Made in 1970–71," in *Speech Genres* (1986: 134)

Unavoidably, therefore, the historian's own condition is recapitulated in the hermeneutical triangles. The historian, situated in a later time, may be skilled at closing the distance, of seeking after the "chronotopic" ideal of Bakhtin; nonetheless, the historian's understanding is conditioned in many ways by his or her experiences within the present world and knowledge of the current artistic traditions. Moving along these triads in the present moment, the historian also attempts to return to the hermeneutical triangles of the past event. The inquiry is an attempt to join the two sets of triads. But besides confronting the gaps in the documentation, problem enough, the historian also struggles with a lack of full and appropriate understanding of the past world and the past artistic heritage. The historian may then misread aspects of the agents' activities and aims, along the triads of world and artistic heritage, as well as aspects of the reception codes and meanings, along the similar triads. A double set of limitations are thus at play: the partial nature of the documentation, the partial nature of the historian's understanding. The lack of historical information filters through the gaps in our understanding. Distance always creates problems in historical inquiry.

Further complicating the recovery process is a dangerous piece of knowledge: historians know what came after, so they unavoidably construct events as if the events were pointing in the direction that history actually developed. But that later realization in time of the supposed potential significance of the event is a meaning that exists in the historian's mind, not necessarily in the event itself. As Paul Ricoeur reminds us, an event could have happened differently.[37] Yet because of our belatedness, we subsequently fix it so that it becomes part of a developmental history – part of a plotted narrative. We turn it into something more than – if not other than – it was at the moment of occurrence, still open to the future.

> My dear fellow . . . life is infinitely stranger than anything which the mind of man could invent. We would not dare to conceive the things which are really mere commonplaces of existence. If we could fly out of that window hand in hand, hover over this great city, gently remove the roofs, and peep in at the queer things which are going on, the strange coincidences, the plannings, the cross-purposes, the wonderful chain of events, working through generations and leading to the most outré results, it would make all fiction with its conventionalities and foreseen conclusions most stale and unprofitable.
>   Sherlock Holmes, in Arthur Conan Doyle, "A Case of Identity" (*Strand Magazine*, September 1891)

In the following chapters, beginning with two case studies in chapters 1 and 2 on Shakespeare's Globe Theatre and Alfred Jarry's production of *Ubu Roi*, I will examine the reasons we have often settled for historical methods based upon the event–context model. I will also offer an analysis of our common division between *documentary scholarship* and *cultural history*. "This dichotomy," which Joseph Roach identifies as a choice between *Theaterwissenschaft* and *theory*, "has to some extent continued to divide the field."[38] In this divisive battle (also identified by some people as a struggle between positivism and post-positivism or theatre history and performance theory), many of us took sides; the arguments defined much about the transformation of the field of theatre studies in the 1980s and 1990s.[39] Thus, in the opening two chapters I revisit some of the key issues and assumptions of the recent decades. It is time, though, to reformulate the strengths and weaknesses of each side in this dichotomy. Are the apparent differences to be accepted as necessary divisions in historical inquiry?

Then in chapters 3 and 4 I will consider the fundamental problems historians face when they attempt to identify and construct historical events, including theatre events, which have some special traits that increase our difficulties in analysis and explanation. What are the defining features of an historical event? How can we recover and reformulate the past aims and actions of people who created performance events? Following this investigation of the construction of events, I will shift to the many challenges of constructing historical contexts for those events. In chapters 5 and 6 I will show how and why we need multiple, not singular, ideas of the historical contexts for events. In chapter 5, which takes up the problem of periodization in history, I will describe the models and analyze the criteria we use for constructing period concepts. Quite often our period concepts provide the primary – and usually unquestioned – basis for our general ideas of cultural context. Then in chapter 6 I will examine the ways we use the idea of politics to establish the interpretive context for historical events. After Marx, after Foucault, after New Historicism, and after our application of various ideas of political order and disorder (from race and gender theory to postcolonialism), how and where should we *locate* the political context for any theatre event? Do we, as historians, share some fundamental procedures and methods, no matter which organizing idea of politics we apply to the past? Finally, in chapter 7 I attempt to pull together a number of the issues and problems in theatre historiography, as I consider twelve major cruxes that all historians face.

My abiding assumption is that certain fundamental concepts – placed in italics in this paragraph – are always operating in our thought processes when we attempt to reconstruct past events. These are *the ideas we think with.* They organize our thoughts; they also organize this book. As we investigate and construct the *archives*, which we analyze on the basis of ideas of *credibility* and *reliability*, we need to *question* the sources that allow us to identify the historical *agents* and their *actions*. We attempt to locate those agents and actions within the appropriate *temporal* and *spatial* dimensions and conditions. We attempt to define not only the *diachronic* and *synchronic* axes for the events but also the shaping conditions of era, epoch, or *period*. Our ideas of *location*, as I will argue, help to place the *events* and put them in their *contexts*. And the location of the historian – in the present and looking backward (if not flying backward like Walter Benjamin's angel) – is part of the challenge?[40] By means of our ideas of identity, we represent the events. Processes of *identification* and *representation* are crucial in historical inquiry. Then, having *constructed* or *reconstructed* the events, as best we can, we attempt to find ways to *narrate* – to describe, explain, and interpret – the basic conditions: *who, what, where, when, how,* and *why.* What are the probable, not just possible, stories offered up by the achieved representations? Can we show how events are related to one another in the dynamic conditions of *change* and *causality?* What are the problems, what are the challenges? What is *possible, plausible, probable,* and even *certain* in our search for the historical *truths* (always in the lower case, but still a matter of accurate and inaccurate, possible and impossible)? In short, how can we do justice to the defining features of the diagram of the four hermeneutical triangles?

Throughout the book I will ask many questions. And I will make critical distinctions. I will, on a number of occasions, point out how and why we have failed to describe and analyze some historical events accurately. I will identify cases of sloppy scholarship, and I will also point out how and why in some cases we misinterpret the definitive traits of an event because of the inadequate ways we construct its context (e.g., formulaic narratives of change, vague period concepts, or reductive models of political analysis). At the same time, as certain cases warrant, I will also show that it is both possible and plausible to carry out research effectively. In many cases, we are quite capable of writing convincing interpretive history of theatre events and their contexts. I will identify a number of historians who deserve our praise for their accomplishments. For all of my questioning and skepticism, I find much to admire in historical study today. My criticism is balanced, I would hope, by not only my full sympathy for the difficulties of the historical task but also my admiration for the many fine achievements. Otherwise, the criticism would be pointless (as would the writing of this book).

> In the wide ocean upon which we venture, the possible ways and directions are many; and the same studies which have served for this work might easily, in other hands, not only receive a wholly different treatment and application, but lead also to essentially different conclusions.
> Jacob Burckhardt, *The Civilization of the Renaissance in Italy* (1990: 19)

Consequently, this book, besides providing a primer on historical methodology, demonstrates that it is often possible to reconstruct historical events and their contexts. We are capable of establishing some of the truths that we pursue and seek to understand. No doubt there are many cases in which we cannot reach certainty. Our explanations of the details and meanings of many events, especially from the premodern eras, will remain inconclusive. We lack sufficient information. But our difficulties are not limited to our lack of evidence. *What* we know is also constrained by *how* we know. In turn, our explanations of *why* depend upon the ways we determine *what* and *how*. That is, our questions, along with our answers, are conditioned by *the concepts we think with*. Indeed, this fundamental problem of the concepts we think with provides the organizing topic and principle for this introduction to theatre historiography. Our procedures of definition, analysis, explanation, and interpretation contribute to our successes and failures as historians.

> In a now somewhat dated study of the best police forces in major cities of the Spanish-speaking world, the key traits of the best detectives were parsed. No single type of police investigator stood out; good detectives emerged from many different training programs and social worlds. Some were well educated; some had dropped out of school before the

age of sixteen. Some were male; some were female. Some came from families that had lived in the same city or region for generations; some were immigrants. Some had access to sophisticated crime laboratories; some depended primarily on street contacts. In their dealings with the pubic, some were cold and hard; some were gentle and soft. Some were admired by their colleagues; some were hated or feared. Some were happily married; some were often divorced. Some always played by the rules; some bent the rules whenever they had the opportunity.

Yet in the descriptions and self-descriptions of these successful detectives, whose accomplishments were defined in part by the percentage of convictions that held up in court (not by the number of arrests), several key verbs recurred regularly to characterize their methods: *track, explore, search, dissect, parse, seek, probe, analyze, pursue, sift, hunt, inquire.* And many of the "re" words also appeared in these descriptions and self-descriptions: *reconsider, rethink, recover, resume, review, retrace, re-examine, rethink.* These defining verbs do not reveal any specific method but collectively they signal a way of perceiving and examining the world. All of these detectives had the defining traits of a kind of behavior: the hunter. And a kind of intelligence: the questioning mind.

Tom Castro (pseudonym of Arthur Orton), *A Universal History of Iniquity* (n.d.: 13)

This matter of uncertainty does not condemn us to a general condition of historical relativism, but it does show that our historical data and historical understanding have their limitations. "Let us not forget," wrote Marc Bloch, "that history is a science in travail."[41] Luckily, the word *travail* suggests not only torturous pain but also hard work. That is a pretty good definition of the historian's task and craft. So understood, the discipline has much in common with good police work: ask the promising questions, then start digging. Effective investigation depends upon how cunning we are in constructing the archive – where and how to look, not just what to look for. Both the historical records and our historical methods confront us with many challenges.

Therefore, in this book I will attempt to answer a basic question raised by Erika Fischer-Lichte: "What are we doing when we pursue theatre historiography?"[42] In order to do justice to this question I must focus on the specific and definitive features of research and writing in theatre history. As we will see, those features have much in common with the procedures and aims that all historians face. In the process of answering this question, I am also guided by a basic principle that applies not only in the general field of history but also in all disciplines of knowledge. In the words of R. G. Collingwood: "A body of knowledge is never merely organized; it is always organized in some particular way."[43] I cannot answer Fischer-Lichte's question unless I also understand the implications of Collingwood's statement. My hope is that the readers of this book, as they reflect upon *the ideas they think with*, will also come to understand how and why Fischer-Lichte's question and Collingwood's statement serve as signposts on the path through this book.

Those signposts confirm that historical inquiry is the pursuit of truths about the past within the conditions and constraints of possible knowledge. Although the full truth eludes us and total agreement is not possible, many partial truths can be attained, verified, and justified. Individually, historians work diligently to describe and explain past events, even though as a group they often disagree about the best way to interpret those events. They even disagree in some cases on the definitive facts and factors for specific events, especially complex events with many defining features. But collectively they participate in a community that adjudicates the descriptions and explanations. The various investigations by the community of historians add to and enhance our understanding of not only what happened in the past but also how and why. Consequently, with Montaigne, we need to agree, "The active pursuit of truth is our proper business." And with Van Gogh, we need to proclaim, "I adore the true, the possible."

Part one

Documentary history vs. cultural history: two case studies

Documentary histories: the case of Shakespeare's Globe Theatre

What do historians do? How do they do it? Two simple questions, but the answers are complex and various. In all fields of historical inquiry, including theatre history, there are established procedures for determining the identity, authenticity, and reliability of the historical sources. These analytical methods guide the initial steps for compiling and organizing the data, and they help the historian to generate questions, ideas, and insights for the research program. At this stage, the guidelines may be as basic as the six interrogatives (who, what, where, when, how, and why). But they can also be as technical as the preservation techniques in papyrology and the dating protocols in numismatics.

By distinguishing between available documents and identifiable facts, historians proceed from "history-as-record," which exists in the sources (e.g., archival records, oral reports, anecdotes, legends, material objects, archeological remains), to "history-as-event," which no longer exists. The recovery process, an act of reconstruction based upon factual data and imagination, depends upon the historian's skills and talent for research, organization, description, analysis, interpretation, and argument. Also, the project usually requires (and rewards) good writing ability, including basic matters of clear prose style, precise description, concise definition, and a sense of narrative. In order to establish the viability of conjectures and interpretations, a historian appeals to the rational principles of possibility, plausibility, and probability. Sometimes a historian can reach a condition of certainty in an investigation, not just over factual data derived from the records (who, what, where, when) but also causal factors (how and why). Yet as soon as one person announces historical certainty, someone else will see good reasons for reformulating both the problem and the answer, especially for large, complex events. Then "history-as-record" and the assumed facts undergo new questions, resulting perhaps in new facts, new motives and causes, new relationships, and new narratives.

To begin this investigation of historical research in theatre, let's take up a specific and familiar historical question, one that theatre historians have attempted to answer since the eighteenth century. How were Shakespeare's plays performed at the Globe playhouse, which opened in 1599? Because this topic has been well researched, analyzed, and debated, it provides a useful introduction to the kinds of documentary records that theatre historians typically draw upon. It also offers many of the challenges and problems that pertain to any attempt to reconstruct a theatrical event, especially when we are confronted with incomplete and sometimes contradictory evidence.

Illustration 1. Swan Theatre, *c.* 1596–1597, copied by Arend (Aernout) van Buchel from a drawing by Johannes De Witt. From Karl Theodor Gaedertz, *Zur Kenntnis der altenglischen Bühne nebst andern Beiträgen zur Shakespeare-Litteratur.* Bremen: C. Ed. Müller, 1888.

This inquiry into Globe performances puts before us a fundamental task that all historians share: the recovery of past events. This basic concept of a *historical event* is at the heart of historical inquiry. Consequently, in order to answer the question about the production of Shakespeare plays, we must be able to represent a historical event (e.g., the performance of *Julius Caesar* at the Globe in 1599).[1] If we know how to recover an historical event – and understand the special challenges and problems of describing a performance event – we have attained one of the fundamental skills in the discipline of theatre history.

There are several related terms – a *presentation*, a *representation*, a *construction*, or a *reconstruction* – for identifying, describing, analyzing, and interpreting a historical event. Historians often use these terms interchangeably. But a distinction needs to be made between the version of the event in the historical records and the version provided by the historian. Accordingly, I will use *presentation* and *construction* to describe the way an event is presented in the sources, then I will use *representation* and *reconstruction* to describe the historian's own version of the event. This usage is a necessary reminder that these events have a double identity: in the records and in the historian's reports. Behind or beyond both is the event itself, referred to or implied by the sources. It may appear *immediate* to some eyewitnesses (e.g., Johannes De Witt sitting in the Swan Theatre while he draws the interior of the building with performers on stage) but it is necessarily *intermediate* for the historian whose access to it is negotiated by the sources. In this sense, the historian is always removed from the event itself, with no ability to gain immediate access to it. Everything is reflected through the sources, dancing images on the wall of the cave. Every source, every image, requires analysis and interpretation in the process of reconstructing the past event.

> . . . the historian's "truths" are derived from analytical evaluations of an object called "sources" rather than of an object called "the actual past."
> Louis Gottschalk, *Understanding History: A Primer of Historical Methods* (1969: 171)

Some historical events are fairly easy to reconstruct. They contain the action of an individual whose intentions are clearly specified in the sources. And the consequences of the action are quite apparent. The basic factors of who, what, where, when, how, and why line up for us, almost as a gift. But this is not the norm. Much of the time historical events are complex rather than simple. Unraveling what happened is difficult, and determining the causes and consequences can sometimes be close to impossible. Because the records, in most cases, are incomplete, various possibilities emerge for description and analysis. The historian, whose first obligation is to stay within the realm of possibility, needs to be not only a good detective in order to find the relevant sources but also a cunning interpreter in the process of developing evidence for an explanation. And the historian must also confront the absences. Weaving together what is and is not known, the historian attempts to craft the most plausible explanation.

The task of reconstructing performances at the Globe Theatre is difficult for two basic reasons: insufficient documentation and the complexity of the historical events, which combined many intentions, decisions, actions, results, and judgements. Numerous individuals, from playwright and players to governmental officials and spectators, serve as potential contributors to the construction and meaning of the overall event. All too often, the motives are unclear, the causes are often inexplicable, and the reactions are contradictory. Yet as theatre historians have demonstrated, it is possible to reconstruct many aspects of theatre in Shakespeare's time. For example, in our attempts to describe the uses of stage space in the London public theatres, such as the Swan, the Rose, and the Globe, our evidence (e.g., a drawing, an excavation, building contracts for theatres, and staging descriptions in the plays) gives us a basic spatial pattern of the thrust stage with doors in the back wall. Our reconstructions combine empirical data and well-reasoned conjectures, as we try to pin down the likely norms and routines of performance methods at the Globe. As much as possible, we try not to impose our own experiences and expectations of stage performance upon the Globe, though this is always difficult. For example, assumptions about spatial relations in the proscenium theatre distorted scholarship for several generations (e.g., an "inner stage," number of doors); modern ideas about acting methods and movement still mislead scholars today; and our suppositions about what spectators understood in the plays and how they responded to performance moments continue to bedevil our understanding of the theatrical experience.

In our search for definitive data and general explanations, theatre historians sometimes depend upon set patterns, even formulas, for describing performance events in Shakespeare's epoch. In our search for clarity and general patterns, we often embrace singular explanations for the building plan for the playhouses, the dominant acting style in the era, the social typology of the audience, or the anti-theatrical mindset of the Puritans and the London city fathers. Accordingly, by applying Occam's razor to the historical conditions, we attempt to achieve a fundamental understanding of the order of things. But at what price? What is the acceptable tradeoff between uniformity and consistency, on the one hand, and complexity and multiplicity, on the other?

In order to answer our question about the performance of Shakespeare's plays at the Globe we need to know how stage space was used. Perhaps the most basic explanation has been put forward by Robert Weimann in *Shakespeare and the Popular Tradition in the Theatre* (1978).[2] Consistent with some aspects of Bernard Beckerman's analysis in *Shakespeare at the Globe, 1599–1609* (1962) and Glynne Wickham's gathering of data in *Early English Stages, 1300–1660*, vol. I (1963), he argues for a model of staging based upon a minimalist principle. The stage space, he explains, was divided into two symbolic areas: *platea* and *locus*. Weimann insists that this two-part arrangement derived from a long history of performance practices that spread from medieval popular culture into the age of Shakespeare. The performance of folk plays, morality plays, and mystery plays throughout England followed this two-part pattern rather consistently. The origins of this practice, he even suggests, can be traced back to the Roman theatre.

The *platea* was a general, unspecified stage area that could represent any place and time. It was nowhere and everywhere for the dramatic action. In turn, the *locus* served as a particular location and setting. With the use of specific stage set pieces and properties, this defined space would help the players and spectators to locate the dramatic action. Typically, the *platea* would be the stage space close to the spectators (e.g., the front of a platform); the *locus* would be set at the back part of the stage. Thus, at the Globe the battle scenes in *Macbeth* would have occurred in the *platea*, but the banquet scene, with a table and chairs, would have been located in the *locus*, close to the back wall and doors. Or, on a center-margin model for the thrust stage of the amphitheatres, some players in a scene could have occupied a central *locus* while other players roamed the marginal *platea* area along the three sides. Thus, the early court scene in *Hamlet* might have featured king, queen, and court people at the center and the moody prince, all in black, at the stage margins, thereby allowing the spectators to attend to his comments. Whatever the dramatic situation, this basic model supposedly distributed players according to a twofold division of stage space: front and back or the center and margin.

Sometimes the *locus* was designated by a stage property (e.g., a throne), sometimes by a booth (e.g., a manger scene). On some stages, which followed the medieval model of the simultaneous stage, there could be several booths across the stage space, each identified with a place that was named or referred to in the dramatic text. The performers would deliver the appropriate speeches from the play while positioning themselves near, onto, under, or within the property or booth. This model of simultaneous staging continued to be used in various kinds of sacred and secular performances (e.g., the French theatre into the first half of the seventeenth century). But in the London public theatres of Shakespeare's time, the players made much less use of the isolated booths and more of large stage properties, which could be shoved out of one of the doors, as needed. Yet despite the development of professional theatre and permanent theatre buildings, the *platea* and *locus* system of staging apparently remained the norm for performances. Weimann's explanation, which has the notable virtue of simplicity, obviously appeals to many literary scholars and theatre historians. It has settled into many surveys and textbooks on English Renaissance theatre.

Performance on the stages in these fixed playhouses [both outdoor and indoor] remained based on a principle of *locus* and *platea*. Despite the fixed dimensions of the stage in a given playhouse (variable, of course, across different playhouses), the stage itself, thrust into and surrounded by the audience, could be used as yet another form of open space, or *platea*, while the tiring house doors or large free-standing props might function as *loci*. This continuing principle meant that the localization of scenes in plays performed in these playhouses was only ever intermittent. Some scenes had a specifically designated location (those in the arbour in *The Spanish Tragedy* (1585–9) or the graveyard in *Hamlet*, for example), but many more are unlocated in any very specific sense, which makes for an open-ended and receptive relation with the audience's time and space.
Janette Dillon, *The Cambridge Introduction to Early English Theatre* (2006: 49–50)

This *platea* and *locus* formula relieves us of the difficult task of trying to formulate distinctive staging practices for each particular case, such as Marlowe's *Tamburlaine* at the Rose, Shakespeare's *The Winter's Tale* at the Globe, or Webster's *The Duchess of Malfi* at the Blackfriars. The same system always operated, despite the variety of playhouses, dramatic genres, and theatre companies. Until the arrival of the proscenium stage and the increasingly elaborated scenic practices of the seventeenth, eighteenth, and nineteenth centuries, the stage space in the London theatre was relatively simple.

Part of the reassuring quality of this explanation is that it fits the spatial configuration of the thrust stage. Shakespeare's plays, written for rapid scene changes, can be effectively staged in a minimalist manner. The players entered and exited quickly through the doors in the tiring house wall. Stage properties were carried onto the stage through these doors (though the procedure was complicated by some properties being lowered from above and others being raised from below). The doors and open stage space established certain playing requirements and conditions that correspond to Weimann's formulation. Also, a simple staging model makes practical sense when we consider the very short time available for rehearsal and the typical need to change plays after one to five performances.

Apparently, then, we have a simple model for constructing the performance event. This formulation of *platea* and *locus* appeals to us because it makes sense of some basic facts. In the most general terms, and without historical research into specific conditions, the *locus–platea* model may seem reasonable because it accords with a basic perspective and experience of spectators in the theatre. Actors are either close to us or far away. And, in turn, stage properties are either present or absent. Weimann's explanation also gains part of its appeal from his broad survey of the centrality and authority of popular culture, which he celebrates as a unifying aspect of English theatre and society from the late Middle Ages to the Elizabethan age.[3] But beyond its reasonableness and general applicability, is the *platea–locus* model historically accurate? It easily satisfies our sense of possibility, but does it also meet historical requirements of plausibility – to say nothing yet of certainty? Were the staging procedures and aims for London entertainment always dedicated to simplicity in scenic representation? Not in the case of court masques or the Lord Mayor's shows, as we know. But are these mere exceptions to the rule? How much reduction in specificity should a historian accept?

> And what is historical research without historical questions?
> Hans-Georg Gadamer, *Truth and Method* (1997: 12)

Between 1450 and 1642 almost all aspects of drama and theatre underwent radical changes, as religious theatre and folk drama were increasingly supplemented – then displaced – by secular, professional, and commercial theatre. The early modern age, in all of its complexity and reforming spirit, had arrived. Various kinds of venues – innyards, amphitheatres, indoor theatres – were used in London. Also, when on the road, the players adapted to many different interior and exterior spaces. Given these various venues and conditions, two possible stage practices seem likely. (1) The players used the same twofold model of staging, no matter what the space, to keep things simple (and to remain true to the heritage of popular culture). The various venues and staging conditions did not allow for elaborate or complex staging. (2) The players, accepting the challenge of many different opportunities, developed several different, sometimes innovative ways to use stage space in order to communicate effectively with various audiences. Despite the busy schedule, as they took on an increasing variety of play types, they sought ways to move beyond the repetitive pattern of *platea* and *locus*. Both modes of reasoning – a typical move of historians – seem possible and thus justified as propositions, but what actually happened over the decades in many different venues? Endless repetition or adaptive modification?

What are the justifications for entertaining a complex rather than simple idea of staging? From the 1570s to the 1640s the theatre companies had distinctive identities, players, plays, and missions. We know that several theatre companies developed distinct identities and attracted particular audiences. The playwrights generated a wide variety of play types and styles. Various performance venues were used. For all of this we have evidence, not just speculation. Can we then speculate that the players, wanting to attract and maintain audiences, encouraged innovation and specialization? As revivals of popular plays became more prevalent, especially in the case of the major companies by the seventeenth century, there were more opportunities to rethink and reformulate the methods of staging. Also, because of the complexity of certain scenes (e.g., the opening of *Titus Andronicus*), the triangulation of stage space would have made good sense (as happens rather easily when three actors or three groups occupy the stage). Moreover, sometimes the *platea*, not just the *locus*, could be used for two, three, and more pieces of stage property. The *locus*, in turn, could become several *loci*. And the added level of the balcony offered additional staging possibilities at the amphitheatres. Many factors point to complexity.

Thus, it is possible to argue, counter to Weimann, that decade by decade the impulse to maintain the repetitive pattern of *platea* and *locus* lost its hold on players and playwrights. The playwrights saw new opportunities and took them. As the playing spaces and kinds of plays changed, the players felt challenged to develop new modes of presentation. Their creative energies fed on change. They were rewarded for their innovations. Is it not likely, then, that some of the players, tired of (even bored by) the same recurring pattern, purposefully embraced innovative modes of presentation? At least on some occasions? Change happens – this is the first principle of historical study.

Sufficient evidence points to a vibrant, changing theatre in London. As Andrew Gurr states in his study of "the Shakespeare company" (his composite name for the Chamberlain's Men and the King's Men), "many features of the company's work changed in the course of their forty-eight years."[4] This should be an obvious point. Many factors allowed for and even demanded innovation: new players, new playwrights, new performance conditions at several theatres, and new spectators. Why, then, should we assume (or deduce) that the company's staging methods remained unchanged across these decades?

Also, before we accept the authority of Weimann's model, we might consider the implications of such a simple, seductive hypothesis for a very diverse and complex era in theatre history. Granted, his model can be made to fit the stage space of the London amphitheatres (and to a lesser extent the private playhouses). Yet because of its vague, two-part division of space, it can also be applied quite broadly to theatre production in not only the early modern age but almost any era. A twofold formula can be made to fit performance practices extending from the Greek amphitheatres to Japanese Noh theatre. Without difficulty, we can describe the platform before the skene building, out of which players exit and enter, as a *locus* and the orchestra as a *platea*. Indeed, most thrust stages, platforms, or open spaces (basic models which manifest themselves in numerous ways in many historical situations and eras) can be divided, all too easily, from front to back or center to margin. This is a division that neatly translates local distinctions into general similarities. At this level of abstraction all theatre spaces generate the same formulaic practice.

Yet if this two-part model fits many different situations equally well (and with equal vagueness), it may be little more than a bland truism that tells us little or nothing historically. It eliminates the need for historical research into specific conditions. If we remain at this preliminary level of description of theatre events (ignoring, for example, the many details that make Greek, Noh, and Elizabethan theatre strikingly different from one another), this formulation reduces all performance to a basic pattern. In this sense, the *platea* and *locus* model is hard to disprove because it fits almost all cases.

> . . . an hypothesis which can explain anything is as useless as one which can explain nothing.
> W. W. Greg, *Two Elizabethan Stage Abridgements* (1923: 334)[5]

Occam's razor is seductive, but the job of the historian is to get down to specific cases. Once we move beyond some basic formulations about theatre and stage space, we know that Greek, Roman, medieval, and Renaissance theatres are not the same. All theatre productions in London during the late sixteenth and early seventeenth centuries were not the same. Historical understanding derives, in great measure, from historical inquiry into differences as well as similarities. Yes, we can write a general history on the basis of a few similar and recurring patterns (e.g., rise and fall of civilizations), but historical understanding is also about differences, variations, distinctions, exceptions, and particularities. History is the narrative of change. The individual case matters. At the very least, as historians, we should entertain the possibility of variety, disparity, and willful contrariety.

Consequently, to the extent that we are interested in discovering the particular identity of events, including the variety of performance events at the Globe theatre between 1599 and 1613, we should be willing, at the very least, to consider some of the questions and doubts raised here. These questions do not prove Weimann wrong (which is hard to do at such an abstract level of historical description), but they do suggest that the simplicity of the *platea–locus* thesis may explain both too much and too little. Instead of being satisfied with a single explanation for staging practices at the Globe, Curtain, Rose, Blackfriars, Inns of Court, Whitehall, royal residencies, and the guildhalls and great chambers around the country, we might entertain the possibility that the players looked for and tapped creative opportunities for diverging from the expected. Indeed, even in the two or three hours of a single production, the players may have been less than satisfied with the repetitive pattern of *platea* and *locus*.

> History begins when we become interested in individual realities . . . The world of the historian is the world of daily life in its immediate totality.
> Raymond Aron, *Introduction to the Philosophy of History* (1961: 29 and 47)

In this investigation of the staging of Shakespeare's plays, let's return to the two questions that opened this chapter: what do historians do? How do they do it? But let's modify the questions slightly: what do historians know and how do they know it? As we will see throughout this investigation of theatre historiography, the matter of "what" we know depends in great measure on "how" we know. Our organizing categories and analytical procedures control our perceptions and knowledge. Our historical knowledge is determined by the questions we ask and the categories that guide our inquiries. How we define both task and terms will determine, in great measure, what we learn. In the process, our emerging clarity about the "how" will also help us to decide if the "what" is worth knowing.

Moving beyond basic assumptions and explanations, what do we think we know about the staging of Shakespeare's plays at the Globe theatre, and how do we know it? Any attempt to reconstruct the performances must consider the potential evidence, explicit and implicit, provided by the quarto and folio editions of the plays. Because we do not have any of Shakespeare's manuscripts (excepting three pages of the *Sir Thomas More* manuscript that may be in his handwriting) or any of his company's "allowed books" that the Master of the Revels approved for the performances of his plays, we must use the published texts as our starting point. But to what extent do the printed plays provide accurate records of performances? What do they reveal, if anything, about the missing playbooks and manuscripts?

In 1623, seven years after his death, thirty-six of Shakespeare's plays were published in the First Folio (1623).[6] Edited by two players in the King's Men, John Heminges and Henry Condell, the folio plays, which include eighteen that had never before been published, may be quite reliable, accurate, or authentic versions of the plays. But what in fact do we mean by these crucial ideas of reliability, accuracy, and authenticity? The folio title page states that the plays were published according to "the True Originall Copies." Were these copies derived from the promptbooks of the King's Men? Or did Heminges and Condell acquire transcripts (i.e., "fair copies" of the original manuscripts) that once belonged to Shakespeare or members of his family?[7] Or did they use intermediate transcripts (copies of copies) provided by Ralph Crane and other scriveners who worked for the company? Shakespeare apparently had little or no involvement with the King's Men after the Globe was rebuilt, and he died in 1616. Consequently, the ten years between 1613, when he retired from the theatre, and

1623, when the First Folio was published, provide many questions but few definitive answers about the sources of the plays.

> It had bene a thing, we confesse, worthie to haue bene wished, that the Author himselfe had liu'd to haue set forth, and ouerseen his owne writings; But since it hath bin ordain'd otherwise, and he by death departed from that right, we pray you do not envie his Friends, the office of their care, and paine, to haue collected & publish'd them; and so to haue publish'd them, as where (before) you were abus'd with diuerse stolne, and surreptitious copies, maimed, and deformed by the frauds and stealthes of injiurious imposters, that expos'd them: euen those, are now offer'd to your view cur'd, and perfect of their limbes; and all the rest, absolute in their numbers, as he conceiued them.
>   John Heminges and Henry Condell, "To the great Variety of Readers," foreword to the First Folio (1623)

In any attempt to reconstruct performances at the Globe, we also need to take the measure of not only the 1623 folio edition but also the quarto texts of Shakespeare's plays, published under various conditions and for a variety of reasons.[8] Between 1594 and 1619 close to twenty of his plays were printed individually in quarto editions (and an occasional octovo). When staging information in the quartos differs from what is provided in the First Folio, which texts should we accept as historical evidence? Some of the quarto plays, such as Q2 (1604) for *Hamlet*, share many features with the folio texts. But other quartos, such as Q1 (1603) of *Hamlet*, are radically shorter and different from the fuller texts. What should we make of the differences between Q1 and Q2 of *Hamlet*? Is Q1 Shakespeare's early draft that he later revised for Q2? Is it a text cut down by players for a two-hour performance? Or is it an unreliable reconstruction by one or more players who provided a version for a printer?[9]

What are the guidelines for separating the reliable information from the unreliable in the various quartos and folios? How should we define and apply this idea of "reliable" texts? For what purpose? One method, prevalent among textual, literary, and theatre scholars, depends upon the principle of divide and conquer. Like King Lear dividing his kingdom, we have attempted to separate the play-texts into three distinct aspects or identities, which we attribute to the determining agency of the playwright, the players, and the printers. And like Lear we have preferences, priorities, and prejudices. We have recognized that all of the published plays, as historical evidence, offer a combination of intentions and agendas – literary, theatrical, and commercial. Accordingly, we have tried to distribute literary aims to the playwright, theatrical aims to the players, and commercial aims to the printers.

Each of the available texts reveals possible contributions by these three "makers" of the texts. Each contains signs and clues that point to the playwright, the players, and the printers. But because of the mingling of intentions, contributions, revisions, and excisions in the published texts, these signs and clues often seem to be at cross-purposes. They do not align in a shared mission; they do not deliver the definitive answers we seek. Our scholarly challenge, as we developed it in the twentieth century, has been to unravel the contending intentions of each maker. Literary and textual

Mr. WILLIAM
SHAKESPEARES
COMEDIES,
HISTORIES, &
TRAGEDIES.

Publifhed according to the True Originall Copies.

LONDON
Printed by Ifaac Iaggard, and Ed. Blount. 1623.

Illustration 2. Title page of the 1623 First Folio of William Shakespeare's works, edited by John Heminges and Henry Condell.

scholars have been committed to the playwright and his poetic text; theatre historians have sought to chart the contributions of the players and their companies; and social historians and some textual experts have attended to the printers and the history of the presses.

In service to the playwright's literary aims, we have attempted to strip away the extraneous layers of textual misinformation imposed by the error-prone printers and the improvising players. By returning to origins, based upon the principle of *vera causa* or primary cause, we have sought to recover the poetic quality of the plays. This textual method reached its apex in the "new bibliography" of W. W. Greg (1955) and his followers. The aim was to provide texts, true to the playwright's poetic intentions, that evoked the original manuscripts, the home of authenticity. But because the manuscripts did not survive, editors had to create surrogate or copy texts that could take the place of the lost originals. In this textual mission, we attempted to honor Shakespeare's artistic integrity even more than he did (for he failed to save his manuscripts or oversee, as Ben Jonson did, a definitive edition of his plays).

This search, however, has ignored or denied the playwright's theatrical and commercial intentions. It has partially blinded us to his accommodating partnership with the intentions of players and printers. For all we know, Shakespeare may have cared more about making theatre and a profit than creating a unified artwork (a formalist ideal that we partially derived from our romantic and modernist sensibilities). We have attempted to construct the literary text by removing impurities, but this mission is based upon an inappropriate division of Shakespeare the poet from the man of theatre and commerce.[10]

By contrast, theatre historians, though quite interested in the literary qualities of the text, have sought clues that reveal the production methods and aims of the theatre companies. Scouring the quartos and 1623 Folio, we have attempted to discover the staging practicalities that determined the uses of doors, traps, balconies, discovery spaces, and stage properties. We have derived clues from all of the extant texts, but in fact we do not know who provided the printed stage directions in these texts: playwrights, scribes, players, or printers. Nor do we know which scenes were removed in performance in order to accommodate the playable time limits of short afternoons, especially in winter. And we don't know how plays were revised over the years (though the multiple versions of several plays reveal major changes). Although some of the "bad quartos," which have troubled literary scholars, may be suggestive about performance practices, we have often been uncertain about how to use these texts. The lack of agreement among textual scholars about the quartos adds to our uncertainties. Are they "memorial reconstructions" by players who, with printers, "pirated" the plays? Are they early drafts by the playwright? Do they reveal contributions of collaborators? If so, who and for what reasons? Also, theatre historians have basically ignored the possibility that some of the published texts were intended for readers.[11] If so, the great length of some plays may mislead us about not only actual performance times but also actual staging decisions and methods.

Desiring a "promptbook," which is a misleading concept for the early modern stage, theatre historians often do not know how to make sense of the supposedly irrelevant layers of "misinformation" that derive from the aims and contributions of playwright, collaborators, and printers. Although neither the plays nor the productions can be frozen into a single identity, theatre historians tend to seek a standard model of production. We want to establish patterns for the uses of doors, traps, discovery spaces, etc. But our models then ignore the shifting venues and the likely revisions from year to year that occurred in scripts and performances. Unfortunately, no matter which text is being examined, theatre historians often ignore the multiple identities of each play. And we often misread the intermingled intentions and contributions of both the playwright and the players. We thus fail to recognize that the apparent signs and clues of performance cannot be neatly separated from the various aims and agendas of playwrights and printers, distributed across the various texts.

As for the third makers of the text, the printers and the compositors who set the type, they are often seen by both literary scholars and theatre historians as nothing but a problem – a hindrance to be overcome. The printers, in our eyes, subverted the intentions of Shakespeare and his genius. They served their own commercial aims because, as G. E. Bentley points out, "English printing and publishing in the late sixteenth and early seventeenth centuries was a closely held monopoly." There was no copyright law that protected the rights of the author. Each publisher attained possession of manuscripts, "by whatever means," and printed it. "There were no requirements concerning his obligations to the author." Consequently, as Bentley assumes (and complains), not one of the nineteen or twenty quarto editions of Shakespeare's plays published during his lifetime "was printed just as he had written it," and some texts are so distorted that if Shakespeare had seen them, "he must have found them either ludicrous or horrifying."[12]

Whatever the source of the printed text – playwright's manuscript, company playbook, scrivener's copy, or actors' recollections – the compositors introduced a series of errors and inaccuracies. Therefore, if we have any hope of recovering the intentions of the playwrights and players, we need to remove the layers of typological mistakes. In the eyes of many Shakespearean scholars, the printers were mercenary businessmen and their compositors were inattentive, sloppy, and lazy workers, aided by incompetent apprentices. At their best, Bentley states, these workers created "many hundreds of mistakes" that are "still uncorrected" in modern editions. At their worse these "piratical Elizabethan publishers" are guilty of "fraud."[13] They turned Shakespeare into a cash cow. Having no intellectual or artistic investment in the printing job, they contaminated the literary and theatrical texts that they failed to understand. Consequently, ever since the eighteenth century, scholars have tried to untangle and remove the false, even fraudulent, contributions of the printing houses.

This is a damning indictment, one that apparently justifies our divide-and-conquer procedures. We need to save the playwright from the commercial aims of the printers, just as many textual editors have also felt the need to counter the theatrical distortions of the players. Anti-capitalist and anti-theatrical prejudices have guided us. Yet this historical perspective reveals its own traits of limited and distorted understanding. In the first place, our frustrated, dismissive attitude hinders our ability to perceive a historical condition and imperative: how and why the printed plays came into existence as a result of the joint intentions of playwrights, players, and printers. By attempting to divide the literary, historical, and commercial documents into three distinct identities, we have fractured what needs to be seen and understood as a whole. Our divide-and-conquer method of inquiry causes us to misread the texts just as grievously as the supposedly incompetent compositors misread their handwritten sources.

In order to reassess the documentary record, we first need to honor the acts of preservation that saved the plays of Shakespeare (and many other dramatists). The credit for the First Folio goes not only to two players, Heminges and Condell, but also to William and Issac Jaggard, father and son, who printed the edition for a consortium of publishers, including themselves. Though we credit Heminges and Condell for their determination to honor Shakespeare and his art, the commitment to the playwright was shared by William Jaggard, who had his own sense of honor: "It touches a Printer as much to maintaine his reputation in the Art he liues by, as a Herald in his Profession."[14] Our simplified opposition between good artists and evil businessmen should embarrass us. The printing of the First Folio was a serious publishing venture on the part of everyone involved.

Without the commercial presses of the era, we would have far fewer plays to consider. We should be beholden to the printers. We owe them a scholarly appreciation of deep gratitude, matching our sense of gratitude to the antiquarians, collectors, and librarians who, over the years, found and preserved Renaissance manuscripts and published texts. Perhaps the fitting irony for Shakespearean scholars derives from capitalist ventures. Our debt for preservation extends not only to Jaggard but to key "robber barons" of American capitalism. Some of the most important archives, such as the Huntington Library in California and the Folger Shakespeare Library in Washington, D.C., exist because of businessmen. From Jaggard to Folger, the commercial side of Shakespearean theatre is an intricate aspect of its documentary existence and its textual meanings.

We would be wiser to recognize that the surviving texts necessarily represent a series of accommodations and multiple agendas that tie together the three makers of the Shakespearean texts. Instead of divide and conquer, whereby we remove the intentions of two makers in order to attain the true aims and actions of a single maker, we need to come to terms with the full complexity of the texts and their mingling of intentions in order to see how and why such texts are delivered to us in this way.

In recent years, a number of Shakespearean scholars have taken a more comprehensive approach to textual editing, theatre history, cultural history, and economic history.[15] When they are not embracing yet another divide-and-conquer model, the new editors (epitomized by Richard Proudfoot, general editor for the Arden Shakespeare, third series) are committed to a comprehensive historical project that does justice to playwright, players, and printers. But sometimes the new textual scholars, determined to attack the flaws of all editors and bibliographers from Edmond Malone to W. W. Greg and Fredson Bowers, remain committed to a divide-and-conquer agenda.[16] Also, some scholars, committed to a materialist analysis, still embrace an either/or model. In recent years, instead of demonizing the printers of Shakespeare's time, they have celebrated the history of the book. But to the extent that they still embrace a divide-and-conquer model by setting up absolute divisions between literary texts and performance texts, they hinder the historical project.[17] Yet despite some reductive ideas based upon an opposition between the material book and the immaterial performance, our textual studies in recent years point to a more holistic analysis. From these reassessments will arise new understandings of the playtexts as historical documents in relation to playwrights, players, and printers.

In our use of the quarto and folio texts as historical documents on performance methods, we face many questions and problems, but few definitive answers.

Nonetheless, Shakespeare's plays are crucial for reconstructing performances because they contain numerous stage directions (e.g., *enter, exeunt, aside, trumpet sounds, upon the walls, gives him a letter, enter dressed as a peasant, enter with a basket, with a torch, in his nightgown, kneel, fall, running, in a chair, attendants follow, flourish and shout,* etc.). They also contain speeches that make reference to and comment upon theatrical practices (e.g., the Prologue and the Chorus to *Henry V*, Hamlet's speech to the actors). Many of the stage directions refer to the dramatic world of the play (e.g., *in his orchard, with their army, upon the walls, the French fly*). And the characters often describe the features of their immediate world.

> Dramatic space is not identical with the stage or with three-dimensional space in general, for it originates in time through the gradual changes in the spatial relations between the actor and the stage and among the actors themselves. Every movement on the part of the actor is perceived and evaluated in connection with previous movements and with respect to the anticipated following movement . . . Dramatic space therefore takes over the entire theatre and is created in the spectator's consciousness during the production. It is the force which establishes unity among the other components of the theatre and at the same time receives concrete meaning from them.
>
> Jan Mukarovsky, *Structure, Sign, and Function* (1978: 214–15)

This kind of information suggests much about the spatial and temporal world of the play, but we need to distinguish between what was actually represented on stage and what was directed to the fancy of each spectator. In *Cymbeline*, Jachimo describes in specific detail the bedroom of the sleeping Imogen: the arras, the window, the pictures, the decorations on a chimney piece, and the "adornment of her bed" (2.2.26). The play was performed by the King's Men in 1610. Should we assume that a full bedroom, with even a painted ceiling of golden cherubs, was displayed on the Globe and Blackfriars stages? We may be tempted to use this description as evidence of staging practices,[18] but there are many uncertainties, as R. A. Foakes cautions us: "I know of no way to establish a boundary between what was done in practice on the Elizabethan stage and what was left to the imagination [of the spectators]."[19]

Still, some stage directions help us because they refer to the playhouse itself (e.g., *enter at one door; Ghost cries under the stage*). Yet other statements suggest both the fictional world and the actual playhouse (e.g., *thunder and lightning* is fictional, but it may also suggest, for example, that a thunder sheet was used for sound effects). These kinds of clues may refer to specific locations within the playhouse, the activities of the players, the staging effects, and the distribution of stage and hand properties. Also, as Francis Teague has shown (1991), we can sometimes determine – or at least make plausible conjectures on – the location of certain stage properties and the uses of particular hand properties (e.g., the bed in *Othello*, the letters in *King Lear*).

In our examination of the quartos and folios, our first task is to determine, as best we can, which stage directions suggest actual performance practices. The various stage directions in the quartos and folio texts are possible but not certain evidence of staging practices; this documentation expresses the possible intentions of playwright and players. We begin with possibilities, move to some probabilities, and, if we are really successful, attain a few certainties.

Beyond the inscribed stage directions, the statements that characters make to one another may reveal staging practices. At the end of *Hamlet*, for example, Fortinbras orders "four captains" to carry away the body of Hamlet. The required activity seems basically clear: the actors who portrayed the soldiers would have lifted the actor who played Hamlet and carried him out through one of the stage doors. A similar kind of action occurs at the end of *Antony and Cleopatra*. Caesar observes the bodies of Cleopatra and her women, then issues a command to his soldiers: "Take up her bed, / And bear her women from the monument" (5.2. 350–51).[20]

Here too, apparently, the actors playing soldiers would depart with the boy actors, who played the women. But would the exit also be through one of the doors? Caesar mentions the "monument," from which the women are carried. What is it? Is it on stage or in the imaginative world of the narrative? If visible to the spectators, what are its identifying features? Many scholars have assumed that Cleopatra and her women were located in the balcony, which served as the location for the monument. But if so, how was the bed taken up by the soldiers, who apparently are not in the balcony? Caesar's command, like that of Fortinbras, is simple, but how was it fulfilled? How were Cleopatra and the women removed from the stage?

This problem derives from a set of perplexing clues in the earlier "monument" scenes of the play. Three times in Act 4, scene 13 Cleopatra and her women announce they are going "To th' monument," where they will lock themselves away from Caesar's soldiers. Then in Act 4, scene 15, when the wounded Antony is brought to the base of the monument (carried, we are told, on his shield), Cleopatra says: "Help, Charmian, help, Iras, help! / Help friends below! Let's draw him hither" (4.15. 13–14). Then Cleopatra – that is, the young male actor who played the role[21] – struggles with the task:

> Here's sport indeed! How heavy weighs my lord!
> Our strength is all gone into heaviness,
> That makes the weight. Had I great Juno's power,
> The strong-winged Mercury should fetch thee up
> And set thee by Jove's side. Yet come a little;
> Wishers were ever fools. O, come, come, come! (33–38)

A stage direction follows this speech: "They heave Antony aloft to Cleopatra."[22]

Where on the stage was the actor playing Cleopatra? Who were the "friends" below? No description of the monument is provided in the text. Some scholars have argued that the word "aloft" meant that Cleopatra and her women were standing within the balcony, located in the tiring house wall approximately twelve feet above the stage floor. That's a daunting distance for heaving an adult male player (such as Richard Burbage in the role of Antony). Other scholars have argued that Cleopatra was located either on top of or within a special booth or raised platform that represented the monument. Or perhaps Cleopatra and her women were in some kind of timber and canvas tent. The monument, whatever its shape, may have provided some kind of intermediate stage level so that Antony could be lifted up only a few feet.[23] Or perhaps, as other scholars have suggested, there was a folding pavilion attached to the tiring house wall; the actors then climbed onto it (and the spectators used their imaginations to identify the pavilion as the monument). But all of these explanations are conjectures without any supporting evidence; there is no mention in the text of any such moveable property, booth, pavilion, tent, or raised platform.

We are, it seems, left to our historical imaginations for the features and size of something that may or may not have existed. Yet we can also draw upon what we know about staging practices in other plays. Lacking sufficient historical evidence, we extrapolate; we infer from the known to the unknown, thereby arriving at our hypothetical conclusion. A parallel situation sanctions an argument by analogy. Such reasoning, by its very nature, can only suggest likely (and unlikely) possibilities; it cannot prove anything. The study of Shakespearean staging provides many demonstrations of the arts of inference and analogical reasoning (ranging from sensible to impossible suppositions).

If Cleopatra's speech is taken as evidence for some kind of physical action by the actors, one thing is clear: wherever the actors playing the women were located, the body of the actor playing Antony had to be lifted up to them. Or at least an attempt was apparently made (or perhaps pantomimed?). Did they kneel and stretch their arms downward over the balcony railing, then haul the body up the wall and over the railing? Did a couple of actors, playing soldiers, lift Antony's body high enough for the boy actors to grab it? The description in Plutarch, from which Shakespeare derived this scene (and follows closely), suggests some kind of rigorous physical action of lifting and hauling. But what exactly does "draw him hither" mean? Did the players have some kind of sling? Ropes and pulley? If so, where was the pulley anchored? Was a block and tackle conveniently hanging in place, ready to be used for such a moment? Speculation takes the place of evidence.

Richard Hosley, for example, posits that a pulley system extended down from the covering roof and hut:

> Antony's chair can be attached by an appropriate harness to one end of a line descending from the stage cover a few feet in front of the upper station, the other end of the line being "returned" from the point of suspension (whether this is the drum of a winch within the stage superstructure or a ring or hook or pulley within or on the underside of the stage cover) to the players in the upper station. Thus Cleopatra and her Maids can "heave Antony aloft", swinging him and the chair into the upper station when they have hoisted him to the necessary height. Antony can then sit in his chair at the front of the upper station until carried off at the end of the action.[24]

But John Orrell, no less insistent, rejects Holsey's conjecture: "Certainly the passage cannot be taken as proving that the Globe possessed a hoist located in the Heavens."[25]

After all of this heavy lifting, no matter how it was done, what was achieved? If the actor playing Antony was lifted into the balcony (Hosley's "upper station"), where was he placed? If Antony's injured body was stretched out on the floor of the balcony, the actor may well have disappeared from view behind the railing, especially for the groundlings. Did he deliver his dying lines from this position of near invisibility? That seems unlikely for a crucial moment in the play. Did he rise up on his knees or stand for his death speech? Or was he raised from stage floor to the balcony, as Hosley and others have inferred, on a "sick chair," a device used in *Richard II*? But the stage directions name a shield, not a sick chair. Was Antony transferred from the shield, then perhaps strapped into a chair, without any guiding stage direction? Did the boy actors lift both body and chair into the balcony, over the railing? If, after having been placed in the balcony, did the actor remain in the chair so that his head would have been visible above the railing? Or was he then removed from the chair and placed on the floor?

This extrapolated chair is a rather forced explanation, adding hypothetical complications to a scene that is already difficult to reconstruct. The solution has become more complex than the problem. Many conjectures have been put forward, but none of these possibilities provides a definitive description of the staging of the death scene between Cleopatra and Antony. We tend to assume that somehow Antony was lifted to Cleopatra, located above in the balcony. But perhaps the balcony was not used; perhaps the actors pantomimed the basic action, thereby leaving to the spectators' imaginations the actual hauling and lifting. This explanation at least makes sense of the concluding stage direction at the end of the scene: "Exeunt, bearing of Anthonies body." If the body of the actor playing Antony had been lifted into the balcony, and was then basically out of sight, why would there be need of this stage direction? Whatever the case, this stage direction, like Caesar's command for the removal of the women, is yet another problem in the many conjectures on how this crucial scene was staged at the Globe.

We still await the discovery of sufficient evidence that reveals what really happened. Until that Eureka, we are condemned to plodding analysis, an awkward blend of inductive analysis and deductive speculation. There is, though, a circumstantial piece of evidence that teases us, as Joan Rees pointed out.[26] In the 1607 revision of Samuel Daniel's *The Tragedie of Cleopatra* (but not in his 1594 version) a passage occurs that could be based upon Daniel having observed a production of Shakespeare's play. The passage describes Cleopatra in her monument:

> She sends with speed his body to remove,
> The body of her love imbru'd with blood.
> Which brought unto her tomb . . .
> She draws him up in rolls of taffaty
> T'a window at the top, which did allow
> A little light unto her monument.
> There, Charmian, and poor Iras, two weak maids
> Foretir'd with watching, and their mistress' care,
> Tug'd at the pulley, having n'other aids,
> And up they hoist the swounding body there
> Of pale Antonius, show'ring out his blood
> On th'under lookers, which there gazed stood.

And when they had now wrought him up half way
(Their feeble powers unable more to do)
The frame stood still, the body at a stay,
When Cleopatra all her strength thereto
Puts, with what vigour love, and care could use,
So that it moves again, and then again
It come to stay. When she afresh renews
Her hold, and with reinforced power doth strain,
And all the weight of her weak body lays,
Whose surcharg'd heart more then her body weighs,
At length she wrought him up, and takes him in,
Lays his yet breathing body on her bed . . . [27]

Is this possible evidence for how the scene was staged in the production of Shakespeare's play? Was the body of the player of Antonius wrapped in taffeta, a fabric of silk, lifted by pulley into the balcony area, and then placed upon a bed? Or is Daniel, who also read Plutarch's life of Marc Antony, merely describing his own version of the passage in Plutarch?

Before we reach any conclusion based upon the 1607 revision of Daniel's *The Tragedie of Cleopatra*, we need to determine when he could have seen a production of Shakespeare's play. When was it first performed? It was not published until the Folio (1623). However, the play was entered in the Stationers' Register, along with *Pericles*, on May 20, 1608, by the printer Edward Blount. Such registry usually signals a forthcoming publication, but no quarto of the play appeared, as far as we know. In order for Daniel's substantial revisions in 1607 to have been influenced by Shakespeare's play, *Antony and Cleopatra* had to be first performed in 1607 or earlier. Perhaps Daniel saw a performance of Shakespeare's play before December 1607. He might have seen a public or private performance (depending upon one's conjectures). Composition, then, of *Antony* would have occurred most likely in 1606 and/or early 1607. But some scholars place it later, in late 1607 or 1608.[28] Was *Antony* written before or after *King Lear* and *Macbeth*? These three plays seem to be tightly grouped in 1606 and 1607. And some scholars argue for the priority of *Antony* and *Coriolanus*. The theatres were closed by plague during much of 1607, so perhaps the play was performed publicly either before March 1607 or in 1608. If 1607, we can use Daniel's play as possible evidence for the staging of the monument scene (unless, of course, Daniel's description is his own enhanced version of Plutarch).

In sum, we have various sources of information that may or may not have factual significance for how the monument scene was staged. This information can serve as possible evidence for our historical reconstructions. It teases us into various speculations about possibilities. This illustration from *Antony and Cleopatra* confronts us with the standard task of historical investigation: examine the available documents, determine their authenticity, test their reliability, and then analyze carefully how the pieces fit together (or contradict one another). From these sources, we identify some possible facts and develop our evidence for the analysis. We ask the right questions; then ask more questions. Slowly, despite some contradictions and gaps in the records, a possible description emerges, and then by means of careful reasoning, a plausible explanation may be developed. However, partial information complicates the task.

> Taken separately, there is scarcely a word in our modern version of the *Oresteia* which we may be certain of reading as Aeschylus wrote it. In its entirety, however, we need have no misgivings that our *Oresteia* is really that of Aeschylus. There is more certainty in the whole than in its parts.
>   Marc Bloch, *The Historian's Craft* (1953: 132–33)

The lack of sufficient documentation on a particular case does not necessarily mean defeat. Paradoxically, in order to understand how any one of Shakespeare's plays was possibly performed, historians must consider his plays collectively, as they were staged at the Globe, from 1599, when the playhouse was built, until 1613, when the first Globe burned down. In our attempts to construct theatre events at the Globe, the search for recurring patterns is crucial. We need to discover norms and patterns of behavior that likely recurred in the playhouses. Even though we may not be able to establish how a particular exit was achieved (e.g., the removal of Cleopatra, Antony, and the women), we can figure out, for example, the basic patterns of entrance and exit for many scenes in Shakespeare's plays. We can also tabulate the recurring uses of the discovery spaces, the kinds of scenes located in the balcony, the likely distribution of the types of stage properties, and the movement patterns of players as they enter and exit.

The texts – stage directions and dialogue – also imply, sometimes rather specifically, the movement patterns for secondary characters in particular scenes (e.g., servants, soldiers, messengers). By calculating their locations and movements, we can often determine, in turn, the locations and movement patterns of major characters. This is, in fact, a good historical principle: solve some of the minor details; then discover the larger ones. Track the movement of the worker bees, out in the world, and then follow them back to the hive and the queen. Historical puzzles, like scientific research or criminal investigations, often get solved in this manner.

> Most of man's actions comprise a *spatial* aspect, in the sense that the objects of orientation are distributed according to such relations as inside and outside, far away and close by, separated and united, and continuous and discontinuous. Space, therefore, is not a particular category of orientation, but an aspect of any orientation.
>   Christian Norberg-Schulz, *Existence, Space, and Architecture* (1971: 9)

Another basic principle in historical inquiry is to attend to the foundational issues and patterns, and in theatre, as in dance, this always means the spatial and temporal patterns. Because the plays provide various codes about the spatial dynamics of the stage, in both the dialogue and the stage directions, we are able to draw a referential map of spatial, temporal, and causal uses of the stage by the characters/players. It may not be a comprehensive map for theatre before the modern era, but it can be quite informative. For instance, a goldmine of lexical information is delivered by the prepositions (e.g., up, down, above, below, behind, before, in, at, outside, with, to, for), the demonstrative pronouns (this, these, that, those), the personal pronouns (he, she, I, we, you, they, it), and the adverbs (there, where, wherein, now, when, whenever, then, whence, next, near, far, later, latest, last, lately). Also, the interrogatives sometimes add to this spatial, temporal, and causal map of dramatic action (who, what, where, when). By attending carefully to these markers of space and location within the temporal sequence of a play, we can accumulate many patterns of dramatic action from the dialogue and stage directions. Thus, despite our problem of describing a specific scene in detail, we still derive and accumulate vital clues on standard procedures from lexical markers, such as *above, aloft, into, up, below.* Without such markers, our historical mission would be impossible.

> The subject posits itself, just as the world shows itself. Pronouns and demonstratives are in the service of this positing and this showing; they designate as clearly as possible the absolute character of this positing and this showing, which are the within and without of language: the world toward which it is directed, insofar as it says something about something; the nonworldly within the ego which radiates in its acts. Language is no more a foundation than it is an object; it is a mediation; it is a medium, the "milieu," in which and through which the subject posits himself and the world shows itself.
>   Paul Ricoeur, "The Question of the Subject," in *The Conflict of Interpretations: Essays in Hermeneutics* (1974: 256)

In addition, the poetic richness of the plays – the images, similes, metaphors, and symbols – may suggest visual codes of action, though we need to proceed with great caution. Much about the poetic register in drama is intended for the ears and imaginations of the auditors rather than their eyes. Only a limited portion of this poetic world is realized materially on stage as dramatic actions. For the theatre historian, who may be most comfortable with the stage directions as historical clues, this poetic and rhetorical richness operates in the realm of teasing, seductive possibility. The danger, of course, is that these literary qualities provide a multitude of possible interpretations for players – as the productions of the plays across the centuries well illustrate. Each performance delivers a rich material embodiment of the text, a materiality of bodies, clothes, and objects that reveals much that we miss in our reading practices (despite the materiality of the book). Yet because many possible, distinct performances exist in the poetic registers of a text, the performance historian must tread carefully in any analysis of the potentialities of the poetic sources for Globe performances. It is all too easy to convince ourselves that our poetic readings of the metaphors accord with the playwright's intentions about a character's actions. Literary critics may be free to speculate, but theatre historians must be circumspect.

Over the years, thousands of literary essays and books on Shakespeare's plays have posited theatrical possibilities for dramatic action on the basis of poetic analysis. In modern times many of these studies have provided production ideas for actors, designers, and directors (e.g., Jan Kott's influence on Peter Brook's *King Lear*). Yet these studies, even when they contribute specific suggestions on the performance codes within the text, should not be confused with historical investigations of Shakespeare's stage. As literary studies they are often brilliant and suggestive of theatrical potential, but as historical studies they are usually quite fanciful. We are left with teasing possibilities (and, even more, with far too many impossibilities). Although we know, for instance, that the poetic qualities of Hamlet's language – the key metaphors and rhetorical tropes – had to contribute to Richard Burbage's preparation of the title role, it is close to impossible to recover aspects of his performance on the basis of a literary and rhetorical study of the poetry. Which actions did he discover? Which metaphors translated into possible stage actions? Paradoxically, the evidence is too rich and plentiful; it tells us too many things – all of which open up the imaginative potentialities of the play yet fail to deliver its historical reality of a particular actor in a specific time and place. Here, too, the historian may be wise to start with the small linguistic sources, such as prepositions; then, if they point to specific actions, the poetic imagery might be consulted – for supplemental, supporting evidence.

In addition to the verbal clues, each of the plays articulates a semiotic system of visual and nonverbal signs. Part of our historical task is to reconstitute the visual qualities and dynamics of performance. In each play a number of these visual and nonverbal signs can be interpreted for possible, even likely, evidence of staging practices, such as the typical uses of sounds, silences, color codes in costumes and banners, the placement and movement of stage properties, and the uses of hand properties such as torches and letters.[29] When examined with care, the verbal text holds clues to its potential visual practices. Some of these signs are quite explicit, and thus carry historical information as valuable as the pointers in the prepositions and adverbs. But when making interpretations, the historian must be far more cautious than the literary critic, the theatre director, or the performer today.

Besides the published plays and a small handful of manuscripts, scholars have examined a wide range of primary sources, including contracts for the construction of playhouses (e.g., the Fortune and Hope), legal records of disputes among actors, playwrights, spectators, and playhouse managers, reports written by playhouse visitors (including foreign eyewitnesses who often note things that may seem too familiar and un-noteworthy to a local observer), records on the publishing history of plays, complaints and attacks of opponents to the theatre, governmental records on the regulation of the stage, inventories of costumes and stage properties (e.g., for Philip Henslowe's Rose theatre), and the wills of actors. The available evidence is a mixture of verbal and visual sources. Also, historians have studied the archeological remains of the Rose playhouse, built in 1587 and renovated in 1592. Four hundred years after the performances, new empirical evidence emerged out of the dirt.

Visual evidence has proved quite valuable. Besides the Swan drawing, discovered in 1888,[30] we have several panorama engravings of London that show the location of the playhouses. Their reliability, however, has been a major problem. But in 1948 I. A. Shapiro demonstrated that while the 1616 drawing by J. C. Visscher is unreliable (despite the widespread use of it in theatre history books), the 1647 "Long View" by Wenceslaus Hollar is trustworthy (despite his reversal of the names of the Globe and Hope).[31] Then in 1982 and 1988 John Orrell revealed how and why Hollar is to be trusted in his details (e.g., height of the Globe) because of the drawing frame and topographical glass he used from the church tower of St. Savior's.[32]

Going beyond the many textual documents and material artifacts, theatre historians have delved into the social practices, economic conditions, and political activities outside the playhouses in order to get a sense of everything from the clothing fashion of the times (which might answer questions about costuming practices) to the operations of the court patronage system (which might reveal not only economic factors and political activities but also social and moral attitudes toward the theatre). Indeed, by examining the documentary record beyond the Globe plays, players, and theatre building, historians have discovered vital information about other theatre companies, actors, managers, spectators, playhouses, and plays. Moreover, theatre historians have investigated governmental procedures, social values, education, the growth of publishing and literacy, the religious beliefs and practices, and economic conditions. The expansion of research into these contextual matters, including almost any aspect of the activities and attitudes of people within the society, may appear tangential, even irrelevant, to the immediate task of reconstructing a performance event. At what point, then, does theatre history become cultural and social history? Has a border been crossed, and if so, does it matter? This set of issues will be a major concern in the following chapters. If theatre historians attempt to expand into and encompass a dozen or more disciplinary fields, what are the needed research skills and knowledge?

In our historical reconstruction of playhouse practices we reason both inductively and deductively. There are, of course, strengths and weaknesses with both methods of historical inquiry. Both can lead to misinformation and misjudgement. Yet collectively induction and deduction complement one another; both are necessary for historical research. All historians, in the process of reconstructing particular events, must often rely upon their ability to discover correspondences, norms, patterns, and habits of the agents and events under study. Our search for these recurring conditions usually follows two distinct paths of investigation and interpretation. One method is based upon the inductive principle of accumulation, whereby we gather a sufficient number of cases of a specific factor, trait, or behavior that allow us to make a general statement about possibility and probability. We compile, for instance, a tabulation of the number of times the Globe plays call for a "discovery space," a trap, or action in the "above" area. We discover recurring patterns, from which we posit our descriptions. The other method depends upon a deductive, analogical, or syllogistic idea, from which we infer or extrapolate our explanations of theatrical practices. We deduce, for instance, the design for all of the amphitheatres from the Swan theatre drawing. Or by means of a manual on fencing we infer the acting method for fight scenes in the plays.

Using the accumulative method, Bernard Beckerman examined the recurring patterns for certain staging practices, such as entrances and exits, in Shakespeare's

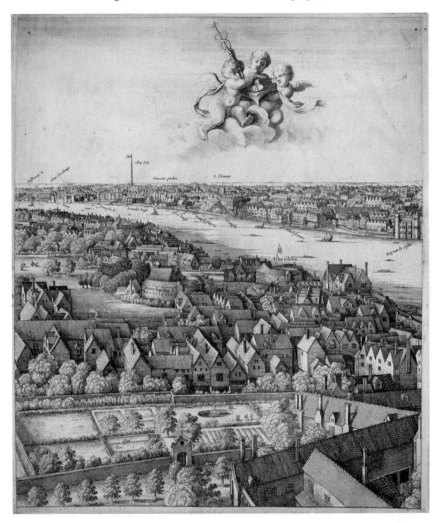

Illustration 3. Wenceslaus Hollar, Long View of London from Southwark (*c.* 1647); the Globe Theatre is mislabeled *Beere bayting h* and the Hope Theatre is mislabeled *The Globe.*

plays at the Globe between 1599 and 1609.[33] On the same principle, T. J. King compiled performance data from all of the plays that were possibly performed at the Globe, 1599 to 1642.[34] By means of these kinds of accumulative investigations, we can make informed suggestions on the specific cases (such as the use of the trap for the witches in *Macbeth*). By examining all of the plays written for the Globe Theatre, we can tabulate how, where, and when various parts of the stage were used. Adapting aspects of King's method for a different purpose, Andrew Gurr has examined all the extant plays that "can be assigned with reasonable confidence to a particular company and playhouse."[35] This data provides the foundation for his study of the practices of each of the theatre companies in the era. Also illustrating an inductive method, Scott McMillan examined the documentary record of players and playing companies, in conjunction with the printing and performance history of key plays, in order to develop his analysis of casting practices and the ties between certain playwrights and certain theatre companies.[36] This method provides part of the strength of the study that he and Sally-Beth MacLean published on the players and plays of the Queen's Men in the 1580s.[37]

The second method for establishing norms and patterns derives from deductions. In a search for correspondences, we take a given or general condition, idea, or practice, then apply it to specific historical cases. Something from one domain justifies a judgement – a deduction – about something in another domain. Ratiocination and discursive reasoning, as basic modes of argument, provide both hypothesis and verification for many investigations in theatre history. Thus, if an actor was strapped into a chair in one play, perhaps, as Richard Hosley argues, this strapping method was used for the production of another play. Or if the Swan drawing reveals two doors, then surely the Globe had two doors. Although there is, in philosophy and rhetoric, a long, abiding tradition of training in the logic of deductive thinking (e.g., *a fortiori* reasoning, *a priori* reasoning, *a posteriori* reasoning, syllogism, apodictic proposition, *enthymeme*), very few theatre scholars today demonstrate an understanding or application of this heritage. Instead, as a poor surrogate, a model of common sense reasoning and inference seems to guide most of us in our deductions.[38]

Historians often have to build a case by means of inferences and analogies. We deduce B from A, and then announce our explanation of a general idea, condition, or principle that operates in theatre production. For example, by studying the sumptuary laws on clothing requirements for each class (e.g., types of hats, fabric, ornaments), historians can deduce (i.e., make conjectures about) the possible types of costumes the characters wore on stage. Likewise, by extrapolating from an inventory of stage properties at Philip Henslowe's Rose Theatre (dated March 10, 1598), historians can infer what kinds of properties were possibly used not simply at the Rose for specific productions but at the other theatres, including the Globe. In this case, deduction and inductive go hand in hand, which is often the case. Henslowe's list tabulates various properties, allowing for some inductive reasoning, yet we still have to deduce from the single list to possible cases.

The dividing line thus wavers between inductive and deductive reasoning. For example, several pamphlets attacking the theatres and players were published in the 1580s and 1590s. Some scholars use them as evidence for a general condition of anti-theatrical prejudice against the theatres. Is this an inductive or deductive argument? Do two pamphlets support a deductive statement, but ten allow for an inductive analysis? Either way, is this evidence sufficient for a historical conclusion about the anti-theatrical status of theatre in London society over six or seven decades at various theatres? To what extent can a few pamphleteers stand in as representative figures for most of the people of the city? Attempts to construct audience reception and values

Item j rocke, j cage, j tombe, j Hell mought	1 rock, 1 cage, 1 tomb, 1 Hell mouth
Item j tome of Guido, j tome of Dido, j bedsteade	1 tomb of *Guido*, 1 tomb of *Dido*, 1 bedstead
Item viij lances j payer of stayers for Fayeton	8 lances, 1 pair of stairs for *Phaeton*
Item ij stepells, & j chyme of belles, & j beacon	2 steeples, & 1 chime of bells, & 1 beacon
Item j hecfor for the playe of Faeton, the limes dead	1 hecfor [?] for the play of *Phaeton*, limbs dead [?]
Item j globe, & j golden scepter; iij clobes	1 globe, & 1 golden scepter; 3 clubs
Item ij marchepanes, & the sittie of Rome	2 marchpanes, & the city of Rome
Item j gowlden flece; ij rackets; j baye tree	1 golden fleece; 2 rackets; 1 bay tree
Item j wooden hatchett; j lether hatchete	1 wooden hatchet; 1 leather hatchet
Item j wooden canepie; owld Mahemetes head	1 wooden canopy; old Mahomet's head
Item j lyone skin; j beares skyne; & Faetones lymes, & Faeton charete; & Argosse heade.	1 lion skin; 1 bear's skin; & Phaeton's limbs, & Phaeton's chariot; & Argus's head
Item Nepun forcke & garland	Neptune's fork & garland
Item j crosers stafe; Kentes woden leage	1 crosier's staff; Kent's wooden leg
Item Ierosses head, & raynbowe; j littell alter	Iris's head, & rainbow; 1 little altar
Item viij viserdes; Tamberlyne brydell; j wooden matook	8 vizards; Tamburlaine's bridle; 1 wooden mattock
Item Cupedes bowe, & quiver; the clothe of the Sone & Mone	Cupid's bow, & quiver; the cloth of the sun & moon
Item j bores heade & Serberoose iij heades	1 boar's head & Cerberus's 3 heads
Item j Cadeseus; ij mose banckes, & j snake	1 caduceus; 2 moss banks, & 1 snake
Item ij fanes of feathers; Belendon stable; j tree Of gowlden apelles; Tantelouse tre; jx eyorn targates	2 fans of feathers; *Belin Dun* stable; 1 tree of golden apples; Tantalus' tree; 9 iron targets
Item j cooper targate, & xvij foyles	1 cooper target, & 17 foils
Item iiij wooden targates; j greve armer	4 wooden targets; 1 greave armour
Item j syne for Mother Readcap; j buckler	1 sign for *Mother Readcap*; 1 buckler
Item Mercures wings; Tasso picter; j helmet with a dragon; j shelde, with iij lyones; j eleme bowle	Mercury's wings; Tasso's picture; 1 helmet with a dragon; 1 shield with 3 lions; 1 elm bowl
Item j chayne of dragons; j gylte speare	1 chain [?] of dragons; 1 gilt spear
Item ij coffenes; j bulles head; and j vylter	2 coffins; 1 bull's head; and 1 vulture [or philtre?]
Item iij tymbrells, j dragon in fostes	3 tumbrels, 1 dragon in *Faustus* [?]
Item j lyone; ij lyon heades; j great horse with his leages; j sack-bute	1 lion; 2 lion heads; 1 great horse with his legs; 1 sack-butt
Item j whell and frame in the Sege of London	1 wheel and frame in *The Siege of London*
Item j paire of rowghte gloves	1 pair of wrought gloves
Item j poopes miter	1 pope's miter
Item iij Imperial crownes; j playne crowne	3 Imperial crowns; 1 plain crown
Item j gostes crown; j crown with a sone	1 ghost's crown; 1 crown with a sun
Item j frame for the heading in Black Jone	1 frame for the heading in *Black John*
Item j black dogge	1 black dog
Item j cauderm for the Jewe	1 cauldron for the Jew

Illustration 4. Property list by Philip Henslowe for the Admiral's Men, Rose Theatre, dated March 10, 1598 (i.e., 1599 according to Gregorian calendar beginning in January, not the middle of March).

from the statements of a few pamphleteers are surely suspect. Unfortunately, many studies of the playhouse spectators, who represented a wide range of Londoners and visitors, are often deductive, even though the arguments introduce a few pieces of inductive evidence. One scholar insists that the playhouse audiences were obsessed with an anti-theatrical prejudice, another scholar constructs an elite audience, and yet another scholar gives us a popular culture. Typically, these formulations are derived from a few pamphlets or a few plays. Then this textual model serves, by analogy, as the basis for a reception model that supposedly represents the audience (often conceived of as a singular entity).[39]

Our evidence for costuming practices comes from several sources, including the plays, inventory lists, drawings, etchings, and paintings, the sumptuary laws, and comments of visitors, such as Thomas Platter. Scholars work both inductively and deductively from these sources. For example, by drawing upon the inventory of costumes and beards held at Trinity College, Cambridge in 1550, Peter Holland suggests, by analogy, what kinds of beards might have been available for Bottom and the mechanicals in *A Midsummer Night's Dream*.[40] And by identifying the costume that a character called Robin Goodfellow wore in *Grim the Collier of Croydon* (c. 1600, published 1662 in *Gratiae Theatrales*, probably written by William Haughton), Holland makes a quite plausible (but of course not certain) conjecture for the costuming of Puck in Shakespeare's *Midsummer*.[41] Savvy historians often reason analogically. Yet without additional evidence, beyond the analogies, the well-reasoned suppositions remain conjectures in the realm of possibility. Promising but not conclusive.

In our deductive methods, the evidence for the specific case we seek to prove is derived from a parallel condition or context. Information taken from the condition or context provides a deductive proof (and sometimes a possible cause) for the theatrical practice. Of course, the search for parallel cases can easily mislead us. Analogies are notoriously inexact and inappropriate. For example, a seventeenth-century manual of rhetoric by John Bulwer called *Chirologia, or the Naturall Language of the Hand* (1644) recommends, with many illustrations, the gestures that speakers should use to express ideas, attitudes, and emotions. By questionable extrapolation, theatre historians have used this book as the basis for generalizations about acting methods throughout the sixteenth and seventeenth centuries. Our joining of rhetoric to acting is not unreasonable, but a 1644 rhetoric book may have little significance for how players in the 1590s developed their craft.

In another kind of deduction, the historian may set up a political text, religious context, or social condition as the basis for a projected description and analysis of a theatre event. A correspondence is proclaimed; then assumed. The context, in this sense, produces an explanation for an event, an action, or a belief. Deductions can be applied generally, thereby allowing for broad explanations. For instance, in his formula of *platea* and *locus*, Robert Weimann depends upon a few limited references to the *platea* and *locus* in a select number of texts. From this limited base, he proposes that a single staging procedure maintained itself, as a controlling idea, for several centuries. He does not base this formulation upon the inductive method of gathering of evidence from a number of documents, texts, or case studies.

Whatever our method, induction or deduction, we must use care when we attempt to identify typical and general patterns in the production of Shakespeare's plays. We face difficulties not only because of the scarcity of detailed information (and because the significance of key sources may be ambiguous and even contradictory) but also

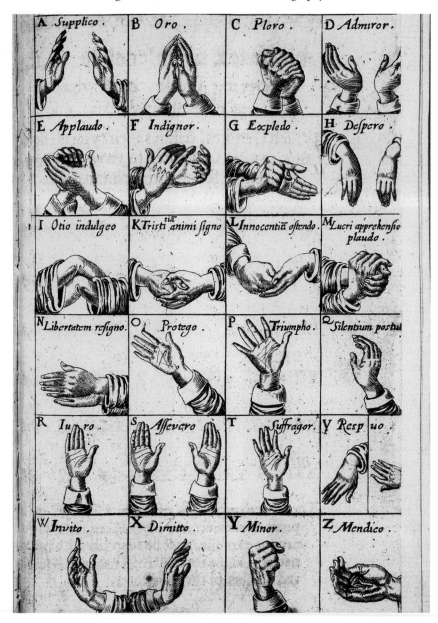

Illustration 5. Hand gestures for orators. From John Bulwer, *Chirologia: or the Natural Language of the Hand.* London, 1644.

because our need to set up typical conditions may cause us to impose an overly general or simplified idea onto the event we are attempting to understand. When undertaken with care, though, the study of the general, the typical, and the contextual allows the historian to move, step by step, from possibility to plausibility to probability – at least in some cases.

In their endeavors to reconstruct performances at the Globe playhouse, theatre historians have asked their questions, analyzed their clues, developed their circumstantial evidence, and reached their conclusions. For example, working inductively, Alan C. Dessen has carefully tabulated and analyzed the many staging directions and character statements within the Renaissance plays.[42] He has been able to pinpoint many details about staging practices. And working deductively, John Orrell has attempted to reconstruct the playhouses and their interior spaces by postulating that the building practices in London followed the same procedures that were used for constructing Roman and Italian theatre buildings, as spelled out in the writings of Vitruvius and Sebastiano Serlio.[43] The humanist tradition, such as Vitruvius' idea of the *homo ad quadratum*, provides the deductive model for Orrell's conjectures. Of course, both Dessen and Orrell combine inductive and deductive methods in their historical study, but Dessen relies extensively on the particular examples he gathers from the plays and Orrell often puts forward a deductive model to make his major arguments.

Yet despite their impressive jobs of inductive and deductive scholarship, the historians may still come up short in some aspects of their accounts of the staging practices. The gathering of evidence, as Dessen insists, is always partial: "a host of uncertainties persist about what actually happened upon the stages within the Globe and other contemporary playhouses . . . Firm conclusions, neat distinctions, and confident truth claims do not emerge from the extant evidence."[44] Andrew Gurr and Mariko Ichikawa, in their attempt to sum up our knowledge of staging in Shakespeare's theatres, concur with Dessen: "Few of the elements that were inherent in the early staging can be identified now with much confidence."[45] In spite of our best efforts, there are many gaps in our knowledge of the Globe playhouse and the production methods of the era.

Theatre scholars, nonetheless, are often unequivocal in their hypotheses, explanations, and suppositions. Questions may exist, but answers continue to be put forward. Apparently, a scholar's authority resides in a confident, even assertive voice. Scholars of Elizabethan theatre, accordingly, are often adamant about the style of acting, the number of doors, the location and use of the discovery space, the methods of staging, the behavior of the audience, or the architecture of the playhouse. But of course other scholars disagree, just as adamantly. The arguments, often intense, are seldom resolved. From generation to generation, even decade to decade, our explanations for most of these staging practices have undergone change. Yet as soon as a consensus – of at least a dominant opinion – is achieved in any matter, an alternative explanation emerges and displaces it.[46]

In the 1950s and 1960s, for instance, Richard Hosley published over a dozen articles on various aspects of the Globe playhouse. In great measure, his views on the Elizabethan stage displaced those of John Cranford Adams, whose model of the Globe

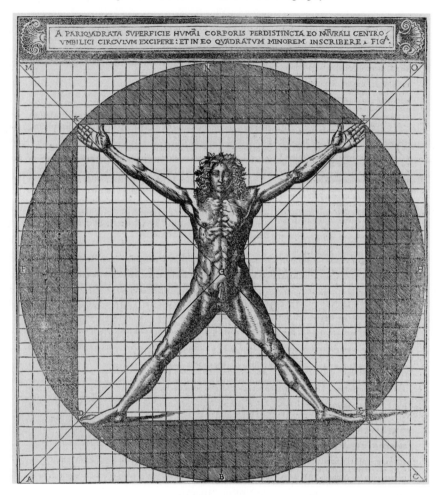

Illustration 6. *Homo ad quadratum,* a drawing from *Di Lucio Vitruuio Pollione de Architectura Libri Dece: traducti de latino in vulgare affigurati* . . . By Augustinus Gallo *et al.* Como, Italy: Gotardo da Ponte, 1521.

had reigned supreme during the 1940s.[47] In fact, by the time Adams published the second edition of *The Globe Playhouse* in 1961, his ideas on the definitive features of the Globe were rejected by most scholars. Yet Hosley's reign as the leading authority was also brief. By 1975, when he presented his description of "The Playhouses" in the third volume of the *Revels History of Drama in English* (1975), some of his ideas, including his analogical mode of analysis that gave priority to the Swan drawing as the typical model for the outdoor playhouses, had lost their hold on the scholarly community. John Orrell, though still accepting the idea of a dominant model for all of the playhouses, argued in the 1980s that their design was dependent upon architectural principles developed by Vitruvius and revived by Renaissance humanism (though carpentry practices in England fine-tuned the methods of construction). Orrell argued determinedly against the prevalent idea that the design features of the theatres had emerged out of inn-yards (e.g., Bel Savage, the Bell, Cross Keys) that players used before the 1570s.[48] Consequently, the new Globe playhouse in London was built in accord with most of Orrell's ideas.[49] But if the disagreements over the new Globe offer a fair measure of scholarly perspectives today, Orrell's status as the reigning authority on playhouse construction will also end in a short time (if it hasn't already).[50] For example, when the foundational remains of the Rose playhouse were discovered in 1989, the building was strikingly at odds with some of Orrell's deductive assumptions about the humanist traditions that guided playhouse construction.[51] As for Adams, he does not even warrant a place in Andrew Gurr's bibliography for *The Shakespearean Stage* (3rd edn, 1992). The scholars, like the kings in Shakespeare's history plays, rise and fall with rapidity. Only one thing is clear: after more than 200 years of research and commentary on the architecture of the playhouses, the scholars still disagree with one another on basic questions and answers.[52]

What do these turns in the scholarly wheel of fortune mean? Is there no advancement in knowledge? Such an explanation cannot be accepted, for without question Andrew Gurr knows much more about the Shakespearean stage than Edmond Malone was able to discover 200 years ago. He also knows things that eluded E. K. Chambers. Yet our progress in knowledge has extended only so far; the things we don't know remain substantial. Alan Dessen estimates that "probably 90 percent or more" of the evidence for the staging of Shakespeare's plays has disappeared in the passage of time.[53] This comment mirrors Glynne Wickham's observation that the scholarly study for the whole field of English Renaissance theatre is 90 percent speculation to 10 percent fact.[54]

> The whole history of the past (what has been called *history-as-actuality*) can be known to the historian only through the surviving record of it (*history-as-record*), and most of history-as-record is only the surviving part of the recorded part of the remembered part of the observed part of the whole.
> Louis Gottschalk, *Understanding History: A Primer of Historical Method* (1969: 45)

Given, then, that a lack of documents is the normal situation for historians of pre-modern eras, disagreements over historical analysis and interpretation are to be expected. But the disagreements actually have a more fundamental explanation than a lack of evidence. Historians have a mandate to interpret, not simply to describe, the historical record. We are asking questions about how and why, not just describing the factual record of who, what, where, and when. Necessarily, the lack of sufficient evidence requires speculations and conjectures. Inductive scholarship may begin with the dictum of William Carlos Williams – no ideas but in things – but nobody, including Williams, makes sense of the world only by means of documentary research and description. Ideas, in their interpretive manner, arise from reasoning and speculation. This is true for inductive as well as deductive reasoning.

There is, though, yet another explanation for the faulty practices of the documentary scholars who sift through the records on pre-modern theatre. In brief, theatre historians, committed to documentary research, are behind the times. Wedded to outdated procedures and assumptions, they have failed to take up new methods of study. Consequently, flawed methodologies rather than insufficient documentation may be the key issue here. This is the view – or indictment – from cultural historians who criticize theatre historians for their empirical procedures and positivist assumptions. According to this indictment, theatre historians have ignored the historiographical issues and problems that animate modern scholarship (e.g., New Historicism, cultural materialism, identity studies, etc.).[55] Guided by an ideal of "fidelity" to the document and a principle of "authenticity," first proclaimed by Edmond Malone but still worshiped, it would seem, by many theatre historians, these diligent antiquarians continue to argue over the diameter of the Globe playhouse but fail to understand the cultural dimensions of the Shakespearean stage and society.[56]

> A people will wherever possible invent its drama according to its own history, spirit of the times, customs, opinions, language, national biases, traditions, and inclinations.
> Johann Gottfried von Herder, *Against Pure Reason: Writings on Religion, Language, and History* (1993: 151)

What should we make of this criticism? What, indeed, should be the place and value of documentary scholarship in the field of theatre history? What are its limitations? In this basic debate, we have two contending evaluations of theatre historians and their accomplishments.

(1) On the one hand, theatre historians have actually done a conscientious job of reconstructing past performance practices, given the many gaps in the documentary record. Though the questions they ask seldom lead them into the areas of cultural and social history, they have advanced our knowledge of the "Shakespearean stage" (e.g., theatre architecture, players, staging methods, organization of theatre companies, printers and publishing procedures, court performances, patronage systems and networks, touring practices, theatrical activities throughout the towns and cities of the country). For example, the building of the new Globe Theatre is a demonstration of what documentary scholars are able to accomplish, despite the partial record. To their credit, a handful of theatre historians persevered; they accepted Sam Wanamaker's mission and they got the new Globe built. They were not deterred by the dismissive critiques of some cultural historians. Now that the Globe exists, most of us are willing to admit (however begrudgingly) that the project was justified and the achievement deserves at least measured praise (though we still have doubts about recovering the "authentic" method of performance).

(2) On the other hand, according to the critics of documentary scholarship, theatre historians, timid to a fault, have remained antiquarians. And the Globe building has been dismissed as a tourist attraction (on the order of, if not the scale of, Disneyland). No amount of crying over the lack of sources can hide the basic fact that theatre

historians have been hindered primarily by their inadequate research procedures and assumptions. If they would abandon their antiquated methods, they would discover that there is much more to reveal about theatre, culture, and society. In short, theatre historians, committed to their empirical methods, have failed to explain how and why theatre events must be constructed in terms of the cultural, political, and social conditions. Having imprisoned themselves in the archive, theatre historians cannot see beyond their piles of documents. They lack the intellectual understanding to see the interrelated world of theatre and culture.

This debate, when set up in this dichotomous manner, implies that we need to take sides: antiquarianism to the right, cultural history to the left. Shall we look backward to nineteenth-century positivism or forward to twenty-first-century performance and cultural studies? Moreover, this way of presenting the basic historical problem – documentary description versus contextual analysis – suggests that we must choose between two scholarly models. Some people are imprisoned within their antiquarian methods; others are liberated by their cultural materialism. It is my hope, however, that we can get beyond this false dichotomy. In this chapter we have examined some of the issues and problems in documentary research and analysis. Our case study has been Shakespearean theatre but it applies to all archival research. Let's turn, in the next chapter, to another case study in order to investigate some of the issues and problems that face cultural historians. We may discover that all of us, as historians, need the disciplinary skills and procedures of both documentary scholars and cultural historians.

Chapter 2

Cultural histories: the case of Alfred Jarry's *Ubu Roi*

Scholars who study modern theatre usually have access to production documents, promptbooks, reviews, interviews, feature articles, letters, and autobiographical statements – all of the things that are unavailable, with rare exception, to the historian of pre-modern performances. For example, the task of describing the staging of Tennessee Williams' *Cat on a Hot Tin Roof* in New York City at the Morosco Theatre in 1955 is almost fail proof. We have the stage manager's promptbook that allows us to track each and every entrance and exit, each sound effect, and each lighting cue. We even know where each piece of lighting equipment was hung and how it was used. We know the details of the scene design, the costumes, and the stage properties. We can describe the movement and gestures of the actors, almost minute by minute, on the basis of the detailed promptbook and a number of photographs. We can even recreate the very inflection of the actors' voices in the delivery of certain lines. And though there are several textual versions of the play, we know which one was used in the Broadway production, directed by Elia Kazan. After the production, which ran for almost a year and won awards, both Kazan and Williams wrote about their disagreements over the versions of the play. We know that Kazan insisted that Big Daddy should appear in the last act, though Williams had originally limited him to Act Two. Kazan won this argument. In sum, we have the full production record that provides all of the information on who, what, where, when, how, and why.[1]

We are thus able to present not only a reconstruction of the staging of *Cat* but also an interpretation of the event in terms of several possible contexts (e.g., the rehearsal process, the professional relationship between Williams and Kazan, the contributions of Jo Mielziner the designer, the development of Williams' career, the talents of the actors, the biographies of participants, the conditions of New York theatre in the decade, the southern themes in the play, and the cultural history of American drama. And because a film version of the play was released a year later, we can compare and contrast stage and screen.

In modern times, when not constrained by a lack of documentation, the theatre historian is able to describe in detail an amazingly wide variety of cultural performances, from play productions to festivals. The range of possibilities extends from the Wayang Golek puppet theatre of Java to the history of American theatre during the Cold War of the 1950s.[2] Likewise, even before modern times, it is possible to reconstruct many details of a complex theatrical event such as the nightly riots that audience members maintained for sixty-seven days against higher prices at John Philip Kemble's Covent Garden in 1809.[3] And beyond the theatre buildings and entertainment venues, we can reveal the ways that performance and political power operated in the street theatre of nineteenth-century Philadelphia or in the series of political performances in Tiananmen Square in Beijing, including the National Day parades before the Cultural Revolution, Mao Zedong's public rally on October 1, 1949, the Communist Party's spectacle *In a Land of Silence* in honor of Premier Zhou Enlai in 1978, the anti-Gang of Four plays of the 1980s, and the students' political performances in the Square in 1991.[4]

Yet before we celebrate our ability to do justice to a wide range of performance events, we need to consider how and why, despite sufficient documentation, we sometimes make mistakes in our research procedures and miscalculations in our contextual analysis. There are, of course, some situations that defy our ability to discover sufficient information. We are also stymied when key witnesses and participants misrepresent the event or attempt to deceive us.[5]

More troubling, though, we often make mistakes and miscalculations in our basic methods of inquiry. Even when the problems are the expected ones of partial documentation – a condition that all historians should be prepared to confront in the normal procedures of research – we find ways to muddle the fundamental task of compiling reliable, accurate information. Compounding our mishandling of the documentary record, we sometimes adopt contextual and causal explanations that are inadequate, even inappropriate. In such cases the difficulties usually derive from the abiding problems in historical inquiry: flawed research methods, inadequate definitions, inappropriate concepts for setting up and organizing a topic, faulty modes of analysis and interpretation, and questionable models for establishing the framing conditions for events. Our scholarship can also be constrained by our ideological biases (often reduced to simplified dictums and dogmas) and our cultural assumptions (often not recognized, reflected upon, and examined).

Consequently, in some cases our historical representations of modern events may be as flawed as those we put forward for pre-modern events. In fact, we can sometimes recover performance methods, in striking detail, from five and six hundred years ago, yet bungle the basic details of a contemporary event.[6] These flawed cases, instead of being caused primarily by inadequate evidence, reveal more complex problems of inappropriate modes of inquiry. To illustrate this point, I want to consider a famous theatre event that has achieved a central place in our historical narratives about avant-garde art and the development of modernism in the theatre: the production of Alfred Jarry's *Ubu Roi* in 1896, produced in Paris by Aurélien-Marie Lugné-Poe's Théâtre de l'Œuvre.[7] This case study features some recurring problems in the handling of the documentary record that all theatre historians face. It also reveals how and why certain kinds of cultural interpretations, including popular narratives and ideological presuppositions, produce misconceived explanations of an event's context and meaning.

The published scholarship on the production contains a surprising number of contradictory statements and misleading explanations. Indeed, the established history, which has been transformed into a series of oft-repeated anecdotes, has contributed to the confusion over what actually happened. These historical lapses result less from the mishandling of specific documents, though that is part of the problem, than from the inadequate analytical methods and assumptions that guide the cultural histories. In the process of describing and celebrating the première, we have been influenced apparently by our guiding ideas on the nature of avant-garde art. We bring to the production a set of modernist narratives, assumptions, beliefs, and ideologies. Consequently, despite the availability of the extensive documentary records, our descriptions and explanations have misrepresented both the event and its context.

> The dramatist, like all other artists, is searching for the truth – which exists in several different versions.
> Alfred Jarry, "Twelve Theatrical Topics," *Selected Works* (1963: 86)

Illustration 7. Alfred Jarry, drawing from 1896 by Caran d'Ache.

The documentary record for the performance of *Ubu Roi* is substantial. Besides the play and its early drafts, we have Jarry's essays on the play, his drawings that represent some of the characters and their costumes, his address to the theatre audience, and his published statements after the production. We also have commentary by some members of the production team and the performers, the reports of various spectators, and dozens of theatre reviews and essays in the newspapers and journals, some appearing in the weeks after the event. Then, in the following years, a number of articles, diaries, memoirs, and historical reflections were published by people directly and indirectly involved in the production. This archive of information, some reliable and some unreliable, was followed by not only key biographies but also the critical and historical scholarship of the last two generations.

How, then, has the production been documented, reported, and interpreted? What is the relationship between the extensive documentary record and the subsequent historical and critical studies? How did the play and production attain a central place in our studies of the development of modern theatre, the avant-garde movement, the modern director, and the history of modernism? Why is *Ubu Roi*, for many commentators, the definitive production in the birth of the avant-garde theatre? Once again, as we did in chapter 1, we start our historical inquiry with a set of historical questions. As we will see, though, many commentators on this event approach it with answers and assumptions already in place.

> The point of departure in investigation is historical interrogation.
>   Johann Gustav Droysen, *Outline of the Principles of History* (1893: 18) (*Grundriss der Historik*, 1867)

Almost without exception, the studies of the production proclaim that it served as a catalyst or turning point in the history of modernism in the theatre. It is widely credited with creating the avant-garde theatre by using art as a weapon of assault against the establishment (which, if identified, is usually equated with bourgeois society and its values). As George Wellwarth proclaimed: "the power to shock is the chief characteristic of avant-garde drama and at the same time its chief source of strength."[8] Or in the words of Michael Kirby, "*Ubu Roi* became the origin of an avant-garde theatre that intentionally attacks traditional taste. This is the mode of *épater la bourgeoisie*."[9]

From our historical perspective, which is aligned with the views of the artists rather than the spectators, both the play and production declared war against the public. The philistines came face to face with a satirical image of themselves in the grotesque figure of Père Ubu. By means of this assault on bourgeois values, Jarry achieved the purpose of avant-garde art, which, as Richard Kostelanetz proclaims in his *Dictionary of the Avant-Garde*, must fulfill two requirements: "esthetic innovation and initial unacceptability."[10] As our historical and critical studies make clear, *Ubu Roi* scandalized the reactionary bourgeoisie. Sitting complacently in their seats, waiting for the performance to commence, they were jolted, even shocked, as soon as the first word was spoken.

Of course, *Ubu Roi* was not the only modern play credited with shocking the spectators and critics. Ibsen's *A Doll's House* (1879) and *Ghosts* (1881) had already generated controversy with several productions before 1896, when Jarry's play pre-mièred. And other works by various writers followed in this manner, including productions of Bernard Shaw's *Mrs Warren's Profession* in New York City (1905), J. M. Synge's *The Playboy of the Western World* at the Abbey Theatre (1907), and the Dadaist performances at the Cabaret Voltaire (1916). We may disagree on which of the controversial events launched the avant-garde revolution in the most significant manner, but we concur that the shock tactics of various artistic works and move-ments, including Futurism, Dadaism, Surrealism, and Expressionism, demonstrate and delivered the adversarial mission of modernist art. Just as censorship and legal battles attended the reception of modernist novels (e.g., Flaubert's *Madame Bovary*, Joyce's *Ulysses*, and Lawrence's *Lady Chatterly's Lover*), so too did public riots testify to the outrageous nature of modernist plays. Historically, then, acts of censorship and riots by spectators helped to sanction the place of the artists in the avant-garde pantheon (though we need to keep in mind that censorship was quite prevalent throughout the centuries, and many artists struggled against it). Consequently, our histories and studies of the avant-garde arts feature each rebellious act, each shocked response, and each manifesto. The innovations and reactions are part of the heritage of modernism.[11] The cultural achievements of the artists – their identities as mod-ernists – depend in great measure upon their roles as rebels with a cause, a cause that provides us with a cultural context for the events we study.

Unlike the philistines, however, we are not shocked. We may even concur with the assaults on bourgeois values. Our refusal to be offended, as is demonstrated in our extensive commentary on *Ubu Roi*, makes us the rightful arbiters of the signifi-cance and value of avant-garde art. As the custodians of the avant-garde events and their cultural history, we chart the development and triumphs of the modern arts over narrow-minded opposition. This historical narrative ratifies not only the value of the ideas and works but also our role as the keepers and defenders of the heritage.

> Historical explanation is to a large degree arrangement of the discovered facts in patterns which satisfy us because they accord with life – the variety of human experience and activity – as we know it and can imagine it.
> Isaiah Berlin, *Selected Writings: Concepts and Categories* (1978: 132)

We feel comfortable, then, with the basic narrative of modernism. Its development in the theatre, as in the other arts, reveals a series of innovations and controversies.[12] Without question, the philistine prudery that led to banned books and closed pro-ductions deserves our dismissal and disdain. In turn, the artists who insisted upon their creative rights and artistic visions deserve our admiration and advocacy. Fine, in general terms. But in the process of identifying with the modernist artists, we

Illustration 8. Title page of *Ubu Roi*, featuring Père Ubu; Paris: Mercure de France, 1896.

sometimes settle too easily into rather formulaic methods of writing history. As keepers of the legacy, we proclaim the new gospel as if we were preaching to the choir. Advocacy takes over. Dividing up the good guys and the bad guys, we repeatedly tell the same basic story of revolt and confrontation. Having little or no doubt about the identity, value, and purpose of the historical narrative of avant-garde art, we insist upon featuring its rebellious acts by the artists and its shocking reception among the unenlightened. No anecdote goes unused.

Perhaps, as historians, we need to ask some basic questions about our assumptions, methods, and narratives. How does our retrospective understanding shape the historical narrative or even distort the way we write history? How and why do the narrative tropes of our modernist story define both our subject matter and our interpretive strategies? Is it possible, at least in some cases, that these innovative and scandalous features are not necessarily the central or whole story? Do we settle into the familiar story too easily? Could it be, just possibly, that our mode of understanding is wrong?[13]

What, in fact, happened in Paris in 1896? An examination of the theatre reviews, biographies, critical studies, and theatre histories reveals that, though everyone seems to agree that some kind of theatre event took place, there is notable disagreement about what actually occurred. Besides the many conflicting reports on what happened before, during, and after the production (both on and off the stage), we disagree on who was responsible for the staging. Some people report that Lugné-Poe oversaw the production, others claim that Jarry took full control, and yet others describe rehearsals with both of them in charge (though sometimes at odds). Scholars also disagree on the size of the audience. Noël Arnaud, a leading French authority on Jarry and the play, places approximately "mille personnes" at the event.[14] Frantisek Deak concurs that "slightly over one thousand spectators" saw the performance.[15] But Annabelle Melzer puts the audience at "two to three thousand people who filled to capacity the Nouveau Théâtre."[16] Several theatre historians and literary critics concur on this larger number. A big riot is preferred to a small one.

Scholars also disagree on the date of the production and the number of performances. In *The Banquet Years* Roger Shattuck states that the première occurred on December 11, 1896.[17] This is the date that shows up in several published editions of the play and in many popular surveys of theatre history. For example, Michael Benedikt, in his introduction to *Modern French Theatre: The Avant-Garde, Dada, and Surrealism*, places the production on December 11.[18] But in *French Theatre Since 1830* Harold Hobson claims that it occurred on December 10, 1896, as does David Grossvogel, Simon Watson Taylor, Frederick Brown, Maurice Marc LaBelle, and Bettina L. Knapp.[19] Whatever the date, most commentators state (or leave the impression) that there was one performance, the première, at which a riot occurred. These scholars all agree on the riot, despite their disagreement on the date. But what in fact is the evidence for the riot? And when did it occur?

Countering the assumption about a single event, Keith Beaumont, Frantisek Deak, Annabelle Melzer, and Claude Schumacher identify not one but two performances on December 9 and 10, 1896 (but nothing on December 11).[20] The first was a *répétition générale* or dress rehearsal for the critics and the "usual audience" of artists and intellectuals who regularly attended productions of the Théâtre de l'Œuvre.[21] The second was the première for the general public. (In the French theatre of this era the reviewers regularly attended the *répétition générale*; their reviews were then usually published a day or two after the official première.) The *répétition générale* might be

Illustration 9. Lithograph by Alfred Jarry of program for *Ubu Roi*, performed by Théâtre de l'Œuvre, Paris 1896.

considered a final preview. Or we could conceive of the event as having two opening performances. Whatever the case, part of the confusion, especially in British and American scholarship, derives from the failure to distinguish between the *répétition générale* and the première. This confusion sets up other misunderstandings and misjudgements.

Jarry himself provides some help on this matter, if we attend to his speech before the start of the play on one of the two evenings. He states explicitly that the actors would perform "pour deux soirées."[22] A few days after the production, he published a short essay, "Questions de Théâtre," that complained about the general public, "illettré par définition," which attended the second evening.[23] He also castigates the conservative reviewers who had attacked the play and production. They were mainly in attendance on the first evening. But Jarry's published judgements on spectators and critics, expressed after the event, do not accord with his statement delivered to the spectators. In this address, he did not display a dismissive or castigating attitude; instead, he appealed to the spectators for understanding and sympathy because the production lacked not only some scenes and proper rehearsal but also an appropriate orchestra of wind instruments, horns, various timpani, kettledrums, bass drum, bagpipes, and even a grand organ. The production had to make do with a piano played by four hands, featuring Claude Terrasse, the composer, and his wife.[24]

Much of the scholarly misinformation stems from confusion over not only the number of performances but also what occurred on each of the two evenings. Despite the evidence that two performances took place, most of the reports, including many standard surveys of modern theatre, describe only one performance, which caused a riot. About this, there is broad agreement. The public was shocked, as J. L. Styan explains in his widely distributed *Modern Drama in Theory and Practice.*[25] As most theatre scholars of modernism assume and report today, the riot began when Firmin Gémier, playing the role of Père Ubu, uttered the first scatological word, *merdre*: "This produced," Styan explains, "an immediate uproar which lasted for fifteen minutes, and many people in the audience walked out at this stage . . . Gémier shouted above the noise, and eventually his fine comic performance held the attention of those who were left, so that something of the satirical spirit of the play came across."[26]

In *The Century of Innovation*, another well-known and widely read history of modern theatre, Oscar J. Brockett and Robert Findlay offer a slightly more detailed version of the opening riot:

> When [Firmin Gémier] spoke the play's opening line – "Merdre" – the audience was thrown into an uproar that lasted fifteen minutes . . . Many spectators walked out; the rest quickly divided themselves into supporters and opponents of the play. Fist fights broke out. Finally Gémier restored order by improvising a dance and reclining on the prompter's box. The play proceeded until the next "merdre" was reached, when the uproar was renewed. This was the pattern for the entire evening.[27]

Both of these standard summaries are apparently derived from the report in Roger Shattuck's *The Banquet Years*, not from the French commentaries on the production.

Shattuck, a leading scholar on modernist French culture, states that Gémier's opening word was greeted with outrage from the bourgeois spectators:

> "Merdre," Gémier said. "Shite." It was fifteen minutes before the house could be silenced. The *mot de Cambronne* has done its work; the house was pandemonium. Those who had been lulled by Jarry's opening speech [before the production began] were shocked awake; several people walked out without hearing more. The rest separated into two camps of desperately clapping enthusiasts and whistling scoffers. Fistfights started in the orchestra . . . Finally, Gémier improvised a jig and sprawled out on the prompter's box. His diversion restored enough order to allow the action to proceed to the next "merdre," when the audience took over once more. The interruptions continued for the rest of the evening . . .[28]

This is the event as it is often reported in studies of the avant-garde theatre, modernism, and French theatre. The description also appears in some biographies and critical studies of Jarry and his works. Variations on this anecdote appear in theatre histories in most of the European languages.[29] The opening word, so shocking to the ears of the general public, scandalized the audience. With one word, according to Maurice Marc LaBelle, Jarry "had struck a blow for artistic freedom." He had "liberated the vocabulary of drama."[30] George Wellwarth, looking back over the history of modern drama, agrees: "With that incredibly simple yet explosively destructive word, Jarry changed the whole course of the future dramatic continuum. Indeed, the theater would never be the same."[31] According to Gérard Damerval, in his book of 1984, *Ubu Roi* was "la bombe comique de 1896."[32] Recently, Williams Hymen Erin has tied the explosive nature of the production to the series of anarchist bombings in Paris in the 1890s.[33] On stage and in the streets, a revolt occurred. Everyone agrees: this single event delivered the anarchist revolt that came to define the modernist age. In the representative words of J. L. Sytan: "This [event] was the beginning of the counter-culture which would display many manifestations of artistic anarchy, and preach a variety of loosely related philosophies, or antiphilosophies, of life and art."[34] Two generations later, it was the precursor, we are repeatedly told in our contemporary theatre books, of the performance art and postmodernism of the 1960s and later. The "contours of the theatrical avant-garde" thus furrow along a modernist arc that extends from Paris in 1896 to our present postmodern theatre.[35] Turn and turn again.

Shattuck also notes that this production, though a catalyst for modernism, had its own precursors, including "the wild première of Victor Hugo's *Hernani* in 1830, when Théophile Gautier and Gérard de Nerval carried the day for romanticism by highly organized demonstrations."[36] That is, modernism, like romanticism, began with a theatre riot. This is the narrative that most commentators insist upon. It's the story we want to tell. Even though the French theatre has a heritage of theatrical turmoil beginning with the seventeenth-century controversy over Corneille's *Le Cid*, we have identified the production of *Ubu Roi* as the quintessential modernist moment. It is a new beginning. Or as Shattuck explains: "No event marks more clearly than this the close of one era and the imminence of another."[37] Thus, the modernist era, launched as an assault that engendered a riot, takes its definition from this production.

Because the production mocked the values of the bourgeois spectators, they felt insulted and assaulted by Père Ubu. This is the argument of David Grossvogel, who also reports that a riot ensued after the first word: "the bourgeois was now to suffer."[38] Jarry was thus the first of *les enfants terribles* in modernist French theatre, followed by Apollinaire, Cocteau, Tzara, Breton, and Artaud. Grossvogel insists that "the single device of shock" defined Jarry's theatrical mission.[39] Following Jarry's leadership, avant-garde artists of the twentieth century, made art, if not everyday life, very uncomfortable for the bourgeoisie. In turn, as the historians of these developments, we both comprehend and approve of the assault on the false respectability of the bourgeoisie.[40]

Jacques-Henry Lévesque, Jarry's biographer, argued in 1951 that the outrage for the unsuspecting spectators was a momentous event:

> Since the action began with this word and was not preceded by anything else, this word resonating with brutality, suddenly crystallized the condemnation of stupidity and cowardice with rage, the indignant rage, of an individual suddenly snatched from his sense of bourgeois well-being, by this loud provocation. The violent surprise caused by such a word, seemingly said completely gratuitously, with no apparent reason, gave it more power, since it became a kind of ideal entity effective by its internal power alone, it is this that constituted the intolerable provocation and inexcusable attack. This word said in this way is charged in its utter simplicity and utmost purity with all the power and seduction of scandal for scandal's sake.[41]

Lévesque's rhetoric is an attempt to evoke the shocking nature of the forbidden word as it invaded the thick skull of the bourgeois spectators.[42] As if he were recapturing a historical truth that must be accepted, Lévesque insists that the general audience, shocked and offended, screamed in pain because modernist art was too difficult to comprehend, let alone to sanction.

This primary narrative not only provides the identity for the production of *Ubu Roi* but also contributes to our understanding of the development of modernism. Yet there is one slight problem with this narrative: the documentation on the première does not support it. For example, Firmin Gémier, who played the role of Ubu, offers a report on the production that is completely at odds with our standard version of the event:

> You know what is the first word of the play. It was well received. The banquet scene amused the audience. Everybody laughed. Some of it was mocking laughter but some amounted to applause. The scenes of the messenger, Ubu's house, the King's palace, the parade ground, the massacre, the scene in the cave with the appearance of ghosts, the nobles and financiers in the great hall of the palace, all went very well, which means, as well as possible in the given circumstances.[43]

In this interview of November 4, 1921,[44] Gémier states that only later in scene 5 of Act 3 did the general public protest, when an actor attempted to imitate a door and Gémier inserted an imaginary key into the actor's outstretched hand and made the noise "cric crac" in imitation of the key turning in the lock. That was too silly. The "joking had been going on for too long," Gémier reports.[45] At that point, the audience hooted and hollered with cat calls. The farce had become inane. But this expression of displeasure had nothing to do with the supposed shocking nature of the play.[46] Apparently then, if Gémier's memory is reliable, the definitive trait of modernist art that we use to reconstruct the event – its ability to scandalize the bourgeoisie – was not a factor in the première.

    In 1921 Gémier was looking back upon an event which he may well have recast in his memory. Yet additional information, which distinguishes between the events of the two evenings, supports his statement. The people who raised their voices in disapproval or approval were not the bourgeoisie but the intellectuals, artists, and critics who played out their familiar and well-established roles in a French tradition of vocal cabals and factions in the theatres. This engagement of cabals occurred during the first night of the production – that is, at the *répétition générale*. In anticipation of the performance, two factions of spectators came prepared to voice their opinions about Jarry and his play. Some of these spectators were quite familiar with the play before they arrived at the theatre. By 1896 Jarry had published at least six fragments of the basic Ubu story, and in the spring of 1896 he published the complete play in Paul Fort's *Le Livre d'Art*.[47] It was widely reviewed in the press. Many people read it. Thus, for a sizable number of people at the first performance there was no surprise; friends and foes alike knew what to expect; they had come prepared to defend or attack the play. They played their roles, as Deak notes, in a tradition of artistic demonstration that had nothing to do with bourgeois distress over a word. "The audience, divided by their artistic loyalties, turned the production into something of a riot. How violent this riot was and when it erupted depends very much on the source of information and on the distance from the actual events: the magnitude of the scandal seems to increase as time passes."[48] The word *riot* may be quite misleading. Instead of a riot, the event had many features of an anticipated cultural occasion, with people prepared to enjoy themselves as they played out their established roles, pro and con. Also worth noting, as Noël Arnaud points out, well over half of the thousand spectators at a typical *répétition générale* or dress rehearsal of a production at Lugné-Poe's Théâtre de l'Œuvre entered without paying. The gathering for *Ubu Roi* was thus an event for invited associates and their friends, identified as several hundred "invités d'honneur" and "les fameuses 'petites femmes' botticelliennnes."[49] Sitting among this throng of festive spectators, including the lovely lady companions, were the critics, reactionaries and supporters alike, ready to fulfill their cultural roles in two claques. The rules of behavior were basically prescribed for many spectators, especially the two adversarial groups.

. . . first nights are attended by those capable of understanding!
    Alfred Jarry, "Of the Futility of the 'Theatrical' in the Theatre" (*Mercure de France*,
    September 1896), *Selected Works* (1963: 69)

If this event qualifies as a riot, it was, for most participants a quite familiar kind of Parisian event. Whatever the case, the actions and reactions of the claques were those of a decidedly un-bourgeois crowd. Yet after the fact, decade by decade, the production has been transformed into what Benedikt calls "one of the most violent theatrical riots of all time."[50]

What, in fact, is the historical evidence for such a decisive judgement about violent behavior? Deak points out that there is only one source for the story that a riot occurred after the opening word. The report came from Rachilde (Marguérite Eymery Vallette), who was Jarry's friend and confidante. Thirty years after the production, Rachilde, a playwright and novelist (among other professional activities), published a book of memories, *Alfred Jarry; ou, Le Surmâle de lettres* (1928). In it, she mentions a riot over the opening word. Yet if we check the many other accounts of the two evenings, as Deak has done, we discover no substantial support for Rachilde's version of the event. Significantly, the theatrical reviewers do not mention a riot. It would seem, then, that a riot over the opening word did not occur on either evening.[51] There were some calculated demonstrations on the first night, as Jarry's supporters and opponents participated in a planned confrontation. But this audience of artists, intellectuals, and critics should not be confused with the general public of the second evening.

Of course, the production was eventful, especially the first-night *répétition générale* which featured the organized factions. Also, there are reasons for us, as historians and critics, to note the innovative aspects of the play and production, including the painted backdrop of several incongruous scenes, the costumes and masks, the unconventional manner of delivering the speeches, and the play's satiric qualities. The play expresses a *jeu d'espirit* that continues to appeal.[52]

And in 1896 it was a special event, but of what kind? Jarry had done much to create a cultural moment that would qualify as a confrontation. He sought attention. Though Shattuck muddles some facts on the production, he does provide a vital description of Jarry's careful and willful preparation for the production. In the months before Lugné-Poe agreed to produce the play, Jarry worked for the theatre company by writing correspondence and helping to select plays for production, such as Ibsen's *Peer Gynt* (in which he also took a role as a troll).[53] During these months, in letters and discussions, he carried on a campaign to convince Lugné-Poe to produce *Ubu*. And once the decision was made, he diligently prepared for the production. "Since he ran the publicity and had a hand in everything, Jarry made certain that his play was not neglected. Posters, announcements, articles, and Jarry's own woodcuts appeared in a steady stream."[54] This suggests that Jarry, despite his unconventional public persona, was quite capable of being a well-organized, dependable, and calculating administrator. He was able to put together not just a production but an elaborate public event, which he achieved with *Ubu*.

. . . if you are absolutely determined to give the public an inkling of something you must explain it to them beforehand.

Alfred Jarry, "Theatre Questions" ("Questions de Théâtre," *La Revue Blanche,*
January 1897), in *Selected Works* (1963: 84)

Determined to make a name for himself, he attempted to engineer a special event, one that we can understand in terms of a long heritage of French controversies in the theatres. Jarry's overall role in the creation of the controversy itself is perhaps the significant aspect of the event, not the response of the supposedly delicate bourgeoisie. Jarry sought to be a celebrity. His efforts to impose controversial identities on himself, his play, and his production were both traditional and innovative. These endeavors were in accord with an established heritage of fame and controversy in Parisian arts and letters (e.g., Voltaire, Rousseau, George Sand, Hugo, Zola, and many others). Perhaps Gustave Courbet, the painter, provided the most immediate model of artistic rebellion and public personality. Yet Jarry was radical in the ways that he committed himself to a fantastical persona. He refined the celebrity game, achieving a model that would influence Marinetti and Tzara, among others. For Jarry, the transformed life was perhaps a more radical accomplishment than the works. His notoriety, which he spent the rest of his life living up to, proved to be a key factor in the event, contributing to (yet also confusing) our historical memory. However much we may be fascinated by his rebellious persona, we need to recognize that he only partially succeeded in making a controversy at the *répétition générale* (and apparently failed to do so at the première).

In this sense, then, the event was not something new, but instead a well-crafted performance – of self as well as art – within an artistic tradition of the nineteenth-century artistic communities of Paris. Vocal claques, organized to support or attack an artistic work, performer, or production, were a common feature of Parisian theatres in the eighteenth and nineteenth centuries.[55] The employment of *claqueurs,* or salaried applauders, was standard business for many theatres. Also, artists regularly caused disturbances at productions of the works of other artists. Hector Berlioz, for example, describes in his delightful *Memoirs* his participation in (and instigation of) several vocal disturbances at performances of new musical works.[56] As occurred with the controversies over Victor Hugo's production of *Hernani* in 1830 and the Paris production of Wagner's *Tannhäuser* in 1861, the production of *Ubi Roi* served as yet another event that allowed artistic factions to voice their opinions.[57] Given the long tradition for cabals in the theatre, this attempt to organize a cultural controversy was almost obligatory for Jarry, who had a well-established practice to maintain and extend. He achieved an evening of factions, but more significantly he turned *Ubu Roi* into an extended debate in the newspapers and journals.

During the weeks after the production, a campaign took place for and against the play, the production, and Jarry. "The real battle of *Ubu*," as Claude Schumacher insists, "was waged in the press," not in the auditorium.[58] The critics hammered out their cultural and political positions in the newspapers and journals, which served as the abiding forum for discussions by and about French writers. Several conservative reviewers, including Francisque Sarcey in *Le Temps* and Henry Fouquier in *Le Figaro,* used the occasion of the production to write yet another negative review about the new plays which failed to satisfy their standards. From Sarcey's viewpoint, *Ubu Roi* was yet one more event within a familiar pattern of critical disputes. Countering Sarcey and others, Jarry's supporters, including Catulle Mendès in *Le Journal* and Henry Bauer in the *Echo de Paris*, wrote articles that praised all aspects of the play and production. They knew quite well their critical roles. Objective, fair-minded appraisal was not the aim of either camp. Predictably, Sarcey, who attended the *répétition générale*, announced that he was offended by the whole matter. Jarry was an insult to his well-honed cultural values, which included a sophisticated appreciation of the well-made play. And just as predictably, Jarry's friend Henry Bauer, who also attended the *répétition générale*, was rhapsodic in his response. He celebrated the play as an assault on authority, and he attempted to stir up controversy over its language: "Scatologie, verbe d'ordure et de malpropreté!"[59] Over the following weeks, the press generated a subsidiary event that retrospectively turned the production into a highly constructed narrative; or actually two separate narratives, with negative and positive valences.[60] Jarry, his play, and the production thus became convenient touchstones for the divisions that existed already in the Parisian cultural communities. This extended exchange of artistic judgements, rather than our popular formula about shocking avant-garde art, is the more appropriate context for the event. But apparently this cultural history of divisions among critics, newspapers, and journals is less appealing to us than a narrative about riots in the avant-garde theatre. We want the event to be the origin of a radical break in culture and values, not a history of continuing cultural relations among artists and intellectuals in Parisian society. But in order to establish our preferred narrative, we must repress a significant part of the historical record.[61]

> The fact that some historical descriptions are disputed does not imply that none can be proved true beyond reasonable doubt. In fact thousands can.
> C. Behan McCullagh, *The Truth of History* (1998: 23)

Given the available documentation on the production of *Ubu Roi*, theatre historians should be able to write a detailed, truthful history. Yet the details of this event have been misrepresented in a number of investigations, not simply because of the seductive appeal of the avant-garde narrative. Some documents are missing. Other sources fail to provide sufficient information on key details. And the reports sometimes contradict one another, as Deak discovered. For example, historians, even those who grant that two performances occurred, have failed to agree on whether Jarry talked to the audience at the *répétition générale* or the première. This issue may appear to be insignificant, but it has contributed to some of our misunderstandings of the event. The French text of his talk was published at the time of the event, then republished on several occasions. The definitive text is in the *Oeuvre completes* (1972). There it has a title but no date.[62] The English translation of 1963 by Simon Watson Taylor includes both a title and a date.[63] The one reads, "Discours D'Alfred Jarry

Prononcé à la Première Représentation d'*Ubu Roi*"; the other reads, "Preliminary Address at the First Performance of *Ubu Roi,* December 10, 1896." Taylor's title adds to the historical confusion. Michel Arrivé, the editor for the *Oeuvre completes,* includes a note, stating that Jarry addressed the audience on "10 décembre 1896, immédiatement avant la première d'*Ubu Roi.*"[64] This would put Jarry before the audience of the première, the second night. Arrivé and Taylor are in agreement on the date that Jarry addressed the audience, but they apparently disagree on whether this happened at the first or second performance. Claude Schumacher, disagreeing with both Arrivé and Taylor, puts Jarry at the *répétition générale* on December 9, talking to the critics, artists, intellectuals, and other invited guests. Which night was it? What is the correct date?

In his description of Jarry's presentation, Arrivé draws upon critical commentaries in the French press of December 11 and 12 that described Jarry delivering a short talk while sitting at a table, a white light above it. But these sources do not specify which performance. Nonetheless, we should note that the critics came to the *répétition générale* on December 9. Even more conclusive evidence is provided by Jarry himself, who, in his address to the audience, mentions that "tonight and tomorrow are the only two evenings" ("c'est aujourd'hui et demain les deux seuls soirs"[65]) that Gémier was free to participate because he was committed to another production. Given this statement, Jarry must have talked to the audience at the first performance (i.e., the *répétition générale*) on December 9 rather than the second performance (*la première*) on December 10. Both Arrivé and Taylor have identified the wrong date, and Taylor (who perhaps believed that there was only one performance) adds to the confusion about the performance and date of Jarry's talk. In order to solve this kind of problem in documentation, a researcher must examine the various sources, not just one source, then work through the confusing terminology and contradictory evidence. Each source has to be checked for the reliability of its information. And the separate sources need to be compared to one another. Contradictions are common in historical sources. (Of course it helps if the researcher has already determined that there were two performances!)

Or consider another problem that remains a mystery: Lugné-Poe reported in 1931 that Gémier, during the performance of *Ubu Roi,* "imposed silence by a wild and startling jig which he danced without a break until he collapsed into the prompter's box with his legs quivering in the air."[66] This is an intriguing piece of information (and a tempting anecdote, as various repetitions of it illustrate). But did Gémier dance a wild jig? Something like this might have happened, on one night or the other, at some point in the production, if not during the opening moment. But is Lugné-Poe's memory, thirty-five years after the event, to be trusted as definitive evidence? Do we have supporting sources? How do we compare his version to Gémier's own report of a calm general public initially or to Rachilde's report of a riot? Perhaps they are recalling two different evenings, but we need to check and double check the documentation. In turn, we need to determine how trustworthy each person's description is – that is, the credibility and reliability of each source, especially if it depends upon a distant memory of a past event. And, to the extent possible, we need to figure out the motives of the person. For example, what should we make of the fact that Lugné-Poe quickly turned his back on Jarry and the play in 1897? Their careers diverged and followed two distinct paths, artistically, socially, and politically. Then, in the 1920s, after Jarry's death, Lugné-Poe tried to claim that he had always been Jarry's champion. Because of these contradictions, we might be skeptical about his recollections of his attitudes and actions.

Should we therefore distrust Lugné-Poe but then embrace Jarry's supporters, such as Henri Bauer and Caulle Mendès, the two critics who wrote rapturous celebrations of the play? Do the supporters, with whom we prefer to align ourselves, have special access to the truth? Perhaps, as a safeguard, we should question our impulse to select and use the evidence that supports our assumptions. Indeed, for a diligent historian, this should be one of the first rules of investigation. The better the anecdote, the better one's suspicions should be. Quite often a striking or clever anecdote has been crafted through a number of retellings and revisions. So, what's the verdict on Lugné-Poe's anecdote? Even after we cross-examine the available sources from these contradictory witnesses, we are left with uncertainty – a situation all too common for historians. Gémier himself does not describe any kind of wild dance at the *première* on December 10; in fact, he describes a calm, engaged audience that second evening (until the silliness of the creaking key). But this does not rule out the possibility that on the first night he might have done some kind of dance in response to the cabals. We don't know, though. This is one of those uncertainties in history. Even modern history has its gaps. Still, this anecdote does not, on its own terms, provide evidence for any hypothesis about a riot by the bourgeois spectators.

The standard narrative of a scandalous event has spread throughout our books on modern drama and theatre. Many fine scholars have thus described and interpreted this event incorrectly. For example, in *Dada and Surrealist Performance* (1994), Annabelle Melzer takes up the *Ubu Roi* production because she wants to locate the origin of avant-garde theatre in Jarry.[67] The grand narrative neatly serves her celebration of dadaism and surrealism. Drawing upon previously garbled surveys, she mixes together information from the two performances. Confusing matters further, she provides commentary from the newspapers, as if these statements were made at the performance in the heat of the moment. She attributes psychological feelings, attitudes, motives, and gestures to people at the event, but often these attributions are only conjectures on her part, ready-made illustrations of the operating assumptions. Dedicated to the standard narrative of avant-garde art, she writes history as a modernist anecdote.

To compound the problem, Melzer's book, like several other surveys discussed here, then serves as a resource for other scholars who want to evoke this famous event. Richard Schechner, for instance, draws upon Melzer as an authority for his own summary of the event, which he features in his book on *Performance Studies* (2002).[68] He too depends upon the familiar assumptions about avant-garde, which *Ubu Roi* supposedly exemplifies. Yet again the riot is described and celebrated. In this way, scholar by scholar and decade by decade, the imaginary primal scene of this avant-garde production is repeatedly described and celebrated, taking its predictable place in our histories of the modern theatre. Melzer and Schechner thus join dozens and dozens of others who have published versions of the basic anecdote. Trusting the previous scholarship, as we all must do on occasion, they perpetuate the received, standard version.

In consequence, even the publication of corrective scholarship has failed to stop or even slow the spread of the false history. Although the primary documents on the production of the play are available, few scholars have bothered to check and verify the sources. The legendary version of *Ubu Roi*, set in place by the 1920s and 1930s, perfectly serves our preferred narrative of the avant-garde theatre and culture. As Deak points out, the inaccuracies on Jarry and the production of *Ubu Roi* continued to circulate throughout the second half of the twentieth century, despite reliable scholarship published in 1952, 1972, and 1974.[69] Also, the complete works of Jarry were published in French in 1972, and new editions of *Ubu Roi* by Maurice Saillet (1962; 1974) and Noël Arnaud (1978) provided a corrective history of many facts about the play and production. Most of these works are also identified in Claude Schumacher's English study of Jarry, published in 1984.[70] And Deak's study in English appeared in 1993.[71] Likewise, Jarry's essays, with corrective information, if one wished to read with care, have been available in English for four decades. Yet despite all of these corrective sources, from the 1950s forward, the production of *Ubu Roi* retains its false significance for most of us. The avant-garde narrative wins out over the facts.

> Context is not given but produced; what belongs to a context is determined by interpretive strategies; contexts are just as much in need of elucidation as events; and the meaning of a context is determined by events.
> Jonathan Culler, *Framing the Sign* (1988: xiv)

Despite the appeal of the riot narrative, along with its supportive idea of avant-garde art, there are other possible narratives about the play, the production, the overall event, and the development of modern theatre. No one narrative contains this event, and no single generalization can adequately explain the history of the avant-garde. In our investigations of the production of *Ubu Roi*, it is possible to make it a turning point or a touchstone (not the same thing) in the history of theatre. It could be placed at the beginning, the middle, or the end of a causal narrative. Depending upon one's perspective and aims, it could be described as the centerpiece of a historical study of Jarry or it might be represented as one of several interrelated events within a set period of Parisian theatre.

Whatever the case, we can do justice to Jarry's inventive accomplishments without need of a riot and scandalized audience. We know, for example, that in his lifetime Jarry did succeed in his campaign of self-creation and celebration. The *Ubu Roi* event was part of that campaign. And subsequently other plays and productions followed, but not merely as a repetition of the same. We also know that Jarry and his supporters contributed to some of the modern developments in the theatre. Jarry intended to challenge not only traditional theatre (e.g., the conventions of tragedy in his parody of

Macbeth) but also the values of traditional society (e.g., marriage, political authority, civilized behavior and taste). In service to these aims, Jarry created his play. He also created an alternative code of rationality which he designated by the name of "Pataphysics." This life project may have been scandalous to some people and confrontational to others, but it was delightfully paradoxical and playful for Jarry's followers. The dadaists and surrealists, two decades later, identified Jarry – or his persona – as an ideal model of the artist-as-outsider. And in the 1930s Artaud named his short-lived theatre after Jarry. There is, then, a developmental narrative of modernism that includes Jarry's activities, works, and persona. In fact, several modernist contexts exist for the production of *Ubu Roi*. Thus, though we might downplay or dismiss the idea of a riot, we could still place both Jarry and the play in a history of modernist theatre.

Just as significantly, as Frantisek Deak demonstrates, *Ubu Roi* also belongs in the history of other artistic events and movements of the nineteenth century. It is part of the symbolist movement of the 1880s and 1890s. For Deak the production of *Ubu Roi* served as a culminating event in the history of French symbolism, not as the scandalous origin of a new avant-garde movement. Yet Deak's study, with its concluding chapter on Jarry, does not rule out the possibility that the production of *Ubu Roi* contributed to the growth of avant-garde movements in the arts. Earlier in the book, before the chapter on Jarry, he makes the following statement: "The end of the nineteenth century saw the invention of a new artistic institution: the avant-garde theater . . . The avant-garde theaters are rightfully thought of in terms of innovation, experimentation, and radical opposition to the existing mainstream theaters."[72] Deak insists, though, that a focus on innovation does not require, in tandem, an argument about *épater la bourgeoisie*. Two distinct perspectives are possible: whereas "the interpretation which dwells on scandal results in an antagonistic model of the avant-garde, the interpretation which emphasizes the originality of the new theatrical language leads to an innovative model of the avant-garde."[73] Scandal and innovation can be understood as separate factors, not necessarily joined historically. It is possible, then, for Deak to argue for the innovative significance of *Ubu Roi*, without any need to construct a riot or a shocked audience for the production.

Even if Deak (or someone else) developed an argument about *Ubu Roi* as an innovative event, this analysis might miss Schumacher's focus on the newspapers and journals as the location of the responses and debates. And if innovation serves as the organizing idea, the interpretation might slight or miss the long tradition of claques in French theatres, a heritage and social practice that modifies any exclusive idea of innovation in the arts. Also, such an approach might not credit Jarry's act of creating a persona, the public iconoclast that fascinates Shattuck. In short, any definition of the avant-garde leaves open many possible avenues of investigation.

Beyond narratives about symbolist theatre or the avant-garde movement, the production of *Ubu Roi* could be seen as part of a long, developmental process of public controversy in the French theatre since Hugo's *Hernani* in 1830 (or even Corneille's *Le Cid* in 1636/37). Or it might be seen as an event in the biography of

Jarry, Lugné-Poe, or Gémier. It would then have a range of meanings from person to person. For example, the event was far more important in Jarry's short writing career than in Gémier's long acting career, as Gémier's memoir makes clear. Or if we were writing a social history of theatre criticism in Paris during the nineteenth century, the event would likely be one among many productions that might illustrate how the reviewers and their journals operated in relation to the playwrights, the performers, the theatre companies, the management, and the audiences of Paris. As is the case with all historical events, the production of *Ubu Roi* fits potentially into many different contexts, each having its own defining features. These quick examples illustrate a maxim of historical research and analysis: change the context, change the meaning. And if we change the historical questions, we may change both the event and the context.

> To ask for the significance of an event in the *historical* sense of the term, is to ask a question which can be answered only in the context of a *story*. The identical event will have a different significance in accordance with the story in which it is located or, in other words, in accordance with what different sets of *later* events it may be connected . . . To demand the meaning of an event is to be prepared to accept some context within which the event is considered significant. This is "meaning in history", and it is legitimate to ask for such meanings.
> Arthur Danto, *Analytical Philosophy of History* (1965: 11–12)

The challenge in all historical inquiries is to figure out effective ways for not only constructing specific events but also providing viable contexts for those events. This case study of *Ubu Roi* has shown that it is all too easy to proclaim that this or that event is "avant-garde," "original," or "revolutionary." No doubt our practices are shaped by the reigning idea of modern theatre history: we prefer to tell the story of a series of new – preferably shocking – events. Accordingly, the works and performances we study all seem to fulfill the requirement that Victor Hugo assigned to avant-garde art. After reading *Les Fleurs du Mal*, he wrote to Baudelaire: "You create a new shudder."[74] In this sense, we have been writing (and rewriting) a popular history of shudders.

All too often we have passed on a reductive story about the developmental history of modern theatre, tied to a ready-made definition of the avant-garde. Once the basic narrative (constructed out of miscellaneous facts, events, assumptions, and theories) was put in place, it has been repeated by three generations of scholars. As an intellectual community, we fulfill the process by which certain ideas, beliefs, explanations, and theories become received truths, a process that Richard Hamilton examines in his book, *The Social Misconstruction of Reality*. Hamilton describes how a received idea, simplified into a basic theory or narrative, can become a social misconstruction. The scholars,

> together with others convinced of its merit, use the scheme in subsequent research and analysis. They also pass it on to others, upholding it, legitimating it, attesting to its merit, and training others to appreciate its special insights. Two processes are involved here: one is intellectual (people attempting to

know or understand a complex reality), and one is social (people passing on and vouching for a given intellectual framework).[75]

The intellectual motive is admirable, of course, but in the processes of serving as the "users and disseminators" of a received idea, we uphold, sanction, and distribute misinformation. An appealing or familiar explanation, based upon inadequate historical study and critical analysis, is embraced. The explanation is accepted intellectually and passed on within one's professional community (e.g., classroom, conferences, and publications). "Underlying the effort, in both processes, is a concern for the adequacy, for the realism, validity, or truth of the schemes in question. The assumption – or hope – is that a theory will provide an accurate portrait, or reflection, of that 'complex reality'."[76] But all too often this assumption is based upon poor or inadequate research – both our own research and that of others. The theory – the set of assumptions, beliefs, ideologies, and narratives – fails to take the measure of the complex reality of the historical events, issues, and problems.

This intellectual process of constructing an explanation is often reinforced by a social process of participating in (and helping to distribute) a familiar narrative or a sanctioned understanding. We join an intellectual community, upholding its received ideas. We gain access to and approval from the community. Since modernist culture by the mid 1920s had developed into a series of movements and manifestoes (e.g., futurism, cubism, dadaism, surrealism, and expressionism), it is not surprising that various people, looking back at the production of *Ubu Roi*, came to see it as the forerunner of these movements. A retrospective construction of seemingly similar events occurred. Historians, by enhancing the details and the significance of what happened in the past, turn an event like the production of *Ubu Roi* into a fitting representation of what a modernist production is supposed to be. Moreover, for some people the event was transformed into the origin of what follows, as if it were the germ out of which the subsequent events developed. At times it was even conceived of as a unique event, a creative moment that has no forerunners, no previous history, no shaping factors. Genius prevails.

Surely, in the historical reconstruction of the production of *Ubu Roi* we can do a better job of research and analysis. The preliminary lesson of this case study should be obvious: we need to verify the evidence we use in our histories of modernism. Reliable documentation always matters. Yet beyond this basic issue of historical accuracy, which cultural historians should seek and honor as conscientiously as a documentary scholar, this case study also illustrates several recurring problems or temptations in historical inquiry and thinking:

(1) the seductive appeal of certain kinds of anecdotes and stories, which tend to simplify yet distort the nature of historical events;
(2) the repetition of key stories, once they had attained their significance and appeal;
(3) the assumption, quite prevalent among historians of modernism in the arts, that artistic innovation and bourgeois sensibility are irrevocably at odds;

(4) the belief that scandalous events in the modern arts deserve to be valued highly for their ability to shock; yet because this aesthetic quality of the works is derived, at least in part, from the scandalous nature of the events, the reasoning is in danger of becoming circular;

(5) the inclination to accept the testimony of key participants in an event because their versions of what happened are consistent with our preconceived narratives of what we want the event to represent; although these participants, to be expected, tend to remember and describe the event in self-serving ways, they are treated as reliable witnesses who sanction the narratives we wish to embrace – yet another circular process of reasoning;

(6) the determination to disregard the details in the sources that fail to align with not only our favorite anecdotes, statements, and descriptions but also our organizing narrative and general assumptions; and

(7) the need to embrace an interpretive model, such as the interrelated concepts of avant-garde and modernist theatre, as a singular, general, and all-encompassing idea that provides a mode of explanation for the historical context of the event being investigated. In this manner, the singular idea, similar to a period concept, holds together and gives identity to the various events of an era – as if they all had to play out in a similar manner.

These assumptions, appeals, inclinations, beliefs, tendencies, and needs recur in all historical study. They are not limited to the case of *Ubu Roi*. They provide modes of reasoning that are typical of not just historians but all of us. As Charles Tilly insists in his valuable little book, *Why? What Happens When People Give Reasons ... and Why?* (2006), reason-giving, as a social and intellectual activity, provides the necessary engine for all human attempts to describe, explain, and understand what happens. The processes of reason-giving address questions of how and why. Often, our reasons, Tilly explains, take the form of conventional formulas, social codes, and stories of cause and effect. And in the case of experts, such as professional historians, our reasons offer accounts that satisfy the basic procedures, terminology, and organizing categories that are shared by the learned community. Despite the patina of learning, they still may be conventional and formulaic.

In the scholarship on the production of *Ubu Roi* we find all of these familiar modes of reason-giving. From key anecdotes derived from documents to the shaping power of the popular definition of avant-garde art, the commentary on this seminal event has become a classic case of reason-giving. The anecdotes provide the "what" and the avant-garde narrative provides the "why." In turn, the seven "temptations" that I catalogue above all find their place in the social construction of our reigning explanation for this production. Accordingly, we all need to be on guard against the seven temptations – the reason-giving assumptions, appeals, inclinations, beliefs, tendencies, and needs in our constructions of the past. The seven temptations can (and should) serve, from the perspective of historiography, as an early warning system for us.

> The historian . . . is prosecutor, attorney for the defense, judge, and jury all in one.
> Louis Gottschalk, *Understanding History: A Primer of Historical Method*, (1969: 150)

Consider, for example, the response of William Butler Yeats to *Ubu Roi*. In 1896, the young poet visited Paris and was taken to the production. Years later in his auto-biography, he crystallized his retrospective assessment of the event: "After us the Savage Gods."[77] What kind of historical evidence is this statement? What can we learn from a close examination of it? Yeats' statement is often quoted in studies of *Ubu Roi* and its production. For example, Michael Benedikt writes that Yeats was "stunned by Jarry's stage effects."[78] But what exactly did Yeats mean by this evocation of the imminent arrival of savage gods? Do they arrive on stage, down the aisle, or in the streets? Who or what qualifies as a savage god? Does Ubu? When do these gods arrive? And how inclusive is Yeats' "us"?

Yeats probably attended the first performance, the night of the claques, because he states that the spectators "shake their fists at one another." He also notes that though his companion needs "to explain to me what is happening on stage," he can see that the "players are supposed to be dolls, toys, marionettes . . . [who] are hopping like wooden frogs." He can also "see for myself that the chief personage, who is some kind of King, carries for a Sceptre a brush of the kind that we use to clean a closet."[79] Did this crude gesture stun him or upset his sense of propriety? That is hard to believe. Or could it be, despite his limited knowledge of French, that he was shocked by the opening word? Whatever the specific cause, he was supposedly shocked. Otherwise, his evidence and the event would not fit the required avant-garde narrative.

His statement about "the Savage Gods" serves well our belief that the production caused a riot. Yet despite his mention of the fist-waving spectators, Yeats does not claim that a riot took place. Perhaps his statement suggests a dark foreboding, but about what? For some commentators it evokes several possible aspects of modernism and modernity, including the spirit of primitivism that came to be associated with certain modernist works (e.g., Picasso's cubism, the performances of Stravinsky's *The Fire Bird* in 1910 and *The Rite of Spring* in 1913). Or perhaps he had in mind the Nietzschean idea of Dionysus? Whatever the specific idea, we need to ask some basic historical questions on reliability and credibility, beginning with this preliminary one. Did this foreboding occur to Yeats during the evening of the performance or a quarter of a century later when he wrote the autobiography? Perhaps Yeats envisioned savage gods in 1896, perhaps he did not; we cannot prove this, one way or the other. What we do know, without doubt, is that the statement was published in 1922, not 1896. It was one of several memories or "pictures" that "come before me without date or order" in this chapter of the autobiography.[80] He may well have reconstructed this event – and his memory of it – out of his subsequent knowledge, ideas, and experiences.

Beyond this basic problem of a belated source, twenty-six years after the fact, what can we learn from the place and significance of the statement within the auto-biography? As an anecdote, the recollection of that Paris evening serves to illustrate key themes in the autobiography about "the trembling of the veil." His 1938

Autobiography is actually constructed out of two separately published books: *The Trembling of the Veil* (1922) and *Reveries over Childhood and Youth* (1936). In his Preface of 1922 he writes: "I have found in an old diary a saying from Stephane Mallarmé, that his epoch was troubled by the trembling of the veil of the Temple. As those words were still true, during the years of my life described in this book, I have chosen *The Trembling of the Veil* for its title."[81] The *Ubu Roi* event, reported in this 1922 book, concludes a section called "The Tragic Generation." This chapter opens with Yeats' memory of another theatre event he attended: the London production of Ibsen's *A Doll's House* in 1889. He states that "I hated the play ... I resent being invited to admire dialogue so close to modern educated speech that music and style were impossible."[82]

Then, sixty pages later at the end of the chapter, Yeats takes up another theatre production that he hates or wishes to reject.[83] The commentary on *Ubu Roi* is the concluding paragraph of Book IV, just as the complaint about Ibsen is the opening paragraph. The two events serve as book-ends for his portrait of the artist as a young man, an artist who was seeking his own voice, his vision, for modern poetry. *A Doll's House* and *Ubu Roi* thus framed his growth as an artist between 1889 and 1896. They are not arbitrary recollections, but instead touchstones for his theme in Book IV.

In his description of the Jarry production, he notes that he and other poets, including Stephane Mallarmé and Paul Verlaine, were committed to a poetic art of "subtle colour and nervous rhythm." From the double perspectives of 1896 and 1922, he wished to place himself in their camp. Accordingly, Jarry's crude comedy, like Ibsen's crude realism, lacked artistic refinement; it was uncivilized and savage. Yeats states that he was "sad" because "comedy, objectivity, has displayed its growing power once more."[84] Jarry is thus, for Yeats, the emblematic figure of the comic or satiric sensibility that deflates and attacks. Set against Jarry are Yeats, Mallarmé, and other poets – the committed voices of the tragic generation in an era of crass compromises with modernity.

As he chose to recall and craft the event, Yeats was disturbed by both Jarry and Ibsen because of what they represented for him: the abandonment of the poetic and tragic vision. Within the European traditions of art and aesthetics, the contemporary generation of artists faced difficult, even tragic, conditions and choices. As Yeats repeatedly says in his poetry, his plays, his essays, and *A Vision* (1938), he conceives of language – its uses and misuses – as the battleground between civilization and savagery in the history of human culture.

> The historian's task is to understand not only what a document's words may formally mean but also what the witness *really intended to say.*
> Louis Gottschalk, *Understanding History: A Primer of Historical Methods* (1969: 124)

Yeats' statement is thus an inappropriate source for a supposedly riotous theatre production in 1896. As historical evidence it is unreliable. First of all, that kind of calamitous moment did not occur in the theatre – except, that is, in later anecdotes about the production, anecdotes well established by the time he wrote his auto-biography. Most tellingly, the statement does not serve our avant-garde narratives, even if we are prepared to believe that he was shaken to the depths of his soul by the behavior of the character of Ubu, the toilet brush, the word *merdre*, or the shouting of some claques.[85]

Why, then, do I give it so much attention? More to the point, if Yeats' statement on the production of *Ubu Roi* does not illustrate or prove what we claim it represents, why have we repeatedly quoted him as an authority? What is wrong with our historical procedures if we are willing to accept and quote his statement? I have focused close attention on the statement because it places before us a basic requirement in historical research – the need to test all sources for their authenticity, credibility, and reliability.

In source criticism, we need to investigate the biographical, geographical, chronological, and occupational or functional meaning of any statement by a historical eyewitness.[86] We cannot just lift a sentence out of a document without first determining how and why it was presented by the person who produced it. We need to ask what it means within its context. We need to determine what is and is not a historical fact. Given these basic requirements, what can we say about Yeats' statement on the Jarry production? He does satisfy the historical requirement of authenticity. We can prove that Yeats, not someone else, wrote the paragraph in his autobiography about the production of *Ubu Roi*. Also, we are probably on safe ground to assume that he actually attended the production, though his descriptions of stage actions and audience behavior could be based on hearsay information.[87] But how reliable and credible is Yeats as a historical witness of an event in 1896? He was an Irishman visiting Paris; he knew little or nothing about Parisian theatre; he knew some French, but had to depend upon his escort to tell him what was happening on stage; he was taken to a performance about which he had very little information. Then, years later, he wrote about the event, which had subsequently gained notoriety. He used it to set up his theme about the tragic generation and his disdain for certain kinds of modernist theatre.

His "reason-giving" and his imaginative memory delivered a gnomic aphorism for us to interpret. He bends these events – or actually his selective memories of them – to his own aims. In like manner, but with far less craft, we have taken Yeats' statement about the savage gods as convenient evidence of a riot. We reconstruct the past event according to our subsequent misunderstanding. We bend the statement to our aims. Perhaps, though, an alarm should go off in our historical sensibilities when yet another historian serves up Yeats as evidence for the avant-garde riot at the production. We should also notice how neatly, almost perfectly, this statement fits each of the seven temptations that I outlined above. It is a ready-made anecdote, delivered by a notable person; it reinforces our ideas about avant-garde art; it has a singular, comprehensive quality; and it has been repeated by many people writing on the production.

In terms of historical methodology, what can we learn from this case study of *Ubu Roi*? Given the basic problems of misinformation, we surely need to relearn – or learn for the first time – the procedures of solid, documentary scholarship (the supposedly retrograde procedures of positivist historians). Historians should be able to describe what actually happened. And did not happen. In order to do this, we have to follow some basic procedures of source criticism. We need to question, not just declare. We also need to take up cultural narratives, such as the stories about the shocking nature of the avant-garde arts, with some care.

It should already be clear, based upon the two case studies in chapters 1 and 2, that I am not offering a critique of cultural history in order to return us to the purity of documentary study. Nor am I suggesting that we must abandon historical narratives that provide a cultural context. Our task remains the same: to describe and to explain, to provide accurate information on a historical event and an appropriate interpretation of the possible conditions and causes that contributed to its historical meanings. Both tasks need to be done well.

If nothing else, this case study of the production of *Ubu Roi* should demonstrate that the opposition between documentary scholarship and cultural history is a false dichotomy. The commitment to documentation is not an antiquarian vice to be overcome; it is one crucial aspect of the historian's sensibility and responsibility. We gain nothing as historians by trying to set up an opposition between documentary and cultural history. Description and analysis go hand in hand with explanation and interpretation. Each well-documented theatre event requires a well-developed contextual understanding.

We need to be clear, therefore, about the basic issues and problems before us. One problem has to do with inadequate and sloppy research. Another has to do with the appeal of a reductive, formulaic narrative. The first problem concerns matters of induction. In solid historical research the gathering of accurate information, step by step, provides an accumulative process for establishing the definitive details of an event. The other problem concerns matters of deduction. Too many scholars, drawn to the neat narrative about the battle between the avant-garde artists and the shocked bourgeoisie, have accepted a general narrative, without careful critical evaluation. We always need to test our general ideas and assumptions against the details of our research project. Deduction and induction should work in tandem. The general and the specific should complement one another. Expansive interpretive ideas often help us to discover the key issues, problems, and questions. But they should not be so conclusive that they dictate the search procedures. In the following chapters I will consider, in some detail, the working relationship between historical events and their possible contexts. The historical event will dominate chapters 3 and 4; the possible methods for establishing contexts will be the primary concern of chapters 5 and 6. Then in chapter 7 I will attempt to reformulate the various issues and problems that we all share in the historical study of theatre.

Part two

Historical vs. theatrical events

Chapter 3

The historical event

Historians who study cultural performances share a familiar and basic problem. Before they can describe and interpret the past actions of their subjects, they must first identify and construct or reconstruct these performances as historical events. Past occurrences take the form and identity of events, of human acts and activities of many types and purposes. Short of merely listing unrelated sources and facts (e.g., a miscellany of documents), historians must construct events, which are the building blocks of historical descriptions, analyses, explanations, and interpretations.

The descriptive mandate of historical study is the recording of actions and events. This is done in order to answer the basic questions of who, what, where, and when. By means of descriptive details, the historian provides a representation of human actions, placed within a shaping context. The explanations provide answers to how and why. In a cumulative manner, the events, when set in relation to one another, provide a developmental order – perhaps contingent, perhaps causal – that may achieve some kind of narrative significance.

And yet as primary as these events are to our historical descriptions and interpretations of theatre, we apparently lack any agreement on how to identify and constitute a performance event. At the level of historical methodology, we are often uncertain about the procedures for establishing the documents, facts, and evidence for an event. Even when we agree upon the documentary record, we may disagree on how an event achieves its identity. In turn, at the level of cultural, social, and political perspectives on history, we are strikingly at odds with one another on how to situate a performance event within a context that is not only consistent with the identity we have given the event but also in accord with other related events and contexts that possibly contribute to its meaning. Part of our difficulty stems from a basic matter of definition and classification. Although we seem to share a common understanding of key terms – event, action, context, identification, presentation, representation, narrative, period – we discover that each of them, as a descriptive and analytical concept, can be quite ambiguous, complicated, obscure, and even contradictory in its denotative and connotative meanings.[1] This unsettling problem of terminology suggests that our ability to construct historical events hinges on two major aspects of historical inquiry: our research skills for digging out the appropriate information and our conceptual skills for defining and organizing the historical task. Indeed, the conceptual problem may be more fundamental than the research problem.

> Identification rests upon organization into entities and kinds. The response to the question, "Same or not the same?" must always be "Same what?"
> Nelson Goodman, *Ways of Worldmaking* (1978: 8)

Let's begin, then, with the definitions and uses of the ideas of *event* and *context*. What comes first, the event or its context, the act or its condition? This problem sends us in search of origins, priorities, and causes, but that inquiry may be misguided because there is, at one level of logic, no way to separate an event from its context in our historical constructions. Events and their contexts are, by necessity, mutually dependent conditions, just as any action must be understood as an aspect of its motivating conditions and its results. Intersecting both synchronically and dia-chronically, the event and context participate together in an historical matrix. Within the vectors of time and space, the event and the context are mutually defining. So understood, they have a singular or joined identity, which we could call the event/ context. But of course this unified idea, which seems to require an omniscient understanding, is pointless for historical inquiry. We need, for various reasons, to give events and their conditions separate identities as we carry out our research, develop our descriptions and analyses, and carry forward our explanations and interpret-ations. The whole consists of its parts. Our task is to identify, describe, and explain the parts and their possible relations. Although, in the final analysis, an event and its context may merge in our understanding, we must, in the preliminary processes of research and identification, make distinctions. We start with the parts of the puzzle, not the completed design. And despite what may be a logical conundrum, we are quite capable, in a practical manner, of distinguishing between an event and its context, just as we can maintain the distinction between past and present, self and other. Typically – and necessarily – we shift our attention back and forth between the two concepts or polarities, as we attempt to describe and explain an historical situation.

> . . . history speaks of particular events.
> Aristotle, *The Poetics*, (1987: 41)
> The spirit of history . . . is contrary to minute exactness.
> Dr. Samuel Johnson, in James Boswell, *Life of Johnson* (1953: 113)

In guides to historical method, it is common practice to divide the professional procedures of the historian into three sequential steps or stages of study, followed by a method of reporting (e.g., lecture, essay, book). First, one investigates the historical topic and subjects in order to discover the relevant sources; secondly, one criticizes, analyzes, and synthesizes the sources by turning artifacts into facts; and thirdly, one arranges the facts as supporting evidence for an argument; in this way, one offers an interpretation of the significance of these facts, placing them in the most appropriate context. Finally, one organizes the study and communicates the results, usually in some kind of narrative. After the information is gathered, analyzed, and interpreted, the report is prepared. Although, as Robert Jones Shafer insists, the three stages of historical research "cannot be delimited precisely into chronological blocks," they are often identified in guides to historical research as the basic steps that historians take.[2] And they are usually presented sequentially within the chapters of these manuals. These developmental steps thus seem to follow a logical progression.[3]

During the first two stages, this model of historical method posits a careful procedure of documentary study. Historians follow disciplinary methods for gathering and testing the potential evidence. Like a police detective, the well-trained historian applies rules of evidence to the data. External criticism determines the authenticity of evidence; internal criticism determines the credibility.[4] All kinds of data, from material artifacts to personal testimonies, are examined and evaluated for their reliability (on a scale of possibility, plausibility, probability, and certainty). Once this crucial task is done, the historian analyzes and synthesizes the information in order to give the event an identity. Only then, with the identity in place, does the historian arrive at a hypothesis about its historical significance. Having discovered its significance, the historian is prepared to explain and interpret it.[5] This explanation provides the basis of the argument in the third stage of inquiry. This whole process is guided by a basic belief that effective and convincing interpretations follow from careful and solid documentation. The hypothesis, derived directly from accumulated data, serves as the interpretive idea for explaining the nature (function, purpose) of the historical subject under investigation.

> Explanation at one level often paves the way for a reinterpretation of the facts at a higher level.
> Georg Henrik von Wright, *Explanation and Understanding* (1971: 134)

After completing the third and final stage, historians have successfully met the two major aims of historical scholarship: to represent the past events by description, explanation, and interpretation. They can then write up the report, accurately describing the data and explaining the significance of the past events and the people who participated in those events. Thus the initial task of identifying, describing, and analyzing *who, what, where, and when* can be followed by the joined tasks of explaining and interpreting *how* and *why* the events occurred. The actions of the participants are explained, their motives are interpreted. This search for meaning extends beyond the event itself to the possible contexts for it. But this search, as several manuals insist, is proscribed by the information that the historian has discovered and analyzed in the first and second stages; the explanations and interpretations, based upon an empirical model of data compilation, remain true to the procedural results of the investigation.

How convincing is this description of the methods of historical research? Do historians actually carry out their research, analysis, and writing in this kind of progressive and logical manner? Perhaps a few operate in this manner, but for most historians this neat, three-step process is an impossible dream. Or a prisonhouse, if not a nightmare, of procedural thinking. Though this methodological description does name the important aspects of historical study, it mainly qualifies as a textbook diagram. The method, as described, is problematic not only because of the complex nature of human events and their causes but also because of the inadequate description of the place and function of interpretive thinking throughout all of the stages, including the process of writing.

Nonetheless, some historians, having committed themselves to the first and second steps in this model, reject the third step. Dedicated to a rigorous program of investigation, they pride themselves on their objectivity. Wishing to avoid (or at least to limit) the problems of subjective or personal bias, these historians attempt to move directly from the first stage of documentation to the final task of accurate presentation. These historians, committed to archival research and the gathering of factual information, are satisfied to write careful, detailed reports on the data. The accumulated facts, arranged in some kind of inherent or conventional pattern such as chronological or alphabetical sequences, speak for themselves. This approach guides certain kinds of historical chronicles, time lines, catalogues, bibliographies, registers, directories, dictionaries, and encyclopedias. Likewise, many authors of classroom texts convince themselves that they are just organizing the facts (from which teachers and students may develop interpretations, if they wish). All conclusions, all acts of inference and synthesis, are supposedly based upon objective procedures that identify facts and ascertain their validity. Some historians are satisfied to represent but not to explain the past. They believe that description can be neatly separated from explanation, as if these are two separate processes of thinking about and representing historical actions and events. They are satisfied with their aim, which is to compile useful information for interested readers (and for other historians).

What is the justification for this documentary mission in historical studies? Is it possible to place brackets around all interpretive matters, and thereby to provide a documentary record on its own terms? Documentary historians, following basic inductive principles of gathering and tabulating data, intend to be trustworthy reporters. They try to avoid preconceived assumptions, prejudices, questionable generalizations, and ideological judgements. The code of reliability – which is applied to all data during the criticism of evidence – serves as the most important value for documentary historians. It is their badge of integrity, justifying their scholarly persona. This code operates as a safeguard against interpretive license.

The empirical truths of eyewitness observation

In the eighteenth century when early voyagers to the new worlds returned to Europe with the plumage of the Bird of Paradise, the skins did not have feet. The displays of the bird fascinated observers. In its exotic beauty and strangeness, the Bird of Paradise had somehow escaped the terrestrial world of all other species. People believed that the birds, lacking feet, never landed; they flew and glided through the air for their whole lives. Almost angelic, they revealed the wonders of the new paradises beyond the distant

horizon. But this judgment, based upon empirical observation of the birds, was wrong. When the dead birds were prepared for shipment, the feet were removed so that they did not damage the beautiful plumage.
British Museum exhibition of 2003 called *The Enlightenment*, and published that year as a book, edited by Kim Sloan

Without question, the commitment to documentary integrity is admirable. It is a code that should guide all research and analysis. Moreover, all of us benefit from the various compilations of data that documentary scholars provide – those dictionaries, encyclopedias, directories, bibliographies, and basic chronicles or surveys. Research would be a more difficult task if we did not have such collections of documents and basic compilations of data. For all of us who draw upon the valuable documentary collections and reference works, such as the *Dictionary of National Biography* in England (recently updated and published by Oxford University Press), the debt to such compilations is enormous. From a reader's perspective, the presentation of the basic facts is greatly appreciated. We depend upon the accuracy of such works.

There are several major projects in theatre history, undertaken by a team of scholars, that seem to realize the aims of documentary scholarship. Among the most notable are the twelve volumes of *The London Stage, 1660–1800* and the sixteen volumes of the *Biographical Dictionary, 1660–1800*. Also, and perhaps the single most impressive documentary project in the study of British theatre, there is the *Records of Early English Drama* (or REED), which was initially funded by the Canadian government. Housed at the University of Toronto and published by the University of Toronto Press, REED is an amazing archival, editing, and publishing venture, under the general editorship of Sally-Beth MacLean and the director Alexandra F. Johnston. It is dedicated to a very ambitious documentary mission: "to locate, transcribe, and publish systematically all surviving external evidence of dramatic, ceremonial, and minstrel activity in Great Britain before 1642."[6] Scholars from several countries have carried out the archival research and edited the separate volumes. They are to be commended for a job well done. Since the 1970s, these volumes have provided a detailed record of the theatrical activities in the cities, towns, and regions of Great Britain. Beginning in 1979 with the two volumes on theatrical activities in York, edited by Alexandra F. Johnston and Margaret Rogerson, REED has published over three dozen volumes. And the project, which is now available electronically online, is still going forward.

REED is thus committed to documentary scholarship in theatre history. As James L. Harner describes it in his *Literary Research Guide*, REED "transcribes – but does not interpret – civic, guild, and ecclesiastical records, wills, and antiquarians' compilations."[7] It would seem to be a perfect example of the commitment and capability of scholars to carry out and publish documentary scholarship. For example, R. W. Ingram, the editor of the volume on theatre in Coventry, describes his determination to be true to what Teresa Coletti calls the "methodological purity the project strives for."[8] In Ingram's words: "The aim of the *Records of Early English Drama* is to collect written evidence of drama, minstrelsy, and ceremonial activity, not to interpret it. The nature of the material gathered here invites interpretation; I hope that I have almost entirely succeeded in resisting that invitation."[9]

Yet this disciplinary logic, though admirable in its commitment to basic procedures for collecting historical documents, may be flawed because it apparently requires – or presumes the possibility of – a methodological division between documentation and interpretation. Grounded in principles of objectivity and positivist analysis, documentary historians seek to be rigorous in their commitment to the facts, which have the integrity of primary truth. The documentary principle that guides such scholarship is quite appropriate for all historians. I am not questioning the basic aim of documentary rigor as a standard in historical research. Nonetheless, this research principle, which is based upon several unwarranted assumptions about both the procedures of historical research and the nature of historical understanding, is self-deceiving. Interpretation is a necessary component of all documentary projects.

For example, the REED project, in order to begin, had to work through a series of interpretive decisions and problems, including the designation of which records should be examined. Also, the decision to stop at 1642, which suggests certain contextual matters of political significance, required a set of interpretations about the nature and purpose of the endeavor. Likewise, the guidelines spell out in detail which kinds of performance events and venues should be catalogued. These decisions reveal certain interpretive ideas about what qualifies as "drama" and "theatre." Thus, in contrast to E. K. Chambers, who attempted in *The Medieval Stage* (1903) and *The Elizabethan Stage* (1923) to focus primarily on London theatre and to separate sacred drama and theatrical activities from the secular development of professional theatre, the REED project covers the whole country and records all kinds of performance events, secular and sacred. In doing this REED offers a corrective interpretation of Chambers' books and aims. Indeed, the interpretive guidelines require special training for the editors, who themselves, as Ingram reveals, are faced with interpretive decisions in their assessment of the documents, even as they follow the guidelines.[10]

All of the historical projects that documentary scholars take most pride in – collections of documents, factual dictionaries and encyclopedias, bibliographies, calendars, and registers – require interpretive choices and statements. In order to begin such projects, judgements must be made on what to include and exclude. These decisions are based upon interpretive procedures and principles. Judith Milhous and Robert D. Hume make this admirably clear in "An Explanation of the Register," which introduces *A Register of English Theatrical Documents 1660–1737.*[11] They are quite explicit about their interpretive decisions on not only what they included and excluded but also why their plan of study is appropriate.

Besides the need to provide an interpretive guideline for what will be covered, the historian must also make hundreds of interpretive decisions on how much space to give to the various entries. This is especially true for dictionaries and encyclopedias, but it applies in all cases of documentary publishing. In these projects, the compiler (and the many contributors) must assess the value and significance of whatever or whoever is being described. As most scholars recognize when they negotiate a book contract, publishers seldom provide enough space for their grand and worthy projects. These constraints on word count challenge the interpretive decisions that have to be made about what to cover and how to cover it. Yet despite all of these decisions, some documentary scholars still insist that their projects are free of interpretation. Readers of such works soon discover, however, that a rather extensive interpretive agenda controlled (or failed to control) the organization of information. It is refreshing, therefore, to read Dennis Kennedy's statement in his "Preface and Principles" section of *The Oxford Encyclopedia of Theatre and Performance*: "The factual material contained in the *Encyclopedia* is expanded by conceptual discussions."[12] Kennedy understands that those "conceptual discussions" occur throughout the two volumes, not just in the long topical essays that he commissioned.[13]

The argument can be made, of course, that some documentary works that cover circumscribed topics, such as calendars or bibliographies, are capable of attaining an exclusive documentary status because the works are comprehensive in their coverage. There is no requirement, accordingly, to trim some entries or exclude anything. Each document and piece of factual information that the scholar discovers appears in the book. The whole point of such works is to list everything that is relevant. For example, *The Colonial American Stage, 1665–1774: A Documentary Calendar* (2001), compiled by Odai Johnson and William J. Burling, intends "to record all the existing material relating to the theatres, productions, and personnel of companies and individuals performing in the American colonies."[14] Locale by locale, from Nova Scotia to the Caribbean, and year by year, 1665 to 1774, the calendar tabulates every piece of evidence that Johnson and Burling could find. Nothing is left out because of a lack of space. The source is identified; the information is recorded. Although new information will be discovered in the coming years by the editors and other scholars, this register is as complete as the editors could make it in 2001.

Thus, *The Colonial American Stage* seems to fulfill the documentary scholar's ideal of presenting the facts, yet leaving interpretation to others. Johnson and Burling, however, make no such self-protective or self-congratulatory statement; instead, they insist that their gathering of information not only documents the available sources but also provides a new interpretive viewpoint on the colonial American theatre. Comparing their work to previous historical surveys, encyclopedias, and collections of documents, such as the *Cambridge History of American Theatre*, 3 vols. (1998–2000), they state: "we offer substantial new evidence not known to the authors of those works, and we interpret in quite different ways some of the data which they present."[15] There, in a nutshell, is the motive for most documentary projects: to correct previous understanding, to make us see things we did not know. In their "Introduction" to this work, Johnson and Burling provide a standard overview on how to use the compiled information, but this preliminary description of what the calendar offers and how it is organized also offers the interpretive justification for what the data shows. In the process, Johnson and Burling demonstrate that the documentary scholar, instead of being a neutral, objective tabulator of information, is usually a person on a mission. Indeed, most documentary scholars are advocates for a cause. The months and years in the archives are often undertaken with missionary zeal. Committed to changing our understanding, they are often among the most argumentative scholars in their discipline.

> In short, the historian's aim is verisimilitude with regard to a perished past – a subjective process – rather than experimental certainty with regard to an objective reality.
> Louis Gottschalk, *Understanding History: A Primer of Historical Method* (1969: 47)

This feisty trait of many documentary scholars should be a tell-tale sign for us that research methods do not divide into a choice between documentation and interpretation. Nor do historical procedures follow a neat two-step or a three-step program. Although it is conceivable that some historians perform their research projects in a methodical manner, most of us, including documentary scholars, have never done so. That's because, in almost all cases, the procedures of interpretive thinking occur at each of the three basic stages of a research project. (And the three stages overlap, and quite often expand into a project with many stages and shifting methods.) Despite the apparent primacy of stage one, the documentary area of investigation usually remains an undiscovered country until the historian has a reason to go there. It is the rare historian who accumulates data before having any idea about why it is being gathered. Almost all, if not all, documentary scholars already have made some definite judgements about the significance of the projects they undertake, before they begin the archival research. And as they discover information, they are busy making interpretations about its significance and about how best to organize and present the data.

This means, then, that historians almost always begin with a version of stage three, an interpretive idea or insight. On some occasions this idea may be little more than a hunch or conjecture; on other occasions it may be a well-articulated hypothesis, a theoretical proposition, or a missionary campaign. Whatever the case, the interpretive idea – an intention to explain something or to counter received knowledge – often launches the historical investigation. The project thus begins with a working hypothesis that guides both the *search* for relevant data and the *selection* of appropriate documents. Most of the time an argument seeks and finds its evidence. Interpretation occurs throughout all of this.

As for the report (usually a written narrative), some researchers are guided from the very start by not only their tentative conclusions and supporting arguments but also their organizational models that provide the narrative form for the studies. Some historians know from the start much about how they want to write the project. And some of them have a highly developed narrative sensibility that contributes to the book they will write. Like a fiction writer, the historian may start with an image, a moment, a person, or an event that demands and calls forth a narrative structure. Even though the historian does not yet know the details and the shape of key sections, he or she may still be driven by a narrative impulse and sensibility. This formal order – and the need for it – often guides the research and the writing. From the initial moment, the narrative begins to take shape. It operates as a design, even an imperative, for the research, analysis, and argument. For many historians, the great pleasure in historical research and writing thus derives from the resolve, right from the beginning, to tell a good story with appropriate style.[16]

For example, some microhistorians are drawn to historical situations that allow for and justify a specific narrative approach to the material. Sometimes they discover in the initiating idea the impulse for telling a story, as was the case for Jonathan Spence with *The Death of Woman Wang* (1978) and for Simon Schama with *Death of a Harvard Man*, one of two investigations in *Dead Certainties* (1991). In both cases, these two historians, inspired by a horrible death, develop a certain kind of narrative that allowed them to mix the modes of historical and fictional narrative. Spence's narrative is presented in the mode of a tragedy, Schama's follows the mode of a detective novel. Both draw upon court records, which evoke the dramatic scene of a culminating trial. Like popular fiction writers, they appreciate the value and power of a court scene in this kind of narrative. And both of them stress the value of focusing on individual lives and actions.

> There is a history in all men's lives.
> William Shakespeare, *Henry IV, Part Two*, 2.2. 80

Spence's book concludes with the image of the dead woman Wang in the snow. This is the very image that initially caught his imagination when he began his project. Having discovered the image of woman Wang while working on another project, he was drawn to it without yet knowing what it might mean. This tragic image had a story in it, but it required extensive research on the history of T'an-ch'eng province in seventeenth-century China. Spence sought the context and some possible causes for what was already known, as he explained in the Preface to his book: "And so the book ends with woman Wang, as it should, for it is with her that it began."[17] His preface, in accord with the circling narrative he tells, serves also as a kind of postscript: the end is in the beginning.

Schama, intrigued by a murder mystery at Harvard College in the nineteenth century, took on the persona of a detective, which allowed him "to follow my curiosity about the death of George Parkman into the archive ... "[18] Inspired in part by Henry James' posthumously published novel *The Sense of the Past*, which "sets out the habitually insoluble quandary of the historian," Schama honed his historical sensibility on the fictional sensibility of James.[19] The rich and complex method that James developed in his fiction thus served as both narrative model and intellectual standard for Schama. The story itself seemed to be pure melodrama, so this provided another reason to turn to James, who was masterful in transforming a melodramatic tale into a complex psychological investigation of human behavior and understanding. The murder mystery evoked the detective within the historian. But instead of reaching the traditional conclusion of a detective story, which reveals all motives and solves all puzzles, Schama honored the limitations of historical research. Because documents are never adequate to the task, Schama had to remain true to the uncertainties and ambiguities of Parkman's horrible death: the dismembered body. Some things remain a mystery; the historian can only deliver so much knowledge. Yet within this limitation he allowed himself substantial fictional liberty in creating situations, dialogue, and personal thoughts for the participants.[20]

Microhistories may offer a special kind of case study, at least in the ways they feature the narrative techniques of dialogue, conflict, and suspense. Certain historians – Spence, Schama, Carlos Ginzburg, Natalie Zemon Davis – are accomplished story-tellers. They are drawn quite often to historical situations that call out for narrative investigation. But microhistories are not exceptional in their use of narrative form. Narrative models are pervasive in most historical works, as a number of scholars, including Paul Ricoeur, Arthur Danto, Louis O. Mink, David Carr, David Perkins, and Peter Burke, have explained and argued in recent years.[21] Perhaps the most familiar figure in this discussion about history and narrative has been Hayden White, who has argued that historians approach their historical subjects in terms of some kind of genre, which serves as a model for the historian's sensibility and worldview (1973, 1978, 1987). In *Metahistory* he describes how four kinds of narrative provide a "mode of emplotment" (e.g., romantic, tragic, comic, satiric), a "mode of argument" (e.g., formalist, mechanistic, organicist, contextualist), and a "mode of ideological implication" (e.g., anarchist, radical, conservative, liberal).[22] Each stylistic model, which accords with the historian's sensibility, encompasses within its "poetical under-structure" certain narrative tendencies that organize figures of speech, formal tropes, plot schemes and codes, argumentative techniques, ideological perspectives, and even mythic assumptions.[23] From White's perspective, accordingly, the narrative model often prefigures and guides the historian's approach to research and analysis. That is, each historian has a predilection to see the world, human character, and actions in certain ways that evoke narrative modes of organization and understanding.

Moreover, as several theorists and philosophers have noted, whatever the beginning point for a research project – a piece of information, a hypothesis, an image, a narrative model – the historian always brings to the task a set of primary epistemological concepts that shape understanding. Historical thinking, accordingly, depends upon certain categorical assumptions and presuppositions, such as concepts of time and space, principles of causality, ideas of contiguity, models of human behavior, and cultural ideologies. These epistemological categories provide the historian with basic modes of comprehension as well as interpretive strategies. In *Historical Understanding*, Louis Mink offers the following explanation:

> There are concepts we think *about*, concepts we *use* in thinking, and concepts (usually called a priori) we think *with* . . . A concept may move (not without change) from one function to another; hence there are no unique examples of each class. But allowing for this we might say that in many contexts the concepts of energy, man, social class, and alienation are concepts we think about; the concepts of quantity, function, value, and change are concepts we use in thinking; and the concepts of time, space, identity, and causation are concepts we think with.[24]

We may disagree with Mink about which concepts belong in which category; and we may wish to suggest other possible epistemological concepts (e.g., operating ideas and assumptions about agent and agency, intentionality, power, position and location, contiguity, boundary, margin, order and disorder, conflict, quantity, quality, direction, probability, necessity). But we all recognize that these kinds of organizing concepts determine how we perceive ourselves, others, the world, and the past. With care, the historian attempts to use these framing ideas and habits of mind without being controlled by them. But often in our research and writing such ideas not only provide an operational mode of understanding but also establish the agenda. They regularly define the basic terms of analysis and direct the argument. They lie so deep in our understanding that even retrospectively we have a difficult time recognizing some of them.

Every research discipline has its organizing categories and discourses. As we will see, for example, one of the primary discourses for history is periodization. Its categories shape our thoughts, as Mink also points out: "Every mode of comprehension tends to generate its own form of discourse, including concepts which take their proper meaning from the way in which they function within the mode."[25] In recent years there has been much commentary on the idea of discourse, especially because of the influence of the writings of Michel Foucault. But the idea has a much broader heritage.

The concept of *discourse* has a complex history in linguistics and philosophy in modern times, beginning most notably with the language theories of Ferdinand de Saussure and Emile Benveniste. Since the 1950s, especially in French linguistics, philosophy, social theory, and Annales history, the idea of "discourse" has been applied in many different ways. For example, as an examination of the writings of Michel Foucault and Paul Ricoeur reveals, two distinct ideas of history emerge in their writings, in part because of their distinct ideas of discourse. Foucault favors Saussure's idea of *langue* (a collective code, often functioning unconsciously), while Ricoeur places emphasis upon Saussure's idea of *parole* (an individual message that is intentional). In Foucault's writings, such as *The Order of Things* (1970), *discourse* is identified as a *discursive formation* that shapes human thought and action. By contrast, Ricoeur uses the concept of discourse to distinguish semantics from semiotics and to characterize a dialectical relation in language between event and meaning.[26] For Ricoeur the subject (i.e., individual consciousness and intention) is a critical factor in the definition and limitation of discourse and its functions. Speech is a performance, an act, an event. "Languages do not speak, people do."[27] But for Foucault the subject is often displaced (or dissolved) into a series of discourses that speak or speak through the individual.

Discourse is the new cultural superorganic – made even more draconian as the expression of a "power" that is everywhere, in all quotidian institutions and relations.
Marshall Sahlins, *Culture in Practice: Selected Essays* (2000: 12)

This controlling idea of discourse shares some features with the concepts of ideology and hegemony in Marxist theory. In anthropology, as Marshall Sahlins points out, the concept of discourse has often replaced the older, all-encompassing concept of culture. So understood, discourse imposes itself through the systems of social order, power, and knowledge. In this sense, knowledge knows the knower. The event, the center of human action, takes its meaning from the discourses operating in and through it, not primarily from the intention and choice of individual consciousness (as Sartre's existentialism proclaimed). But Sahlins warns against this move when applied to history: "Structure is a state; but action unfolds as a temporal process."[28] All too often, the ideas of discourse and structure ignore the temporal, developmental nature of human events. Synchronic time displaces diachronic time. For this reason, Sahlins contends that in both disciplines of anthropology and history there is "an exaggerated opposition between *structure* and *event.*"[29] But even more to the point, Sahlins has identified a logical problem which applies to structuralist and discourse theory as well as Fernand Braudel's model of history: "Once *structure* and *event* are defined in mutually exclusive ways, the one cannot be made intelligible in the terms of the other."[30] Or I would frame the matter this way: we cannot have an idea of event and context or event and structure or event and discourse that depends upon synchronic time to the exclusion of diachronic time. From the perspective of the historical event, then, I am arguing that we need a model of action that includes both motivation and aim within the framing conditions of material culture and cultural conditions. And in a primary way, as I will consider presently in a discussion of the size of an event, we need not only the concept of identity for an event but also an understanding of change – the framing condition for defining events, one from another, and for placing them in some kind of sequence.

Of course, behind the popularity in recent years of the concept of discourse is the abiding question in historical study: do individuals make their own history or do they act and think according to large, expansive, and even deterministic forces? Do certain kinds of *discourses, belief systems, ideologies,* and *discursive formations* shape both identity and action? The kind of history one writes depends, in great measure, upon one's assumptions about the relation between individuals and their systems, including their systems of knowledge and organization. Like other grand concepts that we think with, not just about (e.g., power, time, narrative, identity, and representation), the idea of discourse seems capable of meaning many different, even contradictory, things. Perhaps the idea of history, when trimmed to something specific, can provide some clarity in these matters. The example of microhistory is but one possible way to attempt to do justice to the individual action (which is often of central importance in theatre studies). But even the idea of history, when taken up and applied by some people, can also be imperialistic in its ambitions.

The world is under no obligation to correspond to the categories by which it is thought – even if, as Durkheim said, it can only exist for people in the way that it is thought. Thus, in the dialectic of culture-as-constituted and culture-as-lived, we also discover some possibility of reconciling the most profound antimony of social science theory, that between structure and practice: reconciling them, that is, in the only way presently justifiable – as a symbolic process.

    Marshall Sahlins, *Culture in Practice: Selected Essays* (2000: 290–91)

Unavoidably, these conceptual or epistemological issues encroach upon the pragmatic matter of historical methodology. But they do not – or should not – displace our need to concentrate on our procedures, and to understand how they operate. We need to do justice to both our concepts and our procedures because they are tied together throughout our historical study. So, if we are going to posit, for the sake of convenience, a basic version of the three-step model of historical scholarship (even though we recognize that it is not necessarily sequential), we need to see that at each of the three procedural stages the historian must negotiate a series of dialectical relationships. At stage one, the mode of investigation encompasses both apprehension and comprehension. What historians see – or fail to see – depends upon not only *where* but *how* they look. Information is defined and confined by how they constitute both the field of study and the method of investigation. At stage two, the mode of analysis comprises both empirical and rational thinking; the historian must demonstrate both *a posteriori* and *a priori* understanding. In other words, even the simplest process of historical analysis presupposes certain normative judgements and propositions. Facts always have their reasons in historical discourse, just as acts of induction have their institutional or conventional sanctions. And at stage three, the methods of interpretation transform the data and the facts into evidence for some kind of argument, one that may follow an initial hypothesis or one that may be discovered only late in the processes of thinking.

Then, in the final process of giving form to the research, the analysis, and the interpretation, certain narrative forms and procedures, often well developed, operate in our writing. The historian may be committed to a prose style of lucid description, free of metaphoric conceits and tropes. And the historian may dismiss Hayden White's argument about the modes of emplotment, argument, and ideological implication. But the issue here is not limited to White's particular models, which he derived in great measure from Northrop Frye's *The Anatomy of Criticism* (1957). Whether or not White offers a full and accurate explanation of the place of narrative in historical scholarship, he has demonstrated that historical writing and narrative conventions go hand in hand. White is hardly alone in his discovery of the narrative function in historical writing.

The criterion of unity on which so much emphasis is laid is that of "necessity" or "probability"; which is a principle of the logical and causal relations between actions or events. For poetry to conform to this criterion is for it to produce plots – mimetic structures of human action – which embody generalized patterns of universals, as opposed to the random particulars of history.

    Stephen Halliwell (on the idea of the unity of plot in Aristotle's *Poetics*), *The Poetics of Aristotle* (1987: 79)

All historical writing, as Paul Ricoeur argues so astutely in *Time and Narrative*, depends not only upon rhetorical tropes and narrative techniques but also representational strategies that history shares with fiction writing.[31] The plotting of events, within the realm of possibility, is a shared mission. This does not mean that history and fiction cannot be distinguished in their missions, for I want to insist upon certain crucial distinctions between them. But it does mean that they sometimes share similar methods of description and organization in their representations of life. This relationship between historical and fictional narratives is a complex one, as can be traced in the analytical and theoretical writings of White, Mink, Ricoeur, and others. Ricouer, for example, takes exception to some of White's ideas.[32] The point to keep in mind here, as we consider the relationship between documentation and interpretation, is that the narrative features and functions of history writing reveal yet one more reason that it is impossible to separate representation from explanation in historical scholarship. Interpretation occurs throughout the process of historical research. In brief, the meaning and coherence of descriptive information depends upon the interpretive model that the historian brings to (rather than simply discovers within) the data. Change the model, change the meaning.

Fact and theory, information and explanation, empiricism and ideology, apprehension and comprehension, documentation and interpretation – each opposing pair is joined at all three stages of historical method and understanding. Given this argument (which serves as an operating principle for what follows), I want to return to a preliminary and necessary question in historical study: what is a historical event? Or, in more specific terms, what is a historical event in theatre studies? How do we as historians of theatre, performance, culture, and society constitute historical events? What are the procedures for identification, analysis, and understanding?

When we refer to a historical event, we are considering its four distinct aspects or locations.

(1) The actual or original event occurred in the past. We lack direct access to it – even if it is an event we are recalling from our own experience (e.g., a production we saw and even took notes on). Lacking a time machine, we cannot return to the moment and place of the event, though modern recording technology, such as photographs, recording instruments, and film can document various kinds of events in *immediate* ways. But these *media* documents, like our memories or written notes, must still be treated as *mediating* sources. They are *intermediated* sources between the event and us, contingent markers or clues that must be interpreted. Their documentary value depends upon our ability to distinguish between them and the actual, missing event. They intervene between the event and our method of reconstructing it.

(2) The documented sources, in their many types, provide access to the event. They are fragments to be interpreted. Some of the sources are contemporaneous with the event; some follow after. Some are eyewitness reports; some are hearsay. Historians therefore attempt to distinguish between primary and secondary sources, giving priority to the eyewitness and contemporaneous sources. But sometimes the "primary" eyewitness is wrong and the secondary source is correct. Think, for

example, of the number of people placed in prison on the basis of eyewitness or primary evidence; only the secondary source of DNA testing, sometimes years after the event, provides counter evidence that overturns the certainties of the eyewitness. Skepticism is a valuable trait of mind for a historian (including the willingness to doubt one's own assumptions and certainties). The historical sources take many forms, including human artifacts (e.g., letters, diaries, drawings), oral reports (gossip, anecdotes, stories), and material objects (clothes, furniture, archeological remains).

(3) Historians must delve into the potential sources and determine which ones serve the aim of the research project. The various records have no established identity or meaning until we discover and select the sources that are relevant to our investigation. They attain their significance when we grant it. The relevant information needs to be gathered, wherever it might be located or hidden away. Somewhere, in all of the documents, we discover the pieces of information that may make up the event we seek to comprehend. Sometimes we have a good idea of what we are seeking. But sometimes we do not know until we stumble into the right territory, begin to crack some codes, and start to discover useful data. If we are in the right archive, if we are looking in the right folder or box, if we have figured out where and how to search, then, with some luck, the features of the event may begin to come into view. Then we find some apparent facts and some potential evidence that just possibly will be used to reconstruct the event. At this stage of the process in the making of the event, we are researching history or, as some people say, "doing history."

(4) And then, having done the digging, we separate the relevant sources from the irrelevant ones. We seek a design, an order – that is, we seek a meaningful way to bring the various details into an interconnecting relationship. In this sense we give the events a plot (though unlike fiction, including Aristotle's tragic form, we may not be able to determine the unifying elements of the plotted actions). We spread out the pieces of the potential event and begin to connect A to B to C, and so on. Or, more likely, B and C are missing, so we have to acknowledge the gaps and connect A to D, or even X, Y, or Z. We are constructing a puzzle that is missing a number of pieces. And, in addition, we hold a number of pieces from a dozen other puzzles; if we are savvy, we put them aside, but often we jam them into our constructed event. The event is assembled, but the process is actually one of reassembling, reconstructing, and restructuring the original event, which we represent (not simply present). The puzzle is put together. Partially. We have to work with what is given (unlike the person who constructs a fictional world). Based upon a careful analysis of the available sources, we recreate the event and give it meaning.

The event attains its design and meaning, but it had some potential meanings in the preceding stages of becoming an event. The historian's task is to do justice to those implicit meanings, to make them explicit. The eyewitnesses, for example, express their own meanings, sometimes with certainty. But historians need to provide meanings, drawn perhaps from other sources, that might not have been available to the participants in the event and the makers of the sources. Historians discover and create the truth, to the best extent possible. Each of the stages or manifestations of the event are therefore crucial. Each aspect of an event confronts us with descriptive information and interpretive challenges. Our historical methodology has to be as complex as the event itself; we have to investigate and assemble with shrewd research skills and acute analytical insights.

Given the complex, fourfold identity of any event, our desire for a basic definition of the primary concept of an event may be unwise, if not foolish. But in order to focus in this chapter on some of the key issues and problems in the historical construction of any event, I will venture a working definition. Let's start with this: *a historical event is any single, significant occurrence, large or small, that took place in the past.* In general terms our idea of an event can encompass nonhuman occurrences, including natural contingencies and all kinds of actions by nonhumans. Likewise, our evidence for events can be derived from both human sources and nonhuman remains. But for the most part, we are constructing events based upon human actions. This calls for special considerations.

> In this book an *event* is understood as any past happening. A *fact* is a true descriptive statement about past events. To *explain* is merely to make plain, clear, or understandable some problem about past events, so that resultant knowledge will be useful in dealing with future problems.
> David Hackett Fischer, *Historians' Fallacies* (1970: xv)

For example, while we do not concern ourselves with the motives or aims of a hurricane, such concerns are often primary in the construction of human events. Although physical science has been able to function with the idea of a single cause, such as Newton's *vera causa*, the study of human actions and events needs a more complex formulation, such as Aristotle's four causes: *material, efficient, formal, and final*. A theatre event, for example, has its agents who cause and effect the process; their efficient aims provide the agency for the creative processes. The event has its material features, from scenic and costume elements to the material presence and actions of the bodies of the performers. The event has its formal design or cause in the form of the artistic elements, provided by the participants. The formal design is the basis of the formal description and analysis of critics and historians (hence the emphasis upon formalism in the study of all of the arts). And the event has its final cause or its aims and purposes, which are multiple in any complex event. The participants may share a final aim of creating for an audience a successful production, but the financial aims of the producer may have little to do with the performance aims of the actors. Likewise, the playwright's aims may or may not be realized by the designer or the director. Although, as historians, we do not usually break down the events in this systematic manner, with its four-part separation of human actions and events, we nonetheless attend to the four causes in any theatre event we see. And as historians we try to identity the key aspects of these causes in our process of reconstructing the event.

This method of constructing an event provides a potential measure for the complexity of who, what, where, when, how, and why. Like the pentad of Kenneth Burke's *A Grammar of Motives* – act, scene, agent, agency, and purpose – the Aristotelian four causes not only provide a helpful way to slow us down so that we begin to consider the component parts of human events but also offer the distributive categories that increase the possibility that we will be true to the event's complexity when we attempt to represent it. In Burke's formulation "any complete statement about motives will offer some kind of answer to these five questions: what was done (act), when or where it was done (scene), who did it (agent), how he did it (agency), and why (purpose)."[33] Burke insists that whenever we make an inquiry according to the basic interrogatives – who, what, where, when, how, and why – we are investigating the modes of human action. We are attending to its grammar, its parts, its interrelations, and its motives. Our questions are directed at discovering the nature of human actions. If these actions occurred in the past, they attract the attention of the historian, who, like Aristotle's tragedian, seeks to represent these actions within some kind of plot structure (which has a requisite standard of possibility, and a desire to discover explanations based upon the principle of probability).

Two basic problems confront us initially with this definition of an event: (1) the actual existence of the past event; (2) its size and scope (or its spatial and temporal factors). These two definitive traits – having occurred and having dimensions – are complicated, in turn, by the double perception of the event. Each historical event, whenever it occurred and whatever its size and scope, is constructed not only by the people contemporaneous with it but also by the people, such as historians, who follow after it. Without getting bogged down in paradoxes about past and present identities of events, we can recognize that the sources provide the essential basis for mediating the distance between events and our representations of them. People, including the participants, create the sources for the event, either at the time of the event or subsequently in some kind of report or record. Their testimony and material artifacts certify that an event occurred. We need to establish this basic fact: the event actually happened. Then we can begin to figure out its definitive features and its meanings. In their attempts to identify an event and to establish its significance, the people who provide our sources – participants and eyewitnesses – may also attempt to explain its size and scope. Sometimes these people are in agreement, but only occasionally. In consequence, when historians construct or reconstruct an event, they must judge the credibility and reliability of each witness. The problem that all historians face is that each witness develops his or her own description (and perhaps explanation) of the event. The same event can be perceived in strikingly different ways by a group of witnesses; they may disagree on the basics of its definitive dimensions, scope, and features.

In accord with our definition of an event and its ontological condition, we can establish that it is specific, separate, and unique. But such information tells us nothing yet about the ways we understand and construct events and their meanings. That is, having established an event's ontological identity – it actually occurred – we must then take up the more complex epistemological matters: we must identify, define, describe, explain and understand the event as a human action. We seek its causes: efficient, material, formal, and final. When we take up the epistemological concerns (e.g., definitive features, size, scope, participating and responsible agents, and modes of agency), we are already granting the actual status of the event as something that happened. We are thus ready to move on to the next step as we seek to describe and interpret the event's possible traits and meanings – for the human agents and participants in the event, for other observers and interested parties at the time, for the society at large (however defined), and for any subsequent people, including ourselves, who look back on the event. Quite often, though, previous historians have already constructed the event according to their understanding and purposes. We thus find ourselves contending with several previous versions of the event, each version situated within a spatio-temporal configuration of the maker's design. As we take the measure of each version, we accept, modify, or reject the event as it has been constructed.

How limited and specific do these events have to be for historical identification and description? Are they confined within seconds, minutes, hours, a few days, a few weeks, a few months, or a few years? Do they occur, as drama usually demonstrates, within a specific location such as a room or a street scene? Or do they spread through a neighborhood, a city, a region, a country, or the whole world? As soon as we try to set any such limits, we realize that it is impossible to constrict the time and place for events because they have many different configurations in their lengths of temporal confinements and spatial locations. The identity of the event depends upon our method of determining the temporal and spatial coordinates. As Louis Mink stated, we think – that is, we represent the past – with the concepts of identity, time, and space. Whether or not we actually reflect upon our uses of these concepts, they still provide the direction of our thoughts and the order of our constructions.

Having established that an event occurred, we then confront the problem of its size. It had a starting point, perhaps a turning point, as in the idea of *peripeteia* in Aristotle, and a concluding point. We are able to distinguish events from one another because each event has a "before" and an "after" that frames it for us and gives it an identity (if not necessarily a unity). The event may have happened suddenly, for events can be brief, even instantaneous. Yet they last long enough to have both size and duration. So understood, an event is located in a specific place and time. The boundaries are framed by an idea of change. That is, the action brought about some kind of change – one of the major concerns of historical study. The task of historian, in the process of reconstructing the definitive aspects of the event, is to attend to the moments of change and transformation.

An event can be as specific as the speech of President Chester Arthur at the opening ceremony on the west side of the Brooklyn Bridge on 23 May 1883; but it can also be the whole process of conceiving, planning, designing, and building the bridge, an event stretching from John Roebling's initial proposal in 1855 to the opening in 1883. This full event is the subject of David McCullough's book, *The Great Bridge* (1972). An event can be as minor as a mother's statement to a child or as monumental as the volcanic eruption on the island of Krakatoa (or Krakatau) in the Straits of Java on August 26 and 27, 1883, the subject of Simon Winchester's book, *Krakatoa: the Day the World Exploded* (2003). This explosion and the subsequent tsunami destroyed the island and killed thousands of people throughout the surrounding islands in the

Pacific Ocean. Over the following months the effects of the eruption spread throughout the world, producing a strange blaze of colors in sunrises and sunsets everywhere. It changed the world's climate in the following months. The total event encompassed all of these factors, though the first eruption itself occurred in a distinct moment (the temporal factor) and at a specific place (the spatial factor).

Accepting the basic proposition that events come in all sizes, we use the concept of an event to identify everything from momentary occurrences to grand developments. Typically, we think of an event as something specific, with a distinct beginning and end (e.g., a meeting between two people on a certain day, an individual performance, an arrival or departure of someone). But it can also involve many people, an extended length of time, and several locations (e.g., a Dionysian festival, the *Cid* controversy). And it can even be quite expansive and complex, often with indeterminate origins and conclusions (e.g., the American Civil War, the development of European modernism in the arts). All of these kinds of events, for which we have artifacts, can be established as having occurred, but they cannot be identified, defined, constructed, and explained in the same way. Historians sometimes distinguish between discrete and complex events. But in practice no such separation maintains itself systematically in historical writing. So, each historian must stipulate whether an event being considered is discrete or complex. Depending upon the historian's perspective and the questions being asked, many events, such as a theatrical performance, can be constituted either way. It is possible, though, to break a large event into its component parts, which may then become separate events. There is no set rule or procedure for constructing an event, including its size.

> Paradoxical though it may sound, there is not the slightest possibility of understanding the mechanisms of change unless we understand, or at least recognize seriously, the mechanisms of fixity and persistence in society.
> Robert A. Nisbet, *Social Change* (1972: 6)

Our construction of an event derives from the elements – internal and external – that give it a fixed or persistent identity. Likewise, for the next event. And the next. What separates the events from one another; what gives them their separate identities? What occurs in between each of them? The factor of change. Something changes, and in the process a new event occurs – comes into being, gains an identity. As we will see, the same factors of fixed identity and change will operate in our construction of period concepts. The events, like the periods, are located in a specific time and space. Their identities are tied to our methods of negotiating the relationships between persistence and change.

Anything done or observed by human beings is potentially an event for the historian. And as the Krakatoa example illustrates, anything that happens to human beings also qualifies. Apparently, then, any and everything qualifies as an event. Yet despite the infinite variety of the size and scope of events, can we identify more definitive features? A suggestion from Paul Ricoeur may help, for though "an event may be of any duration," he insists that "what makes it count as an event is its capacity to produce significant change, a 'turning point' in the course of time."[34] This idea of change is crucial to our definition, which we can now modify to read: *a historical event is any single, significant occurrence, large or small, that took place in the past and registered or caused a change.* But here too we face some problems. On what basis is an event a "significant occurrence?" Significant to whom? On what criteria? And how is it changed? Besides needing definitions, the concepts of occurrence and change require judgements – provided, perhaps, by participants and eyewitnesses, then provided as well by the historian. And what kind of occurrence is being changed? Human events? Nonhuman events? Both it would seem, at least potentially. If we are referring to a human event, is the process and cause of change located in the event itself (e.g., the action of a person)? Or is the change located in the perception of the event (e.g., the mode of observation and judgement of an observer)? Action or reaction? Both it would seem, at least potentially. Could the act of observation itself cause a change? It would seem so, for if a person perceives a change in something or someone and believes in it, then it has a historical reality, at least for that person.

And yet the historian's task is to distinguish between true and false events. A perception is often a misperception. Though a person may believe in and testify to a perceived action by someone else, that other person can believe and assert just as strongly that no such action was carried out. Where is the truth? We may grant the belief yet reject the testimony. So the measure of an event cannot be determined by the subjective or personal beliefs of a participant or observer. We still have to test the report for authenticity and credibility. This means that the observation and judgement of the historian is also part of the process of identifying an event, including its elements of location, size, scope, and change. When there are disagreements in the sources, the historian has to judge.

Big or major events, with many participants and witnesses, often attract the attention of historians. We want to provide the big picture. We tend to be drawn to events that represent significant changes (as we saw in the case of the grand explanations for the significance of the production of *Ubu Roi*, which included many participants, on and off stage, and many factors, before and after the two evenings of performance). Yet from the perspective of a microhistorian, the smallest of occasions may prove worthy of attention. Thus, in *The Return of Martin Guerre* (1983) Natalie Zemon Davis can find cultural and social significance in the hoax of a returning husband in a small French village in seventeenth-century France. The initial, seemingly minor event, which led to a court case, provides an occasion for Davis that allows her to investigate many factors of French society in the seventeenth century. Similarly, in *The Cheese and the Worm: The Cosmos of a Sixteenth-Century Miller* (1980), Carlo Ginzburg is able to join microcosm and macrocosm in an investigation of an Italian miller in the Renaissance. Though this event was insignificant in comparison to the decisions and activities of the leaders of church and state, Ginzburg discovered signs of the collapse of the medieval world and the emergence of modern understanding in this situation.

By contrast, the Annales historian Fernand Braudel dismissed such events as completely insignificant in the history of civilizations. They are merely *l'histoire événementielle*, a surface disturbance that changes nothing in the deep, abiding modalities of human life. For Braudel the primary thing that really matters in the course of events is the *longue durée*, the history of what endures: those underlying structures in human history such as economic systems and geographical conditions.[35] These conditions often place individuals in a diminished situation of reaction rather than action.

The Annales historians – or some of them – dismissed the history of events. Braudel criticized the "traditional histories" that present the narratives of individuals and report on the accidents of everyday life, but fail to reveal the essential conditions that shape human lives and destinies. Braudel writes: "Take the word *event*: for myself I would limit it, and imprison it within a short time span: an event is explosive . . . Its delusive smoke fills the minds of its contemporaries, but it does not last, and its flame can scarcely ever be discerned."[36] An event, by this definition, is something insignificant, and thus of limited interest and no importance to the historian. The participants may think that the event is significant, but the job of the historian, then, is to counter their misunderstanding with a more expansive explanation. In this manner, the significance of an event is shifted from the moment to an explanation of a shaping context. The context provides the "true" history.

In his studies Braudel attends to the context of the major economic, geographic, and social factors of material life and culture that shape and determine human behavior. He sets aside the daily acts and thoughts of individuals, including even most (but not quite all) of the political leaders who have usually been the primary subject of history. For example, in his studies of the Mediterranean world during the centuries before the French Revolution, Braudel charts many of the abiding conditions and forces. Yet despite what he has taught us about the *longue durée*, he has not demonstrated that the study of specific events, places, individuals, and groups lacks significance. Indeed, the scholarship of the microhistorians still reveals that significance can be discovered in a history of events. Even some of the other Annales historians, such as Emanuel Le Roy Ladurie, provide ample justification for the study of events: *Montaillou: The Promised Land of Error* (1978) and *Carnival in Romans: A People's Uprising at Romans, 1579–80* (1979). Le Roy Ladurie demonstrates that even for the Annales historians events come in all sizes.

Accordingly, an event can be as specific as a gesture made in a room or as complex and multifaceted as the French Revolution. Although it is possible to describe the French Revolution as an event, any study, sooner or later, narrows the focus, shifting attention from the comprehensive identity to the many acts and incidents of specific individuals and groups that participated in and caused the large event. Because too many factors of change enter into the picture, the historian must retreat from such a broad definition. Likewise, though certain large political, religious, social, and artistic developments and movements are often called events (e.g., the Reformation, the "independent theatre movement"), historical study still needs to investigate the many specific acts, beliefs, and ideas that make up the composite identity of these grand events. Our descriptions of the large event are usually too general, leading us to make vague pronouncements that lack clarity. We have major difficulty holding together the broad identification and the sweeping explanation.

... most universals are so general as to be without intellectual force or interest; they are large banalities lacking either circumstantiality or surprise, precision or revelation ... The search for universals leads away from what in fact has proved genuinely productive, at least in ethnography ...

Clifford Geertz, *Available Light: Anthropological Reflections on Philosophical Topics* (2000: 134)

The temptation to seek a single organizing idea for both identification and explanation is often reinforced by the appeal of systematic theories and method-ologies that can be applied to both event and context (e.g., Marxism, Freudianism, structuralism). The hard sciences justify the search for laws and universals, but the various historical fields, from art history, musicology, and theatre history to literary studies, general history, and anthropology do not. Instead, these fields benefit from the virtues of local knowledge, a recognition of limits, of specific viewpoints, of the concrete and the circumstantial. A method of comparison and contrast, of similarities and differences, serves far better than one dedicated to finding abiding rules and systems of behavior.

The same problem of over-generalization occurs when we invest certain words, thoughts, desires, principles, customs, doctrines, and beliefs with the status of major events (e.g., romanticism). The general designation, sooner or later, requires specific description and analysis. Loosely speaking, such concepts and developments can be considered cultural forces with some kind of causal or contingent power to effect and shape human life. In this sense, almost anything, however large or small, however material or immaterial, seems to serve as a possible historical event. But what is the point of identifying mentalities, periods, and eras as events? Of course, we always need general as well as specific ideas in order to describe and discuss history processes; but when the identity of events become very large and complex, the explanations become too general, even meaningless. For example, the "1960s" was considered a cultural event by participants and now has that status for some historians, who describe it as an event, a period, or a *mentalité*. Depending upon each writer's purpose in writing about the 1960s, it can be an event of various identities – in location, length of occurrence, defining participants, starting date, finishing date, and significance. Until each writer spells out the definitive features of the smaller events that make up the large concept, there can be little or no agreement on the identifying features of the subject and none on its interpretive features, causes, and meanings.

Historians have the responsibility of not only *identifying* an event but also *defining* its distinctive features. The definition makes possible the identification. By the act of stipulation (by which one asserts that here is what I mean and don't mean in this case), historians are able to set the terms for identification. Then it is possible to provide a description, a representation of the event. Only then are we likely to provide meaningful analysis, and, in a cumulative manner, a contextual interpret-ation. We need to make the necessary distinctions in order to go forward in any historical inquiry.

The definition is derived in part from the available documentation. The eyewitness may say one thing, but the historian has to adjudicate. Quite often the eyewitnesses are rather loose and casual about what qualifies as an event, but the historian can still carve out the needed definition that allows for clarifying description and analysis. In our case study of the production of *Ubu Roi* we saw what happens when such adjudication is not done in a sufficient manner. A vague identification – avant-garde theatre – made for sloppy historical study. In sum, though it is possible that events may come in an infinite number of sizes, the identifications need effective and distinctive definitions in order to set the foundation for historical analysis. And when events are identified as large and expansive, this is usually a sign that someone needs to step forward and stipulate what definition will operate in the specific case. Then the study can proceed.

> . . . the historical fact, as it actually exists and as the historian knows it, is always a process in which something is changing into something else. The element of process is the life of history.
> R. G. Collingwood, *The Idea of History* (1946: 163)

What is a historical event? Our answer, it would seem, depends upon our method of identification and definition. Though events can exist in many different sizes, we are able to identify them by defining them carefully. The identification serves to fix or stabilize the event for us, allowing then for clear description, careful analysis, and forceful explanation. We can place the event in its context. But this focus on stability is only half of the equation. Our task of identification requires that we also focus on the factors of change, the historical processes that separate one moment from another, one event from another. At the boundaries of the identity, before and after, change occurs. By attending to the event, by setting its circumference, we can see that certain factors of change and difference are operating in the event – in the efficient, material, formal, and final causes. In turn, by clarifying those causes and their boundaries, we can identify not just the fixed features but also the key factors of change and difference. Those factors, along with their causes, help us to make our definitions and our distinctions as we construct an event. Of course, even when participants and historians agree that a change occurred, they may offer a range of possible explanations for the nature and meaning of the change. As we go forward, let's notice how this matter of change engages related matters, including our construction of the human motivations and aims within the event. Because the crucial matters in our historical study of events often turn on the processes and consequences of changes, we will usually find that questions of causality, including the Aristotelian four causes, play a key role in our methods of defining and analyzing the events.

We can even argue that things that do not happen, such as Sherlock Holmes' dog that did not bark, can be perceived as contributing aspects of an event. In other words, the perception of absence (e.g., of something missing) fills the void with meaning; the lack of signification becomes a locus of significance. Though we seek some sign of change – in action or thought – within events, whatever their size, we can still find significance in the exceptional moment when change failed to happen (but perhaps should have occurred).

Of course, this perceptual problem of presence and absence is not limited to the special cases of things that either fail to occur or do not remain in place. By definition, the historical event, located in the past, is absent. The historian, as Carl Becker points out, "cannot deal directly with the event itself, since the event itself has disappeared. What he can deal with directly is a *statement about the event.* He deals in short not with the event, but with a statement which affirms *the fact that the event occurred*" (his italics).[37] I agree with Becker, though I would note that theatre historians consider more than statements. We also consider such things as archeological remains, scenic drawings, preserved costumes, stage properties, and other material objects. So the concept of "statement" needs to be understood in this expansive manner. And I would also suggest that the statement or document does not affirm the fact that the event occurred. Unless we have additional "statements," of one kind or another, it is most difficult to be sure of one's facts.

> Of course, we must distinguish falsehood and fiction from truth and fact; but cannot, I am sure, do it on the ground that fiction is fabricated and fact found.
> Nelson Goodman, *Ways of World Making* (1978: 91)

We must thus struggle not only to construct the event but also to determine if the historical source provides us with a reliable fact about the event. We must distinguish between a statement or source and a fact. What is a fact? According to Louis Gottschalk, "a historical 'fact' . . . may be defined as a particular [piece of information] derived directly or indirectly from historical documents and regarded as credible after careful testing in accordance with the canons of historical method."[38] Many facts are indisputable, but there are always some apparent facts that are open to doubt. We must question the document and the person who created the document. In order to do so, we place the subject within a defining matrix of biographical, chronological, occupational, and geographical coordinates. We test for credibility and reliability. In *Understanding History* (1969), Louis Gottschalk spells out in some detail the methods for testing the authenticity of documents and the credibility of any historical report. For example, he has not only six tests for the credibility of a witness, including the ability to tell the truth, competence, and degree of attention to the event, but also tests for the willingness of a subject to tell the truth, including self-interest, bias, social conventions, and the desire to please or displease. There are also conditions favorable to the credibility of a witness or testimony. These procedures have become part of the mindset of accomplished historians (just as they are part of the arsenal of prosecuting and defense attorneys in the courtroom).[39]

But even when this kind of rigorous analysis is carried out, there is still a difference between probability and certainty. We can question the documents carefully, but the truths we attain are about the reliability of the sources, not the ontological presence of the actual past event itself. Even the best kinds of written and material evidence – official testimony, a photograph, a material object, a building – are not the event; they are only the possible records of the past. The sources are traces, footprints in the sand. Unlike Robinson Crusoe, we cannot follow the footprints and find Friday, standing before us, down the beach. Our constructions are not the events, which are gone. Like astronomers who read the evidence of the shape of the universe out of light transmissions reaching us billions of years after the events occurred, we are reading events out of the remaining traces, separated from their origin. But these sources are all we have and the constructions are all we can attain.

Necessarily, then, a gap exists between the event and our knowledge of it. Both these sources and the events they evoke for us exist in a conditional mode of articulation. We thus must think and write conditionally. In logic this conditional mode takes the pattern of "if p, then q." The meanings of the events are potential rather than received, not only because the historian cannot avoid interpretation but because the identity of the event depends in part upon how it was constituted as a separate occurrence in the documentation itself. That is, someone else, before the historian, has already given meaning to the event in the process of designating and representing it. The event's documented character results from and is dependent upon a series of initiating conditions: what is recorded, how the event is represented, when and where it was recorded, who did the recording, and why. Moreover, the person who recorded the event understood it from a particular perspective, within the context of a particular condition of identification and designation.

Any kind of historical source (verbal, visual, material) is a possible clue, but not necessarily a reliable piece of evidence. For example, if the source is a human artifact (i.e., something recorded, made, produced, or created by a human being), it already carries an interpretive quality that we must decode as we attempt to look through the source to possible facts, which in turn could be used as evidence of the event itself. The source, constructed by someone at the time or subsequently, provides that person's version of the event (or whatever aspect of the event that he or she may have witnessed, noted, recorded, reported, or recollected). The maker of the document is both a recorder and a participant in the event that we are attempting to construct (not just to discover). A theatre review, a promptbook, a diary entry, a photograph, a letter, an interview – none of them can be taken as neutral, objective, and self-explanatory registers of the event itself.

Consequently, all sources or traces from the past are circumstantial. The trace itself, which designates an event, reveals an act of making, a complex interpretive process by someone who constituted the event for some purpose. In this normal condition, the trace is simultaneously organized (already given shape by someone) and disorganized (not yet given meaning by the historian). In other words, an event resides in the trace in an actual and a potential state, paradoxically having been and yet to be.

One can distinguish the genuine historian both from the layman and the amateur by their views as to what are the "facts". The thoughtful professional will know that every event, no matter how small, is a construction and that for every time and every place many events can be constructed. The layman, the amateur and many amateurs masquerading as professionals, will believe that facts are facts. Ironically, the only hard and fast thing in our knowledge of events is our knowledge that certain events did *not* take place.

Peter Munz, *The Shapes of Time: A New Look at the Philosophy of History* (1977: 32)

Furthermore, an event takes its meaning not just as a separate occurrence but as part of a series of events. We cannot measure change unless we are considering more than one event. All events derive additional significance, for participants and historians, according to what comes before and after. The problem we face with any series, however, is to determine whether the sequence is contingent, contiguous, or causal. Our task is complicated by the fact that the person who provided the testimony has usually designated the sequential order and meaning for the event. At least implicitly, then, even before the historian considers an event, the documentation expresses a set of assumptions, judgements, and values that invest the event with a specific, perhaps exclusive sequential meaning. Both the identity of the event and the factors of change are assumed by the eyewitness. Accordingly, upon examining available documents, the historian is faced with a *constructed* event, which can be either accepted (i.e., interpreted) in a way consistent with the original method of documentation or *reconstructed* in a new way. No matter what the historian's approach, the event is made, not simply found. For this reason the absent event, though recovered through diligent procedures that demand an objective examination of the authenticity of the document and credibility of any eyewitness, precludes even the possibility of a value-free analysis.

While it is possible to use the word *constructed* to describe the version of the event in the sources and *reconstructed* to describe the historian's process of creating a version of the event, this usage (and stipulation) should not imply that the version in the source is the real *presentation* and the version of the historian is a mere *representation*. Just as the stages of historical inquiry cannot be neatly divided from one another according to an opposition between documentation and interpretation, so too must we resist the formula that makes the historical source an objective construction and the historian's version a mere subjective reconstruction. Both the person who created the source and the historian are putting forward versions of the actual event. Both versions may demonstrate a commitment to accuracy and objectivity, but a certain element of subjectivity always enters into the process. All historical inquiry is simultaneously committed to objective analysis yet dependent upon subjective judgements.

A piece of historical evidence can be either involuntary (a skull, a footprint, a food relic) or voluntary (a chronicle, a notarial act, a fork). But in both cases a specific interpretive framework is needed, which must be related (in the latter sense) to the specific code according to which the evidence has been constructed.

Carlo Ginzburg, "Checking the Evidence: The Judge and the Historian" (1994: 295)

Just as no document explains itself, no document contains only one possible meaning. Even as we are constructing the event (from the already constructed documents), we are doing so from a specific perspective, which is derived from a set of assumptions that provide the basis for a possible hypothesis. In Karl Popper's words: "A historical document, like a scientific observation, is a document only relative to a historical problem; and like an observation, it has to be interpreted."[40] At least the experimental scientist can make a direct observation of an event, thereby having an interpretive advantage over the historian, whose event is always absent.

Yet even if the event were directly available (a current event), it still would be open to various observations, depending upon the different possible ways the observer named and represented it. As Louis Mink argues (in basic accord with Arthur Danto, R. C. Collingwood, and Max Weber): "we cannot refer to events as such, but only to events *under a description*; so there can be more than one description of the same event, all of them true but referring to different aspects of the event or describing it at different levels of generality."[41] Or in Danto's formulation, which Mink is echoing: "We do not explain events as such, but rather events under a certain description."[42] Every event is open to a number of descriptions, each of which offers a partial perspective – but not a complete and final description. Every artifact has its codes that the historian must learn to read. Every historian has his or her own codes of understanding that operate in the process of interpreting the documents. At each step of the process, interpretive judgements must be made.

Even in the most austere scholarly report from the archives, the inventive faculty – selecting, pruning, editing, commenting, interpreting, delivering judgements – is in full play.
    Simon Schama, *Dead Certainties (Unwarranted Speculations)* (1991: 322)

Paradoxically, a document is by its very nature a historical register of something, but it is not necessarily a historically accurate fact about the event, occasion, or place to which it apparently makes reference. Whoever produced each source had a motive (an aim, purpose, or agenda) for referring to and representing the event. Moreover, this person also had a set of epistemological presuppositions about basic categories of understanding (e.g., axiomatic concepts about gender, agency, time, space, identity, causality, unity, quality, and quantity) that shaped not only what the observer saw but also how he or she recorded the event. And necessarily, this person had a limited talent for capturing the event (as any theatre review, drawing, photography, or video demonstrates, to our frustration).

Thus, despite the commitment by historians to documentary research, testimony cannot be taken as objective documentation. It must be critically evaluated. Still, there are useful procedures in historical method for testing the reliability of testimony and material artifacts. Original documents or contemporary records can be evaluated, not simply as subjective reports at the time of an event but also as reliable and credible versions of the event. They can be compared and contrasted to other documents on the event. As we saw in our analysis of the historical representations of the *Ubu Roi* production, the purpose of the testimony can be assessed in order to measure its reliability. Likewise, the kinds of information that appear in personal versus public records can be questioned and assessed for authenticity and credibility.

Our primary task, then, is to attempt to understand the knowledge, attitudes, values, and intentions of the source-maker in order to see how and why he or she "documented" the event. In turn, we cannot ignore the ways that our own *mentalité* contributes to the interpretive approach we take to the task of writing history. This condition does not mean that the past is only a grand fiction that each of us constructs, but it does mean that the methodological procedures of the historian must be geared toward plausibility rather than certainty. And though historians are quite capable of offering comprehensive explanations, especially for large, expansive events with many component parts and possible causes, those explanations, as brilliant as they may be, are just possible and plausible interpretations. They may even attain a special status of being probable explanations – which is a fine achievement indeed – but they are not the one and only true meaning for the events. The questions being asked shape the answers being offered.

> Even though we have in many ways moved beyond nineteenth-century historicism, Ranke's overworked dictum that he only wanted to write how it had really been – *Wie es eigentlich gewesen* – remains our standard.
> Peter Gay, "Do Your Thing" (2000: 44)

Obviously, it is rather daunting to consider the many problems that all historians face. And it is equally disconcerting to be aware of the limitations that the surviving historical record places upon research and analysis. But these problems and limitations do not make the task of historical inquiry an impossible undertaking. Many sources exist, and they are full of potential facts. Those facts guide us to possible descriptions of what happened, and they are barriers against misinformation and misinterpretation. As long as we are prepared to do the initial stages of documentary research – the testing for authenticity, credibility, and reliability in the sources – we are quite capable of reconstructing historical events. We can describe and identify them, we can note the factors of change, we can set the events in relation to one another, we can provide reliable representations of those events, we can carry out our analysis, and we can then place each event in an appropriate context that justifies our interpretations and our historical narratives. We are quite prepared, that is, to reconstruct theatrical events. Great care is needed, of course, as we reconstruct our events. But also, as we know, the task rewards those who reveal a certain audacious and imaginative cunning in the making of interesting and significant events.

Chapter 4

The theatrical event

Throughout chapter 3, as my readers may have noticed, I described the historical event and the theatrical event as if they were the same thing. This was justified, in basic terms, because all historians, no matter what their field of study may be, share many of the same tasks and problems – in their research methods, their construction of events, and their need to place events within an explanatory context. But this way of proceeding is not fully justified, at least in certain cases, because theatrical events have some distinctive features that require special modes, means, and manners of representation and understanding.

First of all, in the process of examining performance events, we can study them for their aesthetic or formal qualities, apart from the historical factors that may contribute to their significance. In all of the arts a rich tradition of formal analysis has added to our understanding and appreciation of artistic works. From the study of versification in poetry to the study of harmony in music, artistic critics have developed sophisticated methods of description and analysis that focus exclusively on the formal aspects of the artistic works. And as scholars in theatre studies know, formal analysis has an amazingly rich and long tradition in genre study because of Aristotle's brilliant analysis of mimesis and dramatic form in his *Poetics*. Aristotle does not deny that tragedies represent human actions, and thus point to and interact with the represented world and its conditions, but he makes a clear distinction between the missions of the dramatist and the historian. Both of them construct events, but the procedures and purposes are not the same. He thus provides in the *Poetics* a formal analysis of the six parts of tragic form, including a long section on poetic diction. Though he does offer a few pieces of historical information (e.g., the possible origins of drama) and the names of some playwrights, this commentary is secondary to his primary aim of analyzing the formal traits of tragedy.

> The poet's task is to speak not of events which have occurred, but of the kind of events which *could* occur, and are possible by the standards of probability or necessity . . . It is for this reason that poetry is both more philosophical and more serious than history, since poetry speaks more of universals, history of particulars.
> Aristotle, *Poetics*, (1987: 40–41)

This understanding of the artwork as a formal system has guided much of the scholarship in the field of art history (e.g., the methods of Heinrich Wölfflin and

Erwin Panofsky in the study of Renaissance art). Because art, like theatre, usually represents images of people and material objects in and of the world, it too has both an aesthetic and a historical component. Scholarship in art thus takes up some of the same topics that Aristotle raised in the *Poetics*, including matters of mimesis or representation (e.g., E. H. Gombrich's *Art and Illusion*) and of form, symbolic order, and style (e.g., Nelson Goodman's *Languages of Art: An Approach to a Theory of Symbols*).[1] Formalist issues and questions are paramount to understanding art and its history. And of course the study of music, especially classical as opposed to folk music and songs, has been guided, and often controlled, by formal analysis (e.g., the features of harmony and melody; the kinds of pieces, from sonata to symphony).[2] A special vocabulary must be learned in order to study music and its systems of internal order and development.[3] In dance scholarship, as well, formalist analysis has always been central, not only in the notational vocabulary that practitioners in the field must master but also in the reconstruction of the choreography for specific dance productions (e.g., the recovery of Ballet Russes productions). Likewise, in film studies formalist theory, borrowed sometimes from structuralism and semiotics as well as from narrative theory, has been popular among many scholars. In brief, in the arts it is both possible and quite appropriate to separate artistic works and events aesthetically from the surrounding historical conditions.

The formalist study of art should not be confused with the attempts, since the Enlightenment, to claim that the arts, as the expression of beauty and truth, exist in their own aesthetic realm of pure contemplation – autonomous and serene. This idealism, influenced by Kantian philosophy and the glory of classical sculpture, attempted to celebrate art as timeless and refined. So understood, artworks should be considered with a disinterested aesthetic sensibility. To be expected, this idea of art has been countered by a sustained critique over the last 200 years that places art irrevocably within social, political, and economic systems. Instead of calling for a disengaged contemplation of art, we call for an engaged art criticism that reveals how and why the artwork is related to its representational and conditioning worlds, its shaping heritage, its intentional agents, and its possible audiences, whose judgements are part of its meaning.

The critique of aesthetic theory has been necessary, but a word of caution is needed here because of the negative connotations that the words "formalism" and "formalist" have in some circles today. There may indeed be substantial reason to criticize certain formalist approaches to art, but in general the study of formal systems should not be dismissed, unless of course one wishes to deny all value to formal analysis and theory in various fields (e.g., generative and transformational grammar, neo-Kantian philosophy, symbolic logic, genetics, cybernetics, cognitive science, systems theory, structural sociology and anthropology, and semiotics). Roland Barthes' defense of formalism in the 1950s is still a cautionary warning against what can be a false dichotomy between formal and historical study of art:

> Less terrorized by the specter of "formalism," historical criticism might have been less sterile; it would have understood that the specific study of forms does

not in any way contradict the necessary principles of totality and History. On the contrary: the more a system is specifically defined in its forms, the more amenable it is to historical criticism. To parody a well-known saying, I shall say that a little formalism turns one away from History, but that a lot brings one back to it.[4]

Barthes has repeatedly demonstrated that historical analysis and formal analysis complement one another. The idea of "culture" has both aesthetic and social meanings, and one can choose, quite appropriately, to focus on one or the other in the study of any kind of art. Moreover, cultural analysis of the formal features and styles – in photography, film, fashion, fiction, architecture – takes place within the historical condition of the specific artistic works and the historical sensibility of the one doing the analysis.

Without question, then, any theatre event can be studied for its distinctive formal features. It can be perceived as a special kind of historical event. But of course historians, including theatre historians, are interested in those additional non-aesthetic factors that contribute to the identity and significance of performance events in relation to their several contexts. All theatrical events can thus be studied for their historical significance, over and beyond their complexity of formal features. In doing so, we place such events within the historical conditions that contributed to their identity and meanings. We then take up the same issues, challenges, and problems that we considered in the previous chapter.

But what about the nebulous gray area in which the aesthetic and nonaesthetic factors in theatre events intertwine, yet still maintain a tension (and sometimes an opposition) in their historical relationship? What about the ways that a theatre event is to be understood simultaneously as an aesthetic and a historical event? The double identity of a performance event needs to be recognized in historical inquiry. What are the similarities and what are the differences between these two types of events (or two aspects of events)? There are some notable differences that we recognize without any difficulty. Obviously, when a gun goes off in *Hedda Gabler*, only the fictional character named Hedda, not the actress, dies. The performance itself has a double identity, for it presents a fictional action – the story of the characters – and a real action – the performances of the actors. Thus, in 1891 the London production of *Hedda Gabler presented* an actual performance; it also *represented* the fictional dramatic action of the play. The character of Hedda Gabler and the actress Elizabeth Robins were on the London stage simultaneously in 1891. The spectators read the semiotics codes of performance and the phenomenological codes of the performers.[5] The dramatic action referred to the fictional world, yet it also made reference to and represented aspects of the actual world. For the historian, then, these double identities and references complicate the processes of describing and interpreting the performance event.

This double event – or doubling of action – derives, first of all, from the relationship between a dramatic text and a performance text. The identity of the dramatic text sustains itself over time; the identity of the performance text changes with each manifestation of the dramatic text. Theatre historians are primarily interested in the changeable event, occurring in a specific time and place, but potential clues about the realization are embedded in the play itself. Because a double yet uncertain relationship pertains (and maintains itself), the historian is required to make some fine distinctions in description, analysis, explanation, and interpretation.

In addition to these several factors of doubling on stage, there is also a double consciousness for the spectators. Both the performers and the spectators have roles to play. As Denis Diderot and others have analyzed, the actors both perform a role and observe themselves in the act of performing. Likewise, the spectators carry out a process of splitting their identities by observing the theatrical action and its double identity. They attend to the actors and their characters, which are perceived as joined yet separate. Moreover, the spectators are also capable of observing themselves in a self-reflective manner as they attend to the staged event.

These aspects of performance events suggest that their mimetic (not just illusionist) codes of representation need to be distinguished from the codes of representation in "real life." In this sense, as we recognize, dramatic action and historical action are quite distinct. Also, other kinds of performances events, such as parades, pageants, and spectacles, have actual and imaginative qualities. Even in those special kinds of performances that require a belief in the reality of the action, such as a religious festival, the distinction between the imaginary and the real does not fully collapse or disappear. In terms of Richard Schechner's ideas, the performance needs to be understood as "twice-behaved behavior" or "repetition with revision," a layered process of restored or repeated action.[6] Such actions are complemented by a twice-behaved consciousness.

As historians, we do not observe these doubling aspects directly; we have to reproduce them indirectly, in a piecemeal fashion, based upon the problematic nature of the available sources. Somehow, we have to recover the performance of Elizabeth Robins – a ghostly phenomenological condition for the historian – from aspects of the text (its semiotic codes) and the commentary of anyone, including Robins, who may have left a record of the event. This historical condition, unlike our attendance at a performance, does not confront us with what Alice Rayner calls "ghosts who haunt the representations of the living."[7] Instead, we are dealing with ghosts who haunt the representations of the dead. Everyone from 1891 is dead; the event is long gone. All we have are ghostly messages from the other realm, distributed here and there in the archives. We seek the past event rather than the present engagement. Our problems, from a historian's perspective, are epistemological rather than phenomenological. Absence is the given condition. The historian, it is true, may attempt to evoke the memories of the historical participants or eyewitnesses of a performance event, but the historian is not typically one of the eyewitnesses, engaged in an evocation of his or her own memories of the event. The historical reconstruction – a negotiation of various clues in the mode of condensation, displacement, and substitution – is not an act of perception or consciousness such as spectators experience at a performance. The historical recovery can be achieved only by reading the latent clues in order to make manifest a version, not a repetition, of the past event.

> The philosophy of representation – of the original, the first time, resemblance, imitation, faithfulness – is dissolving; and the arrow of the simulacrum released by the Epicureans is headed in our direction. It gives birth – rebirth – to a *phantasmetaphysics*.
> Michel Foucault, "Theatrum Philosophicum," in *Language, Counter-Memory, Practice* (1977: 172)

Beyond these necessary distinctions between the fictional and the real, there are, however, far more ambiguous factors of doubleness in a theatrical event that effect historical study. A theatrical event is a historical event, yet its historical manner of representation, its modes of significance, and its means of reference sometimes challenge our descriptive and interpretive methods. It is the same as other kinds of historical events yet different. In certain ways it has special or additional features that historians do not normally have to contend with. At the level of potential evidence for an historical analysis, all aspects of a theatrical event offer themselves to us as sources. But of what? How are they to be read? How are they to be tested and used as reliable data for our construction of their historical identities and conditions? In what ways do the aesthetic or formal traits of theatrical events complicate how we might make sense of their historical sources and potential meanings?

Consider, for example, George Aiken's adaptation of *Uncle Tom's Cabin*, which appeared in 1852. Along with several other adaptations, it became amazingly popular, providing the Howard family with stage roles for several decades.[8] Hundreds of other troupes, besides the Howard company, performed versions of Stowe's novel throughout the nineteenth century and into the early decades of the twentieth century. The performance of *Uncle Tom's Cabin* has many identities, many locations, many motives, and many responses. Clearly, it was a major event in the history of American theatre, one that needs to be broken into its component parts as many distinct events, each with its layers of theatrical and historical significance. We can study the definitive features of the 1852 production: first its première in Troy, New York; then its 1853 run at the National Theatre in New York City. Because the play, in its various manifestations, had a complex history as a touring event, we can investigate the distinctive features of these various productions that appeared across North America. And we can also study those representations that appeared in London, Paris, Berlin, and many other cities of the world. The size of the companies greatly varied, as did the scenic effects. Cuts and additions were common. We can also study the formal traits of the other adapted texts and their productions. We can compare and contrast these various productions to one another; we can also compare and contrast them to the novel. Also, the typology of characters can be studied in terms of the conventions of melodrama and in relationship to character types in minstrelsy. Here, too, the formal qualities are paramount, even when we are attending to specific historical factors (e.g., members of the casts, theatre buildings, touring procedures, types of scenery and costume, acting methods).

And yet, beyond the theatrical traits and production histories, *Uncle Tom's Cabin*, as staged, proved to be a major historical event, both nationally and internationally,

Illustration 10. Production poster for American touring companies of *Uncle Tom's Cabin.*

with several lines of political, social, and ethical significance. As a dramatic and performance text, it offered representations of the world outside the theatres. In its various presentations, *Uncle Tom's Cabin* can be examined for what it revealed about the political conditions of the country in the 1850s and later. But here things become more complex, for we need to construct this event with multiple identities as a theatrical and historical event. It entered into the national consciousness (and conscience), catching the attention of almost everyone, from the man in the street to Abraham Lincoln. It has been credited with contributing to the growth of the abolitionist movement and sharpening the political resolve of northern politicians and states, leading up to the Civil War. It was attacked by southerners and forbidden performance in many southern cities, both before and after the war.

A production of *Uncle Tom's Cabin* was a presentation and a representation. It presented white actors in blackface playing the roles of black people, as part of a theatrical event; it also represented some of the conditions of slavery, including the suffering of blacks and the immorality of a racist society. Emotionally and morally this portrayal attained an immanence, an immediacy, a truthfulness; yet the performative nature of the presentation – of showing the suffering of blacks – was merely a mediation, a pretense in blackface. It was a distortion, a condensation, a falsehood. It was an act of playacting and a process of ventriloquism – an act of absence instead of presence for all black people. What are we to make of this act of transference and displacement? It was not the reality of black life; it was a crass substitution. So how should a historian unpack this *action* and the audience *reaction*? How should the historian distinguish among *icon, index,* and *symbol* in the performance codes of representation? What kind of theatrical event is this presentation and representation? What kind of historical event is this presentation and representation?

In turn, how does this division between immediacy and mediation relate to the basic problem of historical study: the actual event is gone; the historian re-presents the past event? Appearance, then disappearance, followed by reappearance. Same but different. Even the eyewitness documents are representations, not direct presentations of the event. The documents mediate between past and present. Is this mediation similar to the ways an actor mediates between fiction and reality? Aristotle claimed that the historian reports what happened, but the poet represents what might happen. A lesser accomplishment, then, for the poet, but Aristotle also claims that the poetic representation is more philosophical, more universal than the specific nature of the historical report. Stage performance, in its basic configuration of actor and audience, requires not only action but the act of witnessing by spectators. How does this key aspect of theatrical witnessing – and its history – relate to two basic issues in historical study: (1) the role and reliability of eyewitnesses for the documentation of past events; (2) the responsibility of the historian to serve as a witness – that is, to account for the reliability of the evidence that sanctions the historical report; its truthfulness? To what extent, then, can the performances of *Uncle Tom's Cabin*, stretching across the country and the decades, be taken as general and abstract, if not universal, pre-sentations? Of what? General in what way? Are the narrative representations, achieved in performance, to be understood as historical portraits of a national condition? What idea of *mimesis* are we prepared to embrace?

As historical events, the many productions of *Uncle Tom's Cabin*, despite their distortions of human realities, may still serve as major documentation for the racial conditions and values in nineteenth-century America, especially widespread racial attitudes and assumptions about black life. Millions of white Americans perceived black people and life through the distorted lens of this popular play. Far more people saw the play than read the novel. And they almost always saw white actors in blackface, for black actors did not appear in the productions until late in the century. Both the novel and the many play versions carried messages about race, slavery, and the south that reflected and challenged many of the prevalent attitudes and beliefs in the country. To this day, many of the racial messages and meanings continue to confront and trouble us, though meanings obviously change over the decades (e.g., the epithet of "Uncle Tom" was applied with negative connotations to accommodating blacks during the civil rights battles of the 1960s).

Explaining how and why the play and its productions carry historical meanings is a major historical task. The challenge, then, for the historian is to figure out how to read the series of double codes of representation. Is it possible, for example, to read the representations of blacks in the productions as historical evidence of black identities in the south? That analysis seems quite wrongheaded, given the blackface tradition that contributed to the formal traits of the performers. It's one thing to write about black life on the plantations based upon plantation documents (e.g., account books, descriptions by visitors, statements by plantation owners, reports by blacks who lived in those conditions). It's quite another thing to derive our historical descriptions from Caroline Howard's impersonation of Topsy in *Uncle Tom's Cabin*. Howard's blackface characterization distorted and falsified historical reality. The problem is not just the normal one of reliable and unreliable sources. The aesthetic features and aims of the play and the productions contribute to the special nature of the theatrical event as a kind of historical source. In part, the representations of black characters need to be understood in terms of the formal typologies of melodrama and minstrelsy. And their actions, tied to the narrative purposes of dramatic representation, cannot simply be lifted out of the play and used as evidence of human actions, events, and people in the southern United States.

And yet, with more subtlety, it is quite possible to study these representations as historical images of certain aspects of American life in the nineteenth century. The representations were not just iconic, but indexical and symbolic. The historical meanings operate at all three levels of representation. The playtexts and productions suggest, directly and indirectly, many aspects of black and white lives in an era of slavery. With care, the productions can be used to reveal much about American cultural, psychological, social, and political values, but this source needs to be tied to additional historical documents. Whatever our historical questions and hypotheses, we need to figure out which aspects of the theatrical event can be taken as direct evidence of historical conditions and which should be interpreted as indirect evidence. This is not a matter of establishing either/or categories, but instead a need to recognize and read the double coding that is simultaneously present. We need to inhabit the metaphoric and ambivalent codes of representation that the performances generated – for the performers, for the spectators, and, subsequently, for us.

Being in two minds, looking both ways, is an approach that has been overlooked in a good deal of structural, and even poststructural, analysis, much of which harks back to a linguistic model of binary opposites, of allocating concepts to one box rather than another, especially where polarities appear in the rows and analogies in the columns of decontextualized tables . . . That failure to be flexible is not remedied by those post-modernist approaches, like that of Derrida, that tend to reject the binary categories, say of orality and literacy altogether. There has to be a third way that treats such concepts contextually.
    Jack Goody, *Representations and Contradictions: Ambivalence Towards Images, Theatre, Fiction, Relics and Sexuality* (1997: 22–23)

As we attempt to use *Uncle Tom's Cabin* as evidence for understanding American society, we need to keep in mind that a production in 1852 carried certain historical meanings that were not present in a touring show of the 1890s. The audience response in a Bowery theatre in New York City must be distinguished from that of audiences in Boston, Louisville, or San Francisco. White spectators did not all see and respond in the same way.[9] And black audiences, when they even had an opportunity to see a production, surely perceived the theatrical codes and understood the historical representations in yet different ways – from various white spectators and from one another. Yes, some historical features of the play may have carried their significance across decades of productions, but other features were modified and transformed. Some features even disappeared. From place to place and time to time, *Uncle Tom's Cabin* was many different kinds of events, with a range of theatrical and historical meanings.

Therefore, our historical interpretation of a theatrical event requires a fine ability to read not only the doubleness that resides in these kinds of documents but also the variety of ways the events were performed and responded to. We need to describe and analyze both action and reaction. At one level, the doubleness exists in the exchange between the dramatic text and the performance text. In this case, two formal systems are operating in tandem. This problem has been central to the scholarship in theatre semiotics. As we considered in chapter 1, the dramatic text may provide many clues about potential staging practices and meanings (e.g., the semiotic codes of location, gesture, and movement in the prepositions). In tandem with other information (e.g., comments on the staging by eyewitnesses), we can join the dramatic text and the performance text in order to reconstruct the specific identity of the theatrical event. We carry out both formal and historical study. Instead of keeping the dramatic text and performance text separate, we slide back and forth between them as we gather information. Their differences do not dissolve, for we always have to keep in mind the distinctions between the two sources, but our historical task requires us to negotiate their relationship. We use both critical and historical skills to read the distinct yet yoked codes of the dramatic and performance texts. Even though we are primarily attempting as theatre historians to reconstruct the specific performance text or event – what was represented, how it was represented, and why – we may discover in the dramatic text (e.g., the characters and themes of the play) certain potential clues that may reveal not only how the performance event was realized but also what it meant in its time and place. Potentiality becomes actuality – if the historian has read the evidence correctly.

At another level, the doubleness points to both the fictional and real nature of the performance. Characters and their actions require role-playing from the performers and a double consciousness from the spectators. Even lifelike representations – the mimetic codes of the natural and the realistic – are not life itself. In our attempt to reconstruct the event, we also investigate the relationship between the imaginary and real actions. We search for evidence on how the actors performed and how the spectators responded. Performers sometimes provide self-reflective commentary on how they played their roles (e.g., rehearsal notes, marked-up script, interviews, autobiographies). Also, spectators, including theatre reviewers, provide descriptions of their experiences. They may focus primarily on the imaginary representations, describing the character's actions instead of the actor's (e.g., "Antony was lifted up to Cleopatra"). But sometimes, to our good fortune, they describe and evaluate the actual behavior of the participants (e.g., "a sling, attached to a pulley and a cantilevered arm, allowed two men dressed as soldiers to lift Richard Burbage into the loft above").

And yet at another level, the doubleness engages historians in the act of interpreting theatrical events for whatever they reveal about their historical topics, representations, characters, social conditions, and ideas. They point to the contextual world and say things about it. Historians need to place theatrical events in their historical context. In order to do this they must use all of their skills in research and analysis, reading all documents for their historical significance. And yet in order to do so, they must recognize and negotiate the important formal qualities of the theatrical codes of the event, codes that stand apart, in some manner, from the rest of the evidence for the historical event. *Uncle Tom's Cabin* is a melodrama, fulfilling many of the conventions and rules of melodrama, yet it is also a distorted yet powerful representation of key aspects of American life.

> Historical writing is metaphorical. It should be remembered, however, that metaphor is not operative here exclusively in the domain of the historical text or in that of the representation: the metaphor ties the past itself to its representation. Theorists (such as Hayden White) sometimes say that historical writing is metaphorical, but they then appear to restrict the activity of metaphor only to the text, to the level of the representation. Actually, however, the scope of metaphor in historical writing comprises both the past itself and its representation.
> F. R. Ankersmit, *Historical Representation* (2001: 14)

Theatre historians are interested in all of these doublings and ambivalences, which are potential sources of historical information about the nature of the theatrical event. Our procedures for occupying, as it were, both realms simultaneously are a crucial test of our skills as theatre historians. Each of the levels needs to be investigated. For the event itself, which we attempt to reconstruct, we need to delve into the significance of the various direct and indirect pieces of potential evidence. Then in order to situate the event within the historical conditions that add to and complete its meaning, we need to figure out which aspects of the formal qualities can be used – not misused and abused – as supporting evidence for our interpretations. At the same time I want to insist that much about the theatrical event must be investigated in the same ways we investigate all other kinds of historical occurrences and actions. That is, we must always attend to the fundamental split in historical study: we are located in the present yet attempting to recover aspects of the past. This is the fundamental condition of doubling that contains the others.

> What will offend simple minds is that my plot is not simple, nor its point of view single. In real life an action – this, by the way, is a somewhat new discovery – is generally caused by a whole series of motives, more or less fundamental, but as a rule the spectator chooses just one of these – the one which his mind can most easily grasp or that does most credit to his intelligence.
> August Strindberg, "Author's Foreword" to *Miss Julie* (1965: 76)

What is a theatre event; how do historians construct such events? In order to consider the problems and challenges that theatre historians face when constructing a theatre event and its possible contexts, let's examine the historical sources for the first London production of Ibsen's *A Doll's House* at the Novelty Theatre, June 7–29, 1889. Janet Achurch played the role of Nora, Herbert Waring was Helmer, and Charles Charrington took on the role of Doctor Rank. The performance was organized by Charrington and Achurch, husband and wife, and staged by Charrington, with the help of William Archer, who provided the translation. Various historical documents exist for this production, including playbills, newspaper stories and gossip columns, advertisements, theatre reviews, personal correspondence, drawings, and photographs.

The production, which Harley Granville Barker called "the most important dramatic event of the decade," is thus a historical event that achieved a notable significance, initially in its time and then retrospectively in 1930 (when Barker made this statement).[10] A series of facts can be derived from the available documentation. But

Illustration 11. Henrik Ibsen in the 1880s.

what kind of event do these facts allow us to construct? We can give it a specific identity, apart from all other events. Yet both diachronically and synchronically it is related to many other events and conditions, including the London theatre season of 1889, the history of the Novelty Theatre in which it was performed, the professional careers of the performers, the career of Ibsen, the activities of William Archer, the performance history of the play, the spectators, the growth of London audiences for Ibsen, the emergence of the professional theatre reviewer for newspapers and journals, the development of the Ibsen campaign in London and in Europe, a history of realism in modernist theatre, the growth of modernism in the arts, the changing status of women in modern society, the bourgeois family in Norway and Europe, sexual attitudes and values of the late nineteenth century, and so on. With all of these various factors and contexts to consider, how should we construct the 1889 production of *A Doll's House* as a theatre event?

> The artwork which is contained in any theater event changes with each performance: some of the difference stems from changes in the actor's behavior, intonation, emotional state, and so on, but an equal part of the theater event's uniqueness stems from the differing composition of its audience, the personal contributions made by each audience member as an individual.
>   Timothy J. Wiles, *The Theater Event* (1980: 183)

If we had sufficient documentation, we could attempt to construct each of the twenty-two performances of the production as separate events. As actors readily acknowledge, each performance, night by night, has its own special features. But we lack sufficient information to construct twenty-two specific events (and, besides, it is hard to fathom who would need or want such a compulsive gathering of data). So, for our purpose of illustrating the challenges, problems, and cruxes of reconstructing a theatre event, we will identify the run of the production, from June 7 to June 29, 1889, as the theatrical event under investigation. Although this complex event is defined in the singular as the production of *A Doll's House*, it still generated potential sources from its multiple performances (and its rehearsals). This paradoxical method of identification (singular yet multiple) is typical of many performance events in theatre history. Historical events may happen only once, but theatre events may be composed of repetitive manifestations.[11]

Our interpretation of the documentation is the initial challenge. As Carlo Ginzburg notes about all historical events, "a specific interpretive framework is needed, which must be related ... to the specific code according to which the evidence has been constructed."[12] This problem of representation is framed actually by another factor. In the words of Marc Bloch: "Reality demands that its measurements be suited to the variability of its rhythm, and that its boundaries have wide marginal zones."[13] The metaphor of "rhythm," like the idea of reality, is vague, but Bloch is purposefully suggesting that events occur within the complex conditions of their variable identities. Historians must be attentive to the unpredictable and changeable qualities of the patterns of clues distributed throughout the documentation. Like a pianist who discovers and achieves the rich tonal potentiality of a Beethoven sonata, the successful historian discovers and makes sense of clues that are distributed in the documents.

Besides factual information, historical documents contain potential meanings that may elude other investigators. Unless, as Bloch suggests, historians can comprehend the variability of the codes of representation that calibrate the statements in the documents, they may have great difficulty in recognizing the "marginal zones" that exist at the boundaries of the documents. The interpretive framework cannot be ready made, before the fact (or just within those facts); it must be derived from the codes that one discovers and deciphers in the investigation. In the potential rhythm that exists both in and between the notes one finds the interpretive reality. *And most crucially, this interpretive reality depends upon the historical questions that are asked of the event and its available record.* Historical inquiry, by definition, requires a questioning mind. Depending upon the questions being asked, the potential aspects of the historical reality may emerge from the shadows and become historical insights. We then see clearly into the marginal zones.

> What is a theatrical event?
>   Willmar Sauter, *The Theatrical Event: Dynamics of Performance and Perception*
>   (2000: 31)

What are the kinds of questions we might ask about the London production of *A Doll's House* in 1889? Let's begin with the historical hypothesis put forward by Granville Barker, who claimed that the production was "the most important dramatic event of the decade" in London theatre. What, actually, does Barker mean? Important for whom; in what ways; how and why? What's the context for this retrospective judgement, made four decades after the event? Barker's proposition would have been rejected by almost everyone in the theatre community at the time. In comparison, for example, to Henry Irving's 1888 production of *Macbeth*, which was celebrated in the press, drew the attention of the full society, and ran for months, the London production of *A Doll's House* was a minor event, taking place at a minor theatre and attracting a marginal audience of London theatre patrons.

Yet within a select community of individuals – which provides a possible interpretive context for the event – this production was important for several reasons. It contributed to the international campaign for Ibsen (a campaign that Bernard Shaw, two years later, call Ibsenism). Although *A Doll's House* lacked the critical controversy that attended the notorious production of *Ghosts* in 1891, it still captured the attention and support of various members of leftist political and social groups, including women who were committed to equal rights for women. By 1889 the topic of a woman walking out on her marriage was not just controversial but socially relevant and timely (whereas the forbidden topic of incest in *Ghosts* lacked any such direct relevance on people's political values). Also, the method of production, with its new realism, contributed positively to the emergence of naturalistic performance codes in acting and design. In this manner it also contributed to the modernist movement in the theatre. Beyond these primary factors, the event directly contributed to the developing careers of key people in the alternative theatre movement in London. The production enhanced the reputation of William Archer as theatre critic and translator; influenced Bernard Shaw's decision, two years later, to become a playwright; and set Elizabeth Robins on a career path to become the great Ibsen actress in London during the 1890s. In similar ways, the ripple effect of the production contributed to the cultural and intellectual transformation of various people in British theatre and society in the coming years (e.g., Harley Granville Barker, Rebecca West, who took her new name from Ibsen's *Rosmersholm*). The boundaries of this event had very wide "marginal zones."

So, if Barker's statement carries weight as a historical judgement, it must be placed within the context of the changing world of modern art and modern sensibilities, not the abiding traditions of the commercial theatre of the West End. By placing the event in what Ginzburg calls "a specific interpretive framework," we are able to stipulate the basis for our historical inquiry and our method of explanation. The evidence for this interpretation, if presented effectively, should support both the basic argument about the growth of modern theatre and the secondary issues concerning the careers of several key people. The historical question that therefore guides this inquiry is this: what made this a benchmark production in the new theatre that we associate with Ibsen?

And yet in the judgements of most theatre historians, the event has not been interpreted in this manner. Why, then, did Harley Granville Barker call it a significant production? How substantial is the evidence for his judgement and our hypothesis? How should we construct the event? What assumptions and narrative models should guide us? In sum, what kind of event should we try to construct? It is important to ask these questions, for as we saw in our consideration of the historical studies of the production of *Ubu Roi*, the failure to ask key questions can lead to historical misrepresentation in our descriptive as well as interpretive scholarship.

There is one other important question to consider. Since we are attempting to make an argument – in order to convince our readers of the major significance of this event – should we highlight some documents and evidence, while dismissing or ignoring other possible documents for this event? Should we, on the model of a trial lawyer, make our argument by means of selective evidence that highlights our case? As we all know, historians mount campaigns for their explanations. In the process they put the focus on their best supporting evidence and they sometimes try to show the weakness of the arguments of other historians (as I did with the case study of *Ubu Roi*). Given the need to make a strong, convincing argument, what is the best way to use the sources?

The answer to this basic question should be clear. We need to bring to bear all of our argumentative and rhetorical skills, but unlike a trial lawyer we must not ignore or suppress any relevant information. A good trial lawyer may manipulate the available information in order to sway a jury. But though the historian always has to be selective – a partial quotation here, a summary statement there – the description and the analysis should be dedicated to the fullest, most accurate representation of the essential information. Besides, unlike a court case, the historical investigation can be tried over and over again, for the case is always open for more study. And of course we should not suppress or "cook" the evidence in any manner. This tactic is not effective arguing; it is cheating. Just as plagiarism is unacceptable for scholars, so too is any act of suppression or modification of evidence. All sources, primary or secondary, should be credited. If a piece of evidence contradicts our hypothesis, we need to confront it, not hide it. And if it is substantial, we may need to adjust or abandon our argument. We are searching for the fullest description and explanation, not calculating points in a rhetorical contest. We seek the historical truth. The best arguments are the ones that do full justice to all available evidence, especially when that evidence presents us with the multiplicity and variety of contributing factors.

Of course, historians often fail to recognize the significance of certain sources. Despite our attempts to describe and explain an event accurately and fully, we sometimes look right past the crucial records. And sometimes we are blinded by our assumptions and ideologies. It is also true that whatever categories and definitions we may use (from period concepts to ideas about human psychology), they impose a certain perspective and understanding. They may make some things visible, yet they make other things invisible. The common problem that we face with historical studies, therefore, is not the cooking or doctoring of evidence, but instead the much more familiar human flaws of incomplete research, inadequate definitions, inappropriate assumptions and categorical imperatives, poor analysis of key sources, and weak arguments.

Many flaws in historical scholarship stem from inadequate analysis of the sources. Consequently, the mission of many manuals and guidebooks on historical methodology is to describe how historians should carry out their research procedures, especially the procedures for establishing trustworthy sources. The principles of authenticity and credibility provide the operating standards for these manuals and guidebooks. Even when historians have a solid piece of information in their hands, they need to question its identity, as Michael Stanford spells out in his *Introduction to the Philosophy of History*.[14] He identifies three requirements for testing sources: (1) examine the relic, the report, and the document to be sure it is what it seems to be; determine whether or not it has retained its original identity; (2) trace its history; consider how it arrived in the archive; determine what changes it has undergone and by what means; and (3) determine its origins; find out how and why it was produced, by whom, and with what intentions; also determine the context for its origin and history; consider the circumstances. Just because something is catalogued in an archive and certified by someone, this does not establish its trustworthy identity. All sources must be tested for authenticity; all statements must be examined for their credibility.[15]

With these cautionary words in mind, what kind of challenges do we face in the reconstruction of the production of *A Doll's House*? In this historical investigation we are not primarily concerned with the *dramatized event* – the action within the play itself (i.e., the fictive story of the characters). Literary critics typically focus on these aesthetic features of characterization and themes, but theatre historians want to understand how such matters were turned into the *theatrical event*. The motives and actions of the characters are secondary to those of the performers, the members of the production team, and the spectators. Typically, when theatre historians have attempted to reconstruct this production, they have depended upon statements made by people who created and attended the performances. Let's begin with three distinct responses to the production.

How did the reviewers evaluate the production? In *English Theatre in Transition*, 1881–1914, James Woodfield explains that the "reviewers were almost unanimous in their condemnation of the play, which they treated with disgust or disdain, finding Nora 'unwomanly' and the morality reprehensible."[16] Such resistance is a common response to modernist works, but is it a fact about this production? If we return to the archive and follow Michael Stanford's guidelines, including the origins, intentions, and circumstances of the eyewitnesses, what do we find? Some reviewers complained about the play, the production, and even the audience. For example, a critic writing under the pseudonym of "Scrutator" in the journal *Truth* characterized the spectators as "a scant audience of unnatural-looking women, long-haired men, atheists, socialists, and positivists, assembled ... to gloat over the Ibsen theory of women's degradation and man's unnatural supremacy."[17] Scrutator's intentions seem clear; his conservative ideology shapes what he sees and says. But of the twenty reviews that I have examined, five were strongly positive, four were basically descriptive and unperturbed, and eleven were negative, to one degree or another. These negative reviews tended to focus on the themes of the play and the behavior of Nora, but some of these reviewers still made some positive comments about the translation and the acting.[18] Many of these reviewers distinguished between the character of Nora and Janet Achurch, whose acting was often praised. The nasty rhetoric of the review by Scrutator was a minority opinion.

Which of the reviews best defines the event? Does the majority rule? Should eleven negative reviews provide the norm for a description and explanation? Despite Woodfield's statement, it is not possible to combine all or most of the reviews into a single perspective.[19] The reviewers are strikingly at odds on what they saw and what the event represented. Is there, however, a way to determine that some reviews are more reliable, more factual, than the others? If so, on what basis do we establish the criteria of accuracy and reliability? How exactly should we determine which reviews qualify as acceptable evidence? Acceptable on what basis? To whom, and what is the measure here of factual information? Even if we are arguing for the major importance of this production, we still need to let the sources have their say.

Let's begin with one of the negative reviews. In his assault on the play and production, Robert Buchanan was appalled at the "jaded appetites" of the kinds of people who would perform or attend such a production. And he attacked the "sluttish young hussies," by whom he apparently meant not only the character of Nora and the actress Janet Achurch who portrayed her so effectively but also the women spectators at the

Illustration 12. Janet Achurch as Nora and Herbert Waring as Torvald, in the London production of *A Doll's House* in 1889 at the Novelty Theatre.

play who looked approvingly upon Nora and her actions.[20] Here we have an historical artifact, but is it a fact? If so, whose fact? What epistemological code is this statement written in? Is it an aesthetic, moral, social, or political judgement? It partakes of all of these registers, but does Buchanan's response help us understand how Achurch acted the role of Nora? What does such a statement tell us about the representation of Nora and her decision to walk out the door? What does it suggest about the possible realism of the production? Or about the audience? Or about the quality of Ibsen's play? Or about the emerging women's movement? Is the response a typical example of the offended sensibility of the bourgeoisie (whom, supposedly, modernist works upset)?

If we don't understand the specific codes and conventions operating here for Buchanan (who was a popular playwright of light entertainment in the West End theatres), how can we use this piece of evidence to construct the event? In other words, under what conditions can an artifact be taken as a fact? What is the fact about? And, granting its significance, what kind of evidence does it provide for our task of constructing a theatrical event?

Almost without exception, theatre historians have decided to give this kind of statement a double identity. In a neat formulation that allows us to have our cake and eat it too, such reviews are unreliable yet reliable; they demonstrate little or nothing about the production, given the small-minded judgements about modern drama, but much about the false values of the reviewers, given the narrow-minded prejudices that reveal the middle-class values of the era (the familiar bourgeois or Victorian culture that modern theatre disturbed).[21] Attributing a misogynist or antifeminist agenda to Buchanan and likeminded commentators, we argue that such statements distort the event.

Should we thus group together all negative comments on the production? For example, Henry Irving, who was invited by Charrington and Achurch to the opening, was also displeased by Achurch and the character of Nora. Privately he stated: "If that's the sort of thing she wants to play, she better play it somewhere else."[22] Such drama does not belong in the theatre community that he represented. Does Irving belong, then, in the same category with Buchanan, given his rejection of Ibsen's drama? Perhaps, but there are conditions of his response that we need to consider. Several months before *A Doll's House* went into rehearsal, Charrington and Achurch had asked Irving for some financial help to prepare a new production, but they did not identify it as Ibsen's play. Instead, they said that they wanted to produce a comedy, *Clever Alice*. He gave them £100, but then discovered afterwards that they were doing Ibsen.[23] Irving's negative response to the production may thus tell us more about his frustration over being deceived by Charrington and Achurch than about his judgement on the values of the play or the production. But of course Irving on several occasions dismissed Ibsen's drama, so we tend to assume that he and Buchanan shared a negative perspective on *A Doll's House* and the production. Yet his anger over the behavior of Charrington and Achurch surely complicates our neat category of negative reviewers, those men who resisted Ibsen and the modern movement.

By dismissing these statements of Buchanan and Irving as unreliable evidence on the production, we seem to be making a distinction (taught in the rules of evidence) between reliable and unreliable evidence; good evidence is factual we say; bad or unreliable evidence is ideological. But this distinction is open to question. Is any evidence free of ideological markers; on what basis can anyone's ideology or beliefs be designated false or incorrect? Despite our problematic distinction, we regularly accept or reject statements as potential evidence because we agree or disagree with the attitudes and values being expressed. In such cases our ideology trumps their ideology. But these kinds of distinctions tell us more about us and our values than about the historical figures and events we are studying. That is, we approve of our own

Illustration 13. Janet Achurch as Nora and Charles Charrington as Dr. Rank in the stocking scene of *A Doll's House*, London, 1889.

values, but we dismiss those of anyone who fails to satisfy our criteria of positive evaluation. Therefore, in this case, anyone who does not praise Ibsen and the production is a reactionary.

In contrast to Buchanan's negative statement, consider a second piece of potential evidence provided by Elizabeth Robins, who in 1891 would become a famous Ibsen actress in the role of Hedda Gabler. She saw *A Doll's House* in 1889, then later wrote:

> The unstagey [*sic*] effect of the whole play ... made it ... less like a play than like a personal meeting – with people and issues that seized us and held us, and wouldn't let us go ... This [production of] *A Doll's House* ... was

not only the most thrilling, it was the most satisfyingly *done* modern play I had ever seen." [24]

No hussies there. Based upon this statement, which we treat as reliable, the play was a model of modern realism, the catalyst for the modern revolution in the theatre. So, we have a neat choice: on one side of this equation, we have philistine male critics, on the other side, we find the avant-garde, feminist artist. And we know where we stand – with modern art, feminism, and the triumph of the Ibsen movement. We take Robins as a reliable witness, not only because her statement accords with our beliefs about the Ibsen productions and the value of the modern, realistic theatre – in playwriting, acting, and staging effects – but also because we approve of who she is and what she accomplished as an artist and feminist. She represents the right values. Yet is her statement really any less ideological than the statement by Buchanan? If not, why do we assume that it is a factual statement but Buchanan's is not? Why do we quote her regularly, but almost never reproduce Buchanan, except to illustrate how the philistines responded?

Here is a third piece of evidence, provided by Bernard Shaw, who became a strong advocate in the 1890s for the new drama, including Ibsen's plays. The production of *A Doll's House* in June 1889 was one of several initiating factors in Shaw's decision to become a playwright, reinforced in 1891 by the production of *Ghosts*, which in turn was the catalyst for the writing of *The Quintessence of Ibsenism*, published in late 1891. Shaw's first play, *Widowers' Houses*, was written in 1892, and produced by the Independent Theatre Society that year.[25] Thus, for aesthetic and personal reasons he had an agenda no less ideological than the agenda of the theatre critics who opposed Ibsen's drama.

Shaw saw the 1889 production of *A Doll's House* several times. He wrote a review for the *Manchester Guardian*, in which he announced that Achurch "achieved a success of a high order."[26] He followed this review with more commentary in one of his music reviews in *The Star*, under the pseudonym of Corno di Bassetto.[27] He used both reviews to make a strong case for Ibsen and the production. But after seeing a performance on June 11, five days into the play's run, Shaw wrote a letter to William Archer in which he complained about the acting:

> In several places, the piece wants playing up ... I was in the fourth row of the pit, which is not unreasonably far back; but I lost several lines, and was conscious of a great relief when they spoke out or made their words tell. One unfortunate pittite [i.e., spectator sitting in the pit] at last cried out respectfully but imploringly "Speak up"; and my sympathies were entirely with him ... [All of the actors] are relapsing into their ordinary stage tricks ... Miss A[church] actually bowed to the applause on her entrance, a proceeding which ... ruined the illusion ...[28]

This statement, which most scholars ignore,[29] suggests that the production may not have been a grand and total triumph of realism for the avant-garde theatre. Because this piece of evidence is a private letter to Archer, it seems to be an unadorned,

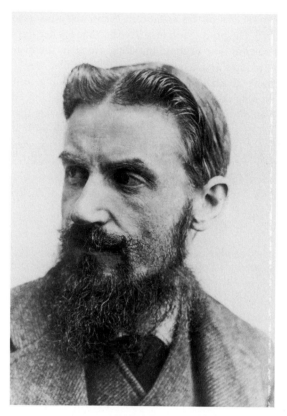

Illustration 14. Bernard Shaw in the early 1890s.

reliable statement. Shaw is apparently being honest here, whereas in his review he is being an advocate for the new drama.

This letter challenges us, therefore, to reconsider the seemingly factual report of Elizabeth Robins. Yet several theatre scholars, when describing the production of *A Doll's House*, are tempted to quote her report because it so precisely makes the event what we want it to be.[30] But consider this: Robins' comment is not a primary document from the time of the event, as is Shaw's letter. Instead, it was written almost four decades later in 1928, as she looked back on the Ibsen movement in which she had been a key figure. In the 1890s she had acted in several Ibsen plays, most famously the first London productions of *Hedda Gabler* and *The Master Builder*. By 1928 modernism had become a successful historical movement, the direction in which the arts had developed. So, for all right-minded people, praising the early Ibsen productions and participants was almost obligatory. Indeed, Robins' 1928 essay, "Ibsen and the Actress," was part of this process of writing the history of modernism as a grand triumph over the philistine world. Is it possible, then, that her memory, in some measure, shaped her version of this significant event, and thus gave the production a kind of halo effect? The production may have become for her – and now for us – an overly neat construction: one of those initiating events in the history of the avant-garde that we now require and tend to construct in similar ways. Also, her description may reveal more about her retrospective understanding in 1928 than about what she actually thought and saw in 1889. But if we come to this conclusion, we probably need to apply it as well to the statement by Granville Barker that I quoted at the beginning of this chapter. It was written in 1930, for an essay with an obvious retrospective understanding, "The Coming of Ibsen." In 1930 Barker knew quite well how the history of the Ibsen movement had progressed. Unlike Robins, however, he did not have any memories of the production, for he was only ten years old then and did not see it. Does this fact make Barker more or less reliable than Robins as a historical source for us?

> For the mind of man (dimmed and clouded as it is by the covering of the body), far from being a smooth, clear and equal glass, wherein the beams of things reflect according to their true incident, is rather like an enchanted glass, full of superstition and imposture.
> Francis Bacon, *Of the Dignity and Advancement of Learning* (1858: 431)

Yet before we reach this unsettling conclusion, based upon these three sources, we should consider the possibility that supporting evidence for our hypothesis can be found in unexpected places. Paradoxically, the theatre critic Clement Scott, despite his general opposition to Ibsen, may be, in this case, a more reliable guide than Robins or even Shaw, the supporters of Ibsen. In his *Daily Telegraph* review of the production, Scott wrote: "Everything was well done. The translation was that of a scholar; the play was perfectly mounted; the acting was really remarkable." He praised Achurch as someone who "acts with her brain." And he announced that "Mr William Archer and the Ibsenites have had their grand field-day."[31] Despite his dislike of – and sometimes disdain for – Ibsen's drama, which he expressed a week late in *The Theatre*, Scott was apparently capable of making the kinds of descriptive distinctions that provide us a window onto the past event.[32] If even someone who was unsympathetic to realism and Ibsen praised aspects of the production, then we might feel justified in constructing the event as a benchmark or turning point in the development of the modern movement in London. And yet almost always we place Scott in the category of unreliable witness whenever the topic is Ibsen and the new drama. We don't have to attend to Scott because we already know where he stands.

Additional support for our tentative hypothesis comes from A. B. Walkley, a theatre reviewer who wrote for *The Star* newspaper in 1889 (under the pseudonym of the "Spectator"). He proclaimed that something new had occurred: "What is being done at the Novelty [Theatre] by this little band of Ibsenites marks the beginning of a dramatic revolution. After *The* [sic] *Doll's House*, we may be of good cheer. The great intellectual movement of the day has at last reached the theatre. There's a future for the stage, after all."[33] This statement – which uses one of our favorite words, "revolution" – offers a positive piece of evidence that a major production took place. Surely, this statement proves, or at least suggests, that the event was decisive in the development of modern realism.

But does it matter that Walkley was William Archer's friend? Archer, who translated the play and campaigned for Ibsen, also spent time pushing his Ibsen agenda with Walkley. Is it possible that Walkley let Archer's advocacy for Ibsen shape how he saw the event? If so, his evidence becomes less definitive than we might assume and wish. His theatre review of the production may reveal as much about Archer's ability to stage-manage the Ibsen campaign as it does about Walkley's judgement. His use of the word "Ibsenites" in 1889 suggests that he already knew that some of the participants, including Archer, conceived of the event as a planned campaign, the first step in a series of related events, for Ibsen's drama (but he may just be echoing Clement Scott's use of the word).

On thing is certain: the role of Archer in this production complicates how we assess the documents. For example, although the theatre program states that the play was "produced under the direction of Charles Charrington," other sources reveal that Archer attended most of the rehearsals and served as a co-director, giving notes to the actors, explaining the play, and helping to develop the blocking. He guided Achurch to a realistic portrayal. Likewise, the program states that the scenery was done by Mr. Helmsley, but Archer took charge, gathering pieces of Norwegian furniture from his own home and a Norwegian white porcelain stove from around London.[34] Moreover, three months before *A Doll's House* opened, Archer had written an essay, "Ibsen and the English Stage," which called for a production of the play (an essay that Walkley likely read). This essay led Charrington and Achurch to ask Archer to provide a new translation – which he did, under the stipulation that he would be allowed to participate in the production. And when the production opened, he then wrote two positive reviews in *The World* (July 12 and 19), and he arranged for his friend Bernard Shaw to do a theatre review in the *Manchester Guardian*. He also stirred up support from a range of people, including Walkley. And he arranged for the publication of a limited edition of his translation of the play, with photographs from the production.[35] One copy was mailed to Ibsen, who expressed to Archer his great appreciation of the London production and campaign.

A month after the production, Archer wrote a summary essay in the *Fortnightly Review* titled "Ibsen and English Criticism." He criticized the shortsighted views of the London critics and made a strong case for the importance of the new Ibsen movement. This essay, which theatre historians today tend to read and use, instead of digging out the many newspaper reviews, constructed the production as a battle in London between the small-minded "despisers of Ibsen" and the open-minded defenders of Ibsen.[36] Archer sought a campaign, so he created one. He provided a narrative, with heroes and villains, which we happily accept. In other words, he not only translated the play and helped with the production but also wrote the initial history of the event, according to his own agenda, a campaign for the new drama in England. Indeed, the first historical construction of the event was provided masterfully by William Archer. Subsequent constructions, not so surprisingly, have many of the same traits because Archer generated many of the critical documents that we now use to describe and interpret the event.

One other thing: does it matter that Archer had a major influence, in the coming years on three of the key witnesses we depend upon for our history of the production of *A Doll's House*? He was a close friend of Shaw's, introducing him to Ibsen plays. Archer also contributed to Shaw's early theatrical activities, including the writing of *Widowers' Houses*. Archer worked closely with Elizabeth Robins on the Ibsen productions in the 1890s, and for a while they were in love, carrying on a secret affair. And he was a mentor for the younger Harley Granville Barker. They wrote a book together advocating a national theatre, first printed privately in 1904 and then revised and published in 1907.[37] Throughout the period that Barker developed as a playwright and director, Archer maintained a close, influential relationship. In other words, in terms of Ibsen and the growth of modern theatre in London, many of the ideas and values that Shaw, Robins, and Barker developed and maintained derive at least in part from William Archer.

Of course, as theatre historians we believe that our historical constructions and interpretations of the production of *A Doll's House* in 1889 are based on solid, dependable facts. We quote Shaw, Robins, Barker, Walkley, and Archer as reliable eyewitnesses. They anchor our descriptions and cultural analysis. Yet what should we make of the documentation provided by Archer, whose activities – and decisive agenda – put in place many of our sources? Are these documents authentic, as per the rules of historical evidence? Are they reliable? Are they to be accepted as the repository of facts?

Is it possible that Archer, instead of being our star witness, was an unreliable witness? We need to keep in mind that despite all of his involvement in the production, Archer was sometimes capable of devious misdirection. For instance, when some people attacked him and Ibsen in July 1889, just after the production closed, Archer denied that he had had much to do with the production. In none of his published writings at the time, including his advocacy for Ibsen and his theatre reviews, did he reveal the extent of his direct involvement in the rehearsals.

As theatre historians, what should we make of Archer's evasive actions? More to the point, how should we take the measure of our historical understanding and judgement of the production, which depend, in substantial ways, on the documentary record that Archer put in place? Was the production a major theatre event, one that made a major contribution to the modernist revolution? Or was it something rather less than this, but then turned into an important event by a publicity campaign successfully engineered by Archer? If it was a "hyped" event, manufactured in key ways, where does that possibility leave us as theatre historians, who must use the available documents to construct the theatrical event?

This event is hardly the only case of participants generating the documentary record in purposeful and often systematic ways. In fact, it is the norm in history for historical agents to record their actions from their own perspectives. From Napoleon to everyman, historical agents provide versions of their activities that accord with their intentions. Public and private documents express someone's agenda. All diaries,

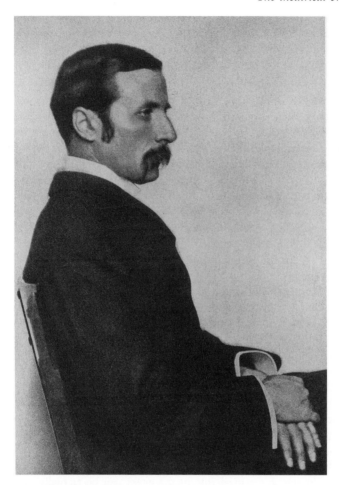

Illustration 15. William Archer in the 1890s.

journals, letters, records, essays, and memoirs are written from a personal perspective. Public figures, such as people in the arts, are no less determined to document key aspects of their lives. Indeed, during the last few centuries theatre people seem to have been quite calculating in their recordkeeping. And increasingly the libraries of the world are prepared to pay the artists for their personal papers.

The historian who ignores this basic fact is, at best, naïve. All sources are problematic and partial. All evidence, to a certain extent, is "cooked." Ambiguities attend all research projects, though some historians may try to ignore them. One thing seems clear: as we test documents for their accuracy and reliability, we must always distinguish between what the historical event might have been and what the documentation, produced purposefully by the participants, suggests about the event. Facts come in many forms, many disguises. The documents we consult are full of information, including facts. But facts about what? Depending upon the questions we are asking of the documents, their reliability may be quite solid in one case and hopelessly unreliable in another.

In the case before us – the production of *A Doll's House* – we must depend upon evidence that Archer, at the time, helped to tilt in a certain direction. We have sometimes acted as if the bias in the records on *A Doll's House* only existed in the negative reviews of some theatre critics. We need to be far more sophisticated about our methods of determining the significance of documents, for we must derive our historical information and interpretations from all of the available sources.

Given the problems with the available sources on this production, is it even possible to gain access to the event itself? As should be apparent, the job of historical investigation requires not only some good skills at detective work but also a discerning eye for analyzing what one finds because the sources are loaded with the perspectives, values, judgements, and motives of each person who provides any kind of source. What are the traits of a reliable document? The answer depends upon not only how we define reliability but also how we negotiate the distinction between our ideas of reliable and unreliable information.

In this case, first of all, we have to come to terms with William Archer because many pieces of evidence point toward his vital role in the making of the event. That's a fact. But what kind of fact? We must conclude that he did help to create and shape part of the documentary record. His contributions to the event are ideological, no less so than the statement by Robert Buchanan or those made by Shaw or Robins. Nonetheless, these sources can still be judged as reliable because part of the meaning of the event is Archer himself. Our job is not to clean up the record by removing or somehow displacing Archer's contributions. Instead of trying to look around or through him to the event we need to locate him fully in the event. Because he is an essential guide to what the event means and how it means, we need to analyze his contributions to what happened.

On thing is obvious: his central role in the event can be factually documented. Operating as a key agent in several capacities, he convinced Achurch and Charrington to perform *A Doll's House* (and guided them away from *Ghosts*, which he calculated would generate the wrong kind of public response). He contributed to the quality of the production by providing an effective translation and by participating in the rehearsals. Then, beyond the stage, he created much of the press coverage that helped to turn the production into the first major Ibsen performance in London. In turn, because of this effort, he set in motion the Ibsen campaign in the English-speaking world. For example, before June 1889 neither Shaw nor Robins had participated in this campaign. They knew very little about Ibsen, for the plays had not yet been translated. But Archer, who knew Norwegian, was already an advocate for Ibsen. Soon, with Archer's support, both Shaw and Robins would become major contributors to the Ibsen movement. In 1891 Shaw published *The Quintessence of Ibsenism* and Robins staged *Hedda Gabler*, playing the lead role – two major contributions.[38] Archer was closely involved in both activities. In other words, we

Illustration 16. Max Beerbohm's caricature of "Henrik Ibsen receiving Mr. William Archer in Audience."

recognize that the ideological nature of the 1889 evidence proves to be a key part of the meaning of the event itself.

> Each act of understanding is an event, a hermeneutical process of discovering and recovering meanings.
>   Richard Palmer, *Hermeneutics: Interpretation Theory in Schleiermacher, Dithey, Heideggar, and Gadamer* (1969: 68)

As this case study of *A Doll's House* illustrates, the task of constructing a theatrical event requires an equally strong commitment to documentary scholarship and cultural history. It is impossible to construct this theatrical event without diligent archival research. Yet that research, as we see with the basic problem of William Archer's activities and aims, extends the task beyond an accurate description of the production itself. Our hermeneutical project of representing what happened, how it happened, and why it happened requires both understanding (*Verstehen*) and explanation (*Erklären*).[39] The event must be placed within its definitive contexts, which we identify and interpret as an expression of our own hermeneutical processes.

We all agree that every event has its contexts, every action has its conditions. But how are these framing conditions to be discovered and defined by the historian? To what extent are they embedded in the documentation or located elsewhere? And how does the distinction between a theatre event and its possible contexts complicate the process of reconstruction for a theatre historian? Basically we are asking how the contexts contribute to the significance of the event, yet what do we mean by this rather vague idea of the *context*? We tend to use the word *context* in the singular, but of course all events have more than one context, condition, or structure. That is, all events can be perceived and constructed from various perspectives, including those that feature biographical, cultural, social, political, economic, and geographical factors. In turn, because all historical events are perceived and understood from the perspective of both the participants and the possible audiences – that is, each of the recorders or documenters of the event – there are many possible contexts that emerge in the descriptions and explanations of the event.

The archive, if we are fortunate in our historical investigation, provides valuable documentation for the various or potential contexts of the event being investigated. Why do I say "potential"? Because even when the documentary record makes possible a well-developed interpretation, the event still needs to be realized and contextualized by the historian. The sources, which suggest a variety of potential meanings, are yet to be analyzed. They need to be tested for credibility and reliability; they need to be compared to and contrasted with the other potential sources. In short, they need to be transformed from artifacts into possible facts that would contribute to the description of the theatrical event and/or the historical event. Each source does not attain its full historical identity or identities until the historian "discovers" the conditions that give the event a viable context. Each historian who attempts to construct the event out of the available sources finds and constructs one or more contexts. No historian, in the process of studying past events, can completely set aside the potential contexts suggested by the sources. Nor can a historian, looking backward through the previous historical constructions of the past events, completely ignore those modes of description and analysis put forward by previous historians. Even when dismissing or arguing against them, the historian incorporates them into the archival repository and the interpretive network. Then, from a present perspective, the historian factors his or her own contextual understanding into the layers of previous descriptions and explanations.

> Every event historically established and presented lives on the fiction of actuality; reality itself is past and gone. This does not mean, however, that a historical event can be arbitrarily set up. The sources provide control over what might not be stated. They do not, however, prescribe what may be said.
> Reinhart Koselleck, "Representation, Event, and Structure," in *Futures Past: On the Semantics of Historical Time* (1985: 112)

Historians have long understood that the context is composed of many factors, as Wilhelm von Humboldt insisted in 1821:

The number of creative forces in history is not limited to those directly evident in events. Even after the historian has investigated them all, separately and in their inter-relationships – the nature and changes of soil, the variations of climate, the intellectual capacity and character of nations, the even more particular character of individuals, the influences of the arts and sciences, and the profoundly incisive and widespread influences of social institutions – there still remains an even more powerfully active principle which, though not directly visible, imparts to these forces themselves their impetus and direction: that is, ideas which by their very nature lie outside the compass of the finite, and yet pervade and dominate every part of world history.[40]

Humboldt was attempting to describe what he called "the historian's task." Long before the Annales historians developed the idea of the *longue durée*, Humboldt understood that historical events are composed of and influenced by many factors, including geography, climate, and abiding social institutions and structures.

In our search for contextual conditions, institutions, and structures, we consider both the diachronic and synchronic dimensions of historical events. We attempt to place events within a sequential or diachronic process, as simple as a chronicle and as complex as a causal narrative. Typically, we attempt to relate events to one another by means of our ideas of motive, aim, change, causality, effect, and consequence. Not surprisingly, various principles of narrative (e.g., the ideas of turning point and climax, the order of beginning, middle, and end) often serve us, intentionally or unintentionally, as we organize the events into developmental relationships.

Synchronically, we attempt to place an event within its specific time and place. We attempt to define its relation to simultaneous occurrences and contributing factors. Far too often, though, we set up this synchronic relationship as an overly neat con-figuration expressed by familiar terms of text and context, foreground and background, situation and condition. In general terms, no one would disagree that we need to name and describe the "outside" factors that contribute to an event, but how do we achieve an understanding of the definitive aspects of these factors? The dead metaphors about cultural *context* and *background* tell us next to nothing. And we are not helped by mirror metaphors (e.g., the actions of this or that person *mirrors* the age; a son's behavior *reflects* the values of the father). This kind of descriptive and explanatory language may suggest that events are located within defining categories and systems of order, but usually the metaphor is dead and the idea is mechanical. Instead of clarifying the meaning of an event, these contextual descriptions reduce an event to a formula about the identifying feature and controlling power of the conditions.

> . . . history can be culturally ordered without being culturally prescribed.
> Marshall Sahlins, *Culture in Practice: Selected Essays* (2000: 27)

Besides using these common metaphors to identify factors of the diachronic and synchronic contexts, we appeal to general concepts, such as our familiar modes of periodization and our theoretical models of human activities and societies. But these kinds of encompassing structures, reified as vague abstractions and formulas, are usually too general. And their singular identities are too reductive. Also, by proclaiming that a certain grand system or authority controls the event, we are in danger of imposing an answer before we have even asked a good question. If we know the answer when we begin, it usually remains in place when we end. On these occasions, the relations between event and context trap us in a tautology as we circle from the one to the other, proclaiming that they define one another. An idea of interchangeability seduces us into an equation that lacks meaning because cause and effect become mirror images of one another, even though we may avoid the explicit use of the mirror metaphor. We confuse a process of nomination with a process of explanation. We ignore the particularity of history, which resists systematic development, because we want the consistency of an expansive idea. The problem is not that we seek an idea of reciprocity; that's part of what we are attempting to discover between an event and its context. But the idea of context needs to be seen as the problem to be engaged rather than the ready-made solution to be imposed upon the event.

The debate that pits the event against the context, as played out between the microhistorians and macrohistorians, shares some similarities with the "nature versus nurture" debate in science. Both oppositions confront us with the dilemma of the chicken and egg – which came first; which is cause and which is effect? Are we the product of our cultural factors and decisions or our genes and physical environment? All too often the debate is presented in this either/or manner. But of course we need to understand how both factors contribute to our existence and to our history. The factors operate in a range of ways from situation to situation. Sometimes culture shapes an act, sometimes biology. And often the mixture is difficult to unravel and distribute, especially when we are attempting to understand causes (another abstract, often confusing idea). Likewise, though it is possible to focus exclusive attention on aspects of a specific event or on aspects of its context, our understanding in the final analysis benefits from seeing how event and context interrelate. The event itself contains participating agents, agendas, and actions; the possible contexts have their contributing factors. But how should we understand these activities and conditions?

As historians, we need to develop models of reciprocity that clarify which of the various contexts (e.g., biographical, theatrical, cultural, social, economic, political, geographical, and receptive) we are investigating in order to locate the event within its descriptive and explanatory conditions. Each context is partial, one possible meaning among many possibilities. As R. W. Vince insists, a theatrical event can be historicized in terms of various factors, some unique, some continuous or coterminous with other events: "The initial performance of the *Agamemnon* … is an event of the Dionysia of 458 BCE; an event in Aeschylus's biography; an event representative of a particular genre, tragedy; an event of the Athenian 'Golden Age'; an event in Greek theatrical history; a 'classical' event; an event in the history of European theatre."[41] In addition, the initial performance of *Agamemnon* is an event that carries religious, political, and social meanings within the order of Athenian culture. Each of these contexts may be appropriate, depending upon the questions we are investigating and the answers we seek to reveal about not only the nature of the event itself but also its place within a diachronic and synchronic order of meaning. Some questions are clear and pursued with great research skill and intelligence. But other questions, even if clearly articulated, fail to provide sufficient guidance for the research and analysis.

In order to provide a theatrical setting and condition for these issues – specifically the matters of event, context, representation, understanding, and explanation – let's consider the intriguing case of the scholarship on classical Greek theatre. Ever since Herodotus, historians have tried to describe and interpret the Mediterranean world in which classical theatre emerged. How have classicists, as critics and historians, tried to explain Greek classical theatre?

The documentary record on theatre in this era is even scarcer than it is for the English Renaissance stage. For example, according to Oliver Taplin there are only two vases from the fifth century BCE that "can plausibly claim to show a play in performance" in the Dionysian festival.[42] Both are from the era of Aeschylus. But some classicists do not agree with Taplin on the nature of the documentary record. J. R. Green, for example, has identified well over a dozen fifth-century vases from various locations that may possibly represent theatrical characters.[43] He claims, for example, that five vases from 460–450 BCE represent scenes from Sophocles' *Andromeda* (for which we only have fragments of the text). Whatever the number of credible vases, the visual evidence for tragedy is slight. Fifth-century vases that depict comic characters are somewhat more plentiful, and we also have some terracotta figurines of comic actors.

Besides the visual sources, which also include the archeological sites for theatres, we have written sources, primarily the plays. We have forty-four complete plays and some fragments. In all, though, we have less than 3 percent of the plays written and performed at the Dionysian festival during the fifth century. Many other plays were performed at other locations, but our documentary record is scarce. Our texts for the plays are based upon manuscripts that are copies of copies of copies. The oldest extant manuscripts are separated from the fifth century by approximately 1,500 years. Besides the plays, we have other written commentaries, such as Aristotle's *Poetics*, that provide some information, however problematic, on theatre. The archeological record on theatre in Athens is also quite scarce, but the remains for close to 200 Greek theatres are scattered across the Mediterranean area.[44]

Working with this limited record, classicists have developed some cunning ways to reconstruct and interpret the performance codes and methods of the Dionysian theatre. Of course, the dramatic texts themselves have been the primary documents. For example, in *The Stagecraft of Aeschylus* (1977) and *Greek Tragedy in Action* (1978), Taplin demonstrates that various staging techniques of classical drama can be identified, at least potentially, by a close reading of the plays. This method is an excellent illustration of how to recognize and read the double identity of the theatrical event. By means of a careful description of the fictional world of the plays, Taplin attempts to recover the possible and probable features of the performances. In *Stagecraft* he reconstructs the performance patterns in each of the seven plays by Aeschylus. And in *Greek Tragedy in Action* he selects nine plays – three each by Aeschylus, Sophocles, and Euripides – in order to identify recurring visual codes of action and emotion in classical tragedy. Although no specific line in the playtexts is necessarily reliable, given the source and condition of the manuscripts, the tragedies still tell us collectively many things about Greek performance. As we saw in chapter 1 where we examined certain patterns of performance at Shakespeare's Globe, historians can mine the plays for the recurring details of performance in the classical Greek theatre. Taplin protests that he is not offering yet "another antiquarian reconstruction of the Athenian theatre," but he does dissect the plays inductively in order to reveal the particular attributes of "the visual dimension of tragedy."[45] He does so by examining exits and entrances, gestures, tokens and objects, tableau scenes, noises and silences, the sequence of scenes, and what he calls "mirror scenes" in plays, actions that reflect and comment upon one another. In the process of teasing out the recurring visual codes of the plays, Taplin demonstrates that a close reading of the texts can offer a semiotics of the implied performance text.

Behind the dialogue of Greek drama we are always conscious of a concrete visual actuality, and behind that of a specific emotional actuality. Behind the drama of words is the drama of action, the timbre of voice and voice, the uplifted hand or tense muscle, and the particular emotion. The spoken play, the words which we read, are symbols, a shorthand, and often, as in the best of Shakespeare, a very abbreviated shorthand indeed, for the actual and felt play, which is always the real thing. The phrase, beautiful as it may be, stands for a greater beauty still. This is merely a particular case of the amazing unity of Greek, the unity of concrete and abstract in philosophy, the unity of thought and feeling, action and speculation in life.
T. S. Eliot, "Seneca in Elizabethan Translations," in *Selected Essays* (1951)[46]

Taplin's stagecraft studies are part of a major new interest in performance among classical scholars since the original publication of A. W. Pickard-Cambridge's *The Dramatic Festivals of Athens* in 1953 (with revised editions in 1968 and 1988). A number of impressive studies of performance and spectacle in classical theatre have appeared during the last three or four decades. Besides maintaining their abiding commitment to metrical and literary analysis of dramatic texts, classical scholars have focused more directly in recent years on the evidence for theatrical performance. The texts themselves provide some information, but classicists, like Renaissance scholars, must also seek elsewhere for evidence. Here, too, Taplin has been a major contributor because of his study of the visual evidence for theatre.[47] Several scholars have reinterpreted the vase paintings, sculptures, terracotta and bronze figurines (some of which were popular souvenirs of performers and performances). Others have reconsidered the problematic evidence in the commentaries that extends across several centuries into the Roman period.[48] And yet others have expanded the archeological investigations, searching for the spatial codes buried in the theatre remains. Decoding, as the semiotician Yuri Lotman states, "is always a reconstruction."[49]

Of special interest, some classicists have attempted to move from the study of the dramatic text to the study of the audience and its potential responses. J. R. Green, among others, has shifted the focus to "the way theatre was received and the influence it had."[50] He is interested in how performance sets up a series of expectations for the audience, but also an interplay of contradictory impulses that shape the possible reactions of spectators at the time. This relationship between performance and spectator also receives attention in *Greek and Roman Actors* (2002), a collection of essays by Pat Easterling and Edith Hall. Hall, for example, shows that despite our popular idea of Greek theatre as a visual medium – in part because of the etymologies of the words *theatai* and *spectators* – it was also a place to listen. From the fifty-strong choruses of men and boys in the dithyramb festivals to the tragedy competitions, singing was a definitive feature of classical performance. Drawing upon dozens of sources, Hall makes a convincing case not only for an operatic tragic theatre but also for the fascinating variety of vocal skills the actors must have mastered.[51]

> In many ways the distinction in Greek historiography between akōe ("hearing") and opsis ("seeing") – what you saw yourself and what you only heard – is still the fundamental one . . . The use of literacy and written record is not obvious or predictable, and therefore it is not enough to observe the presence of literacy without considering its uses; its use is linked closely with the customs and beliefs of the society; and there is a complex mixture of both oral and written processes which persists long after the initial introduction of writing.
>
> Rosalind Thomas (on the interplay between oral and written culture in fifth-century Athens), *Oral Tradition and Written Record in Classical Athens* (1989: 14 and 30)[52]

Besides these attempts to locate classical dramas within a performance tradition, classicists have also placed theatre within its cultural and social contexts.[53] As Edith Hall explains: "The greatest innovation in the study of Greek tragedy over the last thirty years has been the excavation of its historical and topographical specificity."[54] Drawing upon several fields of study, including rhetoric, literature, art history, religious studies, political studies, social history, anthropology, and archeology, scholars have located the Greek plays in a concentric ring of performative influences, from the works of previous artists, the festival traditions, weddings, and funerals to the social, political, and educational systems of Athenian society. Also, some studies take up issues of gender and class that have engaged literary scholars of all languages and periods. The study of Greek myth continues to be a feature of classical scholarship, but in the main the recent studies resist the universal readings of ritual and myth of previous studies that were influenced by J. G. Frazer's *The Golden Bough* (1911–15).

Event and its contextual worlds: the basic mission of placing performances within their cultural conditions guides much classical scholarship today, even though the evidence for staging practice is meager. The investigator faces a methodological challenge because potential evidence for our arguments must be derived from a wide and diverse repository of sources on everything from drama and philosophy to law and religion. Ideally, we make ourselves familiar with the whole classical world. This comprehensive principle is admirable but difficult to serve, even for most classicists. Specialization is the norm in scholarship. And even for scholars of the drama, the problems are substantial. As Christopher Pelling points out, drama is a "particularly delicate source to use" because the dramatic texts were part of the event – the civic festival – that we seek to reconstruct; they are not just a source that points to a historical event. The dramatic text not only "illuminates something beyond itself" in the historical moment; it also illuminates itself because it served as a performative aspect of the event itself.[55] Pelling cautions us: "If we talk of a tragic text as 'evidence' for the civic theatrical experience, it is more like talking of a fragment of a pot as 'evidence' for the original artifact: we begin from a part and reconstruct what we can of the whole."[56]

This double identity defines the relationship between all dramatic texts and their performances. Consequently, whenever theatre historians use a dramatic text as a historical source, they need to note both what it makes reference to and what it embodies. How does it serve both functions? The text signals a double presence (or more to the point, a double absence). We need to understand these texts as historical sources of *performative actions* and *representative events*. They record imaginative actions within the performance, yet they also express performative traits and values of the participants, the spectators, the culture, and the society. They exist simultaneously as aesthetic works and historical records. They are mimetic events, in accord with Aristotle's analysis in the *Poetics*; yet they are also representative events within the historical situation and context.[57] We must therefore ask what they perform artistically and how? And equally important, we must ask what they represent historically and how? The two identities – the aesthetic work and the historical document – are intertwined in a double helix, with each strand reflectively communicating with and against the other.[58]

As I suggested at the beginning of this chapter, the dramatic texts, because of their mimetic features, not only reflect aspects of the civic event, of which they are a part, but also refer to an imaginative human world that each plays represents. The text of *Antigone* thus refers to (and embodies aspects of) an historical event – the performance of the play in Athens. Yet the dramatic action within the play represents and refers to an imaginative event – the political and religious struggle over the burial of Polynices in Thebes. This doubling process is contained within the historical source that we seek to analyze. But what does the political and religious struggle within the play have to do with historical events and conditions at the time of performance? The two aspects should not be collapsed into a single register, but they also should not be separated, as if they were two unrelated matters of historical representation. Although the dramatic text creates an imaginative rather than a real representation of human events, the theatre historian seeks to read between the signs. We investigate the imaginative textual world of the play for clues of the real Athenian world that the playwright lived in and wrote about (however indirectly).

Also, the historian seeks to discover the values and judgements of the spectators within the dramatic actions they witnessed. For example, Pierre Vidal-Naquet asks,

"Can we use Attic tragedy to illuminate the status of foreigners in the Greek world?"[59]
He then proceeds to show how classical scholars have attempted to answer this
question. The argument, of course, is that the registers between the two categories –
imaginary world and real world – can be compared so that representations in the
performative actions may serve as possible evidence for historical events. But as Vidal-
Naquet demonstrates, the question may be simple, but the historical task is complex.
It requires substantial skill (and a measured skepticism) in both literary and historical
analysis. That is, the historian needs to possess an equivocal sensibility, if not exactly a
double identity, as complex as the source itself. In our attempts to derive historical
information from Greek tragedies, we need to proceed cautiously, especially when we
attempt to reconstruct the social attitudes and political values of the audience. "The
dramatic presentation," Pelling points out, "is likely to bear *some* relation to what the
audience might think and do in their extra-dramatic lives; but that presentation may
easily be stylized or simplified, and we must always be cautious about extrapolating in
too straightforward and one-to-one a way [*sic*] from such dramatic 'evidence'."[60]

Just as scholars have often interpreted the Chorus in a reductive way as representative of this or that Greek value or community, so too do they sometimes misread
or over-read the plays for other kinds of historical correspondences. For example,
some scholars wish to argue, on the basis of a one-to-one relationship between
fictional and historical worlds, that Sophocles' *Philoctetes* is about the recall of
Alcibiades to Athens; Aeschylus' *Eumenides* is about the Athenian *demos*. Yet we need
to remind ourselves that allusive references and parallel situations do not necessarily
mirror historical reality and events. Or even if they do evoke the historical figure,
situation, or attitude, we must ask another basic question: who is doing the evoking:
the playwright, the spectator, or the scholar? Even with Aristophanes' satiric comedies
we can be mistaken about the historical references and their intended meanings. Also,
what the playwright intended may have little or no relation to what the spectator saw
in the performance. And in turn what the scholar reads out of the text may be little
more than a projection onto it. Distinctions must be made. Without additional
evidence, how can we know the playwright's intentions or the audience's responses?
We know that each dramatic text has a number of potential performances and
meanings; we need to keep in mind that each dramatic text also has a number of
possible historical meanings. Inadequate and misguided productions are common; so
too are many interpretations of a play's historical significance.

Because of the nature of these doubling relationships within the dramatic text, the
theatre historian should be an accomplished literary scholar, skilled at textual criticism yet skeptical about the potential parallelisms between text and context. Then,
when attempting to reconstruct a theatre event, the theatre historian could use a
special compass for navigating the turns and twists implied by the mysterious historical map offered up by a dramatic text. These texts present to us reflections of
reflections of reflections. All of these doubling relationships in the historical sources
add to the historiographical difficulties that theatre historians must consider when
trying to reconstruct that two-part identity of the performative action and the representative event.

If, for instance, we consider how scholars have attempted to construct the relationship between the tragic text and the religious beliefs of the Athenian audiences, we find a striking pattern of pendulum swings in classical scholarship during the last century. At one time, Greek theatre was explained in terms of myth and ritual. The tragic texts served as indisputable evidence. Not only Nietzsche but also the Cambridge ritualists, who adapted some of the ideas of J. G. Frazer, envisioned a theatre of ritual actions on the theme of dismemberment and rebirth. Gilbert Murray, Jane Ellen Harrison, and Francis M. Cornford, for example, posited that the plays demonstrated a vital process of enacted ritual, whereby the tragic action represented the sacrifice of the god Dionysus.[61] In turn, A. W. Pickard-Cambridge provided a central place for Dionysus in the historical study of the annual festival in Athens.[62] Then, countering these modes of argument, the following generation of classicists, including Gerald Else and Bernard Knox, argued that it is a mistake to understand the Greek tragedies as religious texts and actions.[63] Countering the myth and ritual critics, they placed the plays and productions within theatrical and literary traditions, apart from religious culture. They also insisted that the plays need to be understood in terms of the artistic heritage and mythic narratives, distinct from the religious, social, or political conditions. Euripides writes within and against the tradition of Aeschylus, Sophocles, and the other tragic playwrights.

> We have no way of determining in principle, what an artist may take over from earlier artists, as opposed to what he takes over from other sources within his culture . . . This is not to say that there is no distinction to be made between an artist's relation to past art and his relation to social factors outside his art, but only that there is no general demarcation which can be put, *a priori*, to what can be learned from a work of art by a later artist.
>   Michael Podro (on Rembrandt's painting *Deposition*, 1633, and its artistic heritage), *The Critical Historians of Art* (1982: 131–32)

In recent years, however, aspects of the religious argument have been revived, even though the scholarship of Knox and others remains highly prized. Recent critics and historians, modifying the arguments of some of their mentors, have once again attempted to locate the Greek tragedies within a Dionysian religious event. Thus, J. J. Winkler and F. I. Zeitlin published a collection of essays that places Dionysian religious beliefs back in the relationship between stage and spectators.[64] New evidence and methods of analysis concerning the Dionysian mysteries, Greek religion, and eastern influences have enhanced this revisionist perspective.[65] We are coming to see that Greek culture was directly influenced by Egypt and the east Mediterranean societies, as Herodotus suggested. In this light, Walter Burkert has shown that there is some basis for the Black Athena argument by Martin Bernal about Egyptian contributions to ancient Greek religion (though some classicists at first rejected the whole argument).[66] Even some aspects of Nietzsche's ideas have been revitalized by Richard Seaford, who offers a lucid historical analysis of tragic action and ritual.[67] Yet as P. E. Easterling reminds us, we do not know in what sense the productions might have been experienced by spectators as the "worship of Dionysus," despite all of the scholarship on drama, theatre, festivals, religion, and ritual.[68] We are still speculating about the intentions of the playwrights, the significance of the theatrical representations, and the mindset of the spectators (who should not be reduced to a singular audience, as if everyone saw and thought in the same way).

After a century of classical scholarship on Greek drama, theatre, religion, and society, have we come full circle, arriving at where we began? Not really, for the turns are more on the order of a spiraling upward, an accumulative process of some gains in historical knowledge and a fuller understanding of the complex task of reconstructing Greek theatre performances and festivals. In this sense the historical and critical studies in classics, especially of the last few decades, provide a mirror of the development of theatre historiography today. In the best studies of Greek theatre and history, we find a full engagement with the methodological challenges and problems that pertain to the representation of performance events. To be expected, there are many disagreements over how to interpret the sources, to construct the performance events, and to provide appropriate contextual analysis. Classicists show – and demand of one another – a rigorous examination of the documentary records (e.g., in the study of vases as potential sources of performance evidence). And they also reveal a commitment to contextual analysis in their historical investigation of religion, politics, and society. These studies can therefore serve as demonstrations, from several perspectives, of the possible approaches to the description and interpretation of historical performances. Their methods and their problems are also our methods and problems, no matter what the historical topic and area of study may be.

Part three

Placing events within their contexts

Chapter 5

The criteria for periodization in theatre history: definitive categories for events

The concept of periodization, in its normative if somewhat misleading usage, delineates one aspect of history, the condition of stability (or identity), in relation to another aspect, the process of change (or difference). These two aspects of human events – stability and change – though dynamically interrelated and mutually defining, are organized into a system of classification that allows us to give order and sequence to historical time. Period concepts thus define time as a series of synchronic identities rather than as a diachronic process. Structure and coherence police teleology and difference. The continuous flow of time is organized into heuristic categories. As episodes of our creation, periods are interpretive ideas of order that regulate meaning. Whether we refer to large eras, such as the medieval age, or specific ones, such as the 1920s, the period concept is our way of freezing a segment of time, and giving it an identity. We must remember, though, that the concept is located within us, not within history itself. In short, it is a classification that we create and then project onto the past.

> All thinking involves classification; all classification involves general terms.
> Isaiah Berlin, *Selected Writings: Concepts and Categories* (1978: 113)

Traditionally, in ancient, medieval, and early Renaissance times the theories and models for periodization took several different (though often intermixed) forms:

(1) *cosmological* (e.g., the five ages in Heisod's *Works and Days*);
(2) *mythological* (the distant ages of Cyclops, Titans, herdsmen, and citizens of Atlantis in Plato's writings);
(3) *anthropological* (the various ideas on either progress or degeneracy, such as the movement from primitive to civilized societies or vice versa);
(4) *biological* (Aristotle's life cycles of birth, growth, decay, and death applied to history and empires);
(5) *eschatological* (the Judeo-Christian models, such as the four kingdoms or monarchies of the *Book of Daniel* and the Great Week analogy used by St. Augustine in the *City of God*);
(6) *typological* (the Books of *Luke* and *Acts* as figurative models of reenactment);
(7) *moralistic* (the periodic turns of Fortune's wheel); and

(8) *political* (the six stages of state government in Polybius' *Anacyclosis* and Machiavelli's *Discorsi*).[1]

> All periodization, it may be argued, is arbitrary and artificial. But it is neither entirely arbitrary not entirely artificial. History is a theoretical discipline. To explain why things happen as they happen when they happen, we employ theories of change, explicitly or implicitly. These theories are constantly being challenged and revised.
> W. A. Green, "Periodization in European and World History" (1992: 36–37)

Variations on these models are quite prevalent. For example, Joachim Abbas (*c.*1132–1202) interpreted history by the Trinitarian formula of the Age of Father, the Age of Son, and the Age of Spirit. Plato introduced several possible ages in his writings. An age of Zeus is named in *Gorgias*, a period of heroes in *Timaeus*, and an age of gods and art in *Philebus*. In a piecemeal manner, these incidental ages were given a developmental order by subsequent Greek and Roman writers. We now credit the Greeks – as a whole culture – with dividing time into the *obscure* age (from the origin of things to the Deluge); a *mythic, heroic,* or *fabulous* age (from the Deluge to the first Olympiad); and a *historic* age (from the first Olympiad forward). But these designations merely stabilize the miscellaneous attempts in the works of Plato, the playwrights, and others to identify earlier ages.

These designations are further complicated by the confusing mixture of linear and cyclical time in "Greek classical thought," a concept that usually implies a period, though with little specificity. The dates for this "classical age" are quite various in the scholarship. Sometimes this designation means the whole history of the Greek and Roman civilizations, from the time of Troy, or even earlier, to the final collapse of the Roman Empire. This expansive idea of the time period guides the *Oxford Classical Dictionary* (1970), though the editors and contributors waiver in their procedures for how to handle our archeological knowledge, which expands the period concept. So defined, the classical age covers fifteen, twenty, and even more centuries. Or the term can be limited to the fifth century BCE, as happens with many theatre historians. The period is identified with Athenian drama, from Aeschylus to Euripides and Aristophanes, though, of course, some of the extant plays of Aristophanes were performed in the fourth century BCE, and Menander's plays follow almost a century later. Aristotle, who was born a century after Sophocles, had to take a historical perspective on the previous era. Lacking sufficient documentation, he struggles to reconstruct it (e.g., the definitive traits of the Dionysian festival, the origins of tragic drama). Consequently, all of us who have followed after him also struggle – with his history, with his authority, with his methods.

However we define the classical age, the models of time associated with it are predominately cyclical or recurrent, while the models we associate with Judeo-Christian history are predominately linear. But as Gerald Press points out, this is an overly neat division of ideas in these two complex traditions.[2] In either case, the number of periods has been set usually between two to seven. Thus, while Fortune's wheel alternates cyclically between prosperity and adversity (historical schemes of rise and fall), St. Augustine's Great Week model (a figurative comparison to the seven days of creation) follows a linear sequence of seven periods: Adam to the Flood, the Flood to Abraham, Abraham to David, David to the Babylonian Captivity, the Exile to Christ, Christ to the Last Judgement, and, somewhat confusingly, either the future millennium when the AntiChrist is defeated or a period of rest.

During much of antiquity the period designations were few in number and simple in function. For example, the Roman chronologist Marcus Terrentius Varro, drawing upon Plato and other writers, divided human time into three ages: the obscure, the fabulous (or heroic), and the historical. This tripartite model can be contrasted with the somewhat more complex and purposeful Christian division of sacred history. Part of Giambattista Vico's historic project was his attempt to reconcile these two periodic models. And J. G. Fichte saw world history as five major epochs that followed a developmental order: (1) reason ruling through instinct; (2) reason ruling through law; (3) the emancipation of human beings from the authority of reason; (4) the re-establishment of reason as science; and then (5) reason as art. This developmental model found its fullest expression in Hegel's history of reason. In contemporary historiography, which lacks sacred decisiveness and philosophical wholeness, the tendency is toward even more numerous divisions, with the aim of revealing the definitive attributes of each period and the probable causes for change. The increase in period concepts derives, in part, from our growing historical consciousness since the eighteenth century. Also, the growing number of documents from all ages has contributed directly to our expanded number of periods.

It is inevitable that periodization, in history, should be largely modeled on the nature of the documentation . . . The role unconsciously played by the nature of the documentation in our carving out the historical field must be considerable, and a history of historiography ought to attach a great deal of importance to it.
Paul Veyne, *Writing History: Essay on Epistemology* (1984: 330)

During the Enlightenment, a two-part model of ancient and modern was a common, if inexact, way to designate epochs. This basic division, which operated in the literary battles over neoclassical rules for drama, can be traced from the sixteenth-century Italian studies of Aristotle's *Poetics* (e.g., the idea of the Three Unities) to the eighteenth-century rules on the subject matter of tragedy and *opera seria*. But ever since Petrarch (1304–74) identified an age of barbarism, which intervened between the ancient world and his own age, a three-part model of periodization coexisted with the familiar idea of the ancient and modern worlds. The idea of a *medium aevum*, intervening between the classical and present ages, was necessary to Italian humanists, who made the case for a rebirth of classicism after a long sacred epoch. Many Enlightenment thinkers dismissed this middle period as the Dark Ages. Despite the appeal of this three-part model for history (which was usually conceived of as the story of Western Civilization), there was no agreement on when this middle age began and ended. Nor could people agree on the defining traits of a modern age. In Britain, for example, Samuel Johnson embraced many aspects of neoclassicism, as derived from sixteenth-century humanism, yet he also felt that in England his own modern age was divided from Shakespeare's modern age. 1660 was often the dividing line in British thought (though the works of Milton were assigned to both aspects of the modern sensibility).[3] Of course, 1660 was a meaningless dividing line in France, for Louis XIV's reign extended from the middle of the seventeenth century to 1715. Obviously, in French thought 1789 would become a key turning point, just as 1776 served American ideas for a new period. As we will see, turning points and dividing lines, often tied to political events, are often crucial in the designation of periods. But there is little agreement on the causes of change. And confusion reigns from country to country on the decisive events. These confusions and conflicts are especially problematic when period concepts derived from political reigns serve as period concepts for distinct period styles in the arts.

Although the period designation of the Renaissance did not become established until the nineteenth century, the idea of rebirth was obviously embedded in the many discussions of the classical and humanist features of the new "modern" age, especially from the sixteenth century forward. To complicate matters further, the Latin word *modernus* was used by Roman grammarians in the sixth century to distinguish between ancient and contemporary writing styles. And from the twelfth century forward scholastics distinguished between ancient and modern ways of writing. In short, period concepts based upon either a two-part division between ancient and modern or a three-part division of ancient, medieval, and modern were the norm until the nineteenth century. And even in the nineteenth and twentieth centuries, the basic formula of ancient, medieval, and modern continued to provide a standard method of organizing the history of the West. For instance, W. E. Finer's monumental study of world civilizations, *The History of Government from the Earliest Times* (1997), is published in three volumes: "Ancient Monarchies and Empires," "The Intermediate Ages," and "Empires, Monarchies and the Modern State."[4] Three eras of human history, sufficient for Voltaire, serve Finer as well.

In modern historiography, though cyclical modes of representation did not disappear (Vico, Nietzsche, Toynbee), the prevalent modes are linear, usually developmental, and often progressive. For example, Johann Wolfgang von Goethe, in a short essay called "Stages of Man's Mind" (1817), made the case for four major epochs since humankind emerged from the "primeval phase of the world."[5] In the "pursuit of self-improvement" human history – or the development of the human mind – divides into the "Epoch of Poetry" (distinguished by primitive faith, robust sensuousness, the contemplation of nature, and the power of imagination); the "Epoch of Theology" (stirrings of the ideal, reason dedicated to the sacred); the "Epoch of Philosophy" (intellectual doubt, a growing individualism, the search for general laws of nature); and the "Epoch of Prose"(the dissolution of idealism into the ordinary, the rejection of previous ideals, the principle of the common and the folk). Despite this progressive model, Goethe warns that the search for self-improvement has taken a destructive path in the modern age. The intellect, robust in the earlier epochs, is losing its hold, as vulgar, common, and selfish values justify many false faiths and beliefs. Anyone is capable of sowing follies. In our troubled times, "the value of any mystical idea is destroyed, and even primitive faith is desecrated."[6]

Hegel provided a philosophical justification for dividing history into a series of developmental periods, each of which reveals an organic unity of singular identity. Each epoch of the Hegelian model follows the principle of reason, which moves civilizations forward toward greater and greater intelligibility.[7] In Hegel's philosophy of history, as Daniel Bell points out, each period has "its own realization until broken by the world-historical figures – Alexander, Caesar, and Napoleon – the unwitting instruments of the cunning of reason."[8] Ever since Hegel, even when we have rejected his idea of total history (including the great man theory of change), we have been tempted to identify a series of developmental or evolutionary periods. This is as true for Marxist as for Annalist histories. Also, as our understanding of time has adjusted to geological and biological knowledge, the number of periods has grown.

Whatever our approach, we assume that the history of human events can be separated into specific epochs of temporal identities. Periods are thus discursive models for historical understanding, models based upon the structural idea of maintenance or stability and the temporal idea of divergence or difference. The dividing line between categories or periods serves as a register of change, signaling the end of one era and the beginning of another. It is a turning point of sufficient measure that gives meaning and order to history, though historians have trouble agreeing upon the causes for change. Various taxonomies are possible (if not always probable) for designating periods, but all models, even the simplest ones, follow principles of classification based upon ideas of affinity and distinction, norm and variation, continuity and separation, order and disruption, same and different.

All measurement . . . is based upon order. Indeed, only through suitable arrangements and groupings can we handle vast quantities of material perceptually or cognitively. E. H. Gombrich [the art historian] discusses the decimal periodization of historical time into decades, centuries, and millennia (1974 lecture: "Zeit, Zahl, und Zeichen"). Daily time is marked off into twenty-four hours, and each of these into sixty minutes of sixty seconds each. Whatever else may be said of these modes of organization, they are not "found in the world" but built into the world. Ordering, as well as composition and decomposition and weighting of wholes and kinds, participates in worldmaking.
Nelson Goodman, *Ways of Worldmaking* (1978: 13–14)

In order to understand how and why these taxonomic principles and models have developed and established themselves in cultural history, especially in theatre history, we need to investigate not only the ways that periods have been identified in modern times but also the interpretive ideas that the designations tend to impose upon events. Our understanding of history – both the events and their contexts – derives in great measure from the period concepts that we use. An early clue to modern understanding comes from Augustus William Schlegel in his *Lectures on Dramatic Art and Literature* (1809–11). In discussing the history of the English theatre, for instance, he proclaims that it "divides itself naturally into two periods."[9] The first period begins in the mid sixteenth century and ends when the Puritans closed the theatres; the second period begins with the Restoration of Charles II and continues, with some variations in the era's drama, up to Schlegel's own time. Schlegel pays little attention to medieval drama because it does not fit into his definition of significant dramatic types. Besides, it occurred in the Dark Ages when religion compressed the artistic imagination. His concept of periodization reflects an aesthetic presupposition that aligns drama with the humanistic values of secular culture. It also gives priority to literary texts. Performance and spectacle, such as occurred in medieval religious celebrations, are ignored. Even more basically, it depends upon an idea of causal change in human events. The political activities of the Puritans – that is, non-aesthetic causes – provide the period division.

This division (though not the number of periods) is the same one that James Wright identifies in his *Historia Histrionica* (1699), one of the first theatre histories in English (and a work that Schlegel read). Written as a dialogue between Lovewit and Trueman, this history compares contemporary theatre (of what we now call the Restoration period) with the pre-Civil War theatre, which Lovewit and Trueman praise for its greater plays and players. And Wright, in his preface, notes that the earlier plays, by revealing "the manners and behaviour" of an age, show how times have altered. "For plays are exactly like portraits, drawn in the garb and fashion of the time when painted."[10] This mimetic conceit, which defines a period in terms of a natural correspondence between formal style and social behavior, is a representative trope of Wright's own age. No further explanation is needed, except to point out what seems obvious: the "Rebellion" is the cause for change in both social and aesthetic conditions. The Restoration is a new period – a judgement that subsequent historians from Schelgel forward have had little reason to question, though they may disagree on its causes.[11]

Several aspects of Wright's and Schlegel's ideas on periodization should be noted, for in representative ways – and in basic accord with the growing historical consciousness of the post-Renaissance era – many of their assumptions have carried forward to our own age.[12] First, though they may differ in their explanations for historical change, they both assume that change is in the nature of events. History reveals not just a cyclical pattern of abiding repetitions, but instead a directional process – a series of divergences from what went before.[13] Wright, who derives his history from not only the recent memories of his contemporaries but also John Stow's *Survey of London* (1598) and the *Ludus Coventriae* (1468), attempts to highlight several different theatrical developments since the fifteenth century, and he even traces briefly the changing relations between religion and theatre since "the infancy of Christianity."[14] Schlegel, more comprehensive in his analysis, examines the drama of "particular ages and nations" since the Greeks in order to reveal the distinguishing dramatic traits of each time and place. "The world is wide, and affords room for a great diversity of objects." Second, both Wright and Schlegel assume that changes in the theatre have some kind of relationship to specific social, political, and religious orders. Third, they see this relationship as a causal one, though they differ in how to describe the determining factors in the exchange between art and society. Fourth, they both suggest that each age or period reveals a singular wholeness, a unified identity. In Schlegel's words, the art of each period "constitutes in itself a complete and finished system." Fifth, this coherence, because it occurs within history, can be distinguished by a beginning and an end. And finally, a turning point can (or even should) be found between periods. This last assumption, which returns us to the first point, is based upon the idea of historical change.[15]

Schlegel differs from Wright, of course, in that his *Lectures* put forward not just a comparative commentary on his age but a theory of dramatic history. He identifies a romantic spirit which emanates from the "genius" of an age and gives to art an "organical form" that expresses national character.[16] (From this idea it is only a half-step to Hegel's idea of great leaders providing the genius for each developmental age.) Schlegel attempts in his *Lectures* to reveal the "origin and essence of the romantic,"[17] so as to describe the age of Shakespeare for instance, and to spell out "the history of the development of art."[18] Essentially, his historical periods are the three standard ages of Enlightenment historiography: classical, medieval, and modern.[19] Yet he rejects Voltaire's valorization of the modern age as the rebirth of abiding classical principles and style. Instead, he credits English, Spanish, and, more recently, German dramatic arts with their own original characters, expressive of the intrinsic energy of each national culture. The spirit of an age, which for instance manifests itself in the drama and theatre of Shakespeare, takes shape organically. "Hence it is evident that the spirit of poetry, which, though imperishable, migrates, as it were, through different bodies, must, so often as it is newly born in the human race, mould to itself, out of the nutrimental substance of an altered age, a body of a different conformation."[20] This argument, in opposition to neoclassic principles, implies that the art of one period cannot be understood or judged adequately by the standards of art from another period or culture. History modifies art (though genius sometimes rises above common conditions). Schlegel thus joins Lessing in a rejection of Voltaire's ideas on neoclassical, universal categories for drama and theatre.

Schlegel's metaphor of "different bodies," though not exactly the same one as Wright's "portraits" of manners and fashion, is nonetheless a physiognomic analogy as well as a narrative characterization that credits an age with an identity that is its own, not merely the repetition of the identity of earlier ages. The art of an age is the "speaking physiogomy"[21] of the things out of which it is shaped. Or in Dryden's famous words: "They, who have best succeeded on the stage, / Have still conformed their genius to their age." This assumption, in its general terms, is common to many period concepts. Age and stage somehow "mirror" one another (or they are animated by a spirit of the age). In its simplest form, of course, this idea is but the repetition of Cicero's dictum on comedy: "*imitationem vitae, speculum consuetudinis, imago veritatis*" – a copy of life, a mirror of custom, a reflection of truth.[22] But Schlegel, by examining each period's original character, is describing something other than the oft-repeated purpose of drama; he is explaining how and why historical periods in the arts change and differ from one another.[23]

Schlegel's argument for cultural diversity and change, consonant with historical ideas in the writings of other German critics such as J. G. Herder and F. Schiller, is most fully developed in the philosophy of Hegel. In his aesthetic history Hegel identifies three historical stages in the artistic development of the Spirit or Idea that, after an early age of savagery, correspond roughly to Egyptian culture (a symbolic age), the Greek and Roman classical period (a mimetic age), and the Christian period (the romantic age). In other words, he modifies the three basic ages that Renaissance and Enlightenment thinkers had designated by presenting a progressive history, the unfolding of the Absolute Mind or Reason. And within these three primary ages he notes a series of either tripartite or fourfold phases.[24]

For Hegel the art of each period is not only a historical manifestation of the cultural heritage of an age but also the realization or formulation of the age's worldview. The Spirit finds its expression in the *Volk* (national people), the collective culture of a particular time and place. From this idea it was an easy step in nineteenth-century thought to the concepts of *Volkgeist* and *Zeitgeist* (time spirit), and then but a small step to the argument that a period embodies and expresses a dominant worldview or *Weltanschauung*.

> Every period of civilization which forms a complete and consistent whole manifests itself not only in political life, in religion, art, and science, but also sets its characteristic stamp on social life.
> Jacob Burckhardt, *The Civilization of the Renaissance in Italy* (1990: 230)

These familiar concepts of cultural unity, though often dismissed specifically (when the topic is Hegel or German cultural ideas), have continued nonetheless to operate widely and matter-of-factly in much historical thought – hence the popularity even today of such singular (yet basically static) constructs as the Elizabethan worldview, Greek civilization, the medieval mind, Gothic man, *la mentalité primitive*, the modern temper, and bourgeois society. All artworks of a period are thus interpreted as signs of the times; they represent one all-encompassing mental and social structure (system, *épistème*, *mentalité*, paradigm, ideology, hegemony, discourse). Consider, for example, Jacob Burckhardt's famous work, *The Civilization of the Renaissance in Italy* (1860). As E. H. Gombrich points out, Burckhardt did not see himself as a Hegelian, but he nonetheless based his master work upon many of the assumptions about historical periods, culture, and society that Hegel had put forward. Yet despite the Hegelian influence, which can be traced in Burckhardt's opposition between the medieval and Renaissance mind, his cultural history depends primarily upon a synchronic idea of unity, as Carl E. Schorske points out in his study of the idea of culture in the writings of Burckhardt and De Tocqueville:

> Against the prevailing teleological orientation of history, with its diachronic emphasis, they developed a counterproject: history organized in synchronic tableaux, in which the most diverse, often clashing components of cultural

life – institutions, intellectual and artistic production, mores, social relations – could be displayed in cross section, a horizontal panorama. Burckhardt especially displayed for the first time the colligative power of history, its potential for confronting in coherence the most nonhomogeneous materials of culture. Time certainly did not stop in the constructions of these masters, but it was, one might say, slowed down. Not transformations, but cultural coherence became the focus of attention.[25]

This idea of coherence and wholeness has carried forward to our time.

Although cultural historians for the last 100 years have often disagreed over aspects of Burckhardt's interpretation and conclusion, and thus felt a need to put forward contending definitions of the Renaissance (its beginning and end, its causes, its dominant aesthetic and social traits), they have generally accepted the concept of periodization itself. Today, despite our pervasive criticism of Burckhardt's analysis and our rejection of Hegel's metaphysical history of Spirit or Idea with its teleological design, we have taken up, whether we recognize it or not, much about the idea of a unified period. We may disagree on how best to define a period and to construct the relationship among its component parts, but we still seek a coherent interpretation. This idea of synthesis is our way of organizing history; it is the control on knowledge that shapes our study of the codes of knowledge, the paradigm that underlies our search for paradigms.

> Coherence seems to be a need imposed on us whether we seek it or not. Things need to make sense.
> David Carr, *Time, Narrative, and History* (1988: 97)

Period concepts in modern cultural history, including theatre history, are most commonly established in terms of either the aesthetic attributes of art or the socio-political context. This neat dichotomy between the formal history of artistic and philosophical cultures and their social conditions is not a required opposition, of course, but in various modes of analysis it is well established. Thus, on the one hand, period concepts are defined by formal styles, rules of art, conventions, themes, icongraphic motifs, semiotic codes and systems, and the intertextuality of artistic heritages, while, on the other hand, periods are derived from the social and political orders, economic forces, institutions, ideologies, and mentalities. Cultural historians tend to align themselves with one of these two camps, though obviously many historians take a pragmatic or haphazard approach by making do with whatever period concept is close at hand.

Modern social historians, having had various precursors (Voltaire, Schlegel, Hegel, Comte, Taine, Marx, Burckhardt, Nietzsche, Durkheim, Lamprecht, Dilthey, Spencer, and Weber), offer contending versions of the history of art, but necessarily they all take the idea of periodization as a given. Society is a system, a totality, to be studied in its wholeness. By definition, then, social history explains human activities, including art, in terms of specific, coherent eras of regulative, social systems. The individual artist is not an autonomous creative agent, but is situated, immersed, or confined in social, economic, and political conditions that shape or control his or her work. Consequently, whatever their disagreements on how to investigate an age, social historians assume not only that culture cannot be understood apart from its social conditions but that society and art join together to express a period's identity (or composite identities). The intellectual debate in social history is over which theory best connects everything. Of course, depending upon the theory, the period designations can vary greatly.

Marxism, of the various social histories of art, has proved to be the most systematic in putting forward models for periodization. In the revolt against Hegel and idealism, Marx and Engels transformed a spiritual historiography of periodization into a material one – without abandoning many of the historical assumptions of Hegel's periodic model, developmental narrative, and dialectic conflict. As the material conditions change, the culture changes. Art is shaped, even determined it seems, by the modes of production, not by an immaterial force or idea. Though Marx sometimes rejects a purely materialistic causality, he basically derives his historical categories from his theory of the economic forces that limit, if not totally control, social order and consciousness. Marx identified four major periods corresponding to four historic modes of production: primitive communism, ancient slavery, medieval feudalism, and capitalism. Of course, he predicted a fifth period, arriving in the near future, of social communism.

Some cultural historians have appropriated this developmental model, though most of them – including Walter Benjamin, Georg Lukacs, Arnold Hauser, Theodor Adorno, Jean Duvignaud, Raymond Williams, Fredric Jameson, Joan Kelly, Nikos Hadjinicolaou, and Janet Wolff – have modified it in the process of establishing periods and subperiods. Obviously, most Marxist cultural historians focus on the modern period that Marx called capitalist, but within this broad category there is usually significant need for more specific period concepts that non-Marxist and formalist histories regularly provide (e.g., Renaissance, Restoration, Baroque, Empire, Victorian, Weimar, fascist, modern, postmodern). Surprisingly, there is little attempt in Marxist cultural history to explain how and why these formalist definitions of style and period can be made to fit Marxist theory and its five distinct periods. Still, what can be said for Marxism is that it offers a powerful theory of determination, a method for causally deriving art from economic conditions and social practices. As Nikos Hadjinicolaou argues, "if a historian [of the visual arts] is to study the development of the mutual relations among various different visual ideologies [i.e., styles, formal and thematic elements] over a certain period of time, he must have a rational basis for delimiting this period of time, otherwise his procedures will be completely arbitrary."[26] Marxism, by offering a controlling principle for dividing history into periods, is able to make a specific case for the developmental history of art. Each period, as base and superstructure, generates a unifying principle for artistic practices. As the economic conditions change, the art changes. Marxism thus carries forward the unifying assumptions of Hegelianism without the immaterial causes associated with idealism. Recently, certain historians and social theorists have been struggling with this issue – struggling, that is, against a single interpretation of a period in terms of one spirit, mode of production, structure, ideology, or ruling idea. Yet whatever the approach, most of the social theorists continue to depend upon period concepts that have singular identities.[27]

The drawback to Marxist historiography, besides the continuing difficulty of fully specifying the dialectical relations between infrastructure and superstructure and between subjectivity and system, is its uneasy, revisionist ties to its founder, ties that generate endless disagreements among Marxists over proper interpretation and application. There is a premium on right thinking, even among most revisionist Marxists. Ironically, Marx's texts, which argue that the meaning of ideas and actions must be located within the context of their time and place, are often treated and quoted as sacred texts whose meanings are not at all limited to their historical conditions. In this sense they are read for their essentialist principles.

Many social historians reject this insistence on exclusivity in Marxist theory. For example, Fernand Braudel, comparing his and Sartre's critiques of Marxist history, has this to say:

> Marxism is peopled with models. Sartre would rebel against the rigidity, the schematic nature, the insufficiency of the model, in the name of the particular and the individual. I would rebel with him (with certain slight differences in emphasis) not against the model, though, but against the use which has been made of it, the use which it has been felt proper to make. Marx's genius, the secret of his long sway, lies in the fact that he was the first to construct true social models, on the basis of a historical *longue durée*. These models have been frozen in all their simplicity by being given the status of laws, of a preordained and automatic explanation, valid in all places and to any society. Whereas if they were put back within the ever-changing stream of time, they would constantly reappear, but with changes of emphasis, sometimes overshadowed, sometimes thrown into relief by the presence of other structures which would themselves be susceptible to definition by other rules and thus by other models. In this way, the creative potential of the most powerful social analysis of the last century has been stymied. It cannot regain its youth and vigor except in the *longue durée*.[28]

Of course, it is open to question whether Braudel's emphasis upon the long duration of geography, climate, trade systems, and material conditions offers a viable means for supplementing a Marxian social history of periods. Both models of historical epochs fail to address and explain the multiplicity of artistic works and styles within any specific era. The general theories have trouble accommodating the particularity of artistic developments.

No age can be correctly described by a single, exclusive characteristic. Attempts to do so frequently result in ambiguous and metaphorical use of the characterizing term.
    Louis Gottschalk, *Understanding History: A Primer of Historical Methods* (1969: 214)

In his complex vision of historical orders and disorders, Braudel offers a method for dividing history and periods into a tripartite scheme of overlapping durations: (1) the short term of the individual and the event; (2) the more extended periods, often cyclical or intercyclical, of economic and social history; and (3) the long duration of "long-lived structures" such as geography, climate, trade routes that "resist the course of history and therefore determine its flow." Braudel argues that "science, technology, political institutions, conceptual changes, civilizations (to fall back on the useful word) all have their own rhythms of life and growth, and the new history of conjunctures will be complete only when it has made up a whole orchestra of them all."[29] Suspicious of narrative history, he renounces not only the idea of linear development along a single, developmental line but also all concepts that turn history or civilization in "a being, or an organism, or a figure, or a body, even a historical body."[30] Though we may doubt that his historical vision, method, and style are free of narrative elements (e.g., his metaphor of "life and growth" above), still his tripartite scheme offers one means for getting beyond the pervasive historical practice of giving each period its single identity. In this attention to multileveled sequences of change, his work bears comparison with his German contemporary Norbert Elias, who also has argued for a tripartite division: individual history, social development, and biological evolution.[31] Thus, despite great differences in methods and aims, both of them reject the concept of a single, unified period. In other words, from the perspective of a cultural history of the arts, the social structure of a period, even if definable as a unified system, needs to be understood as existing in functional relation to other structures of organization and meaning. Not so surprisingly, such an idea is difficult to apply in cultural history. Besides requiring a comprehensive historical understanding of human events, this multiple perspective compels the historian of art and culture to maintain simultaneously a tripartite perspective on the causes of the identity of artworks and the causes of changes in these works.

Of course, most theatre historians today, whether or not they take up Marxist theory or Annales models, see theatre as a social art, sanctioned by a social contract and expressive of social values. This social condition applies to the avant-garde drama of revolt no less than to the patronized court masque. In describing this relationship, however, theatre historians often depend upon a few standard analogies about art "mirroring" or "reflecting" society, as if these metaphors provided aesthetic and social explanations. A theatre history textbook, which can go unnamed, classifies each of its thirteen periods (which are arrived at conventionally, if not arbitrarily) with such tags as "reflections of heaven and hell" (medieval theatre), "the gilded mirror" (eighteenth-century theatre), and "a mirror for the masses" (nineteenth-century theatre). Even if the intention of using such tropes is merely to provide convenient titles, the disturbing consequence, for writer and reader, is that these terms not only evade but close off serious thought about the possible relationships between society and theatre.

Not all period concepts carry political meaning, but many do. So, we need to attend to how we locate political meanings in these concepts. We have often assumed that the art of an era is somehow "representative" of either a political figure (e.g., Pericles, Nero, Charlemagne, Elizabeth, James I, Louis XIV, Stalin) or the socio-political order of the era (e.g., the age of reason, modernity, post-capitalism). Each era, whether tied to a great person or a socioeconomic order (or both), is thus seen as an arrangement of power, formulated as a Zeitgeist, a reigning idea, an ideological construct, a dominate discourse, or a discursive formation. Whatever the approach, the age is given a stable, singular identity (i.e., one unified Enlightenment rather than various, diverse enlightenments occurring over a number of decades and countries). By this means, we derive our political categories from our period concepts. Our normal methods of periodization, whatever the set of designations, tend toward homogeneity in the process of identification. If we are not careful, though, the period concepts provide a kind of allegory of totality: classicism, the medieval mind, the Victorian Age. Each of these controlling concepts becomes not simply a compressed formula-tion of a part for a whole (a metonymy), but also a reified structure of thought. Each concept then provides a way to fix in place what in fact is always changing, diverse, and complex.

In general, most theatre historians are quite aware of the problem of reductive explanations, as Oscar Brockett properly cautions: "Interpretation requires that evi-dence be placed in a relevant context. Unfortunately, it is no small task to decide upon the relevant context, for in any period it may include the literary and artistic movements of the time, the social, political, and philosophical interest of the day, the psychological states of the participants, and so on through a multitude of possible determinants."[32] Despite this recognition, Brockett's widely used textbook, *History of the Theatre* (now co-edited by Frank Hildy), struggles to place the extensive catalogue of information into "a relevant context" of "social, political, and philosophical" ideas and values of each era. Brockett attempted to meet this problem by organizing his periods into chapters that are divided into subsections on drama, theatre perform-ance, architecture, and sociopolitical institutions. This strategy of subdivision, while descriptively isolating potential social issues, fails to provide sufficient analysis of the issues, including the relationships among these four parts. And the chapters them-selves, with their various self-contained periods, add to this process of segmentation. Interpretation, hindered by the organizational compartments, becomes something done after the fact or not at all.

Consequently, Brockett's chronicle of information lays out the theatre for the reader as a register of names, places, titles, techniques, terminologies, and events. The substantial advantage of this method of presentation, as Brockett understood, is that it grants to teachers and students the freedom and responsibility to provide their own cultural, social, and political interpretations. The work is not done for them, nor imposed upon them. Teachers can make a virtue out of the absence of contextual interpretation. The disadvantage, of course, is that many classes remain committed to memorization of facts rather than cultural studies and social history. By contrast, *Theatre Histories: An Introduction* (2006), written by Philip Zarrelli, Carol Sorgenfrei, Bruce McConachie, and Gary Williams, attempts to integrate theatre and society by presenting case studies and by drawing attention to the multiple perspectives that historical inquiry brings to the study of theatre. The social and political conditions of theatre, including some philosophical ideas, are identified and, in several cases, explained. Yet even when textbook authors attempt to provide multiple perspectives on theatre history, they still tend to reproduce most of the standard period concepts. So, a seemingly fresh consideration of such topics as popular entertainment, the place of women in theatre, or colonialism and theatre in Asia, still gets presented within familiar – and often formulaic – period concepts. The defining modes of identification for the period concepts carry a register of assumptions that are not engaged directly (and in some cases they are just ignored).

Consequently, most histories of theatre fail not only to consider the reasons for establishing period concepts but also to provide the analysis of the relationship between social history and artistic practices. And the reasons for change are often ignored or reduced to formulaic terms and phrases (e.g., this or that "revolution" occurs). The conditions and causes of history happen in the silent gaps between the chapters. Art and society, introduced to one another by such vague notions as the "milieu" or the "mental climate," do little more than rub up against one another in a brief encounter. Of course, an introductory history book that attempts to record over 3,000 years of theatrical facts has little chance to provide an extensive social history, period by period. But even in most of the specialized theatre histories on particular periods, there is little or no contextual analysis. Usually the period concept is taken without question, as if it were an *a priori* principle for organization and interpretation.

Sadly, and perhaps paradoxically, we make less effort to explain our periods than did James Wright and A. W. Schlegel. Teachers and students still depend upon reductive models for organizing not only time but thought; the singular formulas stay in place: classical age, medieval age, nineteenth-century theatre, and so on. And the "folk" traditions of theatre in many parts of the world are organized into seemingly timeless categories of festive or ritual behavior, as if indigenous theatre in India, Korea, Ghana, Iran, Nigeria, Peru, and elsewhere have, in each case, abiding and singular identities. Folk culture manifests itself in performance practices that supposedly are stable and unchanging; they are, from our perspective, just short of being eternal. The performances, by staying the same, reconfirm a communal identity that is singular. Thus, instead of even depending upon reductive period concepts, as we do for Western theatre, we satisfy ourselves with amazingly simple-minded ideas about unchanging theatre, culture, and society in folk traditions. This allows us to develop sentimental, but actually condescending descriptions of pure, pre-modern versions of cultural performance that we attempt to admire and celebrate in a liberal-minded manner. In turn, we can condemn any and all manifestations of colonial, imperial, and modern development that have intervened and corrupted the integrity of the folk, usually "non-Western" traditions of performance.

Perhaps we need to reconsider Schlegel's basic assumptions, if not his specific procedures and conclusions, since in great measure those assumptions have become our presuppositions. Schlegel assumed that (1) theatre (which for him meant primarily drama) and society are somehow related to one another; (2) both theatre and society go through historical changes; (3) consequentially a "great diversity" occurs in theatre and society; (4) this diversity is not random but more or less systematic to the extent that from time to time (and for a duration) history develops and gets organized (somehow, by means of some principle or cause) into recognizable and definable orders of human culture and civilization; (5) such orders have some kind of unity or wholeness; and (6) these relationships, changes, and orders can be studied and understood by means of period concepts. Most theatre historians take these assumptions as given.

We thus have two ways of proceeding, two choices, in our method of periodization: to take up a period designation deductively as a received category or to develop the designation inductively in order to weave the pieces into a whole. (Needless to say, most historians, using both procedures, tack back and forth to accommodate the prevailing modes of periodization.) Problems attend both approaches. To work deductively often means nothing more than using standard period concepts unquestioningly as *a priori* identifications. Classical theatre, medieval theatre, Renaissance theatre, modern theatre – all are taken as abiding categories into which we pour the theatrical evidence. We are trained to demonstrate that everything fits into a whole, so we "prove" that the art of a period is all of a kind and that art and society correspond no matter what the period designation. Or if we are more theoretically minded, we may apply a social theory (e.g., about capitalism, colonialism, discursive formations) in order to demonstrate that art and the world not only correspond to one another but fit into the systematic divisions provided by the theory. A general process of identification and analysis, unfortunately, produces the logical default of *petitio principii* (or begging the question): our premises assume the question that we undertake to prove. Of course, this kind of circular reasoning is exactly the problem we are attempting to solve when we take up and impose a period concept onto historical events. My point here is not to belittle theory, for it offers the only way out of the current problems of periodization. But I am suggesting that historians might engage history better through a critique of their deductive categories, however arrived at. In this we might well benefit from combining insights and approaches of several theories, what Herbert Lindenberger calls a "multiperspectival method" in historical and literary investigation.[33] The aim is not to lock oneself into a single model, and to find ways to join, if not quite blend, empirical justification and deductive logic.[34]

From an inductive perspective, the gathering of facts, besides providing the descriptive foundation for historical study, should generate the initial basis for constructing period concepts. But this seldom happens. Historians usually assume that the descriptive information is self-explanatory. Especially in theatre history, there is a tendency to pile up information for information's sake: dates, names, anecdotes, productions, plays – all laid out, usually in chronological order, as if enough data, added together, produces a history of the stages of theatrical practices. More promising is the challenge to standard theatre history and its periods that comes from detailed study of facts, people, and conditions that have been ignored usually: as in the case of black theatre history, women's history, ethnic history. In these cases, at least potentially, the conventional assumptions about periods may be challenged by new information, derived from new or different perspectives.

One of the tasks of women's history is to call into question accepted schemes of peri-odization. To take the emancipation of women as a vantage point is to discover that events that further the historical development of men, liberating them from natural, social, or ideological constraints, have quite different, even opposite, effects upon women,
Joan Kelly, *Women, History, Theory* (1984: 19)

Although women's history does not necessarily require that we abandon the period concepts that designate key developments in history, it does put them in question. For this reason information gathered inductively about women's lives raises major questions, at least potentially, about social organization and change. In her influential essay, "Did Women Have a Renaissance?," Joan Kelly calls for a revisionist social theory:

> A theory of social change that incorporates the relation of the sexes [as a category of historical investigation] has to consider how general changes in production affect and shape production in the family and, thereby, the respective roles of men and women. And it has to consider as well the flow in the other direction: the impact of family life and the relation of the sexes upon psychic and social formations.[35]

The theatre offers a rich field for this investigation, for it has proved to be one of the places that the relation between the sexes is not only represented but transformed, especially since the seventeenth century in Europe, when women became prevalent as actresses (though less so as managers of theatre companies).

However we proceed, then, the purpose would be to situate the theatre as fully as possible in its cultural and social dimensions, to follow the traces of documentation both beyond the immediate theatrical occasion to the encompassing conditions and then back again, weaving the complex patterns of theatre and society into one unified fabric. Of course, this method of synthesis does not get us beyond our presuppositions about wholeness of periods, but it does provide a preliminary justification for reflecting upon their appropriateness.

Obviously, as Brockett says, the project of writing a comprehensive social history of the theatre is a difficult task. But how can periods be established and used for framing the social analysis if their definitive features are unquestioned? Whatever our method, we must recognize that the current evasive practice of making "time charts," with theatre events in one section and political events in another, tells us almost nothing. How does theatre follow the basic political history of civilization? What in fact is the relationship between the formal or stylistic qualities of theatre across the centuries and the political, social, and economic developments of history? We might at the very least consider the possibility that the standard periods in political history (dynasties, empires, monarchies) do not always determine (control, delimit) the periods of development in theatre history. Or if they do, we need to show how and why. What indeed are the necessary periods for the history of each of the arts – literary, visual, musical, or theatrical? Are they all subcategories of political divisions of history, developing and changing in the same way and at the same time? Not likely, since even from a formalist perspective the different arts present dissimilar patterns of development and style. And they change in different ways, at different times.

In undertaking this social analysis, two influential concepts are specifically relevant yet problematic: ideology and *mentalité* (or mentalities). Briefly, the primary question about ideology, within the context of periodization, is this: does each period have only one ideology? So asked, we might be cautious about sweeping claims. Whatever our social or theoretical approach, we tend to give the idea of ideology a singular, consuming definition, ignoring the sixteen possible ways of interpreting the concept that Terry Eagleton outlines in his book *Ideology: An Introduction* (1991). The appeal of a singular designation is hard to resist apparently, especially in service to our ideas of ideological coherence and control. Singular ideologies, paradigms, and *épistèmes* are our ideas of order. But is it not possible, even likely, that several aesthetic ideologies coexist during any one period, as Jean Duvignaud argues: "many aesthetic attitudes can exist together in the same period, even when the period officially calls for a single 'style' of expression"?[36] Or in Anthony Giddens' words: "Social systems should be regarded as widely variable in terms of the degree of 'systemness' they display and rarely have the sort of internal unity which may be found in physical and biological systems."[37] Society and art operate simultaneously at various levels of organization and direction. Diversity is common. Though cohesion and conflict are ordering principles, we need to describe and analyze the complexity of this order, without reaching for formulaic versions of ideological totality.

One wonders, for example, when we are going to stop assuming that the Greek classical theatre, the Renaissance drama, or the modernist theatre "reflected" or "expressed" one ideology? In the case of English theatre between the mid sixteenth century and the mid seventeenth century, we have developed period concepts tied to (1) the political reigns of monarchs; (2) the life of Shakespeare; (3) a shaping *Zeitgeist* (e.g., concepts of the Elizabethan world picture, humanism, and the Renaissance); (4) the emergence and organization of professional players in theatre companies (until performance was forbidden); (5) the system of patronage; or (6) the building, maintenance, and subsequent dismantling of theatres. Each of these organizing concepts carries a set of meanings and assumptions. And each excludes other possible meanings and assumptions. But none of them offers a unifying idea, ideology, or mentality. If, however, we sought to be true to the dominant ideology of the era – the religious ideas, institutions, and battles that determined much of European history from Luther and Calvin through the Thirty Years War – we would need to yoke theatrical developments to the religious struggles. But who believes that a singular, coherent, and totalizing period concept based upon religious ideology explains and determined the development of drama and theatre in Italy, Spain, England, Holland, Sweden, and the rest of Europe during the sixteenth and seventeenth centuries? We are wise to reject such reductive periodization, but what is the alternative?

Sometimes, the period concept that a scholar sets up can be quite misleading. For instance, E. K. Chambers titled his four-volume study of English theatre *The Elizabethan Stage* (1923). But despite this title, he did not limit himself to theatre during Elizabeth's reign (1558–1603). Instead, in various sections of the study he carried forward his analysis to 1616, when Shakespeare died. The genius and accomplishments of the playwright rather than the power and influence of the monarchy provided an organizing principle. Yet in other sections, neither Elizabeth nor Shakespeare held sway. Instead, the study expanded to record theatrical events and activities that stretched through the reigns of both James I (1603–1625) and Charles I (1625–1649). All in all, then, this archival study has proved to be a goldmine of information and documents, but it offers a muddled idea of periodization.

In recent years, believing that we have wisely overcome the limitations of not only the positivist ideas that guided Chambers but also such *Zeitgeist* concepts as the rebirth of humanism or the reign of the "Elizabethan World Picture" (which E. M. W. Tillyard, everyone's scapegoat these days, articulated), we have created a new period concept, the "early modern age." Obviously, a scholar who uses humanism as the organizing idea for the era will find quite different political meanings from someone who uses the idea of a material culture of commercial development. The one gives us a period called the "Renaissance," the other gives us the period of the "Early Modern Age." The one looks backward to the classical age, the other signals not only a break from the past but also a turn toward the capitalist future and our own age. Thus the idea of the "early modern age" has the suggestion of a dynamic process, working itself out through time (and culminating, for good or evil, in us). But in practice, as we see in the scholarship of new historicism and cultural materialism, this concept still tends to assume a singular, unified system of textual identity and meaning, a synchronic whole to be analyzed as if it were a masterpiece (written by the age itself). All too often, our period concepts lock us into yet another reductive version of comprehensive identity and ideology.

As for the concept of *mentalité*, developed and applied by certain French historians, including some in the Annales school, the same problem of single-minded explanation pertains. However defined – as collective representations, belief systems, a group mind, a mental collective, or discursive formations – the concept of *mentalité* is in essence a period concept that derives the meaning of the period from the systems of thought and attitudes in a culture. The idea of *mentalité* also bears comparison to ideology, in that both attempt to show how thought is circumscribed by certain values, assumptions, and prohibitions, but its own stamp of identity is more epistemological than economical. It is an attempt to define the commonality of thought and belief in a period – the implicit assumptions, attitudes, and categories of thought that shape everyday life. A period is held together by this collective understanding. We should be careful, however, not to personify this collectivity as a singular agent that determines historical processes. Arnold Hauser's warning against the idea of *Volksgeist* is relevant here: "the group mind, if this concept is to have any satisfactory scientific meaning, cannot designate an originating cause, but only a resultant, not a unitary and original agent, but merely the effect produced by a set of completed actions that on account of their mutual adaptation easily lead us to personify it."[38] A cultural mind or mentality is "posterior" not "prior" to the history it unifies. The categories of thought, instead of being transcendental, are localized in each period. As appealing as the idea of *mentalité* may be, especially when applied by a sophisticated historian such as Jacques Le Goff in his impressive studies of medieval society, we should keep in mind a basic warning by the medievalist Ad Putter: "There were many medieval minds and many mentalities: *mentalité* is not the sum of all of them."[39]

At least in principle (if not always in practice), the study of *mentalité*, as developed by the Annales school, is empirical in its emphasis upon documentation and quantification. Instead of deriving the period designation from the interpretation of major artistic works and philosophies (as is the common method in the history of ideas), a mentalities history gathers extensive information on everyday material life, which then can be analyzed – not just inductively but deductively in terms of the Annales geographic and economic models. Today computers provide organizational procedures for both the empirical data and the theoretical taxonomies. In theatre studies we have only begun to move in this direction, though the databases being prepared on both the eighteenth-century and the nineteenth-century London stage come closest to laying the foundation for a history of mentalities. We yet await the kind of comprehensive analysis that distinguishes the Annales school. No doubt there are arguments to be made against "the tyranny of quantification." And, just as importantly, we will need to investigate the taxonomies that generate the "evidence" of mental collectives for a period. But for now theatre history would welcome a good argument over cliometrics or demographics. Needless to say, we have yet to produce a theatre historian of the stature and influence of Emmanuel Le Roy Ladurie, Jacques Le Goff, or Fernand Braudel.

> Every mode of comprehension tends to generate its own form of discourse, including concepts which take their proper meaning from the way in which they function within the mode.
> Louis O. Mink, *Historical Understanding* (1987: 40)

In contrast to the social history of art, with its emphasis upon external determinates for cultural works and practices, formalist study seeks to define the internal attributes of the artwork. The defining traits of a play, performance, dance, painting, poem, novel, epic, sonata, sculpture, or building are located within both the individual formal system of each individual artistic work and the shared formal traits of groups of artistic works. Individual style and group style are used to define eras of the artistic heritage. In this manner, the period concepts supposedly reveal shared matters of tradition, convention, and typology in the art of the epoch. From a formalist perspective, the period concepts for art should be derived from the artworks of the era. The logic is clear and obvious. First of all, in order to define the artistic traits of any artwork, we must attend to the formal features of the art. And secondly, in order to trace the developmental history of the arts, we should trace how the forms change. Significant stylistic changes should signal new periods.

Although formalist analysis is quite often inductive (e.g., a careful semiotic description of the many communicative codes of a particular theatre performance), the difference between social and formal approaches to periodization should not be seen as a choice between deductive (analytical) and inductive (empirical) methods. Formalism can offer deductive systems, as we see in some aesthetic applications of structuralist theory to literature. Also, from Aristotle to the Chicago neo-Aristotelians, deductive analysis guided some historical attempts, as in the neoclassical theory, to apply Aristotle's theory of tragedy to the writing and study of plays. Besides genre theory, deductive models have operated in various arts, from the principle of harmony in music to the place of perspectivism as a guiding principle in painting for over 300 years. And ideas of natural representation, realism, and naturalism have provided deductive principles for style, often under the banner of mimesis and similitude. It is most difficult, though, to use a comprehensive idea, such as mimesis or perspectivism, to define a specific period. Likewise, an abiding genre concept such as tragedy or comedy offers little help in periodization.

The descriptive method of formalism may aspire to objective principles for generating the period concepts, but as Arnold Hauser notes, "periodization is not a matter of noting, but rather of interpreting facts."[40] The period concepts, as I will presently argue in an analysis of the idea of period style, are no less interpretive than the expansive models of social analysis. Nonetheless, formalism, in its descriptive mode, attempts to present what Heinrich Wölfflin, the nineteenth-century German art historian, called an "autonomous art history."[41] For formalist critics, painting, drama, poetry, music – all can be studied within aesthetic categories of style, motif, theme, pattern, and structure.

These categories, in turn, can serve as the basis of period concepts – not just for the formal study of events, as discussed in chapter 4 – because the transmission and modification of styles and conventions occur historically within the dialectical processes of tradition and innovation in the arts.

We can, for instance, identify and divide up the historical eras of classical music in terms of major composers. Accordingly, baroque music, classical music, romantic music, and modern music can be catalogued as the ages of Bach and Vivaldi, of Haydn, Mozart, and Beethoven, of Chopin, Schumann, and Mendelssohn, and of Schönberg and Stravinsky. In this way, formalist features and artistic figures contribute to our methods for identifying and framing the context for a large group of historical events. This practice has a formalist consistency, but quite often in periodization the aesthetic categories are intermixed with political categories (e.g., the romantic era followed by the Victorian era). And sometimes aesthetic and political categories are used interchangeably (e.g., the age of Shakespeare or the Elizabethan age).

We still must ask, though, how period and style are interrelated in a formalist analysis. How can we move from the individual style of any artist to the general stylistic features that define a period? In the case of drama, formalism throughout the ages has operated as a history or theory of genres – mainly, of course, because of the survival and influence of one formal text: Aristotle's *Poetics*. Especially from the Renaissance through the neoclassical age, the approach was prescriptive in its endeavors to establish abiding formal principles for tragedy and comedy, irrespective of historical conditions. Formal period concepts, to the extent that they could even be developed, were dependent upon and subservient to genre theory. But as the case of

Schlegel illustrates, the study of genres since the romantic age has been descriptive, in part because of a growing historical consciousness of cultural differences among nations and civilizations. In turn, the development of new period designations followed from the study of these formal, cultural differences.

In other words, in the nineteenth and twentieth centuries, formalism did not disappear when neoclassicist theory of drama gave way to descriptive historical study. In fact, if anything formalism was revitalized by its release from prescriptive norms. In great measure, of course, it drew upon and contributed to historical study. But because of its primary focus on internal attributes of art, formalism – from romantic theory and new criticism to structuralism and semiotics – has had a tendency to detach art from social history, either by studying individual plays and performances as self-contained, unified works or by developing formal models of dramatic genre. In these kinds of analysis, formalist interpretation often ignores history and period concepts. Thus, a semiotic analysis of the play and/or the production of *Hamlet* may tell us much about the visual codes of the dramatic text and performance, but it will likely say nothing about the historical origin and development of key stylistic features. Where did they come from? Why these instead of others? Without this larger analysis, any period concept becomes arbitrary. But we should not dismiss formalism simply because some practitioners choose to ignore historical factors in artistic style. Many other practitioners are committed to a formal analysis that not only draws upon the complex historical influences of conventions and traditions but also features the historical analysis of individual careers, the contributions of artistic movements, and the historical traits of audiences (e.g., reception theory that focuses on the horizon of expectation for theatre spectators).

To the extent that a formalist analysis of artworks attends to any historical information, the period concepts in drama, theatre, opera, and dance are derived usually in one of three ways: (1) they are developed out of direct, formal analysis of recurring as well as changing stylistic traits (e.g., the *opera seria*, followed by the classical opera; the naturalistic drama, followed by the expressionist drama in German theatre); (2) they are identified with a dominant artist of the time (e.g., the ages of Shakespeare, Goethe, Ibsen, Garrick, Irving); or (3) they are borrowed and adapted from another field of study, such as general history, literary history, art history, or musical history (e.g., medieval, Renaissance, baroque, romantic, Victorian, modernism). Only the first approach, the study of changing dramatic and theatrical styles, actually qualifies as a formalist method, though there are several problems with this method, as we will see.

In the second case, the romantic idea of the defining genius provides an axiological history, with period categories derived from evaluative judgements, usually canonical. And in the third case, the periods are either received or imposed categories. In the one case, they are taken up as if the definitions and boundaries are well established (and, it is assumed, the artistic conventions are shared by all artworks within a period); in the other case, they are transferred purposefully from another field (often derived from literature and art history). For example, theatre historians often attempt to transfer definitive traits of baroque painting and architecture to baroque scene design, acting, opera, and even singing style in the seventeenth-century theatre and opera).[42] Or in the study of literature, as practiced in universities (and packaged in textbooks by several publishers), poetry, fiction, and drama are normally studied and classified together in a standard set of periods – classical, medieval, Renaissance, romantic, modern – despite the fact that these concepts fail to provide a single, viable period style for the variety of works being studied in each era. The period concepts are more appropriate as shorthand designations for chronology than as measures of stylistic features that an era of writers shared and maintained.

In the formalist analysis of drama, social history is not necessarily lost sight of, for it may provide the subject matter of the plays. Thus, Thomas Dekker's *The Shoemaker's Holiday* refers to historical subjects and events of Dekker's time, from cobblers and merchants to the Lord Mayor. But even though contemporary people, events, and conditions are evoked, they offer little help in the construction of a period concept in terms of formal style. It is possible to relate Dekker's play to a genre type called "city comedy" in the London theatres, but here too subject matter as much as genre traits provides the designation. Consequently, for many formalist critics social history often remains secondary, serving as little more than background material. Although it may help to explain the subject matter (and perhaps some character types), it does not provide a method for describing the definitive formal traits, the ones that supposedly will point to a period concept.

As for the formal traits, they may help to explain the typology of a play but they may also point to other historical times and places. For instance, Shakespeare's *The Comedy of Errors* was likely written and performed in the 1590s, a time that is often called Elizabethan, a period concept transferred from political history. It is quite possible – and perhaps informative – to place the play in the context of the political (or social, economic) conditions, but formal analysis gains little or nothing from this method of identification. Instead, formal analysis seeks to identify the stylistic features that could serve as a period style. Thus, we might attempt to locate *The Comedy of Errors* in the heritage of Roman comedy, a historical designation tied to genre style. Shakespeare has clearly drawn upon this artistic heritage. Tradition, by means of a genre category, provides a formal method, but this period concept is, at best, an overly broad designation. It may be a convenient tag, but it is not a definitive historical marker of style. Because this tradition stretches beyond the borders of an artist's own time and place, it apparently creates a logical contradiction: the period style that is supposed to distinguish Shakespeare's age is derived from formal traits of a distant era (i.e., the time of Plautus). The formal features of the comic genre are too basic (e.g., types of characters, plot techniques) for defining a specific period style for Shakespeare's play.

Instead of a period style, what we discover in *The Comedy of Errors* is basically a matter of individual style in relation to the artistic heritage – what T. S. Eliot called tradition and the individual talent. The history that matters, in this sense, is the art tradition itself which the artist assimilates, modifies, or rejects. Accordingly, we are concerned with how Shakespeare drew upon yet transformed the historical heritage into a separate identity of aesthetic value and meaning, not how his art, conditioned supposedly by genre history, generated a period style. Formalist analysis can tell us much about individual works and theatrical events; this is readily apparent in performance analysis and theatre semiotics today. But we still must wonder how formalist methods will deliver the evasive idea of a period style.

The challenge, and difficulty, of formal analysis of artworks is to identify distinctive features that allow us to locate the style of a group of works within a time period. We attempt to place the works in relation to one another, the decisive issue being their shared formal attributes. If these attributes are to generate a period concept, it needs to be achieved through close analysis of recurring formal traits that add up to distinct "period style." The difficulty remains: how do we get from individual style, which often posits unique or definitive features of one artist (or even one artwork), to a group or period style, which posits a set of shared, recurring features that connect a number of artists and artworks? And then, to complete the circle, how can various artistic works, with their various features, be given a single identity, which becomes for the historian a period style? Even the task of identifying a single formal style for some major artists is daunting (e.g., the definitive, single style of Shakespeare, Goethe, Ibsen, or Strindberg). If each of these artists generates several artistic styles in a lifetime, how can we claim that a collective period style will contain each of them and the other artists of their epoch?

How, then, is it possible that formal analysis could provide a series of period designations? In the study of theatre history itself, formalist analysis typically considers such matters as scenic space, theatre buildings, production modes, scenic and costume patterns, and acting techniques. Often such analysis is limited to a particular time and place (e.g., classical theatre, medieval mystery plays and productions, Victorian music halls). A few scholars have attempted to describe the historical development of theatrical styles and forms across the centuries and cultures (e.g., Marvin Carlson in *Places of Performance*).

Only a few scholars, however, have used formal categories to define and divide up the developmental stages of theatre across the centuries and throughout the world. In *The Seven Ages of Theatre* (1961) Richard Southern took on this formidable task. Though his study is not without problems, it offers a valuable case study of formal analysis in theatre history. For this reason, along with the clarity of his definitions, Southern warrants our consideration. He sets as his objective "an account of the development of *forms* which theatre has taken" throughout human society.[43] For his purposes Southern addresses the concept of periodization by redefining (if not dismissing) it. His seven ages are, as he argues, "*phases* rather than dated periods, for the simple reason that the development of the theatre seems to happen by phases and not by dates." By this questionable formulation he suggests that theatre should be understood by typology not chronology. Though he acknowledges that theatre responds to "the changing course of its civilization,"[44] he makes little connection between art and social history, except for claiming, somewhat curiously, that the rise of the professional actor (his third phase) can be dated precisely in 1576, when James Burbage built The Theatre in London.

The strength of Southern's approach, with its emphasis upon large-scale formal traits of the theatrical arts such as "the costumed player" or "stage illusionism," is that, uninhibited by chronology, political orders, or national lines, he attempts to demonstrate how and why artistic forms and formal systems are (or should be) central to our understanding and appreciation of the history of theatre throughout the world. His mission is to offer a historical perspective not tied to or limited by matters of chronology, national identities, languages, playwrights, and genres – the normal categories that guide most theatre books. By means of formal attributes, Southern is able to connect medieval Christian performances to Tibetan festival theatre, the Elizabethan stage to the Japanese Noh, the continental opera theatre to the Kabuki. The principle of resemblance, not diversity, organizes the history of theatre, which is assimilated into a few formal categories.

The disadvantage, of course, is that these formal categories fail to describe not only the individual style of particular plays, performances, and players within each phase or typology but also the various modifications of stylistic features within each age and from age to age. We cannot describe the specific features of *Hamlet* or *As You Like It*; nor can we compare and contrast the various ways that playwrights within the Elizabethan age wrote tragedies and comedies. Likewise, all Elizabethan players are mirror images of one another, as are all of the theatre buildings. Within each of these typologies no distinctions can be made. Also, Southern purposefully ignores matters of politics, economics, language, geography, or chronology. This strategy disappoints or offends many scholars (e.g., those who see themselves as cultural or social historians). But a critique of him on this basis is unfair, for he quite clearly wants to show that a formal history of theatre can teach us much about theatre. And he demonstrates that formal study need not be tied to the Aristotelian heritage of literary genre. The visual rather than verbal elements of theatre deserve our attention. The actor's relationship with the audience, established by the uses of the body, mask, costume, movement, scenic spectacle, and architectural space, is as significant as the playwright's mastery of plot. In this move Southern frees the study of theatre history from the history of plays.

Still, we pay a significant price for this formal model of theatre history. Without chronological development, the idea of period styles loses its purchase on us. Not surprisingly, then, social historians reject this kind of formalism (and they often expand their rejection to all types of formal analysis). From a social historian's viewpoint, the study of formal typologies displaces not only a chronology of names, dates, and events but also the history of the political, social, and economic forces that shape the theatre. These forces and figures are seemingly insignificant in the making of art, as they recede into the shadows of history. Consequently, in formalist studies the key matters of artistic identity, order, and change are problems in a poetics rather than a history of art. Period styles (or artistic "phases") become the categorical imperative of formalist history. Similar formal traits can be aligned between theatre practices around the world, but the reasons for these similarities are not examined and explained. Unfortunately, the crucial questions about the causes for change are ignored or displaced.

This criticism of formalist analysis is warranted, but we should not lose sight of a crucial formal truth: certain forms or types of art have a history that cannot be limited to the specific social orders of an epoch. Some forms carry across periods and cultures (e.g., the genre of comedy, the masked actor). In some cases, a form or mode can be given specific historical and social origins, as with tragedy or opera, but it transcends those conditions. As even the cultural materialist critic Raymond Williams acknowledges, a genre such as comedy or tragedy "has proved capable of virtually indefinite reproduction in many different social orders."[45] In these cases, therefore, the intrinsic form cannot provide a period designation. But neither can social history. Some forms resist, modify, and limit the control of social conditions, political systems, and ideology. Hence art cannot be contained by or reducible to the ideas of social history – Marxist, Annales, or whatever. Consequently, a distinction needs to be made between certain abiding, if not universal, forms, genres, and modes (e.g., tragedy, comedy, opera) and the different types of distinct manifestations of them that occur in certain periods, however defined (e.g., bourgeois tragedy, comedy of manners, *opera seria*). Within these types, a formal analysis can reveal traits that escape the interpretive power of social history. Such analysis does not rule out the importance of social conditions, but it does sanction certain formal modes of analysis.

> . . . ages [of artistic styles] are simply the names of the influential innovations which have occurred constantly in the history of the arts. Their spirit is thus of no explanatory value whatsoever and its use is misleading both as to what actually took place in a given age and as to the way in which works of art are produced. Let us repeat that we are not arguing that no artists prefer to conform to tradition than to work on their own. Schools of artists, like everyone else, have to face problems which may arise from a variety of sources: philosophic, religious, social, political, economic, and mixtures of them all. There will be conflict in the manner in which such problems are solved. Thus though the problems may be common, the solutions may very well be individual. Variety within an age then is to be thought of as just as normal as uniformity.
>
> George Boas, "Historical Periods" (1953: 254)

In order to proceed in our investigation of the potential yoking of the two concepts of style and period, we need to distinguish the concept of style from the related but not interchangeable ideas of school, art movement, and period. An individual might possess a style that engenders or defines a school; the school may designate itself or become designated by critics as an art movement; a movement might, in turn, be proclaimed as having a collective style and purpose; and subsequently – usually retrospectively – that style might even come to be seen as typifying a period. But this sequence is not necessarily a logical sequence either formally or historically. A period can contain many styles. A style can exist without becoming part of a movement. A movement may be important and yet not produce a definitive period style. Thus, though the phrase *period style* yokes two concepts, they are joined as a proposition, not as a preordained unity. In this manner, one idea (period) is given a possible explanation in terms of the other idea (style), but the argument still has to be made.

Whatever the uncertainties in joining the terms *style* and *period*, at least they are general concepts (if not neutral or objective ones) that can be applied across the historical record. We can use the idea of style to describe acting, drama, scene design, architecture, or costume from any period. But with the terms *school* and *movement* more care is required, for they have specific historical meanings that do not apply equally or even appropriately across all history. Although we might define Futurism or Expressionism as artistic movements that contributed to (influenced, defined) a modern period style, it can be quite misleading to talk of movements in medieval drama or Renaissance acting troupes. Even to apply our modern idea of an art movement (which usually suggests manifestoes, programs, innovations, rebellions) to the eighteenth-century theatre raises serious problems in description and explanation.

Quite obviously we need to clarify our definitions of style. As used by cultural historians, the concept of style has had several different meanings: individual expression, national character, inherent form, material quality, a viewer's perception, an ideal spirit with teleological functions, a product of society, an ideology. At the very least we might specify which meaning we are using when we talk about period style. Some meanings are mutually exclusive.

Assuming some clarity of definition – and, at least provisionally, setting aside the problems of separating theatre periods from social history (or aesthetic culture from social culture) – can we make a convincing case for unified period styles? Do playwriting, acting, costuming, stage design, and kinds of performance spaces all follow the same unified historical sequence? Or do they generate a series of overlapping and even contrasting stylistic periods? Does one aspect of the theatre, such as acting, playwriting, or audience taste, lead or control the period styles of the other aspects? Always? In different ways at different times? In different ways during the same period? Do advances or changes in one aspect necessarily signal new period styles in the others? Or if they are sometimes out of sequence with one another, what causes this, since we tend to describe theatre as a collective art?

If formalism can distinguish period styles and their expressive transformations (which possibly signal and symbolize the changing cultural, intellectual, and social conditions), it should be able to offer some answers to these questions, and thus begin to identify, era by era, the defining traits of the several different styles that possibly exist in complex interrelation. Unfortunately, most formalist historians and critics do not ask these questions; instead, operating on the assumption that each period has its defining style (Roman, baroque, romantic, symbolist), they arrive at a conclusion dictated by their categorical imperatives. Thus, their often substantial achievements in identifying and analyzing specific styles are compromised by the general order that supposedly defines, contains, and explains the formal features.

This is not to say that the concept of period style is without value, especially in the practical considerations of production work. Designers, actors, and directors all benefit from having an understanding of the particular aspects of style that operate in a comedy by Molière, a tragedy by Aeschylus, a melodrama by Boucicault, a tragicomedy by Chekhov. Moreover, not only the specific play but its historical culture may suggest many aspects of style: the cut of a costume, the manner of sitting, the design of a chair, the shape of a gesture, the mode of speaking. For these reasons theatre people in production will continue to use the concept of period styles. But for this very reason the theatre historian needs to question carefully and rigorously the assumptions that underlie the designations of these styles.

Of course, in many cases the critical assumptions and the methodologies for studying period styles in theatre have derived from art history. Leading art historians such as Wölfflin, Warburg, Panofsky, and Gombrich have developed theories and practices for the study of styles that have been carried over into all cultural studies. Some of the formal terminology and the period concepts have seemed especially relevant to theatre studies, since theatre is a visual as well as a literary art.

Certain methodological similarities between theatre and art history should not, however, lead us to believe that art and theatre follow the same developmental laws, rules, conventions, or sequences. Nor should we assume that a key term in art history accurately describes style in the theatre. For example, baroque style in painting is defined, following Wölfflin, as having the four general traits of *painterliness, grandeur, massiveness,* and *movement.*[46] He derived these features from his careful analysis of many paintings in the era (which logically, then, was the baroque era). Art works and the era mirrored one another. Wölfflin argued that a law of stylistic development determined the artistic spirit of an age, and that artists and an age established parallel identities. He argued that styles alternated in a cyclical pattern, with *classical* and *baroque* serving as the models. As Herbert Read explains, Wölfflin "formulated five pairs of contrary concepts – the opposite poles, as it were, between which the artistic spirit oscillates: (1) from *linear* to *painterly;* (2) from *plane* to *recession;* (3) from *closed form* to *open form;* (4) from *multiplicity* to *unity;* (5) from *absolute clarity* to *relative clarity* of the subject."[47] Art history, refining its methods in this empirical manner, was credited with developing a scientific discipline of description and analysis. The history of Western art could be studied, then, according to these fundamental traits of formal style.

Understandably, theatre historians have been tempted to apply these formal definitions to the styles of scene painting (though the cyclical model, as I will note presently, has proved problematic). It is quite possible to find features of Wölfflin's "baroque" style in the scenic representations done by the Bibiena family. We also, apparently, can apply this period style to costume and acting in many different countries over a number of decades. But what if, instead of following Wölfflin, we turn to Werner Weisbach, who identified four somewhat different attributes of the baroque: *formal* (tense, restless, dynamic, polychromatic), *political* (absolutism), *religious* (Counter-Reformation), and *sociological* (first phase of capitalism)?[48] What happens to the concept of period style when it is grounded this way in social conditions? Can a country, such as England, which is not directly under the influence of either absolutism or the Counter-Reformation, still produce baroque art? How so, if these formal attributes are necessary? How should we explain the operas of Henry Purcell? No doubt, there is a complex relationship between some styles in painting and theatre arts. And no doubt some stylistic features in the arts move across national borders (but they often are modified and transformed). But do these similarities in some aspects of the visual and theatrical arts justify the use of period categories based upon one common designation? Are the various arts yoked together, period by period, nation by nation, style by style?

Not surprisingly, when borrowing from art history, we find it easier to use concepts of period style that are purely formalistic. The slide from one field of study to another is tempting. Such slippage, however, is exactly the problem, as the art historian Svetlana Alpers warns:

> Style, as engaged in the study of art, has always had a radically historical bias. It is this that has always impressed, and I think had such an unfortunate effect on, the neighboring humanistic disciplines. Musicologists, literary scholars, and historians following the example set by art historians have felt that the nomination of period styles and sub-styles is a more honorific (because it is scientific) activity than the critical appreciation of and interpretation of individual works. The serious implications of this enterprise are hardly suggested by the endless art historical articles and books which multiply stylistic terms – we have baroque, early, high, and late, and then early, high, and late baroque realism – in order to denote and group art objects. In the handbooks of art history today the denotative stylistic terms, far from admitting to an historical and aesthetic bias, are treated as attributes of the works or groups of works. Thus it is characteristic in art historical discourse to move from the locating of a work in a period style to the analysis of its stylistic (for which read "formal") components and its iconography (for which read loosely "content" or "meaning"). Categories are developed in the interest of externality and objectivity, freeing the observer from any responsibility for them. These presumably objective categories of large historical classifications are then (silently) treated as aesthetic properties of each object. Style, designated by the art historian, is treated as if it were possessed by each object. Thus presumably denotative terms are made to serve as explanations, are pursued ("In what respects is Rembrandt's *Blinding of Samson* baroque?") as leading to the proper interpretation of images.[49]

These tautological procedures are far too prevalent in theatre history. The terms for period style flow into our discipline, and we take them up as objective, general terms that both name and explain theatre styles (in a self-interpretive, that is circular, manner). Ironically, though we intend to situate styles in a historical context of formal traits, we instead dissolve history into an ideal system of formal categories. Our infatuation with formalism turns us away from history. Alastair Fowler provides a needed warning: "the notion of a universally valid systematic correspondence between the arts must be regarded as a chimera. Real correspondences exist and may be worth analyzing. But they change with time, and change so fundamentally as to make diachronic investigation a necessary preliminary to discussing them, if full rigor of method is to be achieved."[50]

Beyond this major problem of establishing and using period styles, there is a related historical procedure of periodization in art history that theatre studies might be wise to resist: the making of dualistic systems for identifying and differentiating styles, motifs, and forms. A common, seductive technique in historical analysis is to establish *a priori* polarities: classical and baroque, idealistic and realistic, naïve and sentimental,

Apollonian and Dionysian, objective and subjective, active and reactive, subordination and coordination, harmonious and disharmonious, Eros and Thanatos, animate and inanimate, optical and tactile, closed and open, additive and integrative, abstraction and empathy, tectonic and atectonic.[51] The spirit of Hegelian dialectic looms over art history, and beyond Hegel a pervasive dualism of aligned oppositions reigns in the aesthetic heritage. This dualism is transmitted in the many guises of the *beautiful* and the *sublime*, as articulated in eighteenth-century aesthetic theory. And it seductively manifests itself in various theories of stylistic change in the arts, such as Roman Jacobson's idea that style in the literary arts swings between the metaphoric and metonymic poles of language.

These dualistic terms can be helpful in analyzing basic contrasts and oppositions that we can discover within and between specific works and styles. They also can help to reveal contradictions, reversals, and paradoxes, especially if one brings to them a sense of ironic understanding. But they have proved much less viable in defining the sequence of cultural periods. For this reason, most art historians have rejected Wölfflin's theory that art history can be reduced to a series of cyclical alternations between classic and baroque styles, just as most historians have rejected dualistic theories of general history. It is true that for well over a century German theorists, from Schiller forward, were especially attracted to neat polarities (to such an extent that a rather comprehensive cultural history of German aesthetic philosophy could be written on the series of different dualistic theories put forward in the eighteenth, nineteenth, and twentieth centuries). And even today some French theorists, especially certain structuralists, have carried forward this love affair of binaries. But history, whatever its measure of periodicity, is surely more than an unending process of pendulum swings between two formal or thematic traits. And likewise, theatre is more than the manifestations of only two styles, alternating in periodic sequence. Even Gombrich's theory of classical *norm* and *variation* settles too neatly into yet one more dualistic pattern. Likewise, the opposition between realism and symbolism comes too easily to theatre historians (especially in their formulations of two types of modernist drama and scenic design). Although it is tempting to organize the complex (and sometimes chaotic) developments of history with dualistic patterns, we need to resist the seductive appeal of these conceptual categories. At their worst they turn history into a reductive melodrama of formulaic oppositions. And even when applied with sophistication, the polarities still provide, at best, a partial and simplified explanation of human behavior.

Social historians are especially critical of formalist history just because of this tendency to set up overly neat categories of formal traits. But of course reductionism, in the name of system building, is a problem that attends both formalist and social histories of art. From the formalist perspective, social history is reductionist when it too readily succumbs to deterministic imperatives that place art under grand systems and controlling ideologies. Most art historians, even Wölfflin, grant art a contextual cultural history. Yet as Wölfflin argues (in a remark that expresses the widespread sentiments of many theatre historians) historical explanations that depend fully on extrinsic social forces as the cause and meaning of art "take us only so far – as far, one might say, as the point at which art begins."[52] A similar point was made more recently by Michael Podro when he stated that art is "both context-bound and yet irreducible to its contextual conditions."[53] Podro may be eliding the issue but at least he reminds us that the various arts and crafts have meanings and values for us beyond the historical conditions of their social modes of production. E. H. Gombrich expresses much the same viewpoint in his commentary on cultural history: "It is one thing to see the interconnectedness of things, another to postulate that all aspects of a culture can be traced back to one key cause of which they are the manifestations."[54] Formalist critiques of such ideas as Zeitgeist or the ideology of a period are prudent reminders against formulaic thinking. Art is not fully comprehended and contained by any one system that would place and explain it, especially a singular period concept. Still, when Gombrich suggests that we abandon the idea of periods and instead study movements and individual artworks, he merely avoids rather than solves a problem.[55]

The relationships between individual styles and a period designation need to be charted carefully so that the part is not mistaken for the whole. Equally important, the many parts need to be identified. To this aim, semiotic analysis of drama and theatre has shown promise because it recognizes the complexity of textual and performance codes.[56] But whether a "morphology" or "grammar" of styles can be spelled out sufficiently to establish a period "discourse" is open to serious question. From semiotics to iconology to structuralism, the attempts to establish methods (and jargons) for describing cultural practices in historic terms have been most successful when honoring the rich multiplicity of theatre communication and least effective when positing a single system.

The concept of period style is inherently paradoxical because it suggests to us both conventional practices and innovative achievements. By definition, a period style for any particular time and place expresses and embodies the standard practices, the rules, the conventions, the common and "natural" ways of representation. In this sense, a period style is familiar and widespread. Otherwise, how could we call it the style of the period? But since we are interested as historians and critics in not only individual styles but also how styles change, we must pay attention to the uncommon and innovative styles in a period, the ones that define a new practice, and perhaps a new period. Unavoidably, we are drawn to major artists and key artistic achievements to distinguish a period, but in many ways these artists and artworks are exceptional instead of standard and common. Shakespeare, Mozart, and Dickens are not the conventional playwrights, composers, and novelists of their eras. We face an unavoidable contradiction, then, when the best or most innovative art (however we might determine such qualities) becomes the norm. Only when we lack most or all of the normal or conventional works, as is the case, in great measure, with classical Greek drama, can we justify the use of great works as a period style.

In our search for period styles, we are caught in a paradox that requires us to construct each style out of what is common and uncommon, what is continuous and discontinuous. Hence, the more neatly we identify a general style as an age's presupposition, the more we fail to explain how period styles come into being, develop, and change. But the more we note the exceptions, the less we are able to identify that common thing called a period style. Our problem, in the opinion of Svetlana Alpers is this: "How, without our notion of style, do we get from a frankly external system of style classification to a discourse that posits art objects possessing stylistic features and validates the originator of those features?"[57] Our definitions of period style are based upon the idea of the persistence of artistic traits, techniques, practices, and purposes, but that idea is maintained categorically in opposition to the stylistic ideas of inventiveness, uniqueness, and change.

Moreover, as George Kubler argues, the concept of style, which gets applied to both visual and temporal arts, may indeed be inappropriate for describing a duration (including historical periods): "no style can entirely fill any period, nor can it resist the alteration of time. Thus, whether we consider duration or style, the same conclusion emerges: that the presence of change precludes assumptions about enduring constancy."[58] At least as a postulate, this statement, which challenges our formal assumptions about period styles, places us in an untenable position. In order to posit a period style we are forced to ignore duration, change, and variety. Moreover, in our attempt to discover the shared and common features of all works within a period, we are reduced to honoring what is commonplace, thereby ignoring the fact that all stylistic analysis requires a recognition of what is distinct in any artist's style.

Underlying all of these concerns about the nature of period styles is, I think, an even more basic problem. *Where in fact is style located*: (1) in the artist's intentions, aims, or purposes; (2) in the referential or representative "world" that the artwork places before us; (3) in the formal codes of the art object itself; (4) in the action or processes of making (such as we get when a play is realized as a performance); (5) in the audience's attitudes, assumptions, values, and interpretive strategies; (6) in the era's social, economic, and political practices and conditions; (7) in the era's values, attitudes, and general mentality or set of mentalities; (8) in the available expressive codes and discourses of the time that shape (limit, determine) how the style is both realized, perceived, and described; or, (9) in the historian's own point of view, that is, the available discourses and discursive formations of subsequent times that give order and meaning to the past? Each of these possible locations would seem to contribute to our understanding of the styles of past artworks, and yet most attempts to describe and interpret period styles has been focused on – limited to – the formal codes. If style is anything more than the formal attributes – those qualities that supposedly are intrinsic to an autonomous artwork – then we must say that most attempts to discover the period style of artworks have been misdirected. And if misdirected, then the period designations derived from formal analysis are suspect, if not completely useless. Perhaps we need a radically new map to get from style to period.

All divisions are arbitrary.
    Luigi Pirandello, *On Humor* (1974: 13)

Formalist or social history – which route should we follow in establishing periods in theatre history? The obvious solution that occurs to many cultural historians, including theatre historians, is to declare this a false dilemma. Consistency is the hobgoblin of small minds. Instead of seeking one, systematic model, we opt for pragmatism: a functional combination of methods. But how does this commonsense approach actually work in theatre history? If we look at some of the representative histories of theatre in English today, the ones used in the classroom, we find an amazing diversity of period designations. For instance, one popular history divides theatre into nineteen sections under period titles such as Roman theatre and drama, English theatre from the Middle Ages to 1642, the Italian Renaissance, theatre and drama since 1960. But do these nineteen historical periods provide a clearer and more accurate notion of theatrical eras than the five periodic sections of another popular theatre history or the twelve, sixteen, or thirty-three of other standard books?

From the viewpoint of periodization, should Italian theatre of the eighteenth century be joined to or separated from French theatre of the same century? One book joins them; another separates them. Likewise, one historian separates the *commedia dell'arte* from the "theatres of renascence Italy"; another historian joins them. How significant are these differences and how do they effect the description and analysis of theatre history? Does it matter, for instance, if Russian theatre of the nineteenth century is set off from or joined to the theatre of Western Europe? Not at all, it would seem, for one book joins what the other separates. Whatever the approach, the number and types of period categories explain little, one way or the other.

Moreover, most of the standard theatre history books, whether they present twelve, nineteen, or thirty-three periods, shift from social to political to formal to chrono-logical classifications as if no problem attends these taxonomic shifts. It makes no difference, seemingly, if a period is defined as a nation, a century, a monarch's reign, an art movement, or even a genre. From book to book, chapter to chapter, and even sentence to sentence, the period concepts and stylistic features vary wildly. Basically we must conclude that a period and a book chapter come to much the same thing – a convenient but finally arbitrary way to package information. One solution, evident in a recent history of western theatre, is to return to the Renaissance model of only three basic periods: classical, medieval, and modern (with a "contemporary age" to close the book). But this retreat into three ages (and the present) – justified by an appeal to Thomas Kuhn's theory of paradigms but actually closer to a vague idea of Zeitgeist – reduces both the complexity of history and the diversity of theatrical activity to vague formulas. Simple classifications masquerade as grand totalities.

Looking at the period categories of most of these standard textbooks, I am reminded of the delightfully bizarre classification system that Michel Foucault borrows from the Argentinean writer Jorge Luis Borges, who in turn attributes the system to a Chinese encyclopedia. Whatever its source, the taxonomy, which appears in Borges' *Other Inquisitions*, distinguishes groups of animals:

> (a) belonging to the Emperor, (b) embalmed, (c) tame, (d) sucking pigs, (e) sirens, (f) fabulous, (g) stray dogs, (h) included in the present classification, (i) frenzied, (j) innumerable, (k) drawn with a very fine camelhair brush, (l) et cetera, (m) having just broken the water pitcher, (n) that from a long way off look like flies.[59]

Obviously delighted, Foucault comments: "In the wonderment of this taxonomy, the thing we apprehend in one great leap, the thing that, by means of this fable, is demonstrated as the exotic charm of another system of thought, is the limitation of our own, the stark impossibility of thinking *that*."[60] Well, maybe. If Foucault had considered the methods of periodization in theatre history, he quite likely would have experienced a similar wonderment. For we have created, without apparent concern for logical contradictions, a collective taxonomy for periods and subperiods that in its categorical disorder challenges the one Borges offers.

Here, for illustration, are some of the current designations we use for defining the periods of theatre history: (1) *political empires and dynasties*: Egyptian, Athenian, Hellenistic, Roman, Holy Roman, Hapsburg, Georgian, Czarist, communist; (2) *monarchies*: Elizabethan, the court theatre of Louis XIV, Restoration; Victorian, Edwardian; (3) *traditional eras*: classical, medieval, Renaissance, enlightenment, modern; (4) *normative attributes*: primitive, ceremonial, festival, mannerist, neo-classical, traditional, amateur, professional, bourgeois, working class, popular; (5) *nationalities*: French, English, Irish, Russian, American; (6) *pan-nationalism*: Soviet, Asian, Scandinavian, German, eastern European, Malaysian, African; (7) *linguistics*: Chinese, Latin, German, Spanish, Turkish, Japanese; (8) *religion*: Hindu, Dionysian, Christian, Protestant, sacred, secular; (9) *philosophical schools, systems or perspectives*: Stoicism, Scholasticism, humanism, rationalism, individualism, relativism, existentialism, absurdism; (10) *chronology*: pre-Greek theatre, *quattrocento*, the seventeenth century, the 1890s, the theatre between the wars; (11) *institutions (religious, political, social, or economic)*: church, feudalism, court societies, capitalism, communism; (12) *modes of institutional support*: clerical, artisanal, municipal, governmental, patronal, commercial; (13) *organizational formations*: bardic, guild, academies, professional societies, professional unions, artistic movements, artistic factions; (14) *art and literary movements*: romanticism, naturalism, avant-gardism, expressionism, modernism, postmodernism; (15) *audience types*: aristocratic, communal, folk, bourgeois, popular, elite; (16) *performance modes and styles*: Atticism, Noh, Kubuki, baroque, realism, theatricalism, illusionism, anti-illusionism; (17) *kinds of architectural spaces*: ceremonial center, free-standing altar, amphitheatre, temple, guild and manor hall, courtyard, unroofed building, roofed building, boxed playhouse, fan-shaped auditorium, performance hall; (18) *kinds of stage spaces*: open, enclosed, facade, picture-frame, round, thrust, found; (19) *famous people*: Aeschylus, Shakespeare, Garrick, Kean, Ibsen, Bernhardt, Barrault; (20) *modes of dramatic representation*: mythic, ritualistic, historical, contemporary; (21) *forms of drama*: classical tragedy, Roman tragedy, Renaissance tragedy, neoclassical tragedy, opera, bourgeois tragedy, naturalistic tragedy, tragicomedy; (22) *styles of visual art and architecture*: classical, baroque, mannerist, rococo, romantic, realistic, modernist, postmodernist.

These categorical riches are no doubt a measure of the complexity of the field of theatre history; they are also, when used in our methods of periodization, a measure of the confusion in the field. This confusion mirrors the idea of order and representation that guided – or failed to guide – the grotesque assortment of forms that Giovanni Rucellai imposed upon the shaped shrubs in his sixteenth-century Villa di

Quaracchi. The shrubs attained, as E. H. Gombrich notes, a perfect "freedom from logical constraints." They were cut to represent "ships, galleys, temples, columns and pillars ... giants, men and women, heraldic beasts with the standard of the city, monkeys, dragons, centaurs, camels, diamonds, little spirits with bows and arrows, cups, horses, donkeys, cattle, dogs, stags and birds, bears and wild boars, dolphins, jousting knights, archers, harpies, philosophers, the Pope, cardinals, Cicero, and more such things."[61] Neither the Argentinean Borges nor the Chinese encyclopedist has anything on the Italian gardener. Yet theatre historians, in our collective wisdom, have devised an even more bizarre system of representation and knowledge.

> We cannot do without the names of periods, because they have become filled with meaning that is valuable to us, even though every attempt to motivate their validity only demonstrates the contrary.
> Johan Huizinga, "The Task of Cultural History," in *Men and Ideas* (1960: 69)

Of course, it is quite possible for a historian, following a specific model of periodization, to chart and analyze the history of theatre architecture; then, with a different model of periodization, to examine the history of audience types. In each case, a consistent period category could be maintained for the subject matter. We may disagree on the value of the system, but at least the interpretive model would be clear. But can one period category – say, audience types – be successfully used to establish the periods for a different category – say, kinds of architectural space? In this case, which is cause and which is effect? Or should both audiences and architecture be subsumed under another period category? If so, which one or ones? Is a hierarchy possible? And upon what principle of ordering? For example, if we select political dynasties as the basis for establishing the periodization of theatre, must we then claim that changes in dramatic genres, staging, and normative attributes are not only subsumed under but derived from developments in political history? Or if we select the formal styles of drama and performance, are we then committing ourselves to aesthetic laws of immanent causation (genius, a Hegelian spirit; a law of alternating forms; the anxiety or dialectic of influence?) that, irrespective of external conditions and events, organize and shape theatre development?

Maybe Gombrich is right; maybe we should abandon the idea of periods. Or, as Lord Acton and other pragmatists have advised, we should study problems, not periods. No doubt, by focusing on details instead of systems, the issue of periodization can be postponed. The historian, committed to the study of a specific subject matter, can then supposedly ignore philosophic issues and instead concentrate on events in their rich, unique particularity. This is chore enough. Such a dismissal may satisfy some people, but sooner or later we are confronted with a simple fact: the way we divide and analyze history *is* the problem. To try to separate periods from problems is a false dichotomy. As Paul Veyne points out: "Events have no natural unity; one cannot, like the good cook in *Phèdre*, cut them according to their true joints, because they have none."[62] So it is hard to see how we can avoid the issue of periodization. Turning away from this problem only maintains the current confusion over periods.

We need to recognize, however, just how pervasive the problem is, and not just in theatre history. In Louis O. Mink's words:

> Periodization is widely acknowledged to be so arbitrary and relative to particular intents of particular histories that it is a rich field for errors, which at bottom consist of starting with the use of a scheme of periodization as an instrument of inquiry, and ending with the claim to have discovered within the field of history as turning-points what actually were imposed on it as conceptual distinctions.[63]

There are, it seems to me, actually two problems with our approach to periodization. Not only do we impose schemes onto history that produce and sanction our conclusions, as Mink points out, but we fail to appreciate how the concept of periodization acts as a controlling generalization, an unconscious or unarticulated presupposition. The first problem comes from having a strong idea of periodization and imposing it willfully on events. The second problem, by contrast, comes from not having a critical idea of system and general principle.

It should be clear that periodization is always more than a descriptive matter because it is a process of concept formation, an ordering process imposed upon the historical data. It is a form of representation, a "representing" that must necessarily balance between documentation and interpretation, reconstruction and deconstruction. The designated periods constitute a pattern of regulation, an interpretive choice and perspective. Yet in theatre historiography today the widespread practice is to act as if the many taxonomies and categories all exist in grand equality and free interchange, to be used or ignored as each historian desires. We jump from category to category or mix them without the slightest sense of logical contradiction. This simultaneous embrace of many propositions, instead of being a sign of a wise pluralism, is rather the evidence of our confusion, our failure to know how our thought is being directed, even conditioned, by the terms and systems we take up. The discourse of periodization is one of the most powerful and pervasive controls on historical inquiry and understanding. Is it not apparent, then, that in the haphazard ways we have mixed and intermingled these categories, we have collectively created an impossible system for periodization in theatre history? The overall result is a taxonomy that is less charming than the one Borges gives us, but hardly less bizarre.

What is to be done? No simply solution exists, of course. But it is time we begin to clarify the criteria for periodization in theatre history. Though my aim in this chapter has been a preliminary one – to suggest the nature of some of our problems – I conclude here with a few very brief and initial recommendations. We must recognize, though, that no formula – no categorical imperative – will eliminate the problems that attend all methods of periodization.

First, whatever the method of periodization we use to group together events, people, works, conditions, etc., we accept the need to provide them with a shared temporal identity. We simplify in order to make general statements. We cannot avoid periodization any more than we can avoid generalization. In fact, period concepts are basic and essential generalizations. Second, the variety and complexity of theatre is a given, so no unitary model of history will be sufficient. No single system of designation – political, normative, aesthetic – can fully comprehend and subsume all other modes of designation. The formal aspects of theatre are not epiphenomena of social conditions; social conditions are not just the background for artistic practices. Therefore, in our period categories we need to join formal, efficient, material, and final causes or attributes. Third, as colligatory terms, period designations are nominal distinctions that we use (constitute rhetorically) to join separate parts or features of history into a community structure. Hence, we must be aware that these terms are only conditional interpretations, even though we use them descriptively to identify apparent morphological and functional features for a series of events, items, occurrences, people, thoughts, values, processes, and localities that are not ontologically joined. Fourth, because all period concepts carry connotative, not just denotative, meanings (even chronological terms: the eighteenth century theatre, the 1920s), the designations should be seen as stipulative, not conclusive. In Johan Huizinga's words:

> Each term that comes into fashion for the indication of a cultural period quickly takes on strong emotional accents, hues, tastes. In that respect it makes no difference what sort of designation one tries to give a phenomenon. Purely arithmetical names such as Old Empire or Tang, or geographical ones such as Mycenean, attract such emotional associations just as well as quasi-significant terms like romanticism and baroque.[64]

Fifth, because the use of more than one kind of designation is often necessary, we need to join and oppose concepts carefully, with clear understanding of how they relate (and fail to relate) logically and causally. For example, instead of thinking that we have solved an interpretive problem by using the concept of early modern age instead of Renaissance, we might benefit from a fuller engagement with both terms, including the places they create ambiguities and contradictions. In the words of Kenneth Burke, *"what we want is not terms that avoid ambiguity, but terms that clearly reveal the strategic spots at which ambiguities necessarily arise* (Burke's italics)."[65] Sixth, this means we need to study and question our classificatory systems, not just take them for granted. Since we are wandering in a labyrinth, we should chart its design. Seventh, because history is a process of change, we need to examine the nature of change – of growths, diversions, anomalies, disjunctions, ruptures, and discontinuities, both within and between periods. We especially need to show care in how we take up the developmental terms of evolution and revolution. Eighth, we need to see just how pervasive the implied narratives are in our models of periodization. Our growth and decay metaphors, our assumptions about unity of design, our emphasis on conflict and dialectic, our language of progress, development, evolution, and revolution, our ways of representing duration – all of these factors and more commit us to narratives that provide some of the key meanings of periodization. And ninth, we should not lose sight of an abiding paradox: though a period is a singular idea, no era, however long or short, has a singular identity. Our period terms always capture too much and too little. Contradiction is in the nature of periodization. Thus, periodization is equally the problem that we cannot solve and the problematic we cannot ignore.

There is no systematic way to proceed. We therefore must stipulate, with as much thoughtfulness as possible, how we are defining and using our period concepts. For example, when Eric Hobsbawn chose the period concept of the "age of empire" for his study of European history at the end of the nineteenth and the beginning of the twentieth centuries (1875–1914), he did not use it as a formula to identify and explain the historical events. Instead, it served as an idea that required substantial explanation and justification, even though European imperialism was an obvious and essential condition of the decades before World War One. Hobsbawn presented the condition of empire as a complex problem to investigate, especially because it served as a key identifying factor in his analysis. When considered fully, it confronted him with a number of questions. That is, the period concept became the problem to investigate, not the condition and cause that already explained what was happening and why. The idea of *empire* provided Hobsbawn with not simply an identity for the age, which could then be pronounced confidently (e.g., Age of Reason, the Medieval Mind), but more significantly with the conditions and problems that produced many of the crises, conflicts, and unresolved oppositions of the era. In other words, he was struggling to get beyond a period concept that stabilized the era, in the way of all period identifications. He was attempting to address the factors of change and transformation. He was thus pushing against the synchronic tendencies of period concepts by defining the age in terms of its diachronic processes that culminated in war.

Within the practices of empire Hobsbawn discovered a series of crises in social, psychological, political, economic, and moral conditions. He delved into each of these in order to not only reveal the nature of these particular situations and events but also to explain what the organizing idea of empire actually meant in the era. He found his illustrations of the condition of identity crisis in many case studies, including the arts: "Perhaps nothing illustrates the identity crisis which bourgeois society passed through in this period better than the history of the arts from the 1870s to 1914. It was the era when both the creative arts and the public for them lost their bearings."[66] In this manner, by examining the manifestations of crisis, Hobsbawn built his explanation of his period concept, which may have initiated his study but also had to demonstrate the nature of the events and conditions before it could justify its potentiality. Hobsbawn justified his period concept by presenting case studies that illustrated how a series of revolutions played out in European and world societies. The danger in this model of conflict is that it may set up a neat polarity between the Victorian world and modernism, between tradition and innovation. For the most part, by attending to many different developments – the new physics, the suffrage movement, the challenges from the new arts, the crises of class, religion, and masculine dominance, the growing militarism, industrialization, the territorial adventures and exploitation in Africa – Hobsbawn has charted various meanings of empire in the era. In the process, he has also shown that his period concept in fact requires a stipulated definition.

The point here is not that Hobsbawn is necessarily correct in his analysis; but he fulfills the required task of a historian to make the period concept part of the investigation, not simply the framing idea that already explains itself as well as the conditions. If used as a self-explaining and unproblematic category, it is merely a tautology. Because he attempts to stipulate, in some detail, how and why he is using the period concept, his readers can then reach their own judgements about not only the meaning of the period concept, which is defined carefully, but also the interpretive value the concept provides for the historical investigation. A period concept may emerge early in a study, but it should not be taken as a clarifying explanation or a framing idea; instead, it should be treated as a provisional idea to be tested throughout the investigation. It may prove to be appropriate, but it may also need to be modified or even abandoned. Only in the process of tacking back and forth between events and contexts do we discover the value of a period concept; we find out what work the period concept is capable of delivering.

> Really, universally, relations stop nowhere, and the exquisite problem of the artist is eternally but to draw by a geometry of his own, the circle within which they shall happily appear to do so.
> Henry James, "Preface" to *Roderick Hudson* (1960: 8)

> When we conceptualize, we cut out and fix, and exclude anything but what we have fixed. A concept means a *that-and-no-other*. Conceptually, time excludes space; motion and rest exclude each other; unity excludes plurality; independence excludes relativity; "mine" excludes "yours"; this connection excludes that connection – and so on indefinitely; whereas in the real concrete sensible flux of life, experiences co-penetrate each other so that it is not easy to know just what is excluded and what not.
> William James, *A Pluralistic Universe* republished in *Essays in Radical Empiricism and A Pluralistic Universe* (1971: 243–44)

In conclusion, I will let the James brothers, William and Henry, provide us with our basic challenge for constructing any period concept. How is it possible to enclose the infinite variety – perhaps chaos – of the world within any system of identity, coherence, and wholeness? Though neither of the brothers comments directly on periodization – Henry James' topic is the unity of the novel, William James' topic is the unity of thought – both of them recognized that we must create, not simply discover, order. Nothing ready-made will serve, including the grab-bag of period concepts. Our understanding of human events depends upon our ability to shape those events into an identity, a representative order that reveals our own interpretive insights. Historians do not create the past, but they do create the categories for describing, organizing, and explaining it. They must find and develop the appropriate categories and ideas that allow them to give meaning to past events. Historical writing does not have to offer us a self-contained and complete unity of beginning, middle, and end. But it still must provide a convincing explanation of the pieces so that their relationships add up to a coherent understanding. The making of that circle of identity – of apparent unity between events and conditions as well as styles and periods – is also the challenge of the historian. Yet identity, though the essential mission of all period concepts, achieves its meaning and value only when it helps us to distinguish one period from another, one event from another. That is, we need as historians not only to construct events and place them within their identifying contexts but also to describe and explain the sequences of change and cause. We need to recognize, in the words of Jacques Le Goff, that "periodization is the main instrument for understanding significant changes."[67] Identity and change: both concepts are required in our formulations of the historical conditions and processes that contribute to our ideas of periodization. Somehow, though we need the generalizing control of a period concept, we also need to allow experiences, in the words of William James, to "co-penetrate each other so that it is not easy to know just what is excluded and what not." Consequently, we must live and think within an irresolvable paradox.

Chapter 6

The idea of the "political" in our histories of theatre: causal contexts for events

What do historians do? How do they do it? These two simple questions have engaged us since chapter 1, but the answers have proved to be complex and various. In our investigation of theatre events and their possible contexts, we have traveled a great distance from the initial polarity that set up an opposition between documentary scholarship (which supposedly limits itself to digging out antiquarian data about theatre events) and cultural history (which supposedly supplies the contextual analysis and interpretations). It should be obvious that scholarship needs to do justice to both the documentary facts and the contextual conditions. As the series of diagrams in the Introduction attempted to suggest, historical study should not be reduced procedurally to a basic, two-part division between the event and its context. But how, then, can we place events within the context of specific factors, such as political conditions?

In the process of constructing a theatrical event, as we have seen, there are many possible meanings that might be attributed to any one of the contexts. The potential contexts provide a way to establish relationships between and among events. By placing events in a relational dynamic, within a specific time and space, we can offer plausible explanations for their relationships. In turn, by examining their sequential patterns, we can attempt to explain some of the causes and reasons for change. Moving beyond chronology, we attempt to explain the interrelationships between theatre and society. Sometimes there are mutual interactions. Sometimes social and political conditions control artistic practices. Sometimes artistic developments influence and change societies. The lines of causality are complex.

One way to proceed is to trace the features and recurring patterns of a key factor that operates in a series of events within a period. As we saw in chapter 5, formal analysis seeks to identify such features and patterns as they contribute to ideas of period style. As we also saw, though, any attempt to unify many different works and events into a unified system is fraught with difficulties. Nonetheless, when we successfully tie together many people and events into definitive norms and interpretive patterns, we may achieve an understanding of major historical developments. We see how and why various agents and events are yoked – perhaps by major traits and models of the artistic heritage, perhaps by controlling factors of the larger world and environment (e.g., social or political arrangements that operate across many events and begin to define an era). We are not limited, then, to the study of single events.

For instance, Tracy C. Davis demonstrates convincingly in *The Economics of the British Stage, 1800–1914* (2000) how the idea of a definitive context, such as the business practices of British theatre in the long nineteenth century, can provide not only a general topic for historical inquiry but also an interpretive model for recurring patterns of behavior. The challenge is to describe accurately how key business practices functioned in the day-to-day activities of theatre in several British cities during the era, and then to identify and analyze the contributory conditions that influenced – and sometimes determined – important aspects of the practice. In this way, with a primary focus on the agents, world, and theatrical practices and events, it is possible to place the actions and values of a number of theatre people, including theatre owners, producers, investors, and managers, in an explanatory context. Then, perhaps, we can understand the lines of development and the forces of change in an era.

Few theatre historians, however, investigate the worlds of economic conditions and business practices. The necessary archival research is daunting, as Davis' extensive notes illustrate. And few of us have sufficient understanding of the basic topic and procedures (e.g., economics, accounting procedures, business and trade laws, statistical research methods). We feel much more comfortable about our ability to explain political conditions and contexts. We regularly seek to understand the political conditions, influences, and controls that operate at any historical moment in the theatre. While very few scholars investigate business practices and economic conditions, hundreds of scholars in theatre and drama studies focus on political topics and issues.[1] Thus, I wish to show in this chapter some of the ways we have attempted to describe and interpret political issues, ideas, and systems. I also want to suggest ways to get beyond our reliance, much of the time, on sets of binaries, including the familiar one of event and context.

In the study of theatre and drama the idea of "the political" (or "politics") can be defined broadly, if perhaps too simply, in two ways. We can investigate the political topics, themes, issues, viewpoints, and agendas that get expressed in plays, productions, theatre groups, and artistic movements. Or, by shifting the focus, we can describe the political conditions within the historical matrix that shape dramatic literature, the theatrical arts, performance events, and cultural practices. Which is to say, the issue before us is not only "political theatre" (i.e., the modes, means, and aims of artistic representation and expression) but also "theatre and politics" (i.e., the relations between theatre and its sociopolitical conditions, including institutions of governance and ideology). The two ideas are not mutually exclusive, but they suggest that we can proceed as scholars from two avenues of investigation, with the assumption that the avenues probably intersect at several points.

In the first case, we usually locate the politics in the dramatic text (e.g., topics, motifs, themes) or the theatrical event (e.g., interpretive features and strategies). Our focus is thus on the ideas and viewpoints of the creators of the artistic work. In the second case, we situate the politics within the shaping environment or culture which the work or event supposedly reflects, embodies, expresses, realizes, fulfills, resists, or subverts.[2] Also, in the first case we tend to grant to the artists a substantial amount of control over intention, motive, purpose, agency, and accomplishment, while in the second case we tend to de-emphasize, limit, circumscribe, or even deny such control to the individual artists. Understood in this manner, the second case sets up the familiar polarity between text and context (or event and structure). But, as I hope to show, this two-part division, although quite pervasive in theatre studies today, fails to explain sufficiently how political factors, values, and forces operate in the theatre. This model usually depends upon an inadequate definition of *politics* or *the political*. What follows, therefore, is a basic primer in the historiography of theatre and politics. In order to focus my analysis, I will draw most of my examples from current scholarship on professional theatre in London in the second half of the sixteenth century and the first half of the seventeenth century. This era goes by several period designations, Renaissance, Early Modern Age, Elizabethan Age, Jacobean Age, and Age of Shakespeare. As will become clear, all of the current period concepts that we use mislead us because of the ways they construct the relationship between theatre events and their contexts.

In basic terms, the concept of a context, such as the politics of a society, is easy to comprehend. We all agree that artistic texts have contexts and that events have their conditions. In the words of Raymond Williams: "It is clear that certain forms of social relationship are deeply embodied in certain forms of art."[3] Therefore, a contextual analysis, instead of situating the politics primarily within the signifying codes of dramatic and performance texts (and thus, rather exclusively, in the political intentions, agendas, and behavior of the artists, especially the playwrights), seeks to describe and interpret the ways drama and theatre respond to, reflect, reveal, or embody the surrounding and controlling context – that is, the sociopolitical conditions of the time and place. Patterns of order and authority outside rather than inside the artwork become the principal object of analysis. But what exactly do we mean by this assumption that events are tied to, representative of, or caused by their contexts? The general idea of representation, despite elaborate aesthetic and social theories of mimesis, usually fails to clarify how politics and theatre are related. Are they yoked by some force (besides the idea of similitude that sanctions the ideas of mirroring, reflecting, and representing)? If, for example, we take up Raymond Williams' containment image of "embodying," which personifies the context, does this actually explain how or why some kind of force or condition joins the event to a defining or surrounding context? Does it carry us any further toward an explanation than the popular idea of mirroring or reflecting? Apparently not, unless the embodying metaphor is developed into an analysis of the actual conditions and processes. This is yet one more formula, as happens with personification in periodization (e.g., Age of Shaw), for imposing a physiognomy on historical events. That is, a poetic trope instead of historical analysis designates the method of yoking together the "features" of the event. All too often, we trap ourselves in familiar terminology that obscures or explains away the initial problem in our interpretive method. Though we seek clarity, our terminology – along with our working assumptions – proves to be foggy and sloppy, delivering evasive clichés and self-deceiving truism. Clear explanations cannot be developed out of unclear descriptions and formulaic metaphors.

By positing a context, we do not necessarily rule out the possibility that playwrights are able and willing to introduce political topics, even controversies, into their works. They can still be seen as agents who (in some capacity) produce the texts and events.

In the case of English drama of the sixteenth and seventeenth centuries, for example, the playwrights often portrayed political issues. Dozens of history plays and tragedies, such as John Bale's *King John*, Marlowe's *Edward II*, Shakespeare's *Richard III*, or Webster's *The Duchess of Malfi*, raised serious concerns about governmental power, and thus these works seem to us – and apparently to people at the time – to provide a narrative representation that draws upon, points to, and judges the political conditions in England.[4] From works of celebration to statements of indictment, it is possible for playwrights, performers, and patrons to engage in political expression.

In the 1590s, for instance, when Elizabeth I was growing old on the throne without a successor, history plays such as Shakespeare's *Richard II* dramatized the problem of royal succession. And the "Elect Nation" drama of the early Stuart years, such as Thomas Dekker's *The Whore of Babylon*, repeatedly campaigned for the English Protestant cause against Catholicism, especially after the Gunpowder Plot of 1605.[5] Likewise, some playwrights, including Ben Jonson and Thomas Middleton, incurred governmental anger and censor because they wrote plays that were felt to be too topical and critical of the government (e.g., *Sejanus, A Game at Chess*).

Granted, these plays can be isolated from their historical contexts, not only by means of formalist (or semiotic) analysis but also by means of subsequent productions which remove them to a later historical period and context. For example, a reading or production today of Marlowe's *Edward II* that places it within our contemporary contexts of gay culture and queer theory may reveal important and timely political issues for us, but the political conditions of the early 1590s will likely be obscured in the process. Consequently, our interpretation of and pleasure in "political drama" does not necessarily require our understanding of the initial – and often initiating – context.

Even if we attend to the political conditions that the play represents, we may still ignore or lose sight of possible contexts that were contemporaneous with the play. Marlowe's *Edward II* is set in the political context of Edward's troubled reign; it also evokes for Elizabethan spectators certain possible political meanings that pertain to their own time. Thus, among the spectators in the sixteenth century, one person may follow the historical reference to the original Edward; another person may know little or nothing about that history, so instead follow the dramatic action on its own formal or narrative terms; another person may pick up (or impose) political references to contemporary politics of the 1590s; and yet another person, perhaps visiting from another country, may understand the politics in terms of a completely different political setting. Then, as soon as we add the perspectives of any and all of us from a later time, we multiply the possible political readings of the play almost to infinity, it would seem. It is even possible for some spectators and readers to ignore any of the possible political references and themes, and instead to consider how the generic traits, poetic language, plot devices, or modes of characterization operate in terms of the tragic tradition that Marlowe is revising in a radical manner. Or as theatre historians we might be primarily interested in what the play reveals about its possible staging at the Rose Theatre. Then the context may shift from any political or formal concerns to Philip Henslowe's commercial practices and motives. In short, for any "political" play, the possible interpretations are many.

In the contextual model of "theatre and politics" all dramatic texts and all theatrical activities (from political plays to comedies without any political intention) can and should be assumed to have – or to be framed by – some kind of political dimension that not only existed at the time but also operated either in concert with or beyond the intentions and talents of the playwright and players. These agents may have been aware of this political context, they may have adapted to it, or they may have been opposed to it, but, nonetheless, it set a number of the major terms for artistic expression. The challenge for historians is to identify and explain these contributory factors, as they operated politically. The topical references in the play may point to some of these framing conditions and forces, but the political significance we seek extends beyond such conscious and well-intended topicality that gets formally expressed or implied. Accordingly, from the perspective of the historian, this context, possibly operating outside of the specific artistic agenda of the initiating agents, provides potential causes and essential meanings of the theatrical event and text. Perhaps these causes and meanings were anticipated in some manner by the playwright, but they could also contribute in ways that the playwright did not conceive or recognize.

But in saying this we have not yet explained anything. Except for these initial choices of identification, our idea of what constitutes a political context must still be developed and applied. We must dig out of the historical sources – of agents, world, artistic heritage, and reception – the possible evidence for any context we wish to discover and interpret. There are many possible contexts, and many possible political meanings for each of them. For example, in 1592 Philip Henslowe paid five shillings a week to the Master of the Revels, apparently as a licensing fee for the Rose playhouse. From one perspective, this information might lead us to construct the political context as a specific situation tied to matters of business practices and playhouse economics. From another perspective, based upon the payment, politics could be understood as a general condition of political directive, oversight, and authority, such as the patronage system and court control that operated for the theatre companies. And from yet another perspective the politics of this payment could be seen as evidence for a pervasive system of political control and court power that operated as a basic ideology or mentality within Elizabethan culture. Thus, in a specific case the political context may be a kind of transaction or calculation in the daily business of theatre. The people involved are all seen as contributing agents in the making of the political context. In a more expansive idea of politics, the process can be seen as actions occurring within a set of limitations and directives, such as the condition of censorship as applied by the Revels Office.[6] And in the most expansive contextual models we can define the politics as a powerful, regulative system of both direct and indirect control, such as the supposedly hegemonic operation of court politics that pervaded all aspects of theatrical activity, from touring companies to the presentation of court masques. The intentions of the artists, accordingly, are subsumed under (or placed within) some kind of comprehensive political system or condition. Agency, defined more abstractly, is then located, in the final analysis, not in the initiatives of individuals or in the mutual transactions of specific groups, but instead within the distributive and discursive forces at work in society. At this level of generalization we often evoke a period concept, such as the Early Modern Age, to frame and perhaps help to explain the general political conditions that somehow shaped and defined the events and texts under consideration. But unless we stipulate how we are using either the controlling idea of power or the period concept, our analysis tends to be overly general and abstract, evoking a dozen different possible meanings (all rather vague) instead of clarifying much of anything about the nature of the theatrical events and the means of operation for the political context.

> Structure and agency are so closely interwoven that to separate either and give it primacy over the other is a fundamental error.
>   Alex Callinicos, *Making History: Agency, Structure, and Change in Social Theory* (1988: 6–7)

According to a general idea of a context – one based upon ideas of power, authority, system, or structure – the political ideas and actions of theatrical artists achieve their significance within the controlling political actions, aims, and practices of rulers, religious leaders, and social elites. And, in turn, these ruling authorities may be seen as figures in a comprehensive ideological condition of systematic authority. Typically, when following this expansive approach, cultural historians have been attracted to one of two ways to define politics: "the politics of power or the politics of contention."[7] Thus, the theatre artist of the Renaissance or the Early Modern Age, usually operating in a patronage system and a court culture, is seen as either a "royal apologist" or a "crypto–subversive" critic.[8] For instance, cultural historians can demonstrate that Shakespeare's *Macbeth*, with its celebration of the Scottish line of descent from Banquo to the Stuart monarchy, presents a "politics of praise" that sanctions the political authority of James I by staging a discourse of "legitimation." Shakespeare thus embraces, if not monarchical authority, at least the principle of political expediency. Yet, by selecting other bits of supporting evidence from the play, we can also show that it reveals a "politics of contention." *Macbeth* then implicitly articulates the possibilities of treason and sedition within the government, dangerous themes in the wake of the Gunpowder Plot. And if we credit Shakespeare with wide reading, as does David Norbrook, the play supposedly makes the case for the republican ideas of "the democratic theorist" George Buchanan, tutor to Montaigne and historian of Scottish politics.[9] These opposing interpretations are not necessarily mutually exclusive – as long as one evokes the familiar principles of contradiction, ambiguity, ambivalence, irony, or duplicity. But, nonetheless, because the play's historical aims and meanings can be understood so variously, it is very difficult, perhaps impossible, to identify and construct a definitive context, political or otherwise, that scholars can agree upon.

These methods of establishing a political context are often flawed. First, a specific hypothesis is set up (based, perhaps, on an organizing idea – the court controlled the theatre – or some text – Buchanan's writings), and then selectively "evidence" for this hypothesis is always found in the play in question, which serves, almost exclusively, as the historical source. Scholars can be quite cunning in their extrapolations from dramatic texts. Of course, from the perspective of theatre production, stretching across the centuries, a multiplicity of possible meanings is justified, for we often relish a new approach to *Macbeth* or any other play from the era. But historians of drama and theatre need to ground their descriptions and interpretations in the initiating conditions and contexts, hence the search for historical documents, such as the writings of James I on the authority of royal rule or those of Buchanan on democratic principles, which can support one's analysis. These texts, by means of a loose principle of correspondence, are identified with the playwright and his presumed political beliefs – not on the basis of direct statement provided by the writer (e.g., documents on the playwright's political beliefs and actions) but instead on the basis of the interpretive speculations and conjectures of the scholar. The procedure has the appearance of historical research but this kind of textual correspondence is a familiar formalist technique in literary studies – the search for similitudes. In this way, it is possible to find supporting evidence in the literary works and possible corresponding documents for any conceivable conjecture about the intentions, beliefs, and activities of the playwrights. We can prove that Shakespeare was both a Catholic and a Protestant; we can demonstrate that Edward de Vere or Marlowe wrote his plays.[10] Even the wildest conspiracy theory can deliver these kinds of corresponding clues as "evidence."

The primary claim of a contextual approach is that social and political relations are not merely represented in plays and productions, but somehow located, situated, embodied, or embedded there in such a manner that the context becomes the primary source of meaning. The political context operates, at the very least, as an instrument or a means of persuasion. And, in its most controlling manner, as some scholars argue, it functions as a fully causal and deterministic force that occasions the work. But in saying this, we must recognize that our vocabulary about being "located, situated, embodied, or embedded" is still a metaphorical rhetoric that remains vague and unexplained.

If the methods for finding politics in plays and productions are questionable, what then should we say about our methods for examining theatre and politics during the Elizabethan, Jacobean, and Carolinian monarchies? The aim would be not simply to analyze key political themes, but to demonstrate how and why the social and political conditions of the times shaped, articulated, and even controlled the theatre.

For instance, Alvin Kernan's historical approach in *Shakespeare, the King's Playwright* (1995) fits within the "politics of power" methodology. In his preface Kernan writes:

> Like many in my generation, I have been slowly converted from a formalist view of literature to a view of the arts as secondary but still important to the ongoing social process of making culture. The theory that seems to fit and instrument [*sic*] best this by-now fairly standard conception is some variety of what is commonly called "the social construction of reality," "construction theory," or "constructivism." I have found this theory elaborated most usefully in the writings of the humanistic sociologist Peter Berger, where it offers no complex Parsonian paradigm of social organization but rather an arsenal of the devices – roles, rituals, philosophies, legal systems, cosmologies, and

arts – by which men and women in society take the given world and make it witness to their own sense of order and meaning.[11]

On the basis of this general theory of society, Kernan finds his organizing hypothesis for the book:

> By now it is possible to see Shakespeare's Stuart plays in the context not only of the English court and its sociopolitical interests but of [the] European developments of the arts as official propaganda for the great kings and their houses . . . Even had he wished to avoid politics, Shakespeare was forced to become a political playwright willy-nilly, by virtue of court performances.[12]

In other words, court politics – a social process that makes culture – determined the writing and meaning for *Measure for Measure, Macbeth, King Lear,* and *The Tempest.* Chapter by chapter Kernan spells out how "the Stuart monopolization of theatre" turned Shakespeare and the King's Men into a political arm of the government.[13] The playwright and theatre company participated in social and political circumstances that "constructed" the plays and performances.

This understanding of Renaissance theatre, which grants not only major influence but substantial control to the court and its agendas, is in accord with the argument in Stephen Orgel's *The Illusion of Power* (1975), which focused on the role of masques in the courts of James I and Charles I: "Dramas at court were not entertainments in the simple and dismissive sense we usually apply to the term. They were expressions of the age's most profound assumptions about the monarchy."[14] By focusing on the topics and scenic traits of the masques, Orgel saw them as "the expression of the monarch's will, the mirrors of his mind."[15] From 1975 forward, Orgel's astute analysis of court politics found sympathetic support in the scholarship of many new historicists and cultural materialists. And some theatre historians concurred in this perspective. For instance, in *English Court Theatre* (1999), John Astington demonstrates that court performances were "occasions of political significance." They were "part of a quite deliberate programme of royal propaganda . . ."[16] Astington describes how some of the court performances celebrated, in glorious display, aspects of royal and aristocratic identity.

It is clear that on various occasions the government used "shewes and pageants" in ceremonial ways to celebrate and entertain itself. We need to question, though, just how much these activities were produced by a unified governmental policy and bureaucracy that directed and controlled the political discourse and activities of the various theatre companies. Neither Orgel nor Astington spells out an absolutist model of power and control over the public theatres, but this basic idea of court power has appealed to some theatre historians who draw up theories and models of systematic power (e.g., ideas derived from Michel Foucault).

Kings are justly called Gods for that they exercise a manner of resemblance of Divine Power upon earth; if you will consider the attributes of God, you shall see how they agree in the person of a King. God hath power to create or destroy, to make or unmake at his pleasure, and to God are both soul and body due. And the like power have Kings: they make and unmake their subjects, and in all cases, yet are accomptable [*sic*] to none but God only. They have power to exalt low things and abase high things and make of their subjects like men at Chess; A pawn to take a Bishop or a Knight, and to cry up, or down any of their subjects as they do their money.

King James I, Statement before Parliament, 1609, in *The Political Works of James I*. Edited by James McIlwain (1918: 307)

This concept of absolutist politics, which scholars often illustrate with statements made by King James I on the divine rights of kings, assumes that a top-down model of power, authority, and control operated with great efficiency.[17] This argument locates the system of control in the censorship powers of the Master of the Revels and the Lord Chamberlain, who worked in tandem with a system of court patronage that was well organized and consistent in its aims and functions. But in his study of the Office of the Revels, Richard Dutton shows that the court was often lax, and even disorganized, in its regulation and censorship of the stage.[18] Tracking the actual practices of the Revels Office, the Lord Chamberlain, and the directives and actions of the monarchs, Dutton shows that no consistent program of political control of the theatre operated. And Dutton is not alone in his skepticism that any systematic political agenda was imposed upon the theatres by the monarchs. Leeds Barroll, for example, offers a distinctly constrained version of the court's political activities and intentions.[19] Expanding his research beyond the standard group of "documents of control" that E. K. Chambers placed in *The Elizabethan Stage* (1923) and that literary scholars tend to use repeatedly, he shows that not only do we lack any decisive evidence that King James sought to establish the King's Men as his propaganda instrument when he took the throne in 1603, but we have counter evidence that strongly suggests that no such political agenda operated in the case of Shakespeare and the King's Men:

> The court and the king were not implicated in the dramatist's professional activities . . . Moreover . . . there is nothing to indicate that plays by professional actors were the king's preferred form of court entertainment, [or] that plays were central to the festivities and – with the ear of the king bent attentively to its script – perhaps politically charged.[20]

At the very least, this counter-argument, based upon evidence of the king's daily activities and decisions over a number of months when the company of the King's Men was established, raises questions about the idea of an absolutist monarchy not only exerting control over the theatre companies but also micro-managing their political activities. It is quite appropriate to note that the court was the center of political power, but surely some distinctions and modifications of the grand model of power and authority are warranted. We always need to distinguish between the desired political agendas of the court and its political ability to impose those agendas.

Is there, then, a clear alternative to the model of central control? Some scholars, though granting that the court sometimes attempted to exert its power over the theatre, seek to discover (even to celebrate) an oppositional idea of politics. A "politics of contention" is located, then, in the resisting attributes of popular or common culture. For example, in his influential study *Shakespeare's Festive Comedy* (1959), C. L. Barber read the plays as expressions of anti-authoritarian attitudes in popular or folk culture. Anne Richter [Barton] also made much of the spirit of play, disguise, and role playing in Shakespeare's plays.[21] Building upon these foundations, Robert Weimann posited in *Shakespeare and the Popular Tradition in the Theatre* (1978) a tradition of folk culture in the Elizabethan theatre and popular culture that provided not only an alternative to literary culture, humanism, and the values of the gentry, but also a spirit of misrule that challenged the political authorities. The plays of Shakespeare, instead of being the organ of the monarch (or, more benignly, the expression of humanist culture), served as the voice of the common people. For example, Weimann claimed that the character of the Fool in Renaissance drama can be traced back to fertility rites and agrarian festivals of pre-Christian times. Thus, "the heritage of ritual embodiment" defined the relationship between actor and audience. The "citizens," already immersed in popular culture and its entertainments, became an ideal audience for the new commercial ventures in the amphitheatres. The theatres thus expressed "dim reflections ... of primitive society [and] immemorial customs."[22] Dionysian traditions and Roman Saturnalia, mediated in medieval times by the Vice figure, reemerged, for instance, as Falstaff, with whom the folk spectators and citizens supposedly identified.

Weimann is hardly alone in conjuring up this folk culture of political opposition. The concept of a "reveling instinct" in "the psychology of the folk" was an organizing principle of the scholarship of E. K. Chambers, who traced the festive spirit through the liturgy of the church, the "festival celebrations of the municipal guides," the "outgrowth of minstrelsy," and the disguisings and masques of the "household of the sovereign."[23] More recently, some literary critics, adapting the ideas of Mikhail Bahktin, especially his study of Rabelais (1968), have celebrated the "carnivalesque" spirit and antics of popular theatre and culture (which can be traced from Aristophanes to Dario Fo). For example, Michael Bristol argues that popular culture offered "the possibility of a meaningful popular resistance to domination by hereditary elites ..."[24] Although the common people and common players faced "the combination of surveillance by state power, hostility from the civic authorities, and religious antitheatricalism," they were able to offer a "threat to the established order" in their entertainments by means of "inversion," "ludic elements," "social dissonance," "excess," and "festival misrule."[25] Bristol points out that "Misrule, inversion, and travesty were typical of the Carnivalesque."[26] Therefore, we are to assume that the carnivalesque spirit served as an "intervention" in the political order. Or, as Leah Marcus has stated in a different context, "a politics of mirth" offsets a politics of power.[27] From this perspective, much of London theatre in this era, from Dekker's *The Shoemaker's Holiday* to the anti-masque sequences in court performances, expressed an oppositional politics of "contestation."[28] Theatre, developing out of popular culture and occurring in the "liberties," those geographical areas that supposedly were beyond the control of the government, found various ways to outwit authority.[29] The Lord of Misrule became the true authority figure.

For some scholars, this approach, which makes a political context out of the antic and subversive dispositions of the folk, suggests an appealing alternative to the three main areas of contextual politics that E. K. Chambers identified in *The Elizabethan Stage*: (1) the government (which included the crown, royal household, nobles, the Privy Council, and court officers such as the Master of the Revels); (2) the city fathers of London who attempted to control theatrical activities; and (3) the "puritans" or religious critics of the theatre.[30]

All three of these groups – the court, the "alienated municipality," and the "alienated pulpit," in Chambers' terms – generated documents, essays, and books which have become the historical texts out of which we build our political contexts. The problem with the common folk is that they produced little in the way of written evidence. So the scholarly attention given to common culture seems to give voice to the voiceless. In a carnivalesque spirit, literary scholars discover a politics of contention, intervention, and opposition (if not revolution) in the plays. Subversion of authority is thus revealed by those of us who can read not so much between the lines, but where there are no lines.

Of course, the spirit of festival can sanction a certain amount of playful disruption of the standard norms and rules of social behavior. This is true across the ages. In some cases, drinking can easily lead to acts against the authorities. Riots can even occur on such occasions. However, we need to distinguish between rather conventional, even traditional celebrations throughout the year (from Twelfth Night to All Hallow's Day) and the actual cases of political action. And we should not equate political disruption with political change. The problem with our scholarly celebrations of the reveling spirit of the folk is that all clowns, fools, festive moments, popular entertainments, and situations of disorder can be made to fit this carnivelesque formula of political subversion. If everyone is a Lord of Misrule, no one is.

Not surprisingly, this scholarly desire or ability to find political contention and intervention in common folk and clowns alike has been challenged by many historians. In recent decades, some scholars have tried to reconfigure how politics contributed to theatrical activities. Faced with the polarity between absolute authoritarian power and manifold acts of oppositional politics in popular culture and the theatre, they have found both positions too reductive. Drawing upon, yet modifying (often with an ironic sensibility), the authoritarian and subversive versions of politics and power, these new historicist scholars have attempted to spell out some kind of middle ground.[31] Governmental power and control, in displaced, energetic ways, still finds expression in the theatre.

For example, in *Shakespearean Negotiations* (1988), Stephen Greenblatt argues that the plays of Shakespeare, despite their subversive motifs or themes, serve to legitimate the power of the crown and its authority. The polarity between two types of politics is turned into an ironic reversal. This textual analysis is, in turn, projected onto all theatre practices of the era: "Elizabethan companies contrived to absorb, refashion, and exploit some of the fundamental energies of a political authority that was itself already committed to histrionic display and hence was ripe for appropriation . . . Theatricality, then, is not set over against power but is one of power's essential modes."[32] In this method of analysis, power is all pervasive and controlling: "the founding of the modern state, like the self-fashioning of the modern prince, is shown to be based upon acts of calculation, intimidation, and deceit. And these acts are performed in an entertainment for which audiences, the subjects of this very state, pay money and applaud."[33] The theatre, despite its apparent separation from court politics, not only justifies the ideological structure of the monarchy but also ratifies and sustains the established order and glorifies authority. Yet theatre itself is powerless, in part because of its theatricality, those "empty" gestures toward the real world. Apparently theatricality in the service of the authorities is all-powerful; but when theatricality is realized in the gestures of players it "evacuates" the very power it represents. All theatrical acts become sound and fury, signifying nothing.

Greenblatt's basic model of a performative society, whereby government and theatre negotiated a political partnership, shared features with other studies in the 1980s and 1990s. For example, the historian Kevin Sharpe posited a balancing act between complimentary rhetoric and calculated criticism in Renaissance theatre.[34] And the literary critic Louis Montrose argued that a text, performance, or event serves "as a site of convergence of various and potentially contradictory cultural discourses."[35] That is, a heterogeneous political "dialectic," which exists within the social dynamics of culture, somehow overcomes the limiting aspects of the subversion–containment model that haunts his analysis.

Yet despite these attempts to conjure into being the heterogeneity of culture and society, the historical context remains a reductive idea of political order. Greenblatt wanted to avoid the idea of a totalizing society, which operates in some Marxist approaches to history, but his own rubric of power – which supposedly circulates throughout society in a discursive and textualized network that reaches into all corners of the era – recapitulates a total, organic system of political authority, on and off the stage. Contingency stretches everywhere, from center to border and back to center again. All transactions are acts of exchange, of "collective production of literary pleasure and interest."[36] They take place within a vast network of social "energy." This is a field theory of culture that is dependent upon the idea of a singular and unified period. Culture and society are joined seamlessly, it would seem, into a *Gesamtkunstwerk*. In sum, Greenblatt's cultural theory is based upon the tropes of similitude, especially metonymy and synecdoche; all of the discrete parts and aspects of the era, including all texts, participate within the organic whole.[37] The job of the historian/critic is to read the half-hidden traces that reveal a "poetics of culture" – as Greenblatt describes his project in *Learning to Curse* (1991). The rhetorical methodology for this poetics is then spelled out in *Practicing New Historicism* (2000), written by Catherine Gallagher and Greenblatt.

The temptation to which the cultural history must not succumb is that of treating the texts and images of a certain period as mirrors, unproblematic reflections of their times.
    Peter Burke, *What Is Cultural History?* (2005: 20)

Resisting the textual methodology of new historicism, Jean Howard (1994) has attempted to offer a Marxist analysis as an alternative approach to contextual analysis. Agreeing with Greenblatt that "power relations" constitute theatrical activities in the era, she too questions the appropriateness of the subversion and containment models. She has reservations about the ability of the "folk" to intervene in and disrupt the power of the elite. So, treading her way between the contending ideas of Foucault and Bakhtin, she "attempts to give an account of why the theatre and theatrical practices were . . . objects of debate and contestation in early modern England . . ."[38] As a "feminist Marxist," Howard argues that: (1) theatre "helped call into being the very bourgeois subjectivity to which it was supposedly opposed;"[39] (2) the drama of the era "disrupted" ideas of patriarchy and heterosexuality;[40] (3) "drama enacted ideological contestation as much as it mirrored or reproduced anything that one could call the dominate ideology of a single class, class faction, or sex";[41] and (4) theatre participated in "social struggles generated by the dual facts of massive social change [i.e., from feudalism to capitalism] and equally massive resistance to its acknowledgement."[42]

Howard's purpose is admirable, for she wants to suggest that political conditions and meanings for the era are more complex than the overly neat opposition between the politics of power and the politics of contention. She wants to reveal the complexity and energy of political ideas and values. She is not merely presenting a rehash of Marxist theory, dressed up in revisionist cultural theory (despite a vocabulary that slides into jargon). But her method lets her down. Why? Like Louis Montrose, she wants to chart a series of "contradictions" in theatre's "total role in ideological production."[43] But, also like Montrose and Greenblatt, in spite of her attempts to evoke a Marxist formulation of "social change," Howard constructs an era called "the early modern age" that holds, embodies, or contains all events and actions within a political condition of theatricalized gestures (e.g., crossdressing, women going to the theatre and being seen, metatheatrical techniques in the plays). In order to justify her analysis, Howard makes large claims for these theatrical gestures, but it is difficult to see how they actually produced any substantial social changes. Crossdressing in *Twelfth Night* or *The Roaring Girl* hardly up-ended patriarchy.[44] Moreover, beyond proclaiming that the politics of plays, playhouses, and playgoing contributed to "ideological contestation and social change,"[45] Howard provides little historical evidence to support her argument. Instead, she just insists that this is so. Despite her evocation of history, she writes primarily as a literary critic (which is also the case with Greenblatt and Montrose). Textual analysis of motifs and themes within the plays and religious pamphlets serves to define the political context, which of course fits neatly within the presuppositions of her theoretical model. In this manner, she finds within the highly selected set of texts what she seeks to argue. Once again, a part stands in for the preordained whole. And the historical process of change lacks agency. Politics is still located in a shaping context, which she derives not from the power of the court or the subversions of popular culture, but the anti-theatrical tracts of a few Puritans.[46] Consequently, despite her resistance to Greenblatt's new historicism, she is still using his textual model of analysis. Both the subversion–containment model and the contestation model, though inadequate for historical explanation, serve literary analysis rather well.

The striking thing about these new historicist and neo-Marxist methodologies, as applied to the drama and society of the "Elizabethan," "Jacobean," "Renaissance" or "Early Modern Age," is the way that everything is a text to be decoded. And all texts, across a large period, are simultaneously available as evidence. In the words of Montrose, the task of the scholar is to study "the Historicity of Texts and the Textuality of History."[47] Charmed by this trope of chiasmus, Montrose claims that "formal and historical concerns are not opposed but rather are inseparable."[48] But to follow such a methodology is to enclose oneself within an internal realm of textual play, without an anchor in the referential world that must exist, the world of historical reality, outside of the textual evidence that the critic analyzes and interprets.

> The fashionable injunction to study reality as a text should be supplemented by the awareness that no text can be understood without reference to extratextual realities.
> Carlo Ginzburg, "Checking the Evidence: The Judge and the Historian" (1994: 295)

At times Montrose and Howard try to overcome the blending of text and context into a single code of intertextuality by evoking what Montrose calls "the dialectic between text and the world."[49] And Howard repeatedly evokes the concept of change, in an attempt to get beyond the synchronic authority of intertextuality. But in this theory of culture the "dialectical" relation between text and context, though supposedly located in historical events and texts, is actually produced by a critical practice of setting up wry textual juxtapositions. Despite her aims, Howard remains within the intertextual methodology as she yokes images and motifs in anti-theatrical tracts with similar ones in *Much Ado About Nothing*. Thus the critic or historian, taking the measure of various texts that the age produced, from plays to pamphlets, reads the textual culture as a series of correspondences, tensions, contradictions, fractures, oxymorons, paradoxes, and ironies.

Moreover, while traditional historical studies of the development of theatre from the late medieval era to the mid seventeenth century have attempted to offer a diachronic model of history,[50] the new scholarly approaches tend toward a synchronic model, locking various cultural elements within a systemic or structuralist method of analysis (even when the scholar's sensibility is post-structuralist). Montrose admits as much: "In effect, this project reorients the axis of intertextuality, substituting for the diachronic text of an autonomous literary history the synchronic text of a cultural system."[51] In consequence, we are confronted with an idea of history that has removed or bracketed the factors of agency, change, and causality. Basically, then, this approach has not only enclosed historical study within the disciplinary methods of literary study but also removed major historical factors from consideration.[52]

> The terms context and text are problematic. We experience the text as a nexus of meanings, and which ones are in the text and which derive from the context cannot be strictly determined.
> David Perkins, *Is Literary History Possible?* (1992: 122)

So, how can we do justice to the diachronic and synchronic factors of the political context? Or, for that matter, how should we construct any context for a theatrical event? How do the textual, contextual, and periodic modes of analysis intersect? Why do we repeatedly get caught in rather formulaic polarities of text and context, event and structure, formal history and social history? What are the problems in our methods? Let me briefly list three basic problems in the models that we use to analyze the relations between theatre and politics. *Underlying all three problems is the basic historical challenge of describing and interpreting historical change.* Though I will merely point to a few of the key issues, we should not lose sight of our primary responsibility to describe historical changes and their causes. This challenge haunts the whole analysis of agency and political conditions. Unfortunately – and fatally – the basic needs to identify and analyze the factors of change are not adequately confronted in the current models of political context. Indeed, they are basically ignored or dismissed.

1. *The problem of singularity.* One of our difficulties is that we often posit a singular identity for the political context, a period, and an artistic style. We unify events, texts, and forces within any historical moment, even though some historians, such as Norbert Elias and Fernand Braudel, have argued for at least a three-tier system of historical analysis (e.g., Braudel's history of events, history of social history or conjunctions, and history of the long duration). Obviously, there are various approaches available to us, including Raymond Williams' ideas of residual, dominant, and emergent practices within any historical time.[53] Whatever our method, we must remind ourselves that no era has a singular identity. Or a single political structure. And no event has a single context. Yet despite the sophistication of our current approaches to theatre, we still tend to identify periods with a single philosophy and political system or – more to the point – with a single theoretical model of analysis. Surely such assumptions undermine much of the textual and contextual scholarship that is being put forward today in theatre and drama studies.

In saying this, I am not attempting to argue that we should avoid all attempts to generalize about movements, decades, generations, and eras. Without question, part of our responsibility as cultural historians is to detect and analyze patterns. Historical study, at its best, is committed to taking the measure of such patterns as we place the major events within their developmental history. Yet no single identity can adequately define the drama and theatre of an era. When we posit a controlling or reigning context (or, by contrast, celebrate a subversive politics), we fail to credit the multiple identities of the operating contexts, which offer us a series of factors in a dynamic relationship between any event and the contexts of agents, artistic heritage, world, and receptions. The idea of a framing or foundational context, put forward as a singular idea (power, authority, ideology, etc.), produces at best a reductive explanation.

Also, the reasoning cannot explain how and why the various events and actions within the same context can be so different from one another. This is the basic indictment that David Perkins makes against the two-part model of text and context: "If we start with the context, we cannot explain how it could determine works to be different [from one another] . . . In other words, if works have the same context, yet are unlike, their dissimilarities cannot be explained contextually."[54] Caught in this circular trap, we are unable to describe or explain the basic conditions and features of history – difference, dissimilarities, and change. When we embrace an idea of a singular context, it logically nullifies our attempts to explain the reasons for the differences and changes that we discover in the historical record.

2. *The problem of correspondence or preordained unity.* We need to examine our working assumptions that theatre and politics somehow always operate as a unit, as corresponding systems. In basic terms this may seem the case, but theatre and political systems also develop apart from one another, with separate factors contributing to their identities and activities. And they do not change necessarily at the same pace or for the same reasons. So, this idea of the unity of art and society continues to be an abiding problem of analysis.

For example, Raymond Williams has much to tell us about the historical relation between dramatic forms and social formations. His argument that "residual, dominant, and emergent practices" exist simultaneously in a period has proved to be an important model that avoids the idea of singular identity for all things and practices within an era. But, nonetheless, he struggles to present an analysis that gets beyond the model of correspondence. This model – in many ways foundational to his idea of cultural materialism – requires that the arts and social practices be joined. As he states: "We cannot separate literature and art from other kinds of social practice, in such a way as to make them subject to quite special and distinct laws."[55] True to his Marxist ideas, for example, he claims that in the eighteenth century, because of the rise of capitalism and a mercantile culture, a new form of drama emerged. For the first time "the material of drama was coming, if hesitantly, to be defined as contemporary (by contrast with all previous drama)."[56] Well, to a certain extent this makes sense; clearly Lillo's *The London Merchant*, which Williams features in his analysis, seems to fit this argument. As a tragedy of contemporary life and common people, it is strikingly different from *Hamlet* or *Coriolanus*. But if we look beyond tragedy to comedy, this causal argument about the required unity of context and text (or social practice and art) collapses. As we know, comedy, starting with Aristophanes, has often represented contemporary life. Various medieval farces give us the contemporary world. And Renaissance comedy, from Machiavelli forward, often staged contemporary culture (e.g., Jacobean city comedies, Molière's *The Misanthrope*). Also, we might note that in the Renaissance some domestic tragedies put contemporary conditions on stage. In brief, drama with a contemporary setting cannot be tied to the emergence of mercantile culture in the eighteenth century.[57]

Williams attempts to escape the limitations of the idea of correspondence by introducing the idea of "disclosure," whereby social practices are disclosed rather than reflected in artistic form.[58] But the basic idea of correspondence still operates in his analysis. The best he can do, consequently, when he tries to explain change in genres, is to evoke repeatedly the all-purpose concept of "crisis" in political and social practices.[59] But "crisis" fails to explain why some formations, such as comedy, do not seem to change significantly across many periods, while other formations, such as certain types of bourgeois or domestic drama, can sometimes be located within a specific cultural formation. To add to our problem, the genre of comedy maintains many of its generic traits across the ages, from Plautus through Shakespeare and Sheridan to Ayckbourn, yet it is still quite capable of presenting contemporary life in its very changeable nature from era to era. Of course, we often recognize this double identity of comedy, but our inadequate models of political analysis and our period concepts often lead us to opposite conclusions, as if the models and the concepts require that we ignore the evidence before us. It would seem, then, that the *processes* of continuity and change are bracketed – if not denied – by our ideas of both identity and correspondence.

We must guard against this collapse into correspondence theory, tied too often to an idea of singularity (or of hegemony). Text and context (or event and condition) all too conveniently add up to the same thing. This condition reproduces, in its own political formation, the same intellectual process we saw in the intertextual model of new historicism or the predictable correspondences in the cultural materialist analysis of textual "dialectics." Despite the appeals to ironic reversals, theatricality, "contestations," or "dialectics," the correspondences are ordained by and subsumed within the textual method that joins a singular context to a unified or organic network. This line of argument always rewards the interpretive tactics of the critic/scholar who connects A to B because they exist within the singular and ordained condition of correspondence.

Although, in our procedures and concepts, we seem to trap ourselves into arguments that make theatre the product of a ventriloquist culture, we know that its development and articulation derive from both endogenous and exogenous factors (often operating simultaneously yet seldom in accord). And anomalies, sometimes of striking originality, emerge. In the supposed "Age of Goethe" (which gets called romantic by one critic, classical by another), we struggle to yoke Goethe and Schiller together as representative artists and models, but the age also confronts us with striking anomalies from the operating norms in art and society (e.g., von Kleist). And somehow we must also accommodate startlingly new and profoundly different artists who seem quite at odds with contemporary art and society (e.g., Büchner). Consequently, it is hard to remain satisfied with an analytical model that makes theatre an epiphenomenon of a definitive socioeconomic and political culture. It is true that Williams and others have countered certain Marxist formulas of a controlling context by demonstrating the reductive nature of the idea of "base and superstructure," but his own ideas of correspondence still fail to do justice to the historical complexity of artistic life and activity.[60] In this case the mirror analogy has returned under cover of a disguised identity, a refreshed but inadequate metaphor.

3. *The problem of location.* It should be apparent that we are overly dependent upon the binarism of text and context which sets up obligatory patterns of correspondence

or formulaic models of resistance. The political force or agency is located in one or the other location. As Norman Bryson, the art historian, has demonstrated in his critique of the prevalent models for placing "art in context,"[61] our foundational ideas of context or network (or ground, platform, etc.) establish the context as the supposed shaping condition for any event, action, or text that we study. So we find what we have already identified (and ignore many other aspects of the social/political world). Context, in this formula, is the active force. But sometimes it occurs to us to make a reversal – by proclaiming oppositional politics and power. We think that we have liberated ourselves from the reductive model, but all we have done is shifted to an equally reductive way of identifying the event and its meanings. We often confuse our own quasi-oppositional politics and sensibilities with the event, work, text, or action we admire and want to celebrate. Three cheers for the folk or women or Shakespeare or whoever we decide to embrace. This reversal hardly solves the problem of a reductive binary category (but perhaps our sense of irony or paradox pleases us sufficiently, so we can ignore the fact that we are still operating in a circular mode of analysis).

Adding to the problem, our period concepts, instead of expanding the possible ways of identifying, distinguishing, and analyzing the aspects of political conditions, collapse text and context together into a singular identity (e.g., the "textuality" model of new historicism). In this totalizing mode we don't even maintain three standard locations for political power and agency: (1) individuals, groups, movements, and specific theatrical organizations; (2) cultural institutions, governments, economic systems; and (3) large historical mentalities or ideologies of an era that define the major operations of a culture, and perhaps even blanket the culture with ideological or hegemonic control over thought, discourse, and practices. Yet even as we try to hold to these three distinctions, we discover that the relationship between and among text, context, and period is not just problematic, but sometimes contradictory. What, then, should we do? As I attempted to illustrate quickly at the beginning of this chapter, our reflections upon the location of politics are irrevocably inadequate as long as they maintain the basic polarity between event and context. The idea of location needs to be multiple. To clarify, I want to close this chapter with a tabulation of some possible locations for politics in our historical study of theatrical events.

> It is the belief men *betray* and not that which they *parade* which has to be studied.
> Charles Peirce, *Collected Papers* (1960: 297)

Here are nine possibilities. By opening up the field of investigation we can get beyond the crippling polarity of text and context, event and structure. In the process of engaging these various locations, we increase the possibility that we will not be constrained by any homogeneous or singular idea of periodization. We also will be able to attend to matters of change and causality – just because we have refused to be satisfied by a synchronic idea of context or structure.

(1) **Politics can be located in the ideolect of each person, dramatic text, performance, or event – that is, in the individual features of the artists, documents, works, and actions that provide specificity and particularity.** For all theatrical events, we need to attend to their topical, local, and unique qualities. We have, for instance, six distinct manuscripts of Thomas Middleton's *A Game at Chess* (written primarily in 1624), each revealing its own idiosyncratic articulation of politics during the writing process, as he responded to current events and incorporated some statements and ideas from the political and religious pamphlets. The earliest of the six manuscripts, probably written between March and June 1624, is 310 lines shorter than one of the published texts. Among other things, it lacks the character of the Fat Bishop, who represented Marco Antonio de Dominus, former Archbishop of Spalatro. This character, likely added during rehearsal, was probably written to accommodate the acting skills of William Rowley, a popular actor.

In turn, we know that the King's Men, in the August 1624 performance at the Globe theatre, added their own political meanings to the play by means of costuming, properties, methods of characterization, gestures, and movement patterns. For example, as Don Carlos Coloma noted in an ambassadorial letter back to Spain, the players took care to dress the Black King to look like the young Philip IV: "the king of blacks has easily been taken for our lord the King, because of his youth, dress, and other details."[62] Likewise, great effort went into representing Count Gondomar, the Black Knight, the villain of the play. Spain, the Catholic Church, and the Jesuits were all given specific political identities by playwright and players. We need to do the diligent historical work that gives us access to the idiolect of signs and codes that made the play and production so controversial. The various topical sources, each expressing its localized significance, offer an accumulative register, both explicit and implicit, of the contributing semiotic signs and codes.

Of course, historians, by the nature of their discipline, are committed to the specificity of events. In this sense we just need to be true to the historical enterprise, but a localized approach to history – and historiography – needs to be applied more rigorously in theatre history.[63] Beyond the value of a refresher course in historical methodology, we might notice how the principle of "localization" ("local knowledge," "thick description," "situated knowledge") operates today in microhistory, anthropology, and ethnography.[64]

(2) **Politics can be located in the intentions, motives, and aims of the individuals or agents who produced the dramatic and performance texts.** By mining the personal documents, we can discover the affective register of the particular choices, values, dispositions, and qualities of presentation of the agents. In a sense, this is what R. G. Collingwood, in *The Idea of History*, calls the "inside" of an event: the thoughts that we try to recover in the process of constructing any historical event. The "outside" is the event itself, what happened (and its consequences). But we need to delve into the "inside." In our research we attempt to determine not only *what* a document means but also *how* and *why*. What does it name; what does it refer to; how so and why? We place the statement in the context of other statements by the agent, and we situate it in relation to other commentary of the time on the same or similar

topics. By reconstructing both the inside and outside of an event, we identify two potential locations of political meaning. We discover the idiolect of the event (its recoverable features) from aspects of the idiosyncratic nature of the intentions of the initiating agents. We recover the locutionary meaning of available statements. As Wilhelm Dilthey stated: "We explain nature, we understand the human mind."[65]

Reading plays for their locutionary statements is difficult, however, because the political thoughts within a play are distributed among the characters. We have to learn to read by indirection, by implication. There may be a preface by the playwright, especially in modern times (e.g., all of those essays written by Bernard Shaw), but for many plays we only have the dialogue and stage directions. We attempt to abstract the playwright's intentions and motives from the speeches and dramatic action, a problematic procedure as we have seen. A dozen different political meanings, for instance, have been discovered in each of Shakespeare's plays. Caution must be the watchword.

We also have the performance, which represents the contributions of the players. For example, the acting styles of certain actors (e.g., Richard Burbage, Edward Alleyn) imbued the characters they played with the aura of their own talent and status. In some cases, their own qualities of presence and performance, operating across a career, expressed values and attitudes that may carry certain political denotations and connotations. This condition adds yet another complication, as we try to distinguish between the signs of the character and those of the actor. But potentially certain political meanings, such as Edward Alleyn's heroic style, may derive from the talent and status of the actor rather than from the topical comments of the character on the page. The actor augments the text but also changes it. In modern times we recognize this quality of presence in certain film and stage actors. And on occasion some of them (e.g., David Garrick, Rachel, Elizabeth Robins, John Wayne, Paul Robeson) achieve in performance a political presence and quality of character or persona that extends, modifies, exceeds, or even challenges – not just supports – the political position articulated in the work itself. Spectators perceive within (or project onto) the accomplished performer a political (and often ethical) quality, identity, or aura. Charisma manifests itself in various ways. Each performer, at least potentially, may embody not simply a dramatic character but also certain political registers, explicitly or implicitly, of authority. Of course, many specific performances and performers may not reveal or realize a particular political presence, but by paying attention to the idiolect of the event and the idiosyncratic features of the intentions, we can sometimes find certain political attributes, apart from many contextual features, that are located in these individual modes of representation and agency.

Also, as we saw in our case studies of the productions of *Ubu Roi* and *A Doll's House*, theatrical events involve the intentions of the various contributors to the events. We must always keep in mind the multiple nature of agency in theatrical events. Whatever the historical situation – distant past or contemporary moment – there are several avenues that may carry us into the inside of the event. Accordingly, we must be on guard against a historical analysis that collapses the agendas and agencies of playwright, players, and patron into one political meaning.

(3) **Politics can be located in the artistic heritage: the conventions, traditions, canons, genres, styles, norms, and recurring patterns of drama and theatre that any specific text or performance draws upon and uses as part of its basic craft.** In short, the artistic heritage provides many of the intertextual codes of any dramatic text and theatrical performance – guidelines to, if not rules for, engagement and expectation. Apart from its specific or local political meanings, a theatrical event or text also carries several layers of political meanings within its conventional and traditional codes. The codes are signaling to us, but we need the historical knowledge that allows us to read the signs and break the codes.

For example, the 1608 quarto text of *King Lear*, besides containing topical allusions to political conditions under James I, also frames this topicality in more general political attributes of the tragic genre (e.g., ideas of authority, social distinctions, power conflicts, the significance of suffering, the tragic downfall of the protagonist). The norms that guide performance and genre (modes of expression and characterization, plot development, and theme) may well supplement the topical attributes, thus establishing political meanings within a text or performance that reinforce the topical politics. But sometimes the conventions and norms of tragedy are quite distinct from other aspects of the work or event, and thus may contradict the topical meanings. These tragic conventions may dominate (or even displace) those other aspects, especially for audience members familiar with the norms, the actors, and the generalizing tradition.

In the process of writing the play, Shakespeare made decisions on what to represent. In turn, the players, as they developed their characters and costumed them, engaged with other possible meanings that derived from their experiences both in the theatre and the political times. Indeed, some of the "contextual" attributes that we might credit to the political times and conditions may have found their articulation only because the playwrights and the players, drawing upon previous experiences, recognized the possible significance of particular conventions, traditions, canons, genres, styles, norms, and recurring patterns of *King Lear*. That is, besides the unique attributes of idiolect and idiosyncratic motives, the politics may have been released by some of the norms that yoke the play and production methods to the inherited traditions. Unfortunately, we may misread the abiding political traits of tragedy as if they are specific statements about English politics in 1608. Care must be taken.

(4) **Politics can be located in the ways a theatrical text or performance may resonate with current events within the community or nation.** Whether intended or not, some theatrical events intersect with current events, and thereby speak to those events, both directly and indirectly. They are timely; they are of the moment. For example, a handful of plays, right after the defeat of the Spanish Armada in 1588, benefited from their immediate engagement with national and religious issues. They captured or spoke to the spirit of the moment. This kind of political significance may not have been intended initially when a playwright began a play in 1588, but as the play got written and the production was staged, the theatre event and the political situation aligned in a special relationship. This kind of serendipity may not be anticipated – by anyone involved or responding – but all at once a special political

register emerges, and it may even dominate the event. A year earlier or a year later, this relationship would not have been established, but the current events opened up the discursive moment.

(5) **Politics can be located in the social and economic organization of theatre itself, its management procedures, its business practices and commercial aims, its institutional qualities, its social and economic place in a theatre culture, a city, and a country.** In addition to tracing the politics of a play, a playwright, a player, a patron, or a producer, we can sometimes attend to the politics of management – a politics of business decisions calibrated to the political times, as the case of Philip Henslowe illustrates. This practice may be a politics of survival or of staying under the radar. Or it may be a more cunning use of the political issues, conditions, and system. Henslowe illustrates both kinds of politics; he operated beyond the political control of the London city fathers, across the Thames river (Rose Theatre) or beyond the north wall of the city (Fortune Theatre). But he also aligned himself with the court, taking on court appointments (e.g., keeper of the royal dogs).

Sometimes, the politics of business, administration, and repertory is rather distinct from the politics of the plays and performance styles. Philip Henslowe's political instincts, ideas, and leanings should not be confused with the politics in the plays at the Rose and Fortune (e.g., those of Marlowe and Dekker). So, even if one does not see the theatre and politics from the perspective of cultural materialism, there are good reasons to attend to business and management practices, especially if one is willing and able to allow localized evidence and explanations to emerge.

(6) **Politics can be located in the social, economic, and political organizations of the society itself, outside of the theatre; that is, in the distinct aspects of communal, national and international systems that define and order human activities.** This larger "context" is where scholars often locate politics in relation to the theatre. Indeed, each of these three subsets of society, economy, and politics are the standard locations and definitions for our general idea of political context. Often we have focused our attention on some kind of governmental identity and practice. In recent years, though, we have also been interested in the politics of race and gender (e.g., our immersion in models and theories of identity politics and our interest in colonial and postcolonial topics). Yet as sophisticated as our investigations may be, they still settle, all too neatly, into a formulaic model of event and structure, text and context. Instead of the unproductive choice between a politics of power and a politics of contention, we need to see that there are dozens of ways that most theatre events are related to social, economic, and political issues?[66] As I suggested in the Introduction with the four hermeneutical triangles, these conditional aspects of the complex "world" outside of a historical event need to be related to the other locations of contextual influence, including the contributing agents, the many aspects of the artistic tradition, and the possible modes of reception.

Also, besides society, economy, and politics, we should add geography to these basic categories. For instance, London, as the urban center, has received much of our attention in theatre history ever since the sixteenth century. But London, inside and outside the city walls, had various neighborhoods with distinct identities and activities. Because each of the playhouses developed in terms of its local geography, the Red Bull plays and audiences were often distinct from those of the Fortune or the Globe. Moreover, theatrical practices outside of London developed not only in terms of the local conditions and geography of the various villages, towns, and cities but also in relationship to London. Beyond ideas of center and periphery, we need to rethink the importance of geography in the making and significance of theatre activities. Our growing knowledge of touring may expand our political understanding of the ways theatre interacted with local and national government in the sixteenth and seventeenth centuries. And in the case of modern theatre, for example, we are beginning to understand the politics of the Royal Shakespeare Company in terms of not simply the political topics and themes of the plays and productions but also the geographic locations of the RSC. The history of the company – with its "home" in Stratford-upon-Avon (Memorial Theatre, Swan) and its "home away" in London (Aldwych, Barbican) – has been defined by a set of recurring political issues, problems, and aims ever since the 1960s. Often divided against itself because of its double identity, the RSC has generated internal politics over its company organization and practices that split its mission between Stratford and London. In turn, these issues and problems have carried over to its external politics because of its complex relationship to the National Theatre Company, the Arts Council, and governmental policy under both the Conservative and Labour leadership. And if we identify the company with its geography, we find ourselves involved in a historical development that goes back at least to Frank Benson's company in Stratford (and occasionally in London) at the end of the nineteenth century. Obviously, any attempt to understand the contextual conditions and contributions of social, economic, and political factors would require us to distinguish between and among these factors. And each factor has its special relation to the geographical issues.[67]

(7) **Politics can be located in the available political and rhetorical discourses of an era.** In other words, the communicative norms and systems, beyond those of theatrical genres, express established, acceptable, and even preferred ways of articulating political thought and meaning, as Quentin Skinner and other scholars of Renaissance political discourse have noted.[68] Skinner has argued that in the process of interpreting political texts and reconstructing historical events, we should describe and analyze the "action" that is expressed or implied in the speeches and essays we study. Our task is to try "to think as our ancestors thought and to see things their way." As much as possible, we attempt to "recover the concepts they possessed, the distinctions they drew and the chains of reasoning they followed in their attempts to make sense of their world." From Skinner's perspective, historical understanding requires us to attend to "different styles of reasoning; it is not necessarily a matter of being able to translate those styles into more familiar ones."[69] Skinner urges us to examine not only the political ideas and rhetorical tropes of individual speeches, essays, and books but also the discourse models and styles that are prevalent within an era. We also need to attend to the speech act and its propositions, the mode of expression that articulates the political intentions, values, and ideas of the speakers and writers. As we try to unpack the ideolect and intentions of historical documents, we often need to

recognize that what might seem to be a personal or idiosyncratic statement of a specific person is actually derived from a more general discourse and rhetoric.

In the Jacobean theatre, for example, the Elect Nation plays of Thomas Dekker derive much of their rhetoric from the heated language of Reformation pamphlets. Whose politics, then, are we discovering: Dekker's or the pamphlet writer's? Other playwrights can be located in the rhetoric of the "Senecan amble."[70] And yet others reveal the influence of Cicero, as taught in the Renaissance universities. Aspects of their statements and styles have a common location in the rhetorical manuals of the age. Consequently, what at first may seem to be a specific political statement by a playwright can actually be one of the standard *topoi* of a pervasive rhetorical tradition. Indeed, the rhetorical manuals spell out common and special topics, types of speeches, stylistic schemes and tropes, and models to imitate. In these cases the politics is situated in the rules and codes of rhetoric.

(8) **Politics can be located in the general mentality, ideology, Zeitgeist, or discursive formations of a culture – its basic system of beliefs, assumptions, and intellectual practices.** This issue carries us back to the problem of periodization, so care must be taken with any singular, expansive idea of ideology or mentality, which often is an overly simplified or reductive process of identification, description, and explanation. Under the cover of the idea of the "spirit," the "Zeitgeist," or the "discursive formation" of an age, much nonsense has been written. Nonetheless, we need to note the ways that abiding political assumptions, beliefs, ideas, and practices are generated by the culture at large. Part of the challenge of historical analysis is to recognize these large processes in action and to find the language (besides the formulaic concepts of power) that explain how and why systems define and express key aspects of a society's politics. Because much of the analysis in chapter 5 on the problem of a singular identity for period concepts applies equally to the uses of the general ideas of mentality or Zeitgeist, I will not repeat myself here.

(9) **Politics can be located in the reception rather than the production of the artwork; that is, in the audience's responses, perceptions, and modes of understanding – those processes of recognition, acceptance, rejection, accommodation, interpretation, and evaluation that are the register and final site of meaning in cultural activities.** How can we construct the political meanings of performance events apart from their reception? In recent years we have begun to analyze reception – horizons of expectation, reading formations, attendance patterns – but we need to expand and refine our methods of research and analysis, including the ways we construct the concepts of audience and community. And we should resist the idea that the audience or the community is a singular entity, a collective mind.

Even when we study specific productions, we are often tempted to construct an abstract or ideal audience that we want to believe is implied by the event and its character. For instance, Leah Marcus (1988) presents a localized study of the St. Stephen's Day production of *King Lear* at court in 1606. Noting, for example, some possible topical references in the Folio text of the play, she reconstructs aspects of the performance before King James I. By focusing on a specific event she demonstrates some of the strengths of a microhistorical study, but her historical analysis is based upon an assumption that the audience interpreted the political statements in the performance in a like-minded manner. Why must we assume that the king and the hundreds of spectators, drawn from different stations and perspectives within court society, would all interpret the mock trail scene in Act 3 as a commentary on the issue of royal prerogative within James' court? Marcus also wants us to believe that the spectators as a group would equate the storm scene with the idea of James as Jove the Thunderer, "who would rain down his terrible punishments if the Project for Union [of England, Scotland, and Wales] were not expedited."[71] In turn, Marcus argues that the spectators would all recognize that this mad scene provides an "echo of James I's actual tactics ... to work his will upon recalcitrant subjects who committed more minor versions of the same infractions [that Lear's daughters have committed]."[72]

The basic problem with this approach is that the learned critic, gathering up extensive historical information about James and British history, becomes the ideal reader and the model spectator. Even if we agreed that the play and production generated these various allusions to James I (a series of propositions quite open to question), there is no good reason to assume that the spectators, sharing a collective mind, would interpret them the way that Marcus does. So, despite her admirable attempt to do a localized historical reconstruction, her analysis fails to localize the spectators. If "localization" is to be applied to each playwright, each play, each player, and each patron, it must also be applied to spectators as well (to the extent that evidence allows us access to members of the audience). Of course, the reception of audiences to theatrical events is one of the key features of the context, including the political context. But the first rule of audience research is that people do not respond in the same way. They bring a diverse knowledge of the *world* to a performance and a diverse knowledge of the *artistic heritage*. Each of them, in the process of negotiating the relation between world and event and between artistic heritage and event, constructs a specific, sometimes unique event. Even though we do not usually have the historical details that would allow us to offer a cross-section of the spectators at a performance, we can still avoid a reductive reconstruction that turns them all into a singular version of a scholar's ideal reader.

History requires distinctions in the construction of spectators. Just as art historians are tempted to create what Norman Bryson calls "the notion of a 'timeless' response to paintings,"[73] so too do theatre historians create an ideal or typical response. For theatre events of the last 200 years or so, it is often possible to dig out one or more reviews. We often grant the theatrical reviewer a special dominion over the reception and its meaning. By this means, we create an authorized reception. But as we saw with the responses to the 1889 production of *A Doll's House*, the various reviews offer a wide range of responses. No single review can serve as the voice of the collective group; no review allows us to construct a singular version of the audience members.

Just as each event has its idiolect, so too does each review. Sometimes we are prepared to grant special significance and status to a particular review, as was the case, for example, with Kenneth Tynan's review of John Osborne's *Look Back in Anger* in 1956. Reproduced in dozens of books, it constructed the event for a generation of scholars, students, and general readers. Then, to be expected, a new generation of scholars had to step forward and proclaim that Tynan should not be taken as the ideal spectator, the source of truth. In order to revise our assessment of the singular importance of *Look Back in Anger*, we had to dismiss Tynan. But have we actually improved our methodology for constructing either the event or the audience?

In brief, then, these are nine possible locations for political meanings, and of course politics can be located in any and all of them. But if all of the locations carry distinct yet overlapping (and sometimes contradictory) sources of political meaning for a theatre event, what are we to think of the standard approach today that divides our choices between text and context? Surely this neat binary is an inadequate model for studying and describing the politics of the theatre. Our solution is not to retreat to a single, all-encompassing idea of periodization, mentality, or intertextuality. But what are we to do? Can we really describe and analyze all nine different locations of meaning each and every time we want to discuss a play, a performance, or an historical event? Not surprisingly, most scholars, faced with such a problem, tend to latch onto one of these specific areas as the basis of their methodology.

Accordingly, theatre semioticians focus mainly on Location 1: the signs and codes of dramatic and performance texts. Biographers key on Location 2: the motives, intentions, and aims of the artists. Marxist historians privilege Location 6: the socioeconomic factors that organize communal, national, and/or international systems. Scholars of the history of ideas feature Location 7: the intellectual heritage of discourses, ideas, and styles among writers. Or perhaps these scholars are drawn to Location 8: the mentalities, discursive formations, and textual systems of representation. Formalist critics gravitate toward Location 3: the artistic heritage of conventions, traditions, and codes of artistic representation, and scholars in audience research specialize in Location 9: the audience's responses, perceptions, and modes of understanding. This selective distribution is typical, with only a few ambitious scholars perhaps taking up three or more options out of these nine locations of politics. A strong case could be made that the various locations complement one another, at least in certain ways, but each of them also defines and identifies the idea of politics in special ways. Therefore, to move from one location to another requires scholarly distinctions. Otherwise, we are in danger of sliding back into a singular idea of politics.

What, then, might we conclude about this search for the location of political meaning in theatre studies? Well, perhaps some readers have figured out that after I have catalogued nine different locations of politics for the reconstruction of theatre events, I could not resist a final turn to the tenth option that intersects with the other nine – the one who does the reconstructing. All of these options imply that meaning must be located not only in these nine possible choices but also in the nature of interpretation itself. As we have seen throughout this study of theatre historiography, all theatre events exist in several states of identity: in the past, in the archive, in the research methods we follow, and in the report the historian develops that is the result of the analysis and interpretation of the sources. Political meanings are thus located in these conditions of historical inquiry, along with the distribution in the nine locations. In other words, although we are attempting as historians to reconstruct the political nature and conditions of texts and performances, we must remember that we are separated from the events that we are studying. And in order to reconstruct them, we must use our own language, assumptions, beliefs, and discourses that operate in our culture in conjunction with the language, assumptions, beliefs, and discourses that operate in the sources. We write from the present, which is yet another location for the reconstruction of past events. As always, theatre historiography identifies itself as a challenge and a problem.

> All history is modern history.
>   Wallace Stevens, "Adagia," in *Opus Posthumous* (1957: 166)

Indeed, I want to recommend, in conclusion, that we should begin instead of end with this condition of historical analysis and political thought. We must reflect upon the ways we set up the whole enterprise of locating our own politics in the theatre we study. Perhaps, then, we can also begin to solve some of the problems and contradictions that the field of theatre studies faces today. Of course, to acknowledge that our present political understanding contributes to our methods of locating and constructing the political contexts of historical theatre is merely to recognize that all historians must negotiate the relation between past and present. In saying this, I am not embracing the facile idea that all history is narrative (and therefore fiction), or the equally jejune idea that we are imprisoned in the present, unable to attain any understanding of the reality of past events. Though we stand in the contemporary moment, looking backward, we are not compelled necessarily to impose a modern sensibility and understanding upon the past. Our task, as historians, is not only to return to the past but to explain it, as best we can. Moving beyond some of our ready-made ideas on texts, contexts, and periods, we might succeed in doing justice to the complexity of the historical events that we are attempting to understand.

Part four

Summing up

Chapter 7

The theatrical event and its conditions: a primer with twelve cruxes

Time to sum up. In order to clarify, but not simplify, the tasks of historical inquiry, I want to describe some of the abiding factors, issues, and conditions that we all face as theatre historians. At the risk of providing an overly schematic summation here, I have identified twelve "cruxes" that historians confront in the interrelated tasks of investigating, analyzing, and reporting an event. These dozen cruxes, though lacking the status of axioms for historical scholarship, are fundamental conditions of the historical project. In order to focus the discussion, I will return to the 1889 production of *A Doll's House*. Our familiarity with that event, including some of the definitive features of both its theatrical and historical identities, should make it an effective illustration of several of the cruxes.

The London production of Ibsen's play involved many intentions, factors, actions, and aims that were distributed among not only the production team and performers but also a highly engaged community of spectators and reviewers. The event, as we saw in chapter 4, was quite complex; and the documentation tied to William Archer revealed his controlling role in the making of the event. As well, a variety of historical factors made the event significant, including the social attitudes and moral values of the spectators and reviewers, the professional and commercial conditions of West End theatre in London, the development of what we now call "avant-garde" or "alternative" theatre, the relation between avant-gardism and various socialist and anarchist movements, the place of women in Victorian culture, the models of marriage in nineteenth-century society, the development of the suffrage movement, and so on. Though it is possible to limit our attention to the aesthetic qualities of this event, my intention is to consider a full range of contributing factors for the production. The theatre historian, in contrast to the theatre semiotician, needs to cross back and forth between the theatrical and historical issues of the event in order to write history. Performance analysis is but the starting point.[1] In what follows, then, I am assuming that a "theatrical event" is also a "historical event." I use the term "theatrical event," therefore, as shorthand for all of the aesthetic and non-aesthetic factors in such an event.

Crux 1: the endogenous features of a theatrical event, including not only the whole or unified action and its codes of representation but also the motivations, aims, and purposes of the initiating agent or agents of an event

All human events can be understood as actions. The two concepts of event and action are often used interchangeably. Therefore, the historian's task of representing past events requires a search through the documentation for the evidence of the actions of the participants in the event. Those actions, in turn, contain and usually express the intentions and aims of the agents. (This way of perceiving an event should be quite familiar to theatre historians because – thanks to Aristotle – both drama, as a genre, and performance, as a kind of spectacle, have always been understood as types of actions.) To the extent that the historian uncovers the component parts of the organizing action (or series of actions) that make up the theatrical event, the task of reconstructing an event can be realized. The miscellaneous evidence for human behavior is presented by the historian as purposeful and unified action, capable of being represented along both the diachronic and synchronic axes.

The collected actions that make up an event contribute to its wholeness or unity. This unity may already be established by the kind of event being investigated. In these kinds of events, such as a theatre production, the participating agents have already given the event its unifying features as an artistic practice. Their actions and purposes are in service to the shared idea that an internal principle of wholeness or completeness guides them. Even if they disagree on which idea of unity they serve or should pursue, they still accept, in most cases, the unifying aim. And if the theatre production is derived from a play, the formal features of drama reinforce the principle of unity. This point may seem obvious, but we need to recognize that many, perhaps most, historical actions lack unity. Indeed, much of the time our actions are partial and incomplete, lacking many of the traits of a completed event and lacking a unifying principle. Events in life, unlike those in the arts, seldom have a self-contained unity of beginning, middle, and end as occurs in narrative, or a definitive frame, topic, and integrated parts as pertains in painting, or a distinguishable pattern of development, variation, and return as occurs musically in the sonata form.

In the case of complex events the historical agents may not have shared a specific aim. Their actions, distributed through the documentation, may seem random, incomplete, or contradictory. Historians, in an attempt to create a unified event – for we do not want to believe that history is only a story of chaos and meaningless actions – gather together the evidence for the meanings of the events and actions. The motives of some of the agents may help, and their actions may reveal some order. But that order does not dictate how historical understanding may achieve additional, sometimes different, ideas of order. If the archive does not deliver a unified event, the historian connects the parts until they deliver a whole – an action that can be described and explained in terms of its internal logic, as understood by the historian. A process of mediation occurs in the making of historical understanding. Past actions and present perceptions interact in the making of the event. The historian is always attempting to be true to what the documentation reveals, but that revealing process is itself a kind of action, a kind of event. Even in the case of an artistic event, such as a theatre production, the idea of order initiated by the participants may not be the one that the historian recognizes. The historian, rejecting the unifying versions provided by the participants (though not rejecting the underlying principle of unity), may decide to reconceive the event and its actions. There are always several possible ways to define and understand the identity of an event, as I noted in chapter 2 on the several different historical narratives that might be written about Jarry's *Ubu Roi*.

The related fields of theatre studies and performance studies have developed, over the years, many methods for describing and analyzing the operating features of a theatrical action or event. The event, in these methods, is submitted to some kind of formal analysis. As early as Aristotle's *Poetics*, with its six definitive elements, a method of formal analysis was spelled out for describing a unified event. Dramatic genres, and Aristotle's way of describing the definitive traits of tragedy, guided critical analysis for centuries. Theatrical performance, as a kind of event, had a place in Aristotle's system, but the elements of spectacle received little attention (and they were relegated apparently to the least significant place). For Aristotle the spectacle was not a separate event, but instead one of six aspects of the dramatic genre. From the Renaissance forward, however, the theatrical event, on its own terms, increasingly became a point of interest in various kinds of commentary. Though the rediscovery of Aristotle's *Poetics* re-established the idea of dramatic genre and unity, the alternative ideas of the theatre event emerged century by century. In modern times, the elements of spectacle have received major attention, from the Prague semioticians to the contemporary advocates of performance studies. Sometimes the defining codes of performance are still derived from the "dramatic text"; at other times, they are given a separate identity (without need of the sanctioning role and control of the initiating text). And of course there are many kinds of performance events, such as festivals, parades, pageants, and processions, that lack a controlling dramatic text.

For the theatre historian, there are many available methods for describing and analyzing the features of a theatrical performance. A useful model is provided by Willmar Sauter's *The Theatrical Event* (2000), which insists that the performance text (which theatre semioticians usually focus on) should not be separated from the spectator's means of perceiving and comprehending. Sauter's method of analyzing the *sensory*, *artistic*, and *symbolic* features of performance events and reception can serve a theatre historian quite effectively. All too often, when we reconstruct performance events, we ignore the ways that various spectators respond to theatrical events. Though effective in identifying the many codes of communication in dramatic texts and "performance texts," the theatre semioticians, with rare exceptions, construct the spectator as an ideal reader of signs, someone just like the semiotician who explicates the many different signs and unifies them into a systematic interpretation. But a communication model that basically ignores the many different ways that spectators perceive and interpret theatrical events is a poor guide for the theatre historian.[2]

In the process of describing the formal aspects of production and reception, the theatre historian tries to understand the motives and practices of the participants in a theatre event. In *The Idea of History*, the philosopher R. G. Collingwood argued that historians must concern themselves with the history of thought. He did not mean the history of ideas (though such study can be useful, especially when constructing the cultural understanding of a time and place), but instead the history of the thoughts of historical agents. "For history, the object to be discovered is not the mere event, but the thought expressed in it." The possible cause of an event is located, in the first place, in the thoughts of "the person by whose agency the event came about: and this is not something other than the event, it is the inside of the event itself."[3] The challenge for the historian is to burrow into the inner sanctum of an event, its motivating causes and purposes that define and explain key aspects of the actions. History is the study of human events, of human agents, of human actions, all of which can be understood at least partially in terms of human thoughts – the beliefs, values, motives, and aims of individuals.

> The historical narrative is a story of changes, of how one event was followed by another. If we want to find out what really happened, we must study how people thought these events were linked to one another and how the thoughts of how events are linked changed [from person to person, from era to era].
> Peter Munz, *The Shapes of Time* (1977: 192–93)

Collingwood's idea of the inside of an event has generated extensive debate since he put it forward. We need to understand that this idea is not a naïve idea of identification with the agent, as if the historian could sweep aside the years and somehow possess the inner thoughts of the historical figure. Nor has Collingwood proposed a kind of emotional empathy that would allow one to enter the minds and emotions of people from the past. Instead, he urges the historian to supplement the discipline of the archive research with an imaginative reformulation of how and why agents acted as they did. Besides describing *how* agents acted, we want to discover, as much as possible, *why* they acted as they did. But we also must keep in mind, as C. Behan McCullagh notes, that "the consequences of an action, event, or practice do not have to be intended to provide their meaning."[4] Actions and events may have meanings beyond what the agents thought and intended. They may not understand aspects of their own actions; they may be blind to forces and conditions that are also operating within and upon the action. And because most documents are created after the fact, sometimes years and decades later, the recollection may be inaccurate, even false and deceptive.

> Recollections . . . do not have existence outside the human mind; and most of history is based upon recollections – that is, written or spoken testimony.
> Louis Gottschalk, *Understanding History: A Primer of Historical Methods* (1969: 42)

Even if we are in accord with Collingwood's basic project, we need to acknowledge (1) the difficulty of gaining access to the truth about the motives of the historical agents; (2) the pervasive doubts that human intentions are the driving force in history, for there are substantial arguments that systems of discourse, power, and material causality control (or have a decisive role in) human actions. Concerning the intentions of agents, David Fischer agrees with Collingwood that the job of the historian is to "measure the motives and purposes that are part of the act itself."[5] Fischer attempts to distinguish between specific motives and general purposes, which express the values and beliefs of agents. This consideration of the shaping and conditional aims of agents enlarges the definition of agency, but it still falls short of Aristotle's idea of the four causes of an event or action: efficient, material, formal, and final causes. If we wish to discover the causal factors of an agent's motives, we need to define the interrelated concepts of intention, motive, purpose, aims, and final ends as comprehensively as possible in an enlarged idea of causes. In a basic sense, each human act has its initiating or efficient cause (which might be related to the concept of a motivating idea, the processes of willing an action into being). This efficient cause, understood usually as an action of an agent or agents, gains its identity in terms of its form, its material features, and its purpose. Of course the action occurs within contextual conditions that need to be explained, not simply identified. Aristotle's basic formulation of the four causes can be adapted and modified in several ways, as we see in the "grammar of action" that Kenneth Burke puts forward in several works.[6]

> Dramatism centers in observations of this sort: for there to be an *act*, there must be an *agent*. Similarly, there must be a *scene* in which the agent acts. To act in a scene, the agent must employ some means, or *agency*. And it can be called an act in the full sense of the term only if it involves a *purpose* . . . [I call] these five terms (act, scene, agent, agency, purpose) . . . the dramatistic pentad.
> Kenneth Burke (on the "dramatistic approach" to action) "Dramatism" (1968: 446)

There are, as well, certain similarities between Aristotle's ideas on causal actions and the five parts of an action that Michael Stanford identifies in historical events (1994).

> It is convenient to distinguish five parts of an action. One [is the] *intention*. When we act we aim to bring about some change in the world or in ourselves. The second part is the *assessment* that we make of the present state of affairs. This state of affairs is not only relevant to why we want to act – our intention; it also helps us to weigh up our chances of success, and to decide how best to achieve our aim. The third is the *means* that we adopt for our purpose. Next, we remember that to do anything at all requires energy, both mental and physical. Hence there has to be some emotion that drives us to act – love, hate, fear, ambition, and so on. (We can easily be mistaken about these.) So the *drive*, or the will, is the fourth element. The fifth contains them all; this is the *context*. By "context" we understand the whole environment – social, physical and cultural – within which the action occurs.
> Michael Stanford, *A Companion to the Study of History* (1994: 24–25)

Whose model is best: Aristotle, Burke, or Stanford? It depends, I suppose, upon the nature of the investigation. But I am not proposing that we adopt any specific model or authority to justify our historical investigations. The point is basic: events can be understood as actions, so let's reflect upon the component parts of any action. By considering the parts of an action, we can begin to reconstruct an event – on the basis of the available documentation and the nature of the event. The issue here is not the reductive one of finding a single theory that can be imposed upon historical events. Instead, we seek some basic ways to appreciate and configure the complex features of human actions.

Whatever our ability to identify the human intentions and motivations of agents, we still must recognize that intentionality cannot be the full and only measure of historical events and their meanings. Intentions take place within framing conditions. As Ludwig Wittgenstein stated: "An intention is embedded in its situation, in human customs and institutions."[7] Or as Georg Iggers notes in his study of European historical methods, "a broad agreement has appeared, shared by historians of very different ideological perspectives, that a history centering on the conscious actions of men does not suffice, but that human behavior must be understood within the framework of the structures within which they occur. These structures often are hidden to the men who make history."[8] This agreement is pervasive today in social history.

Still, in our enthusiasm for the history of determining structures, including those of economics, geography, mentalities, myths, and systems of symbolic order and communication, we need not abandon all studies of individual agency and intentionality. For example, though there has been a tendency to oppose Annales history to microhistory, we should be on guard against false dichotomies. Also, though we may grant that social, physical, and cultural systems exert major influence on human actions, we can still show how and why these actions depend as well upon the willful acts of individuals. The specificity of human thoughts and actions warrants close analysis, especially in the study of cultural history and artistic achievement. The shape of individual ideas, not just the structure of discourses and systems, should attract our attention, as Peter Munz argues:

> If we want to find out what actually happened, we must find out what people thought, what went into their minds. This is true in a double sense. We must find out what they thought in order to understand their actions and plans. But we must also find out their thoughts in order to understand the documents and charters, letters and annals that they wrote down. These documents are their own first attempts to write history.[9]

Moreover, because human actions in speech and writing are speech acts, the historian needs to recover the locutionary meaning of the statements within the historical event (to the extent that those acts can be recovered in the archive).

In order to do this, as Quentin Skinner has argued, we must reconstitute, as best we can, the meanings of the words and ideas for the agents. This process of historical understanding, he insists, requires us to recognize styles or methods of reasoning that may seem strange or unfamiliar to us. We need to honor the ways other people organized their thoughts and the world, without reducing their thinking and their statements to our own assumptions, vocabularies, and formulas. What seems unreasonable or irrational to us was perhaps once quite reasonable. If we find their beliefs, statements, and actions unreasonable, we fail to comprehend a key aspect of the rationality that we confront in the documents.[10] This project carries us into the study of not only the agent's distinctive language (spoken and written) but also the linguistic world of the age that contributes to the discourses. We need to comprehend both the *parole* and *langue* of the historical figures we study.[11] Ideally, we come to understand the linguistics, rhetoric, discourse conventions, the history of ideas, intellectual history, and cultural history of the era. From commonplace statements to philosophical writings, the intentions and aims are expressed within a historical matrix that we attempt to reconstitute. Motives and purposes, directed toward specific actions, carry attitudes and beliefs that shape both thought and action. The specific statements of agents carry their local, even unique meanings, yet in an accumulative manner the historian may be able to trace how the thoughts and motives of individual agents, as expressed in their statements, may participate in the expansive conditions and contexts of ideologies, mentalities, discourses, belief systems, and philosophies that operate within (and sometimes across) an era.[12]

> We must seek to surround the particular statement of belief in which we are interested with an intellectual context that serves to lend adequate support to it . . . It is perhaps needless to add that I am not pleading for historians to re-enact or re-create the experience of being sixteenth-century demonlogists or peasants of Languedoc or any other such alien creatures. I am only pleading for the historical task to be conceived as that of trying so far as possible to think as our ancestors thought and to see things their way. What this requires is that we should recover the concepts they possessed, the distinctions they drew and the chains of reasoning they followed in their attempts to make sense of their world.
> Quentin Skinner, *Visions of Politics: Volume One: Regarding Method* (2002: 42)

Thus, when we turn to the documents for the production of *A Doll's House*, we seek to discover, among other things, the intentions of Achurch, Charrington, and Archer. We cannot describe the event fully without determining how and why it occurred as an expression of their intentions, which we want to comprehend in the fullest way possible. But we can never recover all of the intentions of any historical agent, so we must work toward a partial description and analysis. For example, did Charrington and Achurch, husband and wife, take up *A Doll's House* in order to put forward the new drama or to find a handy vehicle that would bring them some money and fame? Did they want to make a statement about women and marriage? We have evidence that early in 1889 they were planning a world tour to the United States, Australia, New Zealand, and India. They began the tour soon after the June production of *A Doll's House*. When did they select the play for production? Did they select it (either purposefully or haphazardly) because they needed one more play to fill out their repertory for the tour? What came first: the idea of the tour (to which the production then would contribute) or the idea of the production (which would be financed in part by their agreement to do the tour)? Did they share the same aim? Did their purpose remain unchanged? Should we expect to find a clear, unambiguous answer to these questions? Not likely, if we assume – one of our possible presuppositions – that human motivations are seldom singular. They are usually mixed, often contradictory, and sometimes unconscious.[13] And even when we pin down some of the key aims, which are part of the measure of motivation, we still need to determine how those aims took shape and were carried out. The more we know about the purposes, the more we can make viable conjectures about the other causal factors.

Or consider another problem. As we have seen, William Archer was directly involved in the production. We can document many of his activities, and we have his reviews and articles that unequivocally express some of his intentions and beliefs. Many of his speech acts and actions are available to us. But to what extent did his involvement modify the intentions of Achurch and Charrington? For example, we know that Achurch and Charrington begged a gift of £100 from Henry Irving to produce a comedy called *Clever Alice*, but the money went instead into the production of *A Doll's House*. Did this change in purpose occur before or after Archer joined the project? Or was the request to Irving a subterfuge from the beginning? If so, was it part of a plan of either Achurch and Charrington or all three of them?

To answer these questions, we probably need to discover when Archer became involved. In other words, we are faced with one of the most persistent problems in history: identifying the origin of specific decisions and actions within an event. We want to discover the causes, sequential order, and meanings. One possible description of this event would reach back three months earlier, to March 1889, when Archer published the essay "Ibsen and the English Stage" that advocated the production of Ibsen, especially *A Doll's House* instead of *Ghosts*. Charrington and Achurch apparently read this essay, for they asked him for a translation of *A Doll's House*. Then they accepted his offer to help stage the play. Thus, the three of them joined forces, but this does not mean that their intentions were always the same, even though their production aims coincided. The event thus becomes an elaboration of various purposes and origins, stretching over several months.

Most of the time the historian faces great difficulty in identifying, unraveling, and explaining the sequence of aims and actions of the historical agents. Though the attempts to understand the motives of the participants in an event are to be commended, we must acknowledge that there is no single method. Perhaps, as we attempt to discover intentions and motives, we can be guided by certain kinds of dialogical analysis.[14] For example, by tracing, comparing, and contrasting the speech acts and actions of the three participants in production, we may develop aspects of a developing dialogue among them. Or instead of trying to explain away or ignore the contradictory roles that Archer played in this production (advocate for Ibsen's drama, translator, co-director, theatre reviewer, advisor for Charrington and Achurch, close friend of Shaw, etc.), we should set these roles in tension with one another, as we seek ironies and paradoxes, consistencies and inconsistencies, statements and counterstatements, conflicts and crises. The historical dialogue, open to contrary and complex permeations, challenges our ability to accommodate ambiguities and complexities in our methods for reconstructing the actions. As we move from action to reaction among the participants, we remain open to the various events or parts that make up the overall event we are attempting to understand. Our methods must be multiple because of the manifold nature of the agent's motives, actions, and aims.

Even when the event we study seems unified, we can question the nature of its unity. What the participants in the event thought and what we come to understand may be quite distinct ways of achieving a unified event. Whatever the case, we can delay until the end of our investigation the temptation to reach a clarifying and final resolution.

Crux 2: the encompassing or exogenous conditions that directly and indirectly contributed to the event's manifest identity and intelligibility

Whereas crux 1 focuses on endogenous factors that define the inside of an event, crux 2 shifts to the exogenous factors. Initially this shift outward seems to encompass everything that falls under the general (and vague) idea of the context. In general terms these two categories, the event and its context, may initiate our investigation. Human events are a composite of the endogenous features and the exogenous conditions. But as I tried to suggest with crux 1, there are several key features within the endogenous traits of the historical actions. It is also possible – and usually necessary – to separate out and name several types of exogenous conditions. These exogenous factors can derive from the *world* outside the theatrical event, such as the social and environmental conditions. They can reveal the ways that the *artistic heritage* contributes to the making and meanings of the event, for both the creators and the spectators. They can be the aspects of the *receptions* to the event, including the various ways that critics and audiences make and complete their versions of the event. And these exogenous conditions can also reveal, besides the motives of the participants as they create and cause the actions, the ways that the *agents* themselves were conditioned by factors outside of their own immediate intentions. Alfred Jarry attempted to create a controversial event, but despite his careful planning and aims, he could not control or anticipate the many different actions and reactions of the critics and spectators on the first evening. Nor could he anticipate the ways that the "bourgeois" spectators of the second evening accommodated themselves to some aspects of the production, yet grew tired of the farcical traits and the under-rehearsed nature of the production, which had a limited budget and a short rehearsal period.

For all events, there are many possible features and developmental patterns of the exogenous conditions. They can be traced, for example, by two distinct applications of the idea of genealogy. Jacky Bratton, interested in the influence of performance customs and traditions in nineteenth-century British theatre, has applied the idea of genealogy to the history of acting families.[15] These performers inherited and passed on, generation by generation, a heritage of acting practices. The historical continuum, larger than the motives, methods, and aims of individual performers, was the conduit for the exogenous genealogy of acting practices, established and maintained by the families. The performers carried the history in their very bodies, an inscribed set of customs provided, maintained, and carried forward by the artistic heritage rather than initiated and intended by the individual agents. Bratton's insight is striking because she uses this genealogy of families to recover the place of women in the theatre.

> The tracing of families as engines of induction, training and inheritance within the profession, and the exploring of the internal, sometimes hidden, power structures that reveals, brings into focus the historical contribution of women to theatre.
> Jacky Bratton, *New Readings in Theatre History* (2003: 178)

In turn, Joseph Roach has demonstrated how an expansive idea of genealogy, inspired in part by the writings of Michel Foucault, allows the theatre historian to investigate the development of performance in its social and political dimensions.[16] Here too the processes of change are not merely a matter of individual motives and intentions. Nor are the developments located in definitive origins and causes. Instead, genealogy offers a method for studying the transmissions and disruptions of patterns of behavior, belief, and ideology such as the discourses of race and prejudice in public performances in England and the United States since the eighteenth century. An exogenous system of genealogy is thus credited with the power and capability of yoking the stages of London and New Orleans. By means of these two ideas of genealogy, Bratton and Roach reconstitute how historians can discover evidence for people who are often missing from our standard histories of theatre. The danger, of course, is the level of generalization that sometimes informs these ideas of genealogy. One must be careful not to personify the processes, or to manufacture overly grand ideas of causality, periodization, and ideology, delivered by discursive vocabulary.

> Genealogies of performance . . . attend to "counter-memories," the disparities between history as it is discursively transmitted and memory as it is publicly enacted by the bodies that bear its consequences.
> Joseph Roach, *Cities of the Dead: Circum-Atlantic Performance* (1996: 26)

In the case of the production of *A Doll's House*, historians can identify various exogenous or contextual matters, such as the commercial nature of the London theatre in 1889, the management procedures of West End theatres, the widespread model of the actor-manager in London theatres (a model of organization that Charrington was attempting to follow), the early emergence of the director in the professional theatre (a model that Archer was tentatively attempting to offer at the rehearsals without stepping on Charrington's toes), the impact of realism in the arts, the campaigns for an "independent theatre" in Europe, the star system (evident, for instance, in the way the reviewers assessed Achurch's performance), the marginal status of the new drama, the increasing significance of the theatre critic in London (e.g., Archer, A. B. Walkley, Clement Scott), the economics of professional theatre in London, the importance of the long run for a production, the politics of censorship, the socioeconomic regulation of taste and fashion, the cultural milieu that produced and stratified London audiences, the place of theatre in the expanding entertainment industry, the changing status of actresses in British society, the development of Ibsen's career and international reputation in the 1880s, the significance of a play about women's issues, and so on. Each of these theatrical factors might be significant in the representation and interpretation of the production of Ibsen's play, though it is unlikely that any single history of the production would consider them all. They remain, at least in initial terms, outside the event itself. But almost any study of the event will find reasons to bring some of them to bear, as part of the full construction of the event.

Consider, for example, how this event, orchestrated in part by William Archer, was a decisive answer to the few productions and translations that had appeared before 1889. Archer was committed to the idea of the integrity of the playwright's text, a radical idea in nineteenth-century theatre. As translator and critic, he invested Ibsen's text with an artistic sanctity. As soon as the *Doll's House* production opened, he oversaw the publication of a special edition of the play in English, true to the complete Norwegian text. Then, in the next three years, he translated and published five volumes of Ibsen's plays. More people bought and read the plays in the 1890s than saw the plays. Other translators in London, including Charles Archer, Edmund Gosse, Havelock Ellis, Eleanor Marx, and Elizabeth Robins, joined the mission. But Archer established himself as the principle translator, the keeper and defender of the texts. And he attacked any other translation that failed to achieve his high standards. After Ibsen's death, he translated the rest of the plays, which were published in twelve volumes of Ibsen's works (along with some of Ibsen's notes and drafts). Archer also wrote dozens of reviews and articles, in which he often made the case for a theatre true to the text. Thus, in his various roles in the production, as translator, critic, and behind-the-scenes co-director with Carrington, Archer aligned himself with Ibsen's mission. Committed to an idea of theatre that is true to the author's intentions, he helped to define the modern, alternative theatre. This idea of artistic integrity proved to be a shaping discourse and framing idea at work in the era, and this production was a catalyst in the history of modern theatre in London.[17]

The exogenous forces outside the theatre are crucial to historical developments, though they do not form a totality that serves to unify, control, and determine theatrical practices. We have to do the hard work of finding out which ones are relevant and which ones are not. And even with the ones that influenced a production in some manner, the amount of influence is usually difficult to determine. Each historian, in attempting to apprehend and describe the specific event, defines and positions it according to his or her own understanding (or lack of understanding) of these many interrelated, and often contradictory, causes. But no two historians have the same comprehension. Thus, though they may acknowledge, firstly, that the production of *A Doll's House* is not an isolated, self-defining and self-determining event and, secondly, that the production and its circumstances coexist as mutually defining conditions, they still will have trouble agreeing on what the contingent conditions and causes for its occurrence were.

The historian, having so many potential contexts to select from, becomes a context-maker, a manipulator as well as a discoverer of relations and meanings. Each possible way of framing the description and analysis imposes an interpretive meaning, to the partial exclusion of other meanings. Various perspectives are open. Yet each historian, by selecting and privileging specific contextual factors for an event, not only contains the event within his or her own circumstantial perspective but also obscures other explanations. As long as we recognize that our interpretations are partial achievements in historical understanding – no matter how effective our arguments may be – we are not in danger of assuming that we have attained a complete sanction or total fiat for our insights.

Understandably, we wish to situate events within a defining context, but sometimes we have a tendency to grant to conditions more controlling power than the case warrants. To note this possibility is not simply to proclaim the romantic manifesto that genius has its prerogatives. More to the point, specific historical events have a way of occurring unsystematically, even chaotically, despite whatever determining systems supposedly operated at the time. As we are learning from our experiences with bureaucracies, institutions, totalitarian governments, and various communication systems (from television to the internet), complex orders and formations have their anomalies, derangements, and ruptures – their demons and imps, their random fluctuations, their cases of deviancy, their zones of disorder. Chance and necessity coexist in human relations.

> The historical fact is essentially irreducible to order; *chance is the foundation of history* [his italics].
> Raymond Aron, *Introduction to the Philosophy of History* (1961: 16)

Chance is always a factor in complex systems of activity, unpredictable by definition. As for the role of choice and human will within the dynamic relation between endogenous factors and exogenous conditions, the writing of theatre history presumes them. There would be no reason to inquire after intentions if we did not believe that they contribute to the making of events. And unless one believes in the total order and control of certain exogenous conditions, the idea of determinism fails to explain the events we study. From flaws in the systems to grand creative achievements, chance and will power are crucial aspect of human history. At the very least, theatre, though constrained by its own complex organization as well as by the various contextual conditions, can still create forms of irregularity that counter (not just react to) the surrounding order. Alternative options and achievements emerge. The art of theatre can even break free at times, offering not just unexpected but new configurations in the history of human endeavors. So, despite the appeal of grand theories and models for explaining human events, the historian's task is more interesting and more complex than the packaging of systematic analysis. The more we consider crux 2, the more we are required to return to crux 1. And, in turn, there are other cruxes that require our attention.

Crux 3: the signifying codes, values, and systems that constituted the event as a comprehensible occurrence in its own time

Besides considering the history of thought, ideas, ideologies, discourses, and mentalities, which we tend to see as contingent systems of order and power within an era, historians can examine the specific nature of the communicative or semiotic systems – what Marvin Carlson in *Places of Performance* calls "the ubiquity of meaning-making in human society."[18] All forms of communication, from a spoken word to a gesture, from a prayer book to a social gathering, express the behavior, values, beliefs, and ideas of individuals, families, and communities within a culture and its subcultures. In other words, the expansive idea of discourse needs to be divided into its multiple and specific forms (and not just understood as a system of ideological control). Or instead of starting from the general concept and theory of discourse, we need to begin with individual practices.

Historians should recognize that documents articulate their possible meanings according to the specific codes of order, meaning, and rationality for the particular time and place. The documents from the past are not necessarily written in our own codes, even though many aspects of the past carry forward to us. Unless we know how to travel back through time, transforming our understanding as we move through the different layers of historical codes and discourses, we will have great difficulty in comprehending the documents of earlier times. A good etymological dictionary, such as the *Oxford English Dictionary*, demonstrates quite explicitly the layers of time and the transformations of meaning as words have evolved through time. The *OED* tracks the process for each word's usage and meanings, as it moves toward the present. Our task as historians, as we translate and transcribe the signs and codes in our documents, is to comprehend the transformations in all of the cultural discourses, not just those of specific words. Or, to be realistic, our task is to become specialists of the codes and discourses of a few times and places, a select set of cultures.

One of the most effective ways of realizing Collingwood's dictum to get inside an event and to think the thought of the historical figure is to perceive and think within the discourses of an era. We may not be able to enter an agent's mind, but we can enter the discourses in which (and with which) the agent thinks. A medievalist scholar, knowing the church's doctrines on sin, can demonstrate how those doctrines are articulated in a morality play. A classicist, reconstructing the codes of Athenian society, can show how they were articulated in the tragic conflicts of Sophocles' plays. The scholar can reconstitute the codes and discourses, *but only up to a point*. And that point is always where disagreements emerge among experts.

The cultural and symbolic codes of each era and place manifest themselves not only in spoken and written language but also in gestures, body movements, clothes, manners, conventions, traditions, and taboos. Coded communication operates throughout the psychological, social, political, economic, and religious practices of a community. These not so silent languages organize the many temporal and spatial dimensions of cultural behavior. All of these codes and discourses constitute how, what, and why anything means. Moreover, these codes, often specific to the era, transmit certain meanings to the exclusion of others. The manner not just the matter of the code is crucial to the historian. Ideally, the historian is capable of drawing upon several disciplines of knowledge in order to do justice to the codes. But we usually fall rather short of the ideal. Still, the basic task has to be engaged.

> In a word, a historical phenomenon can never be understood apart from its moment in time . . . As an old Arab proverb has it: "Men resemble their times more than they do their fathers".
> Marc Bloch, *The Historian's Craft* (1953: 35)

In attempting to describe the production of *A Doll's House*, we would want to identify the communicative codes and systems of Victorian theatre and general culture. Then, perhaps, we can know what, if anything, distinguished this event from much of the contemporary theatre, especially domestic dramas of the period. For example, if we wanted to make the case that Achurch's acting contributed to the new system of realistic performance, we would need to understand how her acting both reproduced and modified the dominant codes of gesture, movement, speech, and costume that served as the convention for presenting domestic drama. Did she act in a new or different way in this production, or did her established method of acting prove appropriate in this case? What did theatregoers expect to see? In our search for Achurch's style of acting, we might want to analyze how her training in Shakespeare with Frank Benson contributed to or hindered her approach to Ibsen's method of psychological characterization. Within this context, we can begin to place Achurch as an actress – her features, her voice, her physical and sexual presence – in the role.

It is noteworthy that the two leading Ibsen actresses in London, Janet Achurch and Elizabeth Robins, had extensive experience in acting Shakespeare. Robins, for example, toured with Edwin Booth before coming to England; Achurch worked with F. R. Benson at Stratford-upon-Avon. A study of their training and experience might reveal something significant about the development of the new psychological realism. In turn, we might keep in mind that Stanislavsky also trained in Shakespeare before developing his acting program. Could it be that the training in Shakespeare, instead of providing these performers with a rhetorical method they had to put aside, offered a psychological penetration of characterization that they were able to release in Ibsen's plays? Ibsen, too, was influenced by Shakespeare. And of course during the first half of his writing career he wrote poetry and poetic drama, often in the historical mode of Elizabethan drama, with the additional influence of German poetic drama, both romantic and classical. Realism in the theatre was supposedly a radical break from the past traditions. But actually it was possessed by ghosts, as are all artistic practices.

More broadly, we would want to understand how the theatre and the culture shaped the representative ideas and models of womanhood and female sexuality. We cannot assume that our ideas correspond to those of Achurch. And her ideas may not have been in accord with those of Ibsen. And though we may take up Ibsen as a modern thinker, his ideas about women may still be strikingly at odds with the assumptions that we bring to the historical project. All too often the categories and presumptions of our own discourses and codes of behavior distort our historical vision. We then see the documents through a glass darkly. We lack the ability to see clearly, translucently.

> When we concentrate on a material object, whatever its situation, the very act of attention may lead to our involuntarily sinking into the history of that object. Novices must learn to skim over matter if they want matter to stay at the exact level of the moment. Transparent things, through which the past shines!
> Vladimir Nabokov, *Transparent Things* (1972: 10)

Everything about a production expresses the signifying codes, values, and systems of the time and place. So, too, for the surviving documents. These material objects, evocative for the historian because of their specific age and displaced presence, carry us back into the past. Despite – or perhaps because of – their materiality, they seem to be windows through which we can observe the past events. They seem to be "transparent things, through which the past shines." For theatre historians, one of the most enticing material objects is the theatre program. The one for *A Doll's House* notes that a "band under the direction of Mr. W. C. Lamartine" played various musical selections, including Grieg's "Norwegian Melodies," Mendelssohn's "capriccio brilliant," Czibulka's "Italienne" serenade, and Arditi's "Ingenue" gavotte. The materiality of the program delivers the immateriality of the music that the spectators heard in the Novelty Theatre. But how many theatre historians of the late Victorian stage have taken the time to listen to these four pieces?[19]

What was the significance of such music, both for this specific production and for theatre performances in general? How common was the practice of using musical numbers in domestic drama in 1889? Were these pieces played before the curtain rose on Act 1, between the acts, or even during the scenes? How did they contribute to – or work against – the "realistic" style of the acting? A piano was part of the living room set, and it was played when Nora practiced her dance. Which tune? How did the music contribute to Achurch's acting? Did the various music pieces enhance and reinforce the emotional texture of the production in ways similar to how music functions in films? Why were the separate pieces listed in the program? How did this information shape the spectators' responses to the play? In answering these questions, the historian seeks to understand three interrelated but yet distinct aspects of meaning in the program: (1) what it reveals about theatre practices and meanings; (2) what it reveals about the functions of theatre programs for spectators; and (3) what it reveals about theatre programs as historical documents.

Similarly, a theatre review, besides offering an evaluation of the production, may reveal clues about the cultural milieu in which the production occurred. For instance, a reviewer described the Novelty Theatre, at which the play was performed, as "seedy." Should we conclude that the reviewer intended to describe only the interior of the auditorium? Or was he also suggesting something about the cultural status and location of the Novelty, in comparison to most West End theatres, several blocks away? More pointedly, was the reviewer implying that the production was "seedy" or that Achurch and Charrington were "seedy" characters in the theatrical establishment? What, if anything, does the word actually reveal about the production and its reception? Also, what does it reveal about the reviewer and his expectations? And, just as significantly, what does our interpretation of the reviewer's intended meaning suggest about our historical understanding? Since we know that the early Ibsen productions in London were often attacked, are we retrospectively imposing meaning where none was intended?

Production reviews, besides containing descriptions and evaluations of the production, may carry additional information that the historian fails to decode. All reviews are documents about the reviewer, not just the production. The statements express explicit and implicit judgements. Some are aesthetic, but many of the judgements may be moral, social, and political. We may attempt to describe and understand what these reviews say, but our assessment of the production and the reviewer may be restrained by our own values – moral, social, and political. Though we may intend to be true to what the documents reveal, our reading of the documents may be at odds with their expressive codes. Theatre historians often simply lift a statement out of a newspaper or journal, with little or no attempt to investigate the reviewer. Of course, it takes extra time and effort to learn some fundamental things about the reviewers and their newspapers and journals (including the likely audience that the reviewer writes for). But the significance of a review in a socialist journal is surely different from a review in a sporting and entertainment newspaper.[20]

One thing seems clear: the documents express specific meanings for a different time and place, so we must take them up carefully. They are of the past and about the past, but no longer in the past. In our hands they become objects of present perception. They require delicacy in our handling of them. And sensitivity in our interpretations. We need to translate carefully, keeping in mind that translations, at best, are approximations of understanding, evoking a separate realm of being from our own. Past to present, across the borders. Our translations move us in the reverse direction, present to past. But do we get there?

Crux 4: the partial documentation of the event by a limited number of the participants, witnesses, and social organizations

It is always significant who the participants and witnesses are for past events. Our access to the past depends, in great measure, upon the people who produced and passed on historical testimony, the makers of the documentary records. We can only recover a part of the whole. At first we may think that we perceive the past by means of the documents we see. But paradoxically what we see and comprehend, in the final analysis, is – or needs to be – determined by what we don't see. If only we had the missing documents we would see differently. But we lack them, so the acute historian must be prepared to construct the past events out of absences, to credit and allow for what is unknown. We have assumed that those missing from the documents cannot be known. Yet we are finding ways to slide into the gaps and to travel into the invisible realms. Sometimes we return with visions of what we discover there.

The documents always privilege some people and events at the expense of other people and events. Writing the history of those excluded from the records is the great, unfinished project. Much of the time we write the histories of the articulate, the privileged, and the powerful, not the histories of the silent majorities. That is, we privilege the ones, like William Archer, who prepare the archive for us. Their preparation is vitally important, but it is a partial and a distorting picture.

Still, as some recent scholars have shown, sometimes with amazing research skill and determination, we are capable of recovering the social histories of the seemingly invisible and silent participants in history, including the women, workers, and racial minorities, from country to country and age to age. Our scholarly commitment has moved from the material archive into the immaterial past. But how do we do this? How can Jonathan Spence write a book about "woman Wang" when the Chinese records say almost nothing directly about her? How does Emmanuel Le Roy Laudurie recreate peasant culture in the late medieval period in the obscure French village of Montaillou? And what is there about a case of massacred cats in eighteenth-century Paris that would allow Robert Darnton to compose a detailed study of the daily life of workers, their conditions, and their values?[21]

In recent years theatre historians have also attempted to write what Jim Sharpe calls "history from below."[22] For instance, a number of scholars have shown that besides the study of the most famous actresses, it is possible to recover the careers of various women on the British stage during the eighteenth and nineteenth centuries.[23] Errol Hill has written a full history of the Jamaican stage before the twentieth century, though previous scholars had assumed that there was little or no evidence worth consideration. And Krystyn R. Moon, examining the representations of the Chinese in American performance and music from 1850 to 1920, has recovered a racial agenda that hid behind the pervasive idea of "yellowface."[24] These two works are not necessarily representative models of history from below, for there is no single approach; but they signal what has become a major transformation of the field of theatre history in the topical areas of diversity, identity politics, gender, race, hybridity, ethnicity, and class.

The hidden and the invisible emerge before our eyes. People who supposedly had no history are being represented, usually for the first time. We are seeing their actions and hearing their voices, which are being placed in the history of humanity. By asking new questions and searching in new places, we have begun to understand much about what we ignored or could not see in the past. Beyond the acts of recovery, this scholarship is also bringing about a reformulation of many of our historical categories and methodologies. Until recently we had failed to develop broad enough ideas of what qualifies as a document. And we had not realized that even the pieces of documentation that we had before us could reveal surprising new perspectives, if we but tease out the meanings lying just beneath the skin of the visible parchment. Whether we are looking behind the blackface mask in Cuba or the orientalist mask on the British stage, we are discovering new meanings. In the oblique light the face emerges from within the layers of the palimpsest.[25]

Documents respond only to the historian's questions.
Jacques Le Goff, *History and Memory* (1992: 181)

And yet, even when we seek the missing voices, we sometimes come up short. We have our questions, but not always the answers. For example, because we tend to see the production of *A Doll's House* as important in its representation of a woman's emerging self-consciousness, we would like to know how Achurch approached the role of Nora. Did she identify with Nora in certain ways? If so, how so? Why did she choose the play, how did she rehearse it, what did she think about the critical response? Unfortunately, she apparently kept no record of her involvement in the production. Only scraps of information about her participation have survived. We can reconstruct some of the action on stage, but we can't get backstage to her private domain and thoughts.

We do have an angry essay that she and Charles Charrington, her husband, published in 1894 (probably written by Charrington). It is mainly a complaint about the theatre critics, including Archer, who found fault with their attempt to produce plays in 1893, after they had returned from their world tour. In 1889, just before the production of *A Doll's House*, they had signed a contract for a tour to several countries, including Australia. Consequently, they were obligated to fulfill the contract just when they had finally gained artistic recognition in London. Because of the tour, they disappeared from view for over two years. In the meantime, the emergent Ibsen movement had been taken over by Elizabeth Robins, whose 1891 production of *Hedda Gabler* established her as the new Ibsen actress. Archer, as well, had shifted to her camp. When Charrington and Achurch returned to London, they revived *A Doll's House*, along with several other plays; but the critical response was disappointing. They had hoped to attain a West End theatre, so that Charrington could become an actor-manager on the model of George Alexander at St. James's Theatre. No such luck. The title of the 1894 essay gives a suggestion of their frustration and even desperation: "A Confession of Their Crimes by Janet Achurch and Charles Charrington from the Cell of Inaction to which They Were Condemned in the Latter Half of the Year of Grace, 1893." In this essay they make brief mention of their 1889 production of *A Doll's House*, expressing pride in their introduction of Ibsen to the English stage. "We solemnly and conscientiously affirm and declare that we introduced him because we thought he was an artist, not because we thought he was a teacher – an artist who painted his pictures by the light of the coming day – sometimes leaden and sad enough, but still, not the light of the day that is past, or even the day before, and certainly not the light of the studio."[26] They claim to have had no didactic purpose, no desire to convert people to women's rights. They had taken up Ibsen's play just for the challenge of doing a good play. Perhaps, but the lament about critical slights is defensive and combative, hardly the best guide to their intentions four years earlier. It is therefore difficult to determine what Achurch actually believed back in 1889 at the height of her success in Ibsen.

The scarcity of information about and from Achurch surely modifies and distorts our understanding of the event. No doubt, if we had a detailed diary, a major study of Achurch as Nora would be part of our history now. The lack of Achurch's voice creates a gap in our historical studies. We lack a key woman's perspective on *A Doll's House*. Missing Achurch's reflections, we are grateful for Elizabeth Robins' essay on the coming of Ibsen. It gives us a woman's perspective, but as I noted earlier, it was published almost forty years after the event. It hardly qualifies as the woman's perspective in 1889. But nonetheless Robins is still a major voice in the histories of the Ibsen movement. And she was a major participant, producing and performing some of Ibsen's late plays. We have the reviews. Yet one of the key reasons for Robins' centrality in the Ibsen campaign is that she conscientiously produced letters, journals, and books. She was a professional writer and a professional actress. She left us detailed records of her activities for the Ibsen campaign (though it took us several generations to shift our attention from Shaw, then Archer, before we attended to Robins). Her many contributions to modern theatre were substantial, exceeding what Achurch accomplished; but if Robins had not provided so much information, she probably would not have attained such a significant place in our historical reconstructions of the era. Thus, we have two biographies and several historical studies on Robins, but no biography and very few historical essays on Achurch. For the most part, Achurch is only visible to people today as one of the women in Shaw's romantic escapades.[27]

Much of the documentation for the production of *A Doll's House* was provided by men, including the theatre reviewers and Archer. Consequently, we tend to understand the production in terms of how Archer and the male reviewers described its significance. The documentation by men is not evidence of a patriarchal conspiracy, but it surely illustrates that the theatre profession, like almost all professions, was dominated by men. Even those men who were sympathetic to the women's movement, for example, could not set aside many of their blinkered ideas about women. Obviously, the reports and contributions of the various men are vital for our reconstructions of the event. This documentation sanctions our histories of the alternative theatre movement and the birth of modern theatre. Yet despite the great value of these documents, they still require our skeptical analysis of their reliability. Why, for example, should we necessarily see the testimony of Bernard Shaw as any less partial, prejudiced, and opinionated than the conservative reviewers? Apparently we credit and feature his testimony because he was on the "right" side of the debate – that is, the side that fits our historical interpretation (our retrospective ordering of significant events). Two issues converge here: (1) our tendency to write a Whig interpretation of history, the ordained record of the successful events that point toward us and our values; (2) our apparent assumption that only one historical perspective on this production is appropriate or right.

Even when we grant the importance of the Ibsen movement and the emergence of modern acting and staging in the development of modern theatre – a history that should be told – we need to acknowledge that the documentary record, despite its partial nature, could be used for other important social histories about Victorian theatre and its audiences. And if looked at with fresh eyes, the documentation opens up several issues of social change in relationship to the theatre (e.g., the place of theatre in women's lives, the development of the reading public, the shifting nature of middle-class tastes and values, the changing views on marriage by educated people, and so on). Given the growing bourgeois society and readership of newspapers, journals, and published plays, the audience for the play and production extended significantly beyond the small group of social radicals who supported the play (e.g., Shaw, Eleanor Marx, and Havelock Ellis). Many newspapers and journals reviewed the play. We thus might find it worthwhile to shift our attention to the social world of the people who read the many reviews, attended the theatre, and bought the published plays. We know that audiences and their social values are central to our understanding of theatre events. Indeed, as the scholarship on British music halls demonstrates, we have developed an expansive social history of theatre practices and audiences in the neighborhood theatres (e.g., the studies of Peter Bailey, Michael Booth, Jacky Bratton, Joseph Donohue, Tracy C. Davis, and Jim Davis and Victor Emeljanow). But so far these social issues (and the new methodologies of social analysis) have had little purchase on the study of *A Doll's House* and the alternative theatre movement.

Crux 5: the extraneous or extrinsic causes that modify, limit, or distort a document's reliability

Diligence in establishing proof is the first principle for historians, even though no absolute test of verifiability is possible. Historical research depends upon the authenticity of the documents and the credibility of the witnesses. Testimony can always be purposefully falsified – by the person who provides it, by whoever preserves it, by another historian who uses it.[28] This potentiality demands that, whenever possible, we check sources against other sources, as we determine the factual basis of documents. This primary condition allows us to construct the evidence for our descriptions and explanations. But we also need to be on guard against other less purposeful factors than fraud or lying that contribute to the unreliability of documents.

Consider this problem: what can we discover about the set design, which Archer, a decade later, described as the best of the settings developed for the series of Ibsen productions in London between 1889 and 1897? One piece of evidence is the surviving program for the production, which includes the following statement:

Scene.
Sitting-Room in Helmer's house (a flat)
in Christiania.
By Mr. Helmsley.

That seems straightforward and explicit, but who was Mr. Helmsley? What did he know about Norwegian (as opposed to English) sitting rooms? Did he follow Ibsen's descriptions? More to the point, did Helmsley in fact oversee and plan the setting or did he merely arrange the properties on stage, after someone else acquired them?

Bits and pieces of evidence from other sources suggest that Archer provided many, perhaps most, of the suggestions for the set design (including the use of decorative china plates and a Norwegian stove). His familiarity with Norway and with Ibsen gave him a special place in the decision-making for the production. He was the only one who had been in Norway, where he visited relatives during many summers of his childhood. But his contributions to the set design are not recorded in the program. Also, we now know from other evidence that Archer served as co-director, attending the daily rehearsals and handing out detailed written notes to the actors, but the program states that the play was "produced under the Direction of Charles Charrington." Archer's name is missing from the program, except as translator. Thus, the program, usually a reliable document for theatre historians, failed to provide accurate information on scene design and directing (though a few people who attended the production knew about Archer's substantial contributions).[29]

For additional evidence of the set design, we might turn to the five photographs that were in a limited souvenir edition of *A Doll's House* (Fisher Unwin, 1889, 115 copies). But these photographs, though providing almost full-length, close-up shots of the actors, reveal next to nothing of the stage set except for part of a couch on which the actors are seated. Moreover, the photographs present the actors in non-speaking poses against a neutral, empty background, typical of a photo studio rather than the stage. Thus, these photographs provide unreliable testimony because both their final cause or aim (publicity shot) and their formal cause (aesthetic principles of portrait) subvert their documentary potential. Many photographs of performers were taken in the photographer's studio, not in the theatre. We thus cannot assume that the furniture in the photographs was used in the production; nor can we even be sure, based upon these photographs, that the costumes shown were the ones actually worn. We need corroborating evidence.

A document's reliability needs to be tested in terms of its various causes. Just as an archeologist attempts to derive cultural meanings from a pot or a tool, based upon an examination of its material, formal, efficient, and final causes, so too should an historian try to take the measure of the causal nature of evidence. By doing so, we may discover how certain causes, typically understood as means and ends, modify the demonstrative and objective character of the evidence. For example, though a reviewer may be committed to providing an accurate report, the shape and import of the theatre review may be primarily controlled by its formal cause (size limit of 300 words) and final cause (need to sell newspapers).

Additional visual evidence for the production exists in five sketches that appeared in the *Pall Mall Budget*, a newspaper.[30] Three of them show Achurch wearing a fitted, fur-trimmed jacket, similar to what she has on in the photographs. And the evening coats of the men are also similar to those in the photographs. This corroborative evidence suggests, then, that the sketches and photographs together offer reliable documentation on costumes, though limited evidence on set design.

But the most detailed sketch of the five illustrations raises a problem. It shows a scene of Achurch dancing, tambourine in hand, wearing a folk costume. Behind Achurch (and behind a table with a full-length tablecloth) a bearded man, identified as Mr. Waring, sits at an upright piano (apparently playing it). A man with a shaven face, identified as Mr. Charrington, stands next to the piano, watching Nora dance. In

Illustration 17. Janet Achurch as Nora, in the costume for the tarantella dance in *A Doll's House*, London, 1889.

the play Dr. Rank plays the piano, so this sketch implies that Waring is Dr. Rank. But the program identifies Charrington as Dr. Rank. And the photographs in the edition of the play show Waring with a beard, Charrington without. So, the sketch mistakenly reverses the names of the two men, thereby offering unreliable evidence, unless we want to believe that in this production – despite Archer's careful oversight and his commitment to the integrity of Ibsen's text – Helmer, not Rank, played the piano. It is possible that this mistake is the only one that the artist made in the five illustrations, but we cannot know for sure. Visual evidence, though so important in theatre history, raises special problems for us.[31]

Of course, a careful historian, no matter what kind of document is being used, should check it against other sources, for even what seems to be substantial evidence may often prove to be inconclusive, if not misleading. But very few theatre events before the modern era provide us with enough documentation to answer the many questions raised here. It is thus quite difficult to reconstruct a production in the kind of detail we seek. And beyond the difficulty of attaining sufficient, reliable information, we often face the problem of interpreting documents that present not only unintentional distortions and mistakes but willful absences and silences. As the program, illustrations, and photographs for the production of *A Doll's House* reveal, we are forced to construct the event out of partial, often contradictory evidence that often serves causes other than those of accurate documentation. This warning may suggest that we must avoid any undocumented speculations, but this is not the position I am urging here. I do believe that we must be highly skeptical of all sources, and that we need to verify them by rigorous principles of authenticity and credibility. But as historians we still must make conjectures. As long as we clarify that we are making interpretive conjectures, rather than just describing a document, we are doing our job properly. Some of the most intriguing and promising historical analysis is based, at least in part, on conjecture.

Crux 6: the conditions effecting the preservation and subsequent survival, however piecemeal and random, of the documents of record

Various factors contribute to the survival of documents, but seldom is this process systematic and comprehensive. Although concerted effort is often made to preserve certain types of records, as with governmental records, the processes of documentation in the archives are almost always incomplete. And they are often faulty. Large national theatres in modern times do a reasonable job of preserving records, but most theatre companies through the centuries, always short of funds, often fail to maintain sufficient records. And traveling players, from the *commedia dell'arte* troupes to the touring companies of the railroad era, seldom even attempted to preserve records.

Even when records are saved, and perhaps make their way to an archive, they often remain un-catalogued, buried away in boxes. Archivists and librarians in many cases today are very dedicated to their jobs, and many are well qualified to do the work. But because theatre archives are often underfunded and inadequately staffed, the initial task of cataloguing the documents in the archive is incomplete and unfinished. And even if an archive is committed to developing a comprehensive catalogue system, what should it be? What is a proper order for theatre documents? All cataloguing systems are in service to some kind of organizational principle, but theatre collections generate special problems. The categories may provide an effective system of identification and retrieval for some types of documents, yet be ineffective or inappropriate for other types. There is no agreed-upon method for organizing and cataloguing theatre collections. From country to country, the systems – if we can call them systems – are strikingly different from one another. And even within a country, there is no shared rationale that guides the archivists and librarians. In the United States, for example, each of the theatre collections at Harvard, Texas, Princeton, Ohio State, UCLA, the New York Public Libraries, and the Library of Congress has its own logic. And many of the small collections, spread out from state to state, depend upon the memory of one or two people. The researcher has to learn each system, with gratitude for the help the keepers can provide.

> the dispersal of documents is itself part of history. In other words this dispersal is part of the past, and therefore, part of a sequence of events.
> G. J. Reiner, *History: Its Purpose and Method* (1950: 107)

And just as each archive offers its own idiosyncratic method for organizing theatre documents, so too do the separate historical events have their own logic for both how and why some documents survive (and get used) while others do not. Of course, most events throughout history go unrecorded. And in the cases of those events that have been documented, the records, with rare exceptions, are piecemeal, the preservation is inadequate. Much has been lost, destroyed, buried away, and misplaced. The past, in immeasurable ways, is gone and unrecoverable; no amount of cunning can conjure it into historical identity. We must make do with the few traces that we have. And we celebrate those cases of plentitude.

For *A Doll's House* in 1889 we have many documents, but of course a number of key pieces of evidence have disappeared, including most of Archer's rehearsal notes that would reveal much about his behind-the-scenes role. And we have almost no evidence of Archer's conversations with Achurch, Charrington, Waring, and the scene designer, Mr. Helmsley. As noted earlier, we have very little about Janet Achurch and almost nothing by her. We do not know how she responded to Archer's rehearsal suggestions. How, then, could a historian support an argument – an interpretation – that Archer was the decisive figure in the production? One possible tactic would be to analyze the various references to Archer in the theatre reviews, letters, and articles of various other people who wrote about the production and its participants. If a number of different people attack and praise him, then an argument might be made for his importance. In this way, based upon circumstantial evidence, the event gets constructed to fit an interpretive strategy. Secondary evidence may prove more helpful than primary records. But here, as in all cases, the interpretation is limited by the surviving documents.

Crux 7: the contemporary processes that identify an event as noteworthy and significant, thus giving it historical status, often to the exclusion of other events

This process of identification and valuation follows two stages. First, certain events, at the time they occur, get characterized by participants and observers as significant. The event is documented by the participants, who thus provide an extensive record and a specific version of the event's identity and significance. The event attains its initial meaning not simply because of the activities of the participants but also because of the ways they generated documents that describe and explain the event. These events are given a meaning, a place and import in the cultural narratives and practices of the age.

The initiating process is thus both an act of constructing the event itself, thereby giving it a definitive identity, and an act of interpretation, thereby giving it a definitive meaning. Already drawing attention to itself, it produces repeated commentary from people at the time, including commentators who take a historical perspective. Often, because of the attention it receives at the time of its occurrence, the event achieves a definite and substantial identity, one that it then maintains in the future. It also, quite often, then serves to exclude other events from visibility and consideration. Historians accept, often without much question, the importance of a designated event. Even if subsequent historians question its defining traits and disagree strongly over its significance, they still feel the need to add their voices to the commentary. It has to be written about; its importance is unquestioned. Only the interpretations change.

Look Back in Anger presents post-war youth as it really is . . . Mr. Osborne is the youth's first spokesman in the London theatre . . . I doubt if I could love anyone who did not wish to see *Look Back in Anger*. It is the best young play of its decade.
　　Kenneth Tynan, "The Voice of the Young," *The Observer*, May 13, 1956

The English Stage Company changed the course of British theatre almost overnight when it staged John Osborne's *Look Back in Anger*.
　　Philip Barnes, *A Companion to Post-War British Theatre* (1986)

On 8 May 1956, my first play to be produced in London, *Look Back in Anger*, had its opening at the Royal Court Theatre. This . . . date seems to have become fixed in the memories of theatrical historians.
　　John Osborne, *A Better Class of Person* (1981)[32]

No doubt some events have proved to be as significant as contemporary attention to them suggested, but not necessarily. It is not always possible to determine what came first: the significant event or the documentation that proclaims its significance. Which is cause and which is effect? For example, from the perspective of many theatre historians today, the most famous production of Ibsen in London occurred in 1891, when *Ghosts* was staged. Although the successful, almost month-long run of *A Doll's House* had occurred nineteen months before the production of *Ghosts*, which only had two performances (one a dress rehearsal), it is *Ghosts*, produced by J. T. Grein's newly formed Independent Theatre Society (ITS), that has achieved the status of being the decisive or most important event in the Ibsen campaign in London.

In part, this is because *Ghosts* was turned into a controversy by supporters and non-supporters alike (no doubt in consequence of earlier productions of Ibsen). Of key significance, the Lord Chamberlain forbade a production of *Ghosts* because of its subject matter, so it was presented by the ITS as a private event for invited guests. As a censored event, it immediately became a controversial event. Despite being a non-event officially, the production and play received hundreds of reviews and articles over the following weeks. Many of the people who wrote about the production did not see a performance; nor did they read the play. But this restraint on their knowledge did not interfere with their determination to publish their judgements on the play and production. To be expected, the attacks on the play produced a flood of defenses. The event thus occurred in the press, not just on the stage. A few months after this swirl of controversy, Archer published an essay called "*Ghosts* and Gibberings," which brought together in one place dozens of negative statements on the play. By displaying the nasty, often out-of-control qualities of the attacks, he intended to expose the critical bankruptcy of most reviewers and the London theatre establishment. The timing was just right for Bernard Shaw, who was in the process of writing *The Quintessence of Ibsenism*, published in late 1891. He quoted extensively from Archer's essay.

Ghosts was significant, then, not because it introduced Ibsen to London audiences, nor because of the quality of the production, which was amateurish, nor because of the number of performances (only two). Instead, it became – and has remained – important because certain people, supporters and non-supporters, turned it into a controversial event, a well-made test case for the new drama. The constructed controversy (with its cooked evidence) is of historical interest, of course, but the event itself need not be interpreted by us in accord with the initial testimony and aims of the participants. But because we have been given a ready-made controversy, we have accepted the initial version of it.[33]

Crux 8: the commentary that builds up, person by person, age by age, around an event, describing and circumscribing it, to the exclusion of other historical events and perspectives

Once a specific event attains historical significance, through documentation and commentary, subsequent historians are drawn to it. New studies may reinterpret the event, but even revisionist histories seldom question its status as an important occurrence. This chain of commentary is not so surprising, of course, because historians read previous historians, and thus regularly write about the same events that their predecessors described and analyzed.

As the case of Bernard Shaw illustrates, often the actions and statements of well-known people are documented and repeated while the actions and statements of less-well known people go unrecorded. Of course, there have always been clear historical reasons that we feature the actions and events of some people over those of other people. Beyond the modern conditions of a celebrity culture, the processes for according attention to the famous (and infamous) have operated throughout recorded time. For centuries, the actions and statements of royalty and aristocrats were well documented, while common people were ignored. History belongs to those in power. Even after the arrival of the printing press and the spread of literacy, this process of documenting the activities of the few continued. Common people remained invisible in the archives. Not until modern times has this pattern begun to shift.

What has been true for general history has also been true for theatre history. For example, not until the Renaissance did information on performers get recorded in any detail. Previously, only a few names of performers, along with occasional details, made their way into the historical records. Subsequent to the Renaissance, things changed. For several centuries the process was primarily about the most famous performers (though the increasing flow of autobiographies allowed various performers to record versions of their lives). In the main, we have continued to write histories and biographies of the famous until today, with a few exceptions. There is nothing wrong with being interested in the great artists, major works of art, and key productions. But if such interest also excludes others from the historical record and our understanding, as it has, then we have failed in part of our historical mission.

Typically, once a historical narrative gets established, it is repeated in our history books. Scholars may refine the details, but the underlying narrative and the assumptions that support it remain in place. For example, consider the fate of a document that Charles W. Wallace discovered and published in 1913 in *The First London Theatre*. Among the Court of Chancery records in London, Wallace discovered a lawsuit between James Burbage and Margaret Brayne, the widow of John Brayne. Burbage and John Brayne had been partners in the building of the theatre in 1576. After Brayne's death, his widow filed a lawsuit in 1589–90 against Burbage, who had refused to pay her some of the profits from the partnership. Testifying in support of the widow Brayne was John Alleyn, an actor and, most famously now, the brother of the great actor Edward Alleyn. John Alleyn urged Burbage to pay the widow, but Burbage defiantly refused. Also, Alleyn had asked Burbage for the payment due to the actors of the Admiral's Men, who had performed at the theatre, but Burbage refused that recommendation as well. Based upon this legal disagreement, Wallace proposed that the Admiral's Men withdrew from the theatre at this time, shifting back to Philip Henslowe's Rose playhouse. This conjecture, in turn, became the basis for Wallace's argument that a feud and rivalry existed throughout the 1590s between Edward Alleyn and the Burbage family. According to Wallace, the two companies of actors, which in 1594 became the Admiral's Men and the Chamberlain's Men, competed in the commercial market of professional theatre.

The "rivalry" soon became an accepted historical explanation for theatre in this era. As Rosalyn Knutson shows, E. K. Chambers (*The Elizabethan Stage*, 1923) and W. W. Greg (*Dramatic Documents from the Elizabethan Playhouses*, 1931) accepted Wallace's explanation.[34] Subsequently, the rivalry was faithfully reported by the next two generations of theatre historians, who celebrated Burbage and the Chamberlain's Men and dismissed Henslowe and the Admiral's Men. Artistic integrity versus capitalist greed. Many scholars, accepting this basic conjecture by Wallace, developed elaborate explanations for the warring players and playwrights. But, as Knutson also shows, there is little or no reason to accept this narrative, despite the authority of leading scholars and the appeal of the formula of feuds and rivalries. Knutson reviews the evidence for the narrative, but instead of accepting the formula of rivalry, which reduces history to an exclusive idea of quarrelling men, she makes a strong case for the expansive activities of theatre business in the era. Showing how the companies were organized on the model of commercial partnership derived from the tradition of the guild, Knutson presents a revisionist history of not only the available evidence for a few disputes and disagreements but also the additional evidence for the business activities of plays and playwrights at all the playhouses of London. As she insists: "In addition to providing only a partial map of London playhouse enterprises, the narrative of theatrical wars gives a one-sided view of touring."[35] Drawing upon the new evidence from the volumes of the *Records of Early English Drama*, Knutson lays out an entrepreneurial history of the theatre companies that replaces the narrative that conjured up a war between two men and two companies. In the process, a much enlarged understanding of the commercial conditions and practices emerges with Knutson's historical analysis.

Knutson's argument has benefited greatly from the recent revisions in our understanding of the partnership between Philip Henslowe and Edward Alleyn. We no longer feel the need to see commerce in negative terms. When theatre historians, from Edmond Malone to W. W. Greg, wrote about Philip Henslowe, the owner of the Rose and Fortune theatres in Renaissance London, they saw him as a man of commerce, often as a crass businessman. In contrast to Richard Burbage, he lacked the sensitivity of an artist. His famous diary, with its notations of financial transactions, revealed a commercial enterprise. This meant, we insisted, that Henslowe exploited the playwrights, making extra funds off loans with interest. We thus accepted for a century a basic story, whereby Elizabethan theatre was separated into two opposing models: business versus art, Henslowe and Edward Alleyn versus Richard Burbage and William Shakespeare; the Admiral's Men versus the Chamberlain's Men.[36]

A similar kind of historical canonization occurred with our histories of the London production of *Ghosts* in 1891. Because the production was controversial, it fits neatly into our general narratives about the growth of independent theatre companies, the significance of the avant-garde, and the shock value of modern art.[37] As was the case with the production of Alfred Jarry's *Ubu Roi* five years later, the production of *Ghosts* served as primary evidence for our historical narratives about alternative and avant-garde theatre, modernism, bourgeois taste and attitudes, and controversial events. Theatre historians, guided by Archer and Shaw, have made much of the production of *Ghosts*, in part because the event was already given a shape and meaning at the time. The evidence was placed before us, to use as prescribed. Thus, dozens of theatre history books have continued to repeat the same basic history of the Ibsen campaign in London, featuring *Ghosts* (1891) rather than *A Doll's House* (1889), *Hedda Gabler* (1891), or any of the other plays and productions, all of which had more performances and better productions.

In addition, most theatre scholars who write about the Ibsen campaign in London grant Shaw a central place in the fight for Ibsen in 1889, although in fact he was a rather obscure music and art critic in 1891. *The Quintessence of Ibsenism* had a small print run, and few readers. Yet because it was republished in new editions in the coming years, paralleling the growing fame of Shaw, the book provides us with a handy summary on the production of *Ghosts* and the Ibsen movement. He has attained retrospectively an aura of importance and centrality in the whole Ibsen movement. Not surprisingly, in our history books Archer has become a mere lieutenant in Shaw's army. For many theatre historians the production of *Ghosts* qualifies as the origin of the Ibsen movement in London. Consequently, *Ghosts* has not only marginalized the production of *A Doll's House* but also displaced it.

It is certainly a fault for a thinker to be so attached to a hypothesis that he notices only evidence that agrees with it and ignores or denies unfavorable evidence. Popular superstitions of all kinds are protected by this fallacy, but it is common among scientists, historians, and philosophers.

J. L. Mackie, "Fallacies," in *The Encyclopedia of Philosophy* (1967: vol. III: 175)

Crux 9: the codes, discourses, values, and cultural systems of the historian's own time that shape understanding of the past

Our historical methods of thinking and communicating are necessarily of our own time. Even with the best of historical intentions, we find ourselves comprehending in ways that are tied to our contemporary perspectives. Our assumptions, values, knowledge, and beliefs of the present sometimes limit our understanding of assumptions, values, knowledge, and beliefs in the past. Thus, all history is, in some measure, unavoidably anachronistic. And sometimes our contemporary values and assumptions impose an inadequate, even distorting, perspective on the past events. This is not to say that the present perspective of historians has warped their historical research and analysis. Nor does it mean that a network of intertextuality or a handful of powerful discourses must determine and control what we see and how we think. Things are more complex and interesting than these formulaic versions of historical subjectivity.

No doubt many of the questions and issues that occur to us are generated by our modern conditions and understanding. We are all familiar with historical studies that take up and apply a modern theory to the actions and ideas of people in the past. Sometimes the ideas are anachronistic and inappropriate for the historical situation and condition. A decidedly modern idea is imposed inappropriately on the thinking and actions of historical subjects. But it is still possible to analyze previous ages with modes of understanding that only developed in modern times. Just as modern technology and scientific procedures provide valuable new ways to understand the past (e.g., carbon dating, DNA analysis), so too may modern ideas and insights serve the historian (e.g., modern understanding of gender roles, racial identity, migration patterns, health and physical development, conflict theory, ecology). But we sometimes need to make distinctions between our conceptual models and those of the past because systems of meaning, discourse, ideology, hegemony, patriarchy, social institutions, and cultural values change from age to age.

> It is the business of the historian to be always testing his classifications in order to justify their existence, and, if it seems advisable, to revise them.
> Marc Bloch, *The Historian's Craft* (1953: 147–48)

Furthermore, if part of our aim is to discover, as best we can, the intentions of historical figures (so as to comprehend their actions from their perspective and within their own contemporary contexts), we should recognize and attempt to negotiate the distance between our understanding and theirs. The historian's task, then, is the reenactment of past thought in his or her own mind – with the understanding that the past is a different, if not undiscovered, country. A guarded logic of inferential and circumstantial analysis should guide us because we are attempting, on the one hand, to take the measure of similarities and analogies between the past and the present, and, on the other hand, to understand differences and discontinuities. In these terms, we are always investigating, then writing, two histories simultaneously.

Every historical study thus represents a dialogue between documents and historian, between past discourses and present ones. In Robert Weimann's words, we need to find an interpretive balance between "past significance" and "present meaning," which like event and circumstance, are mutually defining.[38] Historical reality (which we discover and construct) and historical consciousness (which shapes the discovery and the construction) are always yoked. But are they – or should they be – in tandem, the one leading the other? And if so, which one leads? When we allow for a dialogue between our present self and the past, the imposition of the present can be addressed. And when we recognize the triangulated nature of the relationship of the three locations of an event – in the past, in the archive, and within the historian – we are anything but reductive historians imposing ourselves on the past events.

In recent years a revisionist history of the Ibsen movement in London shifted attention to the production of *A Doll's House*.[39] But soon the attention on this 1889 production was displaced by a focus on the productions of *Hedda Gabler* (1891) and *The Master Builder* (1893), which were staged by Elizabeth Robins, who served as producer, co-director and lead actress. When Jane Marcus, Gay Gibson Cima, Joanne E. Gates, and, subsequently, Angela V. John published studies of the American actress Elizabeth Robins, we began to get a very new history of the Ibsen campaign in London – a new perspective, based upon a feminist understanding of the era's activities.[40] In this case, a modern perspective, led primarily by women scholars, has challenged the dominant narratives that featured the contributions of Bernard Shaw, William Archer, and J. T. Grein and the Independent Theatre Company. Without question, this new understanding would not have emerged without the intervention of new, modern ideas onto the historical subject.

All to the good, but sometimes these ideas are then embraced as the definitive explanation. This new ideology may, though, reproduce some of the simplified and

Illustration 18. Elizabeth Robins as Hilda Wangel in Ibsen's *The Master Builder*, Opera Comique Theatre, London, 1893.

incomplete features of the old historical narratives that, quite properly, had been challenged. For example, Kerry Powell, in a study of Elizabeth Robins and her "revolutionary aims" in the 1890s, moves Robins to the center of the Ibsen movement, supposedly in league with Oscar Wilde. This revisionist argument displaces all of the usually male suspects. Of course, Robins deserves a central place in the history of the Ibsen movement. She was a great actress, and a great force for change. But in Powell's commendable attempt to revise previous histories (especially the ones that slight Robins), she transforms William Archer into the mere "protégé" of Robins – a reading of theatre history that attempts to correct one flawed historical description, but replaces it with yet another one.[41] If anyone was a protégé in this relationship, it was Robins, who discovered Ibsen a decade after Archer had been carrying out his campaign, including the production of *A Doll's House*, which she saw, and then wrote to Archer to express her interests. But the word "protégé" is inappropriate in either case; it fails to do justice to these two major figures and their work together in the Ibsen movement.[42] Surely, in the process of ridding our history books of one reductive narrative, we do not need to replace it with yet another one. If the next generation of theatre textbooks focus on Robins, perhaps exclusively, we will again highlight one historical explanation while obscuring others.

It is important to note, however, that the revisionist histories of the Ibsen campaign, though shifting attention away from *Ghosts* to different productions and people, still accept the assumption that the arrival of modern, realistic drama is the important issue in the history of London theatre during the 1890s. This is true of my study of Archer as well as the studies of Robins. In the main, we insist upon telling the story of alternative drama and theatre to the exclusion of popular and commercial entertainment. This modernist focus on revolutionary movements and figures ignores, however, hundreds of other productions each year in London that attracted over 99 percent of the audiences and hired 99 percent of the actors. No doubt histories of Ibsen, realism, modernism, the avant-garde theatre, and feminist theatre have substantial merit and justification, but our commitment to this specific history has greatly limited our study of the other theatrical events of this era.[43] Of course, there have been studies of the famous actors and actresses, such as Henry Irving, Ellen Terry, Herbert Beerbohm Tree, and other stars of the West End theatre. Their involvement in Shakespeare helps to keep them in the history books. And in recent years we have begun to study the music halls. This is one clear sign, finally, that we have recognized the need for some alternatives to our histories of the alternative theatre movement.

We might note, though, that this focus on popular entertainment also arises from the contemporary values and ideas of the historians, who see themselves as advocates for popular culture and working-class values. Indeed, many of the theatre scholars today who take a "materialist" or cultural studies approach to historical scholarship are attempting to carry their own ethical and political understanding into the kinds of performance events that justify a cultural studies approach. There is nothing wrong with this, for all historians stand in the present and make fundamental judgements on the basis of their ideas. As long as our categorical understanding is not demanding a single answer, like a theory imposed upon the data, we can avoid tautological analysis. Yet we all need to be aware of how our own values and assumptions guide research projects and our organizing ideas. Some scholars, though, become prisoners of their ideas. Their prose descends into formulaic rhetoric. At that point our alarms should go off because the writer seems to be controlled by popular academic jargon that writes the writer.

Crux 10: the ideas of change that historians use to describe sequences and interpret causes of events

As should be quite apparent by now, these various cruxes unavoidably confront us with the interrelated historical problems of change and causality. Our examination of endogenous and exogenous factors in the construction of a historical event (cruxes 1 and 2) depends in great measure on how we think about change and causality. Whether examining the motives and aims of the historical agents or investigating the determining power of social forces, we are trying to understand how and why historical events occur. We seek to identify the reasons for various changes and causes, which invariably lead us to examine the interrelationships among events.

If, as Jacob Burckhardt claimed, "the essence of history is change," shouldn't we try to understand how and why change occurs?[44] But what is change? What understanding of it does the historian – as opposed to the philosopher – need? How is it to be defined and measured? In looking at it, are we seeing cause or effect? During any particular time, do historical events change in more than one way? Are there certain historical laws governing change? Or does change have its own laws and reasons that govern history? Perhaps the whole search for the laws, rules, and procedures of change in history is misguided, especially if history confronts us with discontinuities, disjunctions, contradictions, and improbabilities rather than with any dialectical, evolutionary, or teleological order.

Instead of focusing only on *change as a process* (a concern of philosophy), we need also to consider *change as an idea*, one of many that we apply to events (or impose upon them) in order to interpret history. History, we might then say, is the sense we make of the processes of change with an idea of change. Not only do we attempt to understand how historical change distances us chronologically and conceptually from past events but we also struggle to comprehend both the process and the idea of change itself.

Consequently, we are concerned with the conceptual ways we link events diachronically in order to understand the relations between and among them. R. G. Collingwood reminds us in *The Idea of History* that "the historical fact, as it actually exists and as the historian knows it, is always a process in which something is changing into something else. This element of process is the life of history."[45] But the process, by itself, is not the essential concern of the historian, who wants to understand primarily how people thought about the process, how they made sense of time and change, whatever the process may actually be. The historian may believe in a specific reason or purpose for historical change (e.g., a religious or a biological explanation); fine, but the primary, or at least preliminary, task of historical inquiry is to discover what the agents thought and believed, as their ideas contributed to their motives and actions in the process of participating in and perhaps causing the sequence of events.

No event stands alone. At the time of its occurrence, it is perceived by participants and observers as part of some kind of series or sequence, not merely as a seamless web of time without significance. Its human meaning develops out of how it is connected to other events. That is, the apparent order of events derives from the observer's own way of thinking about them: (1) how he or she thought the events hung together; and (2) how he or she made sense of changes in the passing of time. Historical agents (as well as the historians who write about them) endow time and the processes of change with meanings. Accordingly, for the historian – as opposed to the physicist – events are joined by thoughts, the thoughts of the agents in the past and the thoughts of the historian in the present. Out of this double perspective on time and change comes historical understanding.

In attempting to comprehend the *process* of change, we must use an *idea* of change to configure events into a meaningful order. And to make sense of the idea of change we need to specify the possible factors, causes, and conditions that define and contribute to change, such as origin, intentionality, motivation, probability, innovation, renovation, progress, linear development, continuity, transition, conclusion, speed, mobility, alternation, dialectic, cycles, crisis, revolution, transformation, and retrospective design. In a variety of ways (often contradictory) these different ideas are applied to events, individuals, works, societies, and systems in order to make sense of change. We need to ask, however, why certain models of change appeal to us (e.g., the idea of progress for the Victorians, the ideas of revolution and crisis for us today). And what kinds of history get written according to these different models?

William Archer, for example, saw the Ibsen campaign as part of the progressive history of drama's development toward realism. He had specific ideas about how to bring about some changes in the London theatre. We need to unpack those ideas as we attempt to explain how and why some key productions of Ibsen contributed to the intended changes. The documents he produced, which serve as our historical traces, express this idea of change (e.g., the 1923 book *The Old Drama and the New* spells out his belief that drama necessarily was progressing toward realism). To understand his place in the Ibsen movement, we need to see that the ideas of evolution and progress were his presuppositions, providing the justification for his advocacy of Ibsen, of realism, of liberalism, and of women's liberation. The productions of the half dozen Ibsen plays that he participated in, from *Pillars of Society* (1880) and *A Doll's House* (1889) to *Little Eyolf* (1896) and *John Gabriel Borkman* (1897), achieved a substantial part of their historical significance from this mindset.

Today, of course, we look with suspicion on an evolutionary theory of drama and theatre history. For instance, we have generally accepted O. B. Hardison, Jr.'s critique of late nineteenth- and early twentieth-century medieval scholars who, under the influence of evolutionary theory, tended to see the history of drama from the medieval to the Renaissance age as a teleological process of development, finding its fulfillment in the drama of Shakespeare.[46] Medieval drama was thus a lesser form, awkwardly striving to become fulfilled by Marlowe, Shakespeare, and the other dramatists (who, supposedly, freed themselves from the shackles of religion and religious topics).

Yet before we pat ourselves on our backs for our superior understanding of history, we might pause over our use of the concept of "revolution." The word is as pervasive in our discourse and thinking as "progress" and "evolution" were in Archer's. Often it operates in quite similar ways. For example, when we consider the history of Shakespearean production, we regularly suggest that the modern "revolution" in performance modes was necessarily an improvement on previous productions. Harley Granville Barker, in his revolutionary manner, overthrew the antiquarianism of Henry Irving (just as cultural studies historians displaced documentary scholars). Apparently, we still have some progressive assumptions, mixed in with our delight in things revolutionary.

In the case of the Ibsen "revolution," which is regularly seen as the beginning of modern drama, we apply the concept of origin to his drama, then from our vantage point we trace a developmental history (which we contain – that is, stabilize by an act of identification – within a period concept called the modern age). We provide a retrospective order, based upon a design we read into the historical events, which become parts of a narrative about significant, consequential changes. The processes of change take their meanings, therefore, from the classification system that is embedded within (and formulated by) the idea of change we use to explain the process of change.

Today, some historians have become aware of our overdependence upon the idea of revolution to explain change; they have shifted to new concepts, such as Thomas Kuhn's *paradigm shifts*, Raymond Williams' stages of *crisis*, or Michel Foucault's *disjunctions* and *ruptures*.[47] As we see in the rhetoric of new historicism, the appeal of things subversive, such as the "counter history" of fractures, ruptures, and disjunctions, seems to sanction the analysis (even when such ideas of change are nonetheless safely contained within a stable period concept of unified intertextuality). Why should we believe that these new ideas are somehow superior to other ideas?[48]

Crux 11: the rhetorical tropes and narrative schemes that historians use to construct the past

The gap between history-as-lived and history-as-written, though not necessarily a chasm, is always wide. As historians, we understand that our history books must provide, by design, orderly meaning that paradoxically is both excessively and insufficiently comprehensive: excessive because we impose coherence, continuity, unity, and closure on past events, insufficient because we can never comprehend the fullness and heterogeneity of human existence. Life may be chaotic; it may be a grand design, but the historian operates somewhere in between these two extremes of representation. And narrative, in its many aspects, provides an essential way to comprehend and organize the great expanse of time and the great variety of existence. The largest models we have for human life are provided by religion and evolutionary theory. Historical writing, though, is selective, and sometimes it is microscopic as we focus on a single or a few events. But even when we attempt large surveys, such as the history of civilizations or the history of theatre from the classical to modern age, we must select, and in doing so we draw upon certain traits and techniques of narrative.

> The most "analytic" historical monograph, one might say and could show, presupposes the historian's more general understanding, narrative in form, of patterns of historical change, and is a contribution to the correction or elaboration of that historical understanding.
>
> Louis O. Mink, "Narrative Form as a Cognitive Instrument," in *Historical Understanding* (1987: 184)

Narrative provides the primary way to organize change. Our ideas of change and our ideas of narrative tend to go hand in hand. Or as philosophers from Aristotle to Paul Ricoeur have pointed out, our task of representation (mimesis) requires us to provide an order for time, a plot for human action. We organize historical events into a sequence or story line that posits contiguous and causal lines of development. We represent some kind of story about human actions, decisions, conditions, and values. This historical representation, committed to truthful description and argument, draws upon a repertory of rhetorical and formal conventions.

These rhetorical tropes (e.g., metaphor, personification, irony) and narrative traits (e.g., voice, characterization, plot structure) help to constitute a history that postulates, explicitly and implicitly, certain working assumptions about temporal configuration, human motivations, causal design, individual understanding, group behavior, representational action, and even world order. Some Annales historians, suspicious of narrative history and its focus on the actions of individuals, reject narrative history as mere fiction. Such narratives turn history into the tragic or heroic actions of grand figures who stride the world's stage like Marlowe's Tamburlaine. Other historians, though acknowledging the pervasive nature of narrative techniques in historical reports, still want to confine narrative to a preliminary stage of historical study. This is the argument of some Annales historians, including Jacque Le Goff:

> Every conception of history that identifies it with narrative seems to me unacceptable today. To be sure, the successiveness that constitutes the fabric of historical material requires us to accord narrative a role that seems to me primarily pedagogical in nature. It is the simple necessity of setting forth the *how* before inquiring into the *why* that situates narrative at the logical foundations of historical work. Narrative is thus only a preliminary phase, even if it has required prolonged preliminary work on the part of the historian. But the recognition of an indispensable rhetoric of history must not lead us to deny the scientific character of history.[49]

By limiting narrative to the presentation of how events unfold, Le Goff attempts to elevate the explanations and interpretations of the events to a separate, scientific realm of judgement, superior to and different from narrative. Description is narrative; analysis is science. This distinction seems at odds with Reinhart Koselleck's claim that "events can only be narrated, while structures can only be described."[50] But both Le Goff and Koselleck are defending an unnecessary dichotomy, similar to the attempts to save history by dividing it into subjective and objective practices.

Even if we accepted a neat polarity between the two stages of historical representation, we are still confronted by a foundational practice in historical writing: descriptions of human events are presented as narrative. But the neat separation cannot be maintained, and need not be defended. No amount of conjuring with the idea of scientific analysis will remove narrative to a preliminary world of description. These attempts to treat narrative as false history or as a set of mere devices for dressing up historical reports miss the essential point about narrative in human understanding. As the philosopher David Carr argues, our understanding of reality and our ways of representing it are dependent upon narrative strategies that are "prefigured in certain features of life, action, and communication."[51] Narrativity is not merely a technique, borrowed from literature, but instead a condition of our temporal understanding of individual and social experience.

> Historical and fictional narratives . . . reveal themselves to be not distortions of, denials of, or escapes from reality, but extensions and configurations of its primary features.
> David Carr, *Time, Narrative, and History* (1988: 16)

The complaint against narrative by the Annales historians stems from their rejection of the traditional narrative histories that told the exciting stories of famous people, who supposedly brought about all events and all changes in history. From this perspective, historians were too adept at using narrative methods. But this complaint fails to address the fundamental nature of narrative in our organization of ourselves – and all others, including historical figures – within our consciousness of time. As Paul Ricoeur insists, "my thesis concerning the ultimately narrative character of history in no way is to be confused with a defense of narrative history."[52] He is not defending, for example, the historians who write about political leaders against the complaints of the Annales historians. All historians, whatever their method of writing about historical events, large and small, depend upon narrative to describe and explain human events.

What strikes me about many historians, besides their avoidance of the basic philosophical issues of time, history, and narrative, is that they are strikingly naïve or even blind to the place of narrative in their own writings and assumptions about change, causality, human motivations, and human actions. From this perspective, then, what most distinguishes the historian from the fiction writer is not so much the historian's commitment to telling the truth about human events – though this is crucial because it demands the research in the archive – but his or her lack of awareness of not only the literary and rhetorical conventions in historical writing but also the ways that narrative shapes all discourse. At least a fiction writer takes up the techniques of narrative consciously and purposefully. The historian, writing about a series of developmental events or about the life of a major figure, incorporates most of the traits of narrative, but all too often without any clear understanding of the narrative traits and techniques that organize and direct the representation.

For example, one of the troubling features of many of the biographies of Shakespeare and Marlowe is that the historians do not acknowledge or even notice how and why the many narrative techniques of genre, voice, characterization, and plot development shape the project. One of the most basic principles of narrative is the distinction between plot and story, yet many historians confuse them and collapse them together. These biographies offer a parade of naïve and often self-deceiving omniscient narrators who insistently proclaim that the world they are representing must be exactly what they proclaim it to be. The biographies attempt to shape a playwright's life into a consistent plot, so that all parts of the narrative accord, thereby delivering a nicely developed *kunstlerroman* or mystery plot. But the historians seem unaware of how genre assumptions guide the writing. And they are equally unaware of key narrative distinctions, such as constitutive and supplementary events. Moreover, in their representations of most of the people in Shakespeare's world, the level of characterization seldom escapes the most obvious stereotypes. Because of this confusion over narrative methods and techniques, large and small, the historical study is a hodge-podge of fictional representation, masquerading as rigorous historical investigation. Consequently, there is as much commitment to historical truth in many novels about William Shakespeare or Christopher Marlowe as there is in many of the biographies of the last few generations.

The message here is not that history writing needs to be saved from the fictional quagmire into which it has sunk. Instead, the point is that we need a far better understanding of *how* and *why* history and fiction share a foundation built on the principle of narrativity in human consciousness. Only when we clarify what they share will we be able also to clarify *how* and *why* they separate at a key point in their methods and their aims. And they surely do. But to understand that crucial point we need to recognize some basics facts about narrative.

It is no accident that the primary terminology that I have used throughout this book, such as *identity, agent, representation, event, action, change,* and *causality,* is also the primary terminology for defining narrative. As Paul Ricoeur demonstrates with convincing philosophical deliberation in *Time and Narrative,* there are irrevocable ties that bind historical writing and fictional writing together, even though the crucial difference of telling the truth about past events (on the basis of documentation) separates the one from the other. For this basic reason, then, young historians who are still learning the task of historical writing might actually benefit from reading and reflecting upon a basic guide to narrative and narrativity such as H. Porter Abbott's *Cambridge Introduction to Narrative* (2002). As least, by considering the nature of narrative, they would understand how to be self-aware of the ways that narrative techniques, such as the methods of plotting (opening, conflict, turning points, closure, narrative coherence), operate in history writing as well as fiction. They might then see how to use description to set a scene and how to control the options of first-person versus third-person narrative voice in their own writing.

Simply put, narrative is the representation of an event or a series of events. "Event" is the key word here, though some people prefer the word "action." Without an event or an action, you may have a "description," an "exposition," an "argument," a "lyric," some combination of these or something else altogether, but you won't have a narrative . . . The difference between events and their representation is the difference between *story* (the events or sequence of events) and *narrative discourse* (how the story is conveyed).

H. Porter Abbott, *The Cambridge Introduction to Narrative* (2002: 12–13)

Historical manuals in the past sometimes proclaimed, for example, that historians should always use the third-person voice (in order to avoid any self-reference, a terrible fall into subjectivity). The neutral, well-measured voice in third person provides a necessary signal of objectivity. By this means, the writer maintains a clear separation between the historian and the representation. Well, this is nonsense. Besides the fact that fiction has a long tradition in the nineteenth century of developing versions of authorial distance for the expressed purpose of achieving a full fictional world (e.g., Balzac, Flaubert, Turgenev, Chekhov), the idea that one achieves objectivity in the third-person voice is a masterful act of self-deception. Flaubert's third-person voice in *Madame Bovary* is no less judgemental and personal than Dickens' first-person voice in *David Copperfield*. Historians do not achieve their control of objective description and analysis any better in one voice than the other. However they may do justice to objective principles, which are worth trying to serve, they do their best when they recognize that subjective and objective are interwoven in all historical study. The objective of historical inquiry is to be as true to the past as one is able – no matter what one's style of writing. Whatever voice a historian uses, the problems and challenges of balancing subject and object remain in operation. Far better is the historian who knows how to shift from first and third person, as the topic and issue may suggest.

If historians recognize the narrative features of their own writing, they might then stop worrying about Hayden White's *Metahistory* (1973), *Tropics of Discourse* (1978), and *The Content of the Form* (1987). Misconceiving his analysis, they feared that they had to choose between history or fiction, facts or fabrications. Not only are reports by historians written in narrative modes of representation; so too are the documents from the past, such as most descriptions of specific events. And some documents, such as autobiographies, reveal themselves to be organized in great measure according to narrative features of description, plotting, theme, and characterization. Auto-biography is a well-developed narrative mode, displaying many generic types. Not surprisingly, then, most of our biographies and theatre histories, based upon these documents, reproduce some of the narratives forms and explanations that exist in the documents. For instance, when using an actor's autobiography, most theatre biog-raphers may balk at this or that anecdote but still accept much about the overall narrative plot structure and modes of characterization that organize the work's representation of the life and events of the actor.[53] Or in the case of our histories of almost all modern playwrights, directors, and designers, we tell a familiar generic story of innovation and revolution, thus recording yet one more time the triumphant battle of individual genius against the resisting forces of traditions, conventions, and societal values.

Instead of attempting to defend historical scholarship from the false modes of representation in narrative, we need to recognize that narrative form, which is inherent in human understanding and the organization of human time, is an unavoidable aspect of historical documents and studies. As historians we need to become more aware of the various narrative devices and designs that we use to structure events. Perhaps, then, we can at least recognize some of the presuppositions built into our narrative forms and the documents themselves.

> Time becomes human time to the extent that it is organized after the manner of narra-
> tive . . . Narrative, in turn, is meaningful to the extent that it portrays the features of
> temporal experience.
>   Paul Ricoeur, *Time and Narrative* (1984: vol. I: 3).

However we identify the key participants in the London production of *A Doll's House* and represent the processes of preparation and presentation for the production at the Novelty Theatre, we are describing two, interrelated narrative actions: (1) the dramatic action within the play, which narrates a story about developing conflicts and a crisis within a troubled marriage; and (2) the historical actions of all of the participants in the event – agents and spectators – who participated in the making of a performance that generated conflicts between, on the one hand, supporters of Ibsen, the new drama, realism, women's rights, and the social and political forces of change, and, on the other hand, defenders of established drama, melodrama, the commercial theatre of the West End, and a patriarchal idea of marriage and social stability. The story within the play represented, in key ways, the possible and potential conditions that might emerge in the world outside the play. In this capacity, the dramatic action narrated a kind of potential historical event that carried significance for the theatre people who made the production and the spectators who observed it. Both felt they were caught up in not just an artistic representation but a possible action that entered into the lived world of their experiences. This possible or parallel action was thus perceived as either an action to champion or an action to resist, even deny.

The theatre historian of this event is confronted with many documents, all of which reveal aspects of the possible narratives that define the production as a *conflict*, a *battle*, a *crisis*, and even a *revolution*. Each of these words appears in one or more of the documents. As we have seen, Archer, along with others, purposefully conceived of and participated in an event – the making of the production of *A Doll's House* – that could be dramatized as a cultural narrative about change and conflict in the London theatre. Archer's willfulness in creating not just a theatre event but a historical moment of change and confrontation was no less calculating than Alfred Jarry's careful preparation for the controversial nature of the *Ubu Roi* production. Obviously, their tactics were very different from one another, but not their basic strategy. Archer hid himself, as much as possible, behind the scenes, as he attempted to pull the strings for the event; Jarry displayed himself in every way possible, turning himself into a revolutionary figure for a quintessential Parisian event – art at the barricades.

Surveying the sources, the theatre historian selects from the abundance of details to craft the kind of historical narrative that he or she wants to tell. Some historical narratives have their origin in the actions and intentions of the participants, but other narratives find shape and meaning in the designing perceptions of later observers. A range of possible stories is possible: a narrative about the origin and development of the new drama, a narrative about Ibsen, a narrative about the campaign for Ibsen, a narrative about the arrival of modern drama, a narrative about Ibsen's vision of Nora, a narrative about a crisis in contemporary marriage, a narrative about the importance of *A Doll's House* in the campaign for women's rights, a narrative about Shaw, a narrative about the London theatre at the end of the Victorian era, a narrative about the aims and careers of Achurch and Charrington, a narrative about the divisions in the London theatre community, a narrative about Elizabeth Robins and her discover of Ibsen and her artistic mission, a narrative about Shaw's shift from being a novel writer to a playwright, a narrative about Shaw's relationship with Achurch and Robins, a narrative about the alternative theatre movement, a narrative about Henry Irving's resistance to the new drama, a narrative about Clement Scott and his central place in the theatre community as the leading theatre critic, a narrative about the development of professional theatre criticism at the end of the nineteenth century, and, of course, a narrative about William Archer.[54] Many stories are possible, including no doubt some that do not occur to me.

Whatever the case, our historical explanation and understanding will find ways to represent and refigure human events as narrative actions – either fulfilled or unfulfilled, complete or incomplete – that reveal intentions and actions of agents, a temporal frame of sequential development, possible speech acts and performative acts, a process of doing (of actions and reactions within a condition of time-consciousness – for the agents, and retrospectively for the historian), an articulation of goals in terms of their means and circumstances, a struggle (combining help and resistance, success and failure), and perhaps an accomplishment, even a resolution.[55]

> To ask for the significance of an event in the *historical* sense of the term, is to ask a question which can be answered only in the context of a *story*. The identical event will have a different significance in accordance with the story in which it is located or, in other words, in accordance with what different sets of *later* events it may be connected . . . To demand the meaning of an event is to be prepared to accept some context within which the event is considered significant. This is "meaning in history", and it is legitimate to ask for such meanings.
> Arthur Danto, *Analytical Philosophy of History* (1965: 11–12).

Crux 12: the reading formations, assumptions, values, and expectations of each person who, as audience for the historical report, attempts to understand what is written about the event

When we read a historical report or book, we are thrice removed from the event itself. We are reading readings that are readings of readings of the event. The first reading is the document, which refers to the original event; the second reading is the historian's interpretation of the document; and the third reading is our own interpretation of the historian's report.

Often, a historical document succeeds in finding or calling forth its desired reader, someone who is prepared to interpret it according to the aims of the person who provided the testimony. For instance, in his drama criticism Bernard Shaw has often succeeded in creating his desired readers, who nod in agreement with his witty version of plays, players, and playwrights. He documents for us exactly what the London theatre was like in 1895 – as seen from his perspective. We willingly put aside just how much he reshapes his subject matter in service to his own values, judgements, and prejudices. His judgements on Ellen Terry or A W. Pinero become ours, just as his version of the production of *Ghosts* determines aspects of our historical understanding.

A great voice, with its control of rhetoric and narrative, is a delight for us as readers. Each of us can name figures from the past whose voices we are most willing to trust. The world that these voices create becomes true for us. And, in turn, we find historians whose reports and interpretations fulfill and even exceed our expectations of historical scholarship. Readers of this book can predict, I am sure, some of my own favorite historians. I have become the desired reader for their writings. The key question is always *why*? Is my best judgement still guiding me?

All kinds of historical reports can generate their desired readers. A positivist transcription of a document, offered without apparent reinterpretation, can evoke its desired reader. Indeed, the method of presentation, with its apparent objective aim of delivering nothing but the facts, appeals to us because it implies that we are trusted to make our interpretation, to find our own meaning. We are not being browbeaten by an insistent voice that tells us what to think. The document, in a straightforward manner, delivers its meaning, its truth. We are seduced by the neutrality of it all. But a resisting reader may be the better historian. Then, if one is not an ideologue, one can at least acknowledge that historical documents are open to various readings, that they contain a number of potential meanings, depending upon each person's understanding. Then we recognize that all documents express a point of view, a perspective, a subjective understanding.

Just as historians bring presuppositions, codes, values, and inclinations to the task of reading and writing history, so each of us reads historical studies from his or her own "horizon of expectations." Discourse analysis, reader-response theory, and reception theory are all showing us that a dynamic and complex process of interpretation occurs in the act of reading. There is no reason to assume, therefore, that a historical text is somehow exempt from this coded condition of understanding (and misunderstanding). We can become increasingly self-aware of our own individual perspective, but we cannot step beyond it to a place of value-free judgement and comprehension. A basic paradox or contradiction always pertains: our subjective judgement determines how objective we find the report.

Consequently, in addition to all the possible ways of constituting and writing about historical events, there are at least as many ways of reading history. The reader constitutes the historical text according to the various factors that have shaped his or her understanding up to the moment the reading begins. No matter how talented the historian is in directing and controlling the reader's understanding (e.g., with a fine control of narrative voice, effective characterization, clear and convincing plot, and satisfying conclusion or summation), the reader always adds to, subtracts from, modifies, and even nullifies what the historian writes. This is true for the reading of all historical events, including the histories of the Ibsen campaign in London. Some studies attract fully sympathetic readers. Yet can they also attract resisting readers? Which voices and which narratives appeal to us, and contribute to our historical knowledge and understanding? Which ones do we accept, question, resist, or reject?

A representative case study is close to home. When I wrote about the London campaign for Ibsen, I had to negotiate the many studies of Bernard Shaw, which in great measure placed him at the center of the events. There was plenty of information about Shaw's activities, including his own writings, but there was almost nothing available, I felt, about Archer's central role. By the mid twentieth century Archer had been pigeonholed as the Victorian translator of Ibsen, the man who tamed and contained Ibsen's vibrant prose. Following the complaints of T. S. Eliot and others, the theatre and literary historians who wrote about Ibsen had decided that Archer was a minor figure, even a regrettable one, in the modernist movement. In his last book, *The Old Drama and the New* (1923), he huffed and puffed, his critics complained, as he attempted to make an unimaginative justification for realism, which was supposedly the progressive culmination of dramatic style and purpose. Archer was apparently blind to the more radical aspects of modernism. These studies provided the initial lens for my perspective onto the Ibsen movement. They were my reading formation, but I was a resisting reader.

My mission, then, was to rescue Archer from his detractors. In the process, with discoveries in archives in London, including the British Theatre Association library on Fitzroy Square (an organization that no longer exists), I discovered the evidence for his involvement in the productions. And in New York, at the Fales Library, I discovered some of the love letters between Archer and Robins. In other words, I gathered the pieces of a new narrative about Archer, Robins, and the Ibsen campaign. My book, published in 1986, then became a historical text that subsequent historians would read, a reading formation that they might accept or reject.

Soon after I published the book, a new wave of scholarship emerged, focusing primarily on Elizabeth Robins. In key ways, some of the scholars, including Joanne Gates and Gay Gibson Cima, took issue with my analysis and interpretation, as they presented a fuller case for the significance of Robins in the Ibsen campaign. They revealed a sympathetic perspective on Robins that matched my sympathetic perspective on Archer. On some issues we were divided. In this way, the historical record provides layers and layers of texts that determine, in one way or another, the reading formations of the next generation of scholars. And likewise, when Peter Whitebrook wrote his biography of Archer, though he agreed with many of my discoveries and insights, he still headed in some new directions. He felt no need to quote me as an authority. Initially I felt that I was being marginalized by these newer studies, but of course the process of adding new histories was following many of the procedures of cruxes 8 and 9. Historians are readers of previous histories, and if they bring to the text their own understanding, they are then prepared to carry out their own research on the topic and to write their own representations of the events. The task of historical inquiry thus goes forward, never finished. This basic condition is actually formulated, piece by piece, in each of the twelve cruxes, as each historian recapitulates the path of the previous historians.

What is a historical event? The question is basic, but as we have discovered, it is not simple. In the process of answering this question, we have generated a parallel question that is equally important: *Where is a historical event?* We cannot answer the *what* question unless we confront the *where* question. Historical events reside in no one place: not in the specific past, nor the documents, nor the codes and discourses, nor the history books, nor the historians, nor the readers of history, but instead in a complex and dynamic interrelationship among all of the possible locations of historical meaning. The grand thing called "history," as noted in the Introduction, has many meanings, in part because of the many locations. History happens and re-happens, as we continue to reconstitute the past each time we comprehend it. We are always rewriting and rereading history.

Therefore, I want to insist that we must ground ourselves in the protocols of historical research. Without question, we need to make a rigorous commitment to archival investigation and analysis. As I attempted to illustrate with the two case studies on the Globe Theatre and the production of *Ubu Roi*, accurate documentary research is paramount, for without it our interpretations fail us and our readers. In turn, we must not only analyze the sources and establish the facts but also reflect upon the assumptions and methods that lead us to set up certain kinds of evidence to support our arguments. Our assumptions, including the categorical ideas we think with, determine much about the success or failure of our historical inquiries. Accordingly, our descriptions and explanations for events depend directly upon the ways we construct the conditions, the circumstances, and the contexts for those events, from political causes to period concepts.

For theatre events we need to investigate the agents, the world, the artistic heritage, and the receptions. We need to move beyond basic binaries in order to see how an event is triangulated among these four contributing factors. Both the event and its contexts have multiple identities, resulting from multiple locations. As we carry out our research, from initial conception of a project until the final report, we move through the twelve cruxes, whether or not we actually think explicitly about them. The cruxes, like the organizing ideas of agents, world, artistic heritage, and reception, are also basic conditions of historical thinking. They help us to recognize the ideas we think with, and thus they cannot be reduced to a numerical checklist. But to the extent that we internalize, as historians, the basic ideas and categories of historical understanding, we have prepared ourselves for the tasks of research, description, analysis, explanation, and interpretation.

We must recognize, accordingly, that the issue of credibility is not merely a procedural matter of following the rules of evidence for documentation. It is also the standard by which historians are judged. Our sources provide the credible witnesses to the events we attempt to construct, but each of us who works as a historian is also a witness to history. In our scholarship – our historical narratives – we perform our own acts of witnessing. Our credibility, like that of the documents we consult, is always in the witness box. We are under oath to tell the truth yet we must also remain open to questions, doubts, and challenges.

Notes

Introduction

1. Although the basic methodologies and problems that I investigate apply to all historical fields, I focus my investigation on the performing arts and performance events. I do not attempt, however, to cover all of the psychological and social activities that might be considered under the broad idea of performance. Such matters as speech acts, the presentation of self in everyday life, sexual and gender roles, the performing self, and the nature of social roles in organizations and communities will not be examined in this book. Nor will I take up matters of performance and modern technology. I recognize that some people wish to describe and analyze all of these activities as modes of "performativity" or "theatricality," but when a concept means almost anything, it is in danger of meaning nothing. See T. Davis and T. Postlewait (2003: 1–39).
2. Peter Novick (1988: 8).
3. R. G. Collingwood (1993: 209; 218).
4. S. Toulmin and J. Goodfield (1972).
5. Donald R. Kelley (2003: x).
6. Despite this empire of knowledge, historians recognize that their colleagues in the other disciplines are not prepared to anoint history as the queen of the disciplines. The reorganization of the university, with history in charge of everything, is an unlikely revolution in the modern research university (though historians can still entertain the fantasy that the transfer of power should occur).
7. Also, I happily leave to others the epistemological challenges of understanding and explaining the foundational concepts of time and historical consciousness that guide such fields as physics (e.g., Einstein's theories), geology (the catastrophic changes between eras), biology (Darwinian evolution), and astronomy (the distribution of matter since the Big Bang). Clearly, the idea of history encompasses far more than any individual can address.
8. See R. G. Collingwood (1946), Arnaldo D. Momigliano (1966; 1977; 1990), Ernst Breisach (1983), Michael Stanford (1994), Michael Bentley (1997), and Donald R. Kelley (1998; 2003). There are also several collections that provide a selection of writings by major historians across the centuries. See, for instance, Hans Meyerhoff (1959), Fritz Stern (1972), and Donald R. Kelley (1991).
9. See Carol Fink (1989) and Susan Friedman (1996) on Marc Bloch, Friedrich Meinecke (1936; translated 1972) on historicism in the Enlightenment, and Stephen Bann (1984, 1995) on history writing and romanticism.
10. Georg Iggers (1984; 1997); Michael Bentley (1999).

11. For studies in historical method and approaches, see Leonard Mendes Marsak (1970), Peter Burke (1990; 2001), John Tosh (1991), Michael Stanford (1986; 1998), and Eric Foner (1997). I also found the following studies most instructive on historiography: C. Behan McCullagh (1984; 1998; 2004), Michel de Certeau (1984; 1986; 1988), Joan Kelly (1984), Dominick LaCapra (1983; 1985; 1989), Roger Chartier (1990), Joan Wallach Scott (1988), Geoffrey Hawthorn (1991), Philippe Carrard (1992), Beverley Southgate (1996), Bonnie G. Smith (1998), Mary Fulbrook (2002), and Elizabeth A. Clark (2004). For an annotated catalogue of historical research, primarily in English or translation, for all areas of world history, see Mary Beth Norton (1995). It is an excellent place to begin a search for contemporary scholarship.

12. Raymond Aron (1961) and Paul Ricoeur (1965; 1974; 1981; 1984; 1985; 1988).

13. *Ibid.* (8 and 24).

14. *Ibid.* (88 and 91).

15. *Ibid.* (265–316).

16. Both Aron and Ricoeur provide an epistemological basis for going forward while acknowledging the problematic nature of objectivity in historical inquiry. For a comprehensive survey of the battles in the American history profession on the question of objectivity, see Peter Novick (1988). On the issue of objectivity in several disciplines, see the collection of essays by Allan Megill (1994). Megill's opening essay on "Four Senses of Objectivity" is a good introduction to the issues and debates.

17. T. Postlewait and B. McConachie (1989). See the bibliography for representative works in theatre historiography. For example, a quick introduction to theatre studies is available from James Arnott (1981). Key scholars, such as Bruce McConachie (2001; 2004; 2007) and Tracy C. Davis (1993; 2002; 2007), have continued to write regularly on theatre historiography. For recent work on theatre historiography, see the forthcoming Charlotte Canning and T. Postlewait (2009).

18. A few representative works may suggest the range of studies in theatre historiography: Marvin Carlson (1989; 2004), Greg Dening (1996), Robert Hume (1999; 2002), Christopher Balme (1994; 1999, 2008), Michael Quinn (1991; 1995), Joseph Roach (1996), Erika Fischer-Lichte (1997), Michal Kobialka (1999), Freddie Rokem (2000), Susan Bennett (1997; 2000), Richard Knowles (2004), Shannon Jackson (2004), Steve E. Wilmer (2004), Alice Rayner (2006), and Peter Holland (2004–07).

19. In three valuable books, R. W. Vince has described and analyzed the historiographical features of theatre scholarship in the study of classical and medieval theatre (1984), Renaissance theatre (1984), and the "Enlightenment" theatre (1988).

20. R. W. Vince (1989).

21. Here, for example, is a very brief list of representative works: Sue Ellen Case (1988; 1992), Sue Ellen Case and Janelle Reinelt (1991), Tracy C. Davis (1989; 1991), Charlotte Canning (1993; 2001), Laurence Senelick (1992), Elin Diamond (1997), Maggie Gale and Viv Gardner (2000), Harry Elam and David Krasner (2001), Xiaomei Chen and Claire Sponsler (2000), Ann Dils and Ann Cooper Albright (2001).

22. See, for example, Susan Leigh Foster (1995; 1996), Alexandra Carter (1998; 2004), Susan Manning (2004).

23. J. Reinelt and J. Roach (1992; new edition 2007). See also Chris Balme (2008).

24. Marvin Carlson (1996; revised 2004). Also see Phil Auslander (2002–03).

25. See Elizabeth Burns (1972), Erika Fischer-Lichte (1997), Willmar Sauter (2000; 2004), Josette Féral (2002), and Tracy C. Davis and T. Postlewait (2003).
26. Stephen Toulmin (1958: 1).
27. Richard Kostelanetz (1993: xiv).
28. I should note, however, that this book does not qualify as a primer in the mechanics of research. I am not offering a guide to research procedures in the libraries and archives, such as Thomas Mann (1998). Nor am I writing a manual on scholarly practices, such as Mary-Claire van Leunen (1992). And I am not attempting to present a guide that assists students in their college research papers, such as Jacques Barzun and Henry F. Graff (1992) or Wayne C. Booth *et al.* (1995). Yet despite this disclaimer, I will have things to say about archives, scholarly practices, and the basics of research and writing. And I urge students and teachers alike to maintain a research program that takes advantage of basic primers and handbooks on library research. Of course, guides to and training in internet research are also essential today.
29. We could say that the relationship is *dialectical*, but this word, so overused in critical and historical study, has become a buzz word that usually diminishes rather than enhances our attempts to explain.
30. See M. H. Abrams (1953).
31. That is, the significance of *An Enemy of the People* should be located not only in its text and performance but also in a precursor event and its reception, a year before *Enemy* appeared on the scene. Yet despite Ibsen's attack on closed-minded communities and hypocritical values, he was still capable of representing his individualist, Dr. Stockmann, with ironic detachment and some pointed criticism.
32. See T. S. Eliot (1951).
33. Elin Diamond, *Performance and Cultural Politics* (1996: 1).
34. See, for example, W. Jackson Bate (1970) Harold Bloom (1973).
35. See the trained eye of Marvin Carlson in *Places of Performance* (1989); and the analysis of time and space in Sarah Bryant-Bertail (2000).
36. Consequently, there is no agreement on the meaning of the basic concept of a *performance space*. From Peter Brook's "empty space" and Tadeusz Kantor's "other spaces" to Michel Foucault's "heterotopia" and Henri LeFebvre's "production of space," the possible definitions and theories multiply exponentially. Gaston Bachelard attempted to offer a "poetics of space" (but performance remain marginal in his reflections). Complicating matters further, while some people locate the features and meanings of the performance space within the nature of the space itself; others insist that a performance space is always a matter of perception (e.g., a gaze, a projected attitude and judgement, or a neurological negotiation), whereby the perceiver always constructs space in the process of his or her engagement with events that occur beyond (outside of) the perceiver's consciousness. The idea of *performance space* appears to be a thousand and one ideas.
37. Paul Ricoeur (1984: I: 97).
38. Joseph R. Roach, in J. Reinelt and J. Roach (2007: 192).
39. Along with many others, Bruce McConachie and I participated in the transforming endeavors with our collection of essays, T. Postlewait and B. McConachie (1989) See also B. McConachie (1985) and Michael Quinn (1991).
40. See Walter Benjamin, "Theses on the Philosophy of History" (1968; 1996–2003).

41. M. Bloch (1953: 185). Perhaps the word *science* is too exacting for historical scholarship. In English it seems too grand; but it has maintained its place among French historians.
42. E. Fischer-Lichte (1997: 340).
43. R. G. Collingwood (1946: 249).

1 Documentary histories: the case of Shakespeare's Globe Theatre

1. See James Shapiro (2005) and Steve Sohmer (1999) for two energetic yet quite different attempts to provide significant information on *Julius Caesar* at the Globe in 1599.
2. Weimann refined his ideas in *Author's Pen and Actor's Voice: Playing and Writing in Shakespeare's Theatre* (2000).
3. Crediting major aspects of Shakespeare's plays and theatre practices to popular culture instead of humanism, Weimann grounds his case for the *platea–locus* model on this heritage. Yet because of his rather expansive representation of theatre history (e.g., the history of comic types, Greek to modern) his arguments are open to criticism. See, for example, Brian Vickers (1993).
4. Andrew Gurr (2004b: 49).
5. Laurie E. Maguire (1996: 7) quotes Greg's statement as she argues against the idea of "memorial construction" as an all-purpose explanation for the "bad quartos" of Shakespeare and other playwrights.
6. Three other folio editions of the plays were published in the seventeenth century, hence the title First Folio now for the 1623 edition. It did not include all of the plays we now credit to Shakespeare. For example, *Pericles*, which had appeared in quarto in 1609, was excluded. Seven additional plays, including *Pericles*, were added to the third and fourth folios, but the other six have not, so far, been accepted into the canon.
7. In the language of textual editors, "fair copies" of a text are derived from "foul papers" of an author's draft of a manuscript. Adding to the complexities, a "prompt copy" – an anachronistic idea for the playbook – may be derived directly from the "foul papers," but more likely it is derived from a "fair copy" or a transcript, which becomes a copy of a copy. Various people could have done the copying.
8. For scholarship on the quartos, see Alfred W. Pollard (1909; 1923), who distinguished between the fourteen "good" quartos and the five "bad" quartos, which included *Romeo and Juliet* (Q1), *Henry V*, *The Merry Wives of Windsor*, *Pericles*, and *Hamlet* (Q1, 1603). For well over half-a-century, scholars, including W. W. Greg (1955a), accepted this idea of good and bad quartos. Recently, though, various scholars have questioned the "bad" quarto concept and the historical research that supports this interpretation. See, for example, Randall McLeod (1982), Maurice Charney (1988), Kathleen O. Irace (1994), Laurie E. Maguire (1996), Peter M. W. Blayney (1996), and Paul Werstine (1982; 1999).
9. On the first quarto of *Hamlet*, see collection of essays by Thomas Clayton (1992).
10. For revisionist ideas on the "new bibliography" of W. W. Greg and his generation, see, for example, Gary Taylor and Michael Warren (1983), Stanley Wells and Gary Taylor (1987; 1997), G. Thomas Tanselle (1987; 1989), Jerome J. McGann (1983;

1991), Randall McLeod (1994), D. F. McKenzie (1986; 2002), Laurie E. Maguire and Thomas L. Berger (1998), Ann Thompson and Gordon McMullan (2003), and Steven Urkowitz (1980 as well as essays in other collections listed here). Many others have joined the critique of the "new bibliography" of W. W. Greg and his era.

11. See Richard Dutton (2000) and Lukas Erne (2003).

12. G. E. Bentley, 1961: 160–61; 183.

13. *Ibid.*, 191–92. Bentley's sympathies are with the professional playwright or the player, not the printer and publisher. See his two books on playwrights (1971) and players (1984).

14. From Augustine Vincent's *A Discovery of Errors*, London, 1662; quoted by Gary Taylor in his "General Introduction" to Stanley Wells and Gary Taylor (1997: 47).

15. For introductory essays to the "craft of printing" and the "publication of playbooks" in the era, see Laurie E. Maguire (1999) and Peter W. M. Blayney (1997). For theatre as a business, see William Ingram (1992; 1999), Douglas Bruster (1992; 2004), and Andrew Gurr (1996; 2004). For representative studies of the printing of plays, see Douglas Brooks (2001; 2005), D. F. McKenzie (2002), Paul Werstine (1982), George Walton Williams (1985), and Richard Proudfout (2001).

16. Fredson Bowers, like W. W. Greg, did much to define the principles of textual editing for Renaissance plays. See, for example, *On Editing Shakespeare and Other Elizabethan Dramatists* (1966). See also his other works listed in Works cited (1964) and (1978).

17. A sophisticated study of Shakespeare and the book has been put forward by David Scott Kastan. And yet he still feels compelled, in the process of honoring the printers who preserved Shakespeare's plays, to blame or dismiss the players, who fail to do so. Kastan argues that "the pliancy of his plays in the hands of theater professionals" serves the "tendentious interpretations" of the players rather than the intentions of the playwright (2001: 7). Texts are durable, but performances are evanescent. Theatre engenders multiple, unreliable identities. The material texts and the immaterial performances are incommensurable. Kastan thus insists upon a separation between text and performance: "The printed play is neither a pre-theatrical text nor a post-theatrical one; it is a *non*-theatrical text, even when it claims to offer a version of the play" (2001: 8). By embracing this materialist mandate, we must write two separate histories: the book, uncontaminated by performance; the performance, divorced completely from the book. Literary scholars can embrace the material book; theatre historians can chase after the immaterial performances. In accord with Kastan's logic, theatre history is a "non-theatrical" discipline, even when it claims to present a version of the play.

18. See, for example, Frederick Kiefer (2003: 4–5).

19. R. A. Foakes (1993: 341).

20. I am using the 1998 Cambridge University Press text, edited by Richard Madelaine.

21. Most scholars assume that a boy played the role of Cleopatra, but we do not know for sure. A young man in his late teens or early twenties could have played her. Or even an adult male might have taken on this demanding role. Or in later years for revivals the boy might have become a man, and still performed the role. For convenience sake, I will refer to this actor as a young male or boy, but this is a conjecture, not an assertion of fact.

22. The play exists only in the Folio edition. It contains this stage direction.

23. For a summary of the scholarly debate on the lifting scene, see Richard Madelaine's edition of the play (1998: 288–92). For additional commentary on the possible method of staging, see Joan Rees (1953), Albert B. Weiner (1961), Richard Hosley (1964), Leslie Thompson (1989), Janette Dillon (1999), and Andrew Gurr and Mariko Ichikawa (2000).
24. R. Hosley (1975: 192–93).
25. J. Orrell (1988: 270).
26. Joan Rees (1953).
27. Samuel Daniel, *The Tragedie of Cleopatra*, 1607; passage quoted in Gamini Salgado, (1975: 27–28).
28. It is possible that the episode of the adder at Cleopatra's breast in *Antony and Cleopatra* may have influenced Barnaby Barnes' *The Devil's Charter* (Stationers' Register on October 16, 1607). If so, this would place Shakespeare's play in late 1606 or 1607, not 1608. But an earlier play by George Peele has a similar scene, so Barnes may have been influenced by Peele, not Shakespeare.
29. As Bruce R. Smith has shown (1999), the "acoustic world" of early modern theatre, including the players' voices, sound effects, music, and other sounds of the playhouse, holds riches for the astute historian. Besides sounds, there are prescribed silences in the plays that reveal performance codes.
30. See Karl Theodor Gaedertz (1888).
31. I. A. Shapiro (1948).
32. John Orrell (1982: 153–54) and (1988: 83–92). For some further commentary on the visual sources for the London theatre of this era, see R. A. Foakes (1985), John Astington (1997, 1999), Peter Thomson (2000), Tarnya Cooper (2006), and Thomas Postlewait (2009). Many documents on English professional theatre, 1530–1660, are available in G. Wickham, H. Berry, and W. Ingram (2000), but this collection is deficient on visual evidence.
33. B. Beckerman (1962).
34. T. J. King (1971).
35. A. Gurr (1992: 232).
36. See Scott McMillan (1972; 1992).
37. S. McMillan and Sally-Beth MacLean (1998).
38. A basic introduction to aspects of deductive argument and rhetoric can be found in E. P. J. Corbett 1971. Also helpful is Stephen Toulmin (1958), which has generated a scholarly following and debate: David Hitchcock and Bart Verheji (2006). A good refresher manual in research methods in the humanities is available from Wayne C. Booth *et al.* (1995). On Aristotle, see his *Rhetoric* in the edition by George A. Kennedy (1991). See, also, Robert J. Conners *et al.* (1984). Logical argument, such as matters of probability in evidence, is still taught in many law schools; see, for example, Joseph Horovitz (1972) as a model text. The shelves of college libraries are full of books on classical rhetoric, logic, and deductive analysis and argument.
39. An inductive approach to audience construction can be seen in Andrew Gurr's helpful gathering of documents (2004a). See, by contrast, Laura Levine's deductive construction of the audience out of a few antitheatrical texts (1994), Ann Jennalie Cook's elite audience based upon a social idea of class and ticket prices (1981), and Annabel Patterson's use of Shakespeare's plays for a version of a popular audience (1989). Both Cook and Patterson attempt to blend inductive and deductive analysis,

but their arguments are over-generalized. More promising is the approach of Anthony Dawson and Paul Yachnin (2001), though their study would be enhanced by more documentary sources.

40. Peter Holland, editor of *A Midsummer Night's Dream* (1994: 151).

41. *Ibid.*, 154–55. On costumes and their potential significance in Shakespeare, see Jean MacIntyre (1992). On clothes and material culture in the era, see Lena Cowen Orlin (2000) as well as Peter Stallybrass and Ann Rosalind Jones (2000). Likewise, Robert Lublin (forthcoming) reveals much about the costuming of gender, social status, and religious figures.

42. Alan Dessen (1977; 1984; 1995; 1999).

43. John Orrell (1982; 1988).

44. A. Dessen (1996: 44 and 62).

45. Andrew Gurr and Mariko Ichikawa (2000: 12).

46. For surveys on our historical knowledge of theatre in London during this era, see M. C. Bradbrook (1982–89), A. Gurr (1992), Peter Thomson (1992), A. Kinney (2003), and J. Milling and P. Thomson (2004). These overviews tend to ignore, however, the many areas of disagreement and doubt among scholars. For example, to this day we cannot agree on the doors in the tiring house wall of the amphitheatres – the number, kinds, and uses. See the recent arguments and counterarguments by Leslie Thompson (1989), A. Gurr (1999; 2001) Janette Dillon (1999), Andrew Gurr and Mariko Ichikawa (2000), T. Fitzgerald and W. Millyard (2000), Tiffany Stern (2001), and M. Ichikawa (2006). The journals are full of the continuing debates on lighting, acting methods, discovery space, properties, types of audiences, sound effects, uses of the balcony, architecture, etc.

47. In the mid twentieth century various people built small models of Adams' Globe (e.g., one was on display for decades at the entrance to the Department of English, University of Georgia). And Adams' model guided the building of several Elizabethan theatres in Canada and the United States, from Stratford to Ashland. The ideas of John Cranford Adams were also contending with those of Joseph Quincy Adams (1917), adding to the confusion over the Globe among literature professors and students.

48. See John Orrell (1988).

49. See Andrew Gurr and John Orrell (1989). Also see A. Gurr, R. Mulryne, and M. Shewring (1993) and R. Mulryne and M. Shewring (1997) as historians and advocates for the new Globe theatre.

50. Also, just before Orrell put forward his ideas in *The Human Stage* (1988), Herbert Berry (1987) presented his own analysis of the playhouses. For more differences of opinion, see the two collections of essays by Franklin Hildy (1990) and John Astington (1992).

51. For example, in the disagreement on the size for the rebuilt Globe theatre – twenty sides and 99 feet diameter or eighteen and 90 feet – the scholarly advisors for the new building voted fourteen to six in support of Orrell's argument for the larger model (A. Gurr *et al.*, 1993: 12–13). A list of the advisors appears on pp. 1–2. In 2003 radar surveys of the foundation for the old Globe suggested a diameter of 72 feet, not the 100 feet that Orrell deduced. See R. A. Foakes (2004: 31) and John Gleason (2003: 15). For a brief survey of the shifting scholarly ideas over three generations, see Gabriel Egan (1999).

52. Of course this is a quick summary, but if I were to add a dozen other scholars who have put forward their versions of the Globe and the other amphitheatres, the disagreements would multiply. From W. J. Lawrence (1913; 1927) to the present, the battle has gone forward without a resolution. For example, Alexander Leggatt's historical summary of our knowledge of the public playhouses (1992) attempts to adjudicate the disagreements, but despite his skillful summary he cannot resolve the disagreements. A similar condition of constant disagreement and contending explanations pertains in Shakespearean biography, as S. Schoenbaum demonstrated (1991). Indeed, an inverse ratio seems to operate: the increase in biographies over the last 200 years has led to a decrease in agreement over not only the meaning of key developments in Shakespeare's life but even the basic question of who wrote the plays. The perfect answer to the endless speculations running through the interpretations of the Stratfordian and anti-Stratfordian is provided by Rodney Bolt, who has written a delightful send-up of the whole biographical enterprise (2004). Perhaps the playhouse controversies need an equally ironic narrative.
53. A. Dessen (1996: 63). For a perspective on Dessen's historical method and assumptions, see the essay by Cary Mazer (1996).
54. Wickham's observation is reported by Michael Jamieson (1990: 39).
55. For example, in the mid twentieth century, textual editors sought the holy grail of the copy text, the one true version of each of Shakespeare's plays. By eliminating printing errors in the quartos and folios, by rejecting interpolations by irresponsible players, by identifying "bad" quartos, and by conjuring the intentions of the playwright, they believed that it would be possible to produce a single, trustworthy edition of *Hamlet* or *King Lear*. They gamely chased after this impossible dream. But during the last few decades textual editing – no longer "new" but "new new," – has relinquished the search for the one, true text. Instead, editors proudly proclaim that they honor the multiple texts of the playhouses. Consequently, there are two versions of *King Lear* in the Oxford Shakespeare, edited by Stanley Wells and Gary Taylor.
56. For a critique of Malone and his principle of authenticity, see M. de Grazia (1991); for a response to her critique, see Thomas Postlewait (2003) and Peter Martin's biography (1995).

2 Cultural histories: the case of Alfred Jarry's *Ubu Roi*

1. Much of the information on this production is readily available in the published production text from Dramatist Play Service, which publishes promptbook texts of Broadway productions.
2. See Peter Buurman (1988) and Bruce McConachie (2003).
3. Marc Baer (1992).
4. Susan G. Davis (1986), Xiaomei Chen (2002).
5. These cases sometimes generate various kinds of conspiracy theories, as occurred, for example, with the investigations of the assassination of John F. Kennedy. I am purposefully avoiding these conundrums in this study, though the conspiratorial mindset operates in all fields of historical study.
6. As Shelley Fenno Quinn demonstrates (2005: 154–97), it is possible to reconstruct many aspects of the celebratory Waki play *Takasago* (or *Aioi*) of Zeami Motokiyo

(1363?–1443?), as it was originally performed for Kyoto elites and is realized today in the performances of the Noh schools and companies.

7. For the purposes of this case study, which examines how and why a century of theatre histories have misrepresented the 1896 production of *Ubu Roi*, I draw primarily upon the extensive scholarship published in English, including works by specialists in modern French theatre, yet I also tap key French sources, critical writings, histories, and biographies. I have examined both the historical scholarship and the critical analysis on *Ubu Roi* and its performance, but in order to do justice to the interpretations and narratives of this major theatrical event, I also draw upon key French sources, including the writings of Alfred Jarry and Aurélien Lugné-Poe. Jarry's play and documents are in *Oeuvre complètes*, edited by Michel Arrivé (1972). I also have used Noël Arnaud's valuable French edition of *Ubu* (1978). For information on Jarry, I have consulted the 1951 French biography by Jacques-Henry Lévesque. The piano music for the production, provided by Claude Terrasse, was published as the *Marche des polonais* in 1898. Several translations of the play are available (e.g., Simon Watson Taylor in 1968). And Jarry's major essays are also translated in an edition by Roger Shattuck and Simon Watson Taylor (1963). Because most of the French sources are cited in the English scholarship, it is possible to track the ways that certain anecdotes and narratives emerged and established themselves in the cross-cultural exchanges. See, for example, Roger Shattuck (revised edition, 1968), Claude Schumacher (1984), and Frantisek Deak (1993). Deak's commentary on this event has served as the catalyst for my own investigation. I sometimes disagree with him on specific details, and of course my historiographical purposes extend beyond his own aims in reconstructing the development of symbolist theatre in France. Nonetheless, I am indebted to his analysis of the confusing historical record. He has done much to correct the historical picture of the production.

8. G. Wellwarth (1971: 2).

9. M. Kirby (1987: 97). Kirby notes that avant-garde art, often different from traditional or popular art, "is apt to cause those who appreciate the other work to become defensive and antagonistic. Thus any innovative work might be shocking to someone who has only the most general, most popular, most widely held view of art." But he also insists that "the tradition of *épater la bourgeoisie* explains only one aspect of the avant-garde." Besides the antagonistic model, the avant-garde also produces works for an exclusive audience; he calls this other avant-garde the hermetic model. It is also innovative, but it turns away from the general public and is content to be exclusive. His examples of the hermetic model, based upon his experience as a New York critic since the 1960s, are the artistic works of Grotowski's Polish Laboratory Theatre and, less convincingly, the performance artist Laurie Anderson. The Living Theatre, by contrast, serves as the model of antagonistic avant-garde (1987: 100).

10. R. Kostelanetz (1993: ix).

11. For the sake of this quick survey, I am equating avant-garde art and modernist art, but I recognize that these two concepts are not interchangeable. Some modernists were "avant-garde" in their sensibilities and artistic practices, some were not. Some modernists revolted against bourgeois values; others made key accommodations. I would agree that the term *modernism* can be used to encompass various movements in the arts of the nineteenth and twentieth centuries, including those of

the self-proclaimed avant-gardists. And the historical idea of *modernity* takes in far more than the arts, for it refers to modern transformations in industry, communication, science, business, technology, etc. For some helpful qualifications on these concepts, see Matei Calinescu *The Five Faces of Modernity* (1990). Also see Astraudur Eysteinsson on modernism (1988) and on postmodernism, see Johannes Willem Bertens (1995) and M. Calinescu and Douwe Fokkema (1987). Alistair Davies published a bibliography on modernism in 1982, revealing how extensive the scholarship and criticism is. The scholarship of the last twenty-five years has, if anything, accelerated.

12. In most, but not all, of our studies, we are not much interested in the various accommodations that modern artists made to the heritage. We tend to ignore the ways the traditions were modified yet continued. Our focus on innovation and confrontation usually rules out a history of continuity. The key exception to this historical agenda is our interest in the ways that modernist artists responded to one another; this new tradition of mutual influences does receive our attention.

13. In making this preliminary critique of our popular understanding of avant-garde art, I am not claiming that the idea of the avant-garde lacks any historical truth. But the two-part model of invention and scandal is only, at best, a partial description and explanation for an event such as the production of *Ubu Roi.*

14. Noël Arnaud (1974: 321).

15. Frantisek Deak (1993: 236).

16. Annabelle Melzer (1980; reprint 1994: 114). Her uncertainty about the number of people leads her into unfortunate phrasing in this sentence, which seems to imply that the capacity of the theatre building could vary by a 1,000 people.

17. R. Shattuck (1968: 206).

18. Michael Benedikt (1966: ix).

19. Harold Hobson (1978: 22); David Grossvogel (1958: 335); Simon Watson Taylor (1968: 12); Frederick Brown (1980: 285); Maurice Marc LaBelle (1980: 88); and Bettina L. Knapp (1988: 145). And Brian Singleton, in what must be a typing or editing error, puts the single performance a year later in 1897 (D. Kennedy, 2003: vol. I: 642). Something seems to be missing in this entry, which makes Jarry fifteen years old in 1897. At that age he was still contending with his teacher Professor Hébert, whom he was later to make fun of in the figure of Ubu.

20. Annabelle Melzer (1994: 230), Claude Schumacher (1984: 68), Keith Beaumont (1987: 59), and Frantisek Deak (1993: 236).

21. F. Deak (1993: 236).

22. Alfred Jarry (1972, vol. I: 400) and (1963: 77).

23. A. Jarry (1972, vol. 1: 415).

24. For the piano music, see Clause Terrasse (1898).

25. J. L. Styan identifies "two momentous performances," but not the dates (1981, vol. II: 45).

26. *Ibid.* (vol. II: 49).

27. (1973: 138). Brockett and Findlay also state that the production received two performances, though like Styan they misreport and confuse what happened on the two evenings. Also like Styan, they draw upon the scholarship of others. Their primary sources appear to be Roger Shattuck (1961, not the 1968 revised edition) and Gertrude Jasper (1947).

28. R. Shattuck (1968: 207–08).
29. I've consulted theatre history colleagues in more than a dozen countries, and they all report that the narrative about the opening of *Ubu Roi* usually gets described in the familiar manner in the histories of modern theatre published in their countries. Because of the dominance of the English language in the international scholarly communities, many of these theatre historians depend upon the publications in English. Not surprisingly, then, these sources are often the basis of the repeated anecdote about the opening of *Ubu Roi*.
30. Maurice Marc LaBelle (1980: 90).
31. G. Wellwarth (1971: 14).
32. G. Damerval (1984).
33. W. H. Erin (2005: 101–22).
34. J. L. Styan (1981: vol. II: 50).
35. See, for example, James Harding's collection of essays (2000).
36. R. Shattuck (1968: 206).
37. *Ibid.* (209). Unfortunately, this evocation of the two shocking riots in 1830 and 1896 ignores the fact that there were dozens of demonstrations and riots in the French theatres during the nineteenth century.
38. D. Grossvogel (1958: 19).
39. *Ibid.* (27).
40. We celebrate Père Ubu as the forerunner of all offensive and objectionable characters in modern art. But we tend to ignore his own place in a scatological heritage of Aristophanes, Chaucer, Rabelais, Shakespeare, Molière, Balzac, and many others before the modern era. This long heritage, the model of continuity, does not fit our avant-garde narratives.
41. Translated and quoted by Frantisek Deak (1993: 235). He misdates Lévesque's book, which is 1951, not 1967. Here is the full statement, which Deak silently trims in a few phrases:

> Sur ce mot, le premier de la pièce, qui, sans doute, n'avait jamais été prononcé, auparavant sur un théâtre, et qui, lancé au visage des spectateurs, semble les atteindre personnellement, puisque l'action débute par là et n'a été précédée par rien d'autre, sur ce mot, rayonnant de brutalité, subitement se polarise la condamnation de la bêtise et de la lâcheté avec la fureur, la fureur indignée, de l'individu arraché brusquement, par cette provocation retentissante, à sa niaise quiétude bourgeoise. Une surprise aussi volente, produite par un tel mot, qui semble dit, tout à fait gratuitement, et sans raison apparente, ce qui lui confère encore plus de force, puisqu'il devient en quelque sorte une entité idéale efficace par sa seule puissance interne, c'est bien là l'intolérable provocation, l'impardonnable attendat.
>
> Ce mot, dit ainsi, dans ces circonstances, se trouve bien chargé, dans sa simplicité terrible – et le plus purement possible – de toutes les puissances et de toutes les séductions du scandale pour le scandale. La sale debout hurle.   (1951: 39–40)

42. Lévesque has no doubt about this argument. Indeed, he opens his study with the following statement: "*Merdre*, c'est par ce mot de six lettres que commence *Ubu Roi*,

et il semble qu'aucun autre ne pourrait mieux convenir pour commencer un livre sur son auteur: Alfred Jarry" (1951: 9). By the word we know the man. Everything comes down to the one word.

43. Translated and quoted by F. Deak (1993: 234).
44. Deak names the journal *Excelsior*; Melzer names it *Commoedia*. They agree on the date. I have not dug through the French journals to resolve this contradiction.
45. F. Deak (1993: 235).
46. Keith Beaumont, though aware of Gémier's statement and the scholarship of both Noël Arnaud and Claude Schumacher, does not want to believe that the bourgeois audience failed to play the role assigned to it by avant-garde theory, so he decides to treat both performances as scandals (1987: 60–64). He does not, however, provide any evidence to counter Gémier's explanation. And to confuse matters further he shifts details from the second night to the first night. Deak's subsequent review of the evidence shows that Beaumont is wrong.
47. See R. Shattuck (1968: 203).
48. F. Deak (1993: 233).
49. Arnaud has provided a report on the audience for the dress rehearsal:

> à tous les spectacles de l'Oeuvre, les six cents spectateurs des galeries entraient gratuitement: amis des auteurs et des décorateurs et des machinistes et du concierge, étudiants, rapins, compagnons anarchistes, fournisseurs qu'on dédommageait ainsi de vieilles dettes impayées, petites amies des amis de tout ce monde-là, un monde bruyant, beuglant, applaudissant à contretemps, déversant quolibets et injures sur les journalistes réactionnaires assis au parterre; trios cents des spectateurs du balcon et de l'orchestre sont des invités d'honneur, des critiques bénéficiaires d'un "service" permanent qu'accompagnent leurs propres invitées, les fameuses "petites femmes" botticelliennnes.   (1974: 321)

50. M. Benedikt (1966: ix). Theatre historians have identified a number of violent riots in the eighteenth and nineteenth centuries, causing physical damage to the interiors of the theatres and sometimes resulting in deaths. And at the Astor Place riot in New York City in 1849 approximately twenty people were killed by the police and soldiers. By comparison with many theatre riots, *Ubu Roi* was a decidedly contained, well-behaved demonstration.
51. For a basically reliable description of the event, see F. Deak (1993: 231–38).
52. In spirit and energy, with its anti-authoritarian themes and its antic disposition, it is a play that delights young people. Not surprisingly, it is regularly revived by college students.
53. Jarry's fascination with *Peer Gynt*, written three decades before the production of *Ubu Roi*, should signal to us that some of the innovative features of Jarry's play have their heritage in Ibsen's far more significant play.
54. R. Shattuck (1968: 204).
55. On nineteenth-century French theatre, see F. J. W. Hemmings (1993); on the claques, see F. J. W. Hemmings (1987).
56. Hector Berlioz (1969: 96–97).
57. Victor Hugo prided himself on not needing to hire *claqueurs*; instead he invited many young artists to be his defenders. See James D. Bruner's introduction to the play (1906: 21). Charles Baudelaire saw the *Tannhäuser* performance in Paris, which

drew vocal claques, and then wrote a spirited defense, *Richard Wagner et Tannhäuser à Paris*, in April 1861.
58. C. Schumacher (1984: 75).
59. Reprinted in Charles Chassé (1947: 17).
60. For a brief, informative summary, see R. Shattuck (1968: 209–11).
61. From our modern perch, we may sneer at Sarcey because of his conservative advocacy for the well-made play, but our embrace of the simple historical narrative, with its melodramatic opposition of good artists and bad bourgeoisie, seems even less defensible.
62. See A. Jarry (1972: vol. I: 399).
63. See A. Jarry (1963: 76).
64. A. Jarry (1972: vol. I: 1165).
65. A. Jarry (1972: vol. I: 339).
66. Quoted by Christopher Innes, (1993: 235).
67. See especially pages 116–17, A. Melzer (1994).
68. Richard Schechner (2002: 208).
69. See Deak (1993: 285).
70. See Schumacher (1984: 192).
71. Moreover, since Deak's book was published in 1993, revisionist perspectives have been provided by Aurélie Gendrat (1999) and Sylvie Jopeck (2007).
72. F. Deak (1993: 134).
73. *Ibid.* (237).
74. Quoted by Leo Steinberg, "A Symposium on Pop Art," in Steven Henry Madoff (1997: 71).
75. R. Hamilton (1996: 199).
76. *Ibid.*
77. W. B. Yeats (1938: 297).
78. M. Benedikt, in M. Benedikt and G. Wellwarth (1966: xiii).
79. W. B. Yeats (1938: 297).
80. *Ibid.* (295).
81. *Ibid.* (97).
82. *Ibid.* (237).
83. In Book IV he also discusses Bernard Shaw and Oscar Wilde, two Irishmen he struggled against in his artistic engagement with the theatre. Here is his famous statement about Shaw's ability "to write with great effect without music, without style, either good or bad . . . Presently I had a nightmare that I was haunted by a sewing machine, that clicked and shone, but the incredible thing was that the machine smiled, smiled perpetually. Yet I delighted in Shaw the formidable man" *Ibid.* (241).
84. *Ibid.* (297).
85. Even if we still insisted that Yeats did recall an evening in Paris when a riot occurred, his recollection, so understood, would reveal as much about Yeats' own experiences during the turbulent developments at the Abbey as about that one evening in Paris. Having participated in the making of a similar narrative for Synge's *Playboy of the Western World*, Yeats' was thus primed to represent his memory of Paris in similar terms. But to argue this way is to ignore the careful organization of the tragic generation section of *The Trembling of the Veil*.

86. For a basic review of procedures for establishing both authenticity (external evidence) and credibility (internal evidence) of sources, see chapters 6 and 7 in L. Gottschalk (1969).

87. People often claim attendance at events that in fact they never witnessed. If we discovered that Yeats reports some pieces of information in his autobiography that he did not actually witness, we would then have to wonder about the neat formulation of his representation of the production of *Ubu Roi*, for he uses it purposefully to make his point about the tragic generation. This suspicion may seem excessive, but historians need to be on guard against manufactured statements, plagiarism, and the doctoring of documents. More to the point, all sources should be examined for their authenticity, credibility, and reliability.

3 The historical event

1. I noted in the Introduction that the familiar term *theatre* has over a dozen distinct meanings. We should not be surprised, then, that a similar complexity haunts our use of these other familiar terms. Of course, those of us in theatre studies should be prepared for some of the complexities and contradictions in the idea of *representation* because we have had to confront the many ways the basic idea of *mimesis*, since Aristotle and Plato, has been translated and applied. A lengthy bibliography can be compiled on the studies of mimesis and representation. See, for example, S. Halliwell (2002) on mimesis and C. Prendergast (2000) on the idea of representation.

2. Robert Jones Shafer (1980: 39).

3. Besides Shafer, see the guides to historical method by Marc Bloch (1953), Louis Gottschalk (1969), and Jacques Barzun and Henry F. Graff (1992). Also, Michael Stanford (1968) presents a developmental model that includes events, evidence, the constructed argument, writing, and reading. See, also, John Tosh (1991), Joyce O. Appleby, Lynn A. Hunt, and Margaret C. Jacob (1994), Beverley C. Southgate (1996), C. Behan McCullagh (1998; 2004), Frank Ankersmit (2001), and Elizabeth Clark (2004).

4. See, for example, Louis Gottschalk (1969) on internal and external criticism of sources.

5. Although some historians (e.g., C. Behan McCullagh) and philosophers (e.g., Georg Henrik von Wright) attempt to make a distinction between explanation and interpretation, I do not maintain a neat separation between the meanings of the two words as I describe how historians represent the possible significance of their sources, which serve as evidence for their arguments. I appreciate, though, that *explanations*, as C. Behan McCullagh defines the concept, "are constrained by the questions they are designed to answer" (1998: 6), whereas *interpretations* offer "one of several possible accounts which can be given of a subject, which usually gives significance or meaning to its parts" (1998: 7). In this sense, explanations often spell out the factual significance of the sources; interpretations offer a potential meaning for these explained facts. I hope that my use of both concepts is clear within the context of my statements.

6. Quoted by Teresa Colletti (1990: 248).

7. James C. Harner (2002: 227). Harner's guide, as his subtitle states, is "an annotated listing of reference sources in English literary studies." It is, then, a model of documentary scholarship. But as any reader knows, and as Harner fully understands,

the annotations are necessarily interpretive. These valuable explanations of the value of the various works fulfill the mission of the documentary project.

8. T. Coletti (1990: 248).
9. *Ibid.* (249).
10. Teresa Coletti (1990) provides an astute analysis of the interpretive features, assumptions, and mission of the REED project.
11. See J. Milhous and R. Hume (1991: xiii-xxii).
12. D. Kennedy (2003b: vol. I: ix).
13. For a detailed explanation of the making of the *Encyclopedia*, see Dennis Kennedy (2003a), who puts a lie to "the false sense of objectivity that encyclopedias foster" (2003: 32).
14. O. Johnson and W. Burling (2001: 9).
15. *Ibid.* (10).
16. Of course, our narratives are sometimes beneficial in the procedures of research, but as we saw in chapter 2 with the avant-garde narrative, some stories mislead us. They subvert the mission of historical inquiry.
17. J. Spence (1978: xv).
18. S. Schama (1991: xiv).
19. *Ibid.* (319).
20. Schama's approach to writing history has its critics, of course, but that is not the issue here.
21. See Paul Ricoeur (1984; 1985), Arthur Danto (1965, 1985), Louis O. Mink (1987), David Carr (1988), David Perkins (1992), and Peter Burke (2001).
22. H. White (1973: 29).
23. See *Ibid.* (105)
24. Louis O. Mink (1987: 205).
25. *Ibid.* (40).
26. See P. Ricoeur (1976; 1981).
27. P. Ricoeur (1976: 13).
28. M. Sahlins (2000: 287).
29. *Ibid.* (293).
30. *Ibid.* (295).
31. See P. Ricoeur (1984; 1985).
32. Although both Paul Ricoeur and Hayden White have important things to say about the place of narrative in historical writing and understanding, there are key ways that they differ from one another in their explanations. See, for example, David Wood (1991: 140–59; 188–200) for White's analysis of Ricoeur's *Time and Narrative* and Ricoeur's response.
33. K. Burke (1969: xv).
34. Quoted in David Wood (1991: 185).
35. See Fernand Braudel (1980).
36. *Ibid.* (27).
37. C. Becker (1959: 124).
38. L. Gottschalk (1969: 140).
39. See *ibid.* (chs. five and six).
40. Karl Popper (1969: 196): quoted by Robert D'Amico (1989: 29).
41. L. Mink (1987: 200).
42. A. Danto (1965: 250).

4 The theatrical event

1. Without question, many art historians insist upon placing artworks in their cultural and social contexts, as is also the case in theatre history, but this does not nullify the importance of aesthetic study in art. For an astute analysis of the idea of "representation" in art history, see David Summers (2003). On these issues of artistic form, representation, and historical context, see E. H. Gombrich (1969), David Carrier (1974), Michael Ann Holly (1984), Norman Bryson, Michael Ann Holly, and Keith Moxley (1991), Mark A. Cheetham, Michael Ann Holly, and Keith Moxley (1998), Robert Nelson and Richard Shiff (2003).
2. Even popular songs, tied to historical moments, can be studied for their formal features. In the 1960s, the songs of Bob Dylan were often treated as historical documents for reading the significance of current events, yet some commentators specialized in the study of the songs as poetry, using the same methods that they applied to symbolist poetry.
3. Songs almost always have a complex representational agenda. They make reference to the world beyond the artwork, create a persona that goes with the words, often tell some kind of story, and take on some of the traits of the performer. But music without words creates its own internal system that requires formal study and analysis. Of course, the whole history of classical music can be related to factors outside of the music – the lives of the composer, the performers, the audiences, the critical responses, the economic conditions of patronage versus commerce, the nationalist agendas that effect music. In all of these cases formalist study gives way to contextual matters of historical conditions and causes.
4. R. Barthes (1982: 96–97).
5. For a succinct survey of semiotic and phenomenological codes in the theatre, see Marvin Carlson (2007). See, as well, Bert O. States (1985; 2007) on the phenomenology of theatre and Willmar Sauter (2000) on the sensory and symbolic aspects of performance.
6. See R. Schechner (1985).
7. Alice Rayner (2006: 15). Rayner provides a subtle psychoanalytic reading (by way of Freud, Lacan, and Derrida) of the ghostly features of a spectator's consciousness of performance. Theoretically astute, in the tradition of Bert States' investigations of the phenomenology of theatre, her analysis complements Marvin Carlson (2001). She probes the paradoxes of representation (e.g., the Mobius strip of the real and the idea, or the material and the immaterial) and time (e.g., Augustine's ideas about past, present, and future), but her investigation of history writing (by way of M. de Certeau and M. Kobialka) is primarily philosophical, with limited application to the basic conditions and methods of historical research, including the primary need to reconstruction the absent event.
8. The Howard family included George C. Howard, who played St. Clare, his wife Caroline Emily Fox, who played Topsy, and their daughter Cordelia as Eva. George Aiken, who adapted the novel, was a cousin.
9. Nor did white, working-class men bring the same racial prejudices and sexual fears to the representations of blackface characters in minstrelsy and the play. See Eric Lott (1993) for an overly ambitious attempt to use theatrical events for a general explanation (part Freudian, part Marxian) of racial beliefs in nineteenth-century America.

10. H. Granville Barker (1930: 59).
11. This historical problem of singular yet multiple identities also occurs in the other arts. There is one *Mona Lisa* yet thousands of copies. There is only one *Moby Dick*, yet it has been printed in dozens of different editions. There is one *Citizen Kane*, yet an endless supply of film stock. And for every famous photograph, there is the original yet the possibility of a seemingly infinite trail of reproductions. Related to these complex issues of reproduction and repetition, all musical scores and plays can be performed by many different musicians and actors. *Hamlet* remains the same yet always changes. And of course any singular literary work can be edited, thereby extending the identity by modification. Walter Benjamin's famous essay on "The Work of Art in the Age of Mechanical Reproduction" (1968) takes up some of these issues. That essay in the last few decades has been reproduced and translated often (thereby extending yet changing it); it has also been quoted and re-quoted, thereby adding another intellectual echo down the academic canyons, as the original idea gets repeated until it apparently loses all attachment to an essential idea. See Andrew E. Benjamin (2005), Beatrice Hanssen (1998), Michael Steinberg (1996), Vanessa R. Schwartz (2001), and T. Dant and G. Gilloch (2002). See also Roland Barthes (1980) and Susan Sontag (1977).
12. Carlo Ginzburg (1994: 295).
13. Marc Bloch (1953: 189).
14. Michael Stanford (1998: 64–65).
15. On the problem of credible sources and evidence, also see C. Behan McCullagh (2004).
16. James Woodfield (1984: 37).
17. Quoted by Tracy C. Davis (1985: 24).
18. T. Postlewait (1986: 42).
19. Of course, if one were putting together a casebook on the production, it would be possible to reproduce all of the reviews. By doing so, one is preparing the material for someone else to make the judgements. Usually, though, historians must select from the data. But how so; on what basis?
20. *Pall Mall Gazette*, June 14, 1889; quoted by T. Postlewait (1986: 45).
21. The words "bourgeois" and "Victorian" thus carry, almost always for us, negative connotations.
22. Quoted in Lawrence Irving's biography (1952: 535).
23. *Ibid.*
24. E. Robins (1928: 10–11; 12–13)
25. In the 1880s Shaw wrote five novels, realizing slowly that his creative talent pointed in a different direction. Finally, at the age of thirty-five in 1892 he launched his playwriting career with *Widowers' Houses*. By contrast Mozart's whole career was compressed into thirty-six years. Shaw is a model for all of us who are slow starters, tortoises instead of hares. There's hope, however belated, of finding one's voice, style, and mission.
26. Bernard Shaw (1991: 106).
27. *The Star*, June 21, 1889; quoted in T. Postlewait (1986: 42).
28. Bernard Shaw, letter to William Archer, June 11, 1889 (1965: vol.I: 213–14).
29. I included myself in this critique, for I did not quote it in my 1986 book on the Ibsen campaign in London.

30. Both Peter Whitebrook (1993) and I (1986) quote the Robins statement as if it were a contemporary response.
31. *Daily Telegraph*, June 8, 1889; quoted by P. Whitebrook (1993: 87–88). Whitebrook's biography gives a fairly balanced assessment of the production, though he too sets up a neat opposition between Buchanan and Scott, on the one hand, and Shaw and Archer, on the other.
32. Clement Scott's article in *The Theatre* (July 1889) is an attack on the play's representation of immoral men (Dr. Rank, Krogstad) and Nora, who abandons a marriage and her children. This action appalled Scott.
33. A. B. Walkley. June 9, 1889, *The Star*; quoted in T. Postlewait (1986: 42).
34. See T. Postlewait (1986) for documentation.
35. 115 copies of this special edition were published by Fischer Unwin in the summer of 1889.
36. William Archer, "Ibsen and English Criticism," *Fortnightly Review*, July 1889; reprinted in Thomas Postlewait (1984: 15).
37. William Archer and Harley Granville Barker (1904; 1907).
38. The production of *Hedda Gabler* in London ran for about a month; Shaw's *Quintessence* had a small publishing run initially. The 1913 edition, revised and enlarged, sold more widely because by then Shaw was a major figure in the modernist theatre.
39. Georg Henrik von Wright makes the case that explanation (*Erklären*) is the aim of natural sciences, while understanding (*Verstehen*) is the aim of the historical sciences. The one seeks general and covering laws, the other seeks to investigate particular cases of intentions, semantics, and symbolic meanings. I appreciate the distinction, but I am insisting that historians also seek explanations, but not universals, not systematic knowledge. Historians put forward explanations as a way of reaching understanding. I agree with Wright that understanding requires a form of empathy from the investigator.
40. Wilhelm von Humboldt (1973: 19).
41. R. W. Vince (1997: 111).
42. O. Taplin (1997: 70). We also have a few other vases that seem to represent actors in costume and with masks, but not in performance. And after the fifth century, we have many more vases, especially from southern Italy, that show actors, tragic and comic. "The problem – and the challenge – is to ask to what degree any particular painting reflects the theatre," (*ibid.* 76). Taplin himself has responded to this challenge of 1997. Recently, working with the Getty Museum, he has carried out a major reassessment of vase paintings and their relationship to theatre production. His project, expanding beyond the classical age of the fifth-century tragic playwrights, examines fourth-century vases discovered recently in the colonies of Sicily and southern Adriatic coast. He argues that some of the scenes on these vases are plausibly informed by not just the myths but also the tragic plays, especially those of Euripides, and their possible productions throughout the Mediterranean. See his masterful, yet controversial study (2008).
43. J. R. Green (1994: 16–48). For the vase-paintings, sculptures, and other monuments that illustrate the theatre, see O. Taplin (1993; 1997; 2008), A. D. Trendall and T. B. L. Webster (1971), T. B. L. Webster (1967; 1978; 1995), A. D. Trendall (1987; 1989), K. Neiiendam (1992), and J. R. Green and E. W. Handley (1995).

44. For some recent and valuable reviews of the documentary evidence on Greek theatre and staging practices, see Oliver Taplin (1993; 1999), R. W. Vince (1984), J. R. Green (1994; 1999), Eric Csapo and William J. Slater (1995), and David Wiles (1991; 1997; 2000).
45. O. Taplin (1978: 9).
46. Taplin used this statement by Eliot as the epigraph for *Greek Tragedy in Action* (1993: 1).
47. See O. Taplin (1993; 1997; 2008).
48. For a sense of how scholarship on the performance of Greek drama has developed since the mid 1970s, see, besides O. Taplin, David Bain (1977), J. Michael Walton (1980; 1984), R. Halleran (1985), M. Kaimio (1988), P. D. Arnott (1989), David Wiles (1991; 1997), R. Rehm (1992), M. L. West, (1992), J. R. Green (1994; 1999), E. Csapo (1993), E. Csapo and W. J. Slater (1995), C. Ashby (1999), P. Wilson (1999), P. E. Easterling (1997), and P. E. Easterling and Edith Hall (2002). For a more detailed bibliography on performance of classical drama, see Easterling and Hall.
49. Yuri M. Lotman (1990: 218). I am suggesting that Lotman's method of reading the semiotics of culture has definite potential for theatre history, including the study of classical Greek theatre, although I see little evidence so far that his methods have been combined with the archeological and performative practices of classicists.
50. J. R. Green (1994: xii).
51. We should also keep in mind, however, that dance was joined to the singing; the visual and aural elements were clearly joined. On the importance of dance by the chorus, see Albert Henrichs (1995).
52. On oral traditions and history, see also Jan Vansina (1985).
53. The scholarship is extensive; I identify here a few representative studies of recent years: B. Gentili (1979), Erica Simon (1982; 1983), J.-P. Vernant and P. Vidal-Naquet (1988), E. Hall (1989; 1997), J. J. Winkler and F. Zeitlin (1990), J. R. Green (1994), E. Csapo and W. J. Slater (1995), M. S. Silk (1995), C. Pelling (1997), P. E. Easterling (1997), S. Goldhill and R. Osborne (1999); Christiane Sourvinou-Inwood (2003).
54. E. Hall (1997: 94).
55. C. Pelling (1997: 213).
56. *Ibid.* (214).
57. Stephen Halliwell provides an astute reading of the mimetic qualities of tragedy; see his translation of the *Poetics* (1986), his commentary on the *Poetics* (1986), and his study of the aesthetics of mimesis (2002). Also, on mimesis see Erich Auerbach (1968), Paul Woodruff (1992) and Arne Melberg (1995).
58. Paralleling this relationship between the written text and the oral performance, there are other dynamic dualisms in the Athenian world, including the doubling process for spectators of hearing and seeing a performance that Edith Hall (1997) analyzes and the dependence on oral tradition and written record that Rosalind Thomas (1989) investigates. In this light, we should keep in mind that Herodotus not only drew upon oral traditions probably more than written records in the writing of his *Histories* but also performed sections of the work in public forums. We do not know when he wrote out the parts of his *Histories*, perhaps subsequent to the public performances in some cases. Even our distinction between public and private needs to be modified if we are to understand the crucial dialectics of Greek thought and experience.

59. Pierre Vidal-Naquet (1997: 109).
60. C. Pelling (1997: 215).
61. See G. Murray (1935), Jane Ellen Harrison (1927), and Francis Cornford (1923). For a full bibliography of the "Cambridge Ritualists," see Shelley Arlen (1990). For an assessment of the ritual school, see Rainer Friedrich (1983) and Robert Ackerman (1991).
62. See A. W. Pickard-Cambridge (1927; 1946).
63. See G. Else (1965) and B. Knox (1979; 1993). Brian Vickers (1973) provides a useful summary of the key arguments against ritual theory. See also scholarship of A. M. Dale (1969).
64. See J. J. Winkler and F. Zeitlin (1990).
65. See Walter Burkert (1985; 1987; 1992; 2004); Jan Bremmer (1994); Sarah Iles Johnston (1999; 2004; 2007), and Sarah Iles Johnston and Fritz Graf (2007).
66. See W. Burkert (2004); he is responding to M. Bernal (1987) and M. Bernal and David Chioni Moore (2001).
67. See R. Seaford (1994). Also see Simon Goldhill's strongly positive review of Seaford's book (March 1995): 226–29. And on Nietzsche and tragedy, see the revisionist analysis of M. S. Silk and J. P. Stern (1981).
68. P. E. Easterling (1997: 39).

5 The criteria for periodization in theatre history: definitive categories for events

1. The scholarship on concepts of history, time, progress, cycles, and change is extensive. Of special note, see G. W. Trompf (1979). For a summary of various approaches to periodization, including attempts to move beyond the Western world picture, see W. A. Green (1992). I have also found helpful the studies of Lawrence Besserman (1996), Robert Stalnaker (1967), Gerald A. Press (1982), Ernst Breisach (1983), Simon Hornblower (1994), Donald R. Kelley (1991), Anthony Kemp (1991), and Joseph Mali (2003).
2. Gerald A. Press (1982), especially ch.1.
3. For eighteenth-century British perspectives on sixteenth-century England, see Jack Lynch (2003), who uses the old formula of identifying an age with a great person, hardly a "modern" way to construct a period.
4. For the development and uses of the idea of the Renaissance as a period designation by the novelist Balzac and the historians J. Michelet and J. Burckhardt, see Peter Burke (1998).
5. Johann Wolfgang von Goethe, (1986: 203).
6. *Ibid.* (204).
7. See G. W. F. Hegel (1902; 1953).
8. Daniel Bell (1997: 112).
9. A. W. Schlegel (1846: 448).
10. James Wright (1876: 401).
11. We might keep in mind, however, that despite the separation between the two periods, the plays performed in the early 1660s were by Fletcher, Beaumont, Jonson, Shakespeare, Shirley, Brome; the theatres included the Red Bull and Salisbury

Court, built before the Rebellion; and many of the actors were still those from the Jacobean age. Moreover, though most commentators claim that theatre disappeared during the Cromwell years, private performances continued to occur selectively and quietly in London and about the country. Also, some touring English players shifted to the continent, performing in several countries. And some players went to Paris, where they appeared before Prince Charles. See not only Leslie Hotson (1928) but also Judith Milhous and Robert D. Hume (1991). Even a dividing line of two decades is not entirely definitive for separating two periods.

12. For a survey of this larger movement, see Ernst Breisach (1983).

13. This is not to say that only progressive ideas of change were put forward between 1699 and 1811. Vico, Montesquieu, and Gibbon are strongly cyclical in their historical theories. But even these historians, within their narratives of the rise and fall of civilizations, traced patterns of periodic change.

14. James Wright (1876: 413). Although Wright evokes, in vague terms, the popular myth of a fall from a golden age, he does not find the standard model of Christian historiography – or, for that matter, the four-empire scheme from the Book of Daniel – at all relevant to his task of describing theatre history, which, like Schlegel, he sees primarily as a secular activity. For *Ludus Coventriae*, see Peter Meredith (1990).

15. A. W. Schlegel (1846: 18 and 23).

16. *Ibid.* (340).

17. *Ibid.* (342).

18. *Ibid.* (29).

19. Within this tripartite history, Schlegel defines subperiods or subgroups based upon national cultures.

20. A. W. Schlegel (1846: 340).

21. *Ibid.*

22. Epiloque to "The Conquest of Granada" in John Dryden (1957: 162) Cicero's statement was repeated by Donatus in his *On Comedy and Tragedy*, which was included in many copies of Terence's comedies during the medieval and Renaissance eras; by this means the statement spread across the ages as a neat formulation. See Barrett H. Clark (1965: 34).

23. The claim that periods have identities is hardly exclusive with Wright and Schlegel. Erwin Panofsky, for example (1960), asserts that periods have a "distinctive physiognomy." Noting this, the historian Robert Stalnaker points out that "the claim that the period has a distinctive physiognomy is the same as the claim that it has an essence or an identity." Moreover, for such a claim to have any content, "some distinction between differences in degree and differences in kind, or alterations of the same substance and changes in substance must be drawn. These distinctions are questions of decision rather than discovery, pragmatic questions rather than simple questions of fact, but the decisions are not arbitrary or indifferent; there are reasonable and perverse ways to choose categories" (1967: 172).

24. G. W. F. Hegel (1975). My basic concern here is not an interpretation of Hegel's theories of history and aesthetics, but a description of the historical model that he put forward for periodization, a cultural model that was taken over, modified, or rejected, for example, by the major German art historians, from Schnaase, Riegl, and Wölfflin to Panofsky, Hauser, and Gombrich. See Michael Podro (1982) for an

examination of how art historians from Schiller to Panofsky developed their aesthetic theories based upon ideas of freedom and cultural variation. Also see Arnold Hauser (1958) and E. H. Gombrich (1969; 1979).

25. Carl E. Schorske (1990: 414).
26. Nikos Hadjinicolaou (1978: 190).
27. For an attempt to yoke the scientific and humanistic features of modern social theory, see the works of Anthony Giddens.
28. F. Braudel (1980: 50–51).
29. *Ibid.* (30).
30. *Ibid.* (200).
31. See, for example, Norbert Elias ch.1.
32. Oscar Brockett (1982: 723).
33. H. Lindenberger (1984: 22).
34. For an epistemological approach that attempts a synthesis of inductive and deductive thinking (and to avoid the skepticism of Richard Rorty and other "poststructuralist" philosophers), see Susan Haack (1993; 1998).
35. Joan Kelly (1984: 10).
36. Jean Duvignaud (1972: 65).
37. Anthony Giddens (1984: 377).
38. Arnold Hauser (1985: 135).
39. Ad Putter (2006: 7).
40. A. Hauser (1985: 164).
41. Wölfflin articulated his formalist methods in three major works: *Renaissance and Baroque*, which first appeared in 1888, *Classic Art*, which was published a decade later, and *Principles of Art History* (1915). English translations, with dates, are listed in Works cited.
42. Note that I have made an evasive move here by beginning with the idea of the "baroque" as the period concept, but then I shift to the more neutral identity of the seventeenth century, a matter of chronology rather than style. On several occasions in this chapter I depend upon chronology to provide a basic period concept; this allows me to avoid the troubling connotations of many period concepts.
43. R. Southern (1961: 17).
44. *Ibid.* (32).
45. R. Williams (1981: 194), especially chs. 3 and 7. Also see Janet Wolff (1981), chs. 4, 5, and 6. Both Williams and Wolff attempt to offer a modified Marxist analysis of the relation between artistic works and the social modes of production in an epoch.
46. See Heinrich Wölfflin (1932).
47. H. Read, "Introduction" to Wölfflin's *Classic Art*, 3rd edn (1968: vi).
48. Werner Weisbach, "Barock als Stilphanomen," *Stilbegriffe und Stilphanomene* (Vienna: Schrool, 1957), 53; quoted by Niko Hadjinicolaou (1978: 91).
49. S. Alpers (1987: 137–38).
50. A. Fowler (1972: 487).
51. For a critique of this dualism in German art history, see Arnold Hauser (1985), chs. 3 and 4.
52. Heinrich Wölfflin, *Classic Art*, pp. 287–88; quoted by Michael Ann Holly (1984: 84 and 49).

53. M. Podro (1982: xix–xx). Janet Wolff, a Marxist art historian, also resists the equation of aesthetic value and meaning to ideology: "Indeed, the central theme of this book is the irreducibility of 'aesthetic value' to social, political, or ideological co-ordinates. This has become an increasingly worrying problem among sociologists of art and Marxists aestheticians, who, while rightly refusing to reinstate any essentialist notion of 'aesthetic', have begun to see the need to accord recognition to the specificity of art" (1983: 11–12).
54. E. H. Gombrich (1979: 46).
55. See also Gombrich (1974).
56. The field of theatre semiotics has been central to the study of drama and theatre, especially for many Russian, Czech, Italian, French, German, and Israeli scholars. Even a short list of theatre semioticians signals how vital formalist study has been in performance analysis: Jean Alter, Roland Barthes, André Bazin, P. Bouissac, Umberto Eco, Keir Elam, Martin Esslin, Erika Fischer-Lichte, Ernest Hess-Lüttich, Roman Jakobson, Tadeusz Kowzan, Yuri M. Lotman, Mario de Marinis, Ladislav Matejka and Irwin R. Titunik, Christian Metz, Jan Mukarovsky, Patrice Pavis, Dinnah Pladott, Freddie Rokem, Eli Rozek, and Göran Sonesson. And the Americans who have applied aspects of semiotics to modes of performance usually have a European heritage or reveal a strong grounding in European scholarship (e.g., Sarah Bryant-Bertail, Marvin Carlson, Michael Quinn).
57. S. Alpers (1987: 139).
58. G. Kubler (1987: 167).
59. Jorge Luis Borges (1968: 103).
60. M. Foucault (1970: xv).
61. E. H. Gombrich (1978: 20–21). Gombrich quotes directly from the description provided by A. Perosa in *Giovanni Rucellai ed il suo Zibaldone*, London: *Studies of the Warburg Institute*, 24 (1960: 22).
62. Paul Veyne (1984: 37).
63. Louis O. Mink (1971: 111).
64. J. Huizinga (1960: 74–75).
65. K. Burke (1969: xviii).
66. E. Hobsbawn (1987: 219).
67. Jacques Le Goff (1992: 127).

6 The idea of the "political" in our histories of theatre: causal contexts for events

1. See, though, William Ingram (1992), Theodore B. Leinwand (1999), and Douglas Bruster (2004) on business practices in Elizabethan and Jacobean theatre. Also, some studies of Philip Henslowe provide analysis of commerce and economic systems, topics surely as important as political conditions and influences.
2. These are all problematic verbs, as will become apparent presently.
3. R. Williams (1982: 148).
4. For representative works, see D. Bevington (1968), J. Goldberg (1983), J. Dollimore (1984), Philip J. Finkelpearl (1990), Kim Hall (1995), Donna B. Hamilton (1992), M. Heinemann (1980; 1990), and D. Bevington and P. Holbrook (1998).

5. See Julia Gasper (1990).
6. In the words of Karl Marx: "men make their own history but not under conditions of their own choosing." Ideology shapes practices. For an application of this assumption in Renaissance studies, see, for example, Ivo Kamps (1991: 5). Marx's statement, which is from the *Eighteenth Brumaire of Louis Bonaparte*, is quoted by Kamps (15). For a trenchant (and sometimes self-ironic) critique of the idea of ideology as it is used today in renaissance studies and literary theory, see Edward Pechter (1995: ch. 6).
7. Richard Taruskin (1993: 32).
8. Alvin Kernan (1995: xx).
9. David Norbrook (1987: 78).
10. All literary scholars and theatre historians, no matter what their areas of specialization, would benefit from reading Rodney Bolt (2004), a delightful send-up of historical speculations and certainties. With his tongue in his cheek, Bolt imitates the documentary and interpretive methods of both the Stratfordians and the anti-Stratfordians, while also having great fun with the current scholarship on Marlowe and the supposed spy network he participated in. Perhaps, after reading Bolt, all of us would be less prone to wide-eyed conjectures that fit our own assumptions rather than the available evidence.
11. A. Kernan (1995: xii). For Kernan, then, literature is part of "a social institution that changes over time in response to political and technological circumstances, and in turn participates in the great social game of which it is a part by helping to remake the world in ways that seem plausible and useful" (xii).
12. *Ibid.* (xii and xix).
13. *Ibid.* (10).
14. S. Orgel (1975: 8).
15. *Ibid.* (45).
16. J. Astington (1999: 1).
17. For a succinct survey of scholarship on censorship, see Dutton (1997); this survey is based upon his two major books on these issues (1991; 2000). Also consult A. Patterson (1984). On the disarray and corruption of the court, see the solid historical study by Linda Levy Peck (1990). Peck's study puts in doubt the neat absolutist models of power that appeal to literary historians.
18. See Richard Dutton (1991; 2000).
19. Besides J. Leeds Barroll (1991), see his two essays (1988, 1996).
20. Barroll (1991: 69).
21. See C. L. Barber (1959) and Anne Righter (1962).
22. R. Weimann (1978: 19). Weimann's historical overview in chapter 1 of this study seems to share some of the attitudes about folk culture and lore that can be traced in nineteenth-century Germany from the Grimm brothers, who gathered and published folk tales, through the evocations of *das Volk* in Richard Wagner's essays.
23. E. K. Chambers (1923: vol.I: 268, 3). The theme of reveling and festival shows up in not only *The Elizabethan Stage* but also *The Medieval Stage* (1903) and *The English Folk-Play* (1933). For my analysis of Chambers and theatricality, see T. Postlewait (2003).
24. Michael Bristol (1997: 233).
25. *Ibid.* (235, 245). This tightly written essay captures the spirit and aspects of his argument in his influential book *Carnival and Theatre* (1985).
26. M. Bristol (1997: 235).

27. L. Marcus (1986).
28. M. Bristol (1997: 233). This word "contestation" has become a popular buzzword in literary studies, to the point that almost any disagreement, debate, or even dialogue is characterized as a contestation, which usually occurs at a "site."
29. See Steven Mullaney (1988) for an overly expansive version of this concept.
30. Even though Chambers identified a reveling spirit in medieval and Renaissance life, he did not turn this spirit into a cultural force of political subversion. Because of his evolutionary ideas, tied to the concept of progress, he saw folk culture primarily as a precursor of professional theatre, not as the basis of its foundational identity. His studies provide a historical investigation quite different from the interpretive ideas of Weimann, Bristol, and others who celebrate the oppositional qualities of Shakespeare's plays.
31. Besides Stephen Greenblatt (1980; 1988), see, for example, Jean Howard (1994), and Louis Montrose (1989; 1996).
32. S. Greenblatt (1988: 40, 46).
33. *Ibid.* (52–53).
34. See K. Sharpe (1987).
35. L. Montrose (1996: xii). Montrose's clear articulation of this approach can serve as a touchstone for the method of many of the leading cultural historians writing on the Shakespearean age and theatre.
36. S. Greenblatt (1988: 4).
37. See Alan Liu (1989) on Greenblatt and other new historicists, especially their relationship to the "new criticism," against which they are supposedly revolting. In key ways, new historicism – as a cultural poetics of politics – offers a new formalism, not a new historicism. It is, in Tony Bennett's words (1987), a "reading formation" which joins text and context within a discursive relationship, to be read and interpreted as a unified or organic work created by the whole epoch.
38. J. Howard (1994: 14).
39. *Ibid.* (14).
40. *Ibid.* (17).
41. *Ibid.* (7).
42. *Ibid.* (10).
43. *Ibid.* (4).
44. *Ibid.* (128).
45. *Ibid.* (18).
46. See T. Postlewait (2003: 90–126).
47. L. Montrose (1989: 23).
48. *Ibid.* (1989: 17).
49. L. Montrose (1992: 392). See his *The Purpose of Playing* (1996) for a full application of his intertextual method of analysis.
50. See, for example, E. K. Chambers (1923) and Glynne Wickham (1959–1981).
51. L. Montrose (1989: 17).
52. I want to insist that I focus on Weimann, Greenblatt, Bristol, Montrose, and Howard because they are some of the most articulate and intelligent advocates for the new approaches to the historical study of drama and theatre in the late sixteenth and early seventeenth centuries. If, as leading scholars, they are having difficulties in constructing the political contexts for theatre, the problem is quite widespread.

53. See Raymond Williams (1982: 203–05) and (1977: 121–27).
54. David Perkins (1992: 126).
55. R. Williams (1980: 44).
56. R. Williams, (1982: 166). He repeats this claim in *The Politics of Modernism* (1989: 83).
57. Even an argument tied to the representation of colloquial speech will have problems, for *commedia dell'arte* and other comic modes before the eighteenth century used everyday speech.
58. R. Williams (1982: 158).
59. *Ibid.* (57, 72–77, 157–58, 171).
60. For a succinct criticism of this Marxian idea, see Raymond Williams (1977), but also see Terry Eagleton's critique of Williams (1989).
61. Norman Bryson (1992: 18–42).
62. Letter reprinted in T. H. Howard-Hill's edition of Middleton's play (1993: 194).
63. See Henry James' "In the Cage" (1958) for an astute cultural perspective on the practice and significance of localization.
64. See James Clifford and George E. Marcus (1986); Clifford Geertz (1973; 1983); Giovanni Levi (2001); George E. Marcus (1988; 1999).
65. Wilhelm Dilthey, *Die Geistige Welt* (Leipzig, 1924), quoted by E. Breisach (1983: 282). This is the familiar distinction between explanation (*Erklären*) and understanding (*Verstehen*) that I noted in ch. 4; it is prevalent in the German hermeneutical tradition, stretching from J. G. Droysen to G. H. von Wright. See Johann Gustav Droysen (1893) and G. H. von Wright (1971).
66. For example, in my essay (2007b) on *A Game at Chess*, I provide a catalogue of sixteen socio-political factors that operated in England during 1624.
67. On the geographical locations and performance spaces of the Royal Shakespeare Company, see Christina Ritter (2007).
68. See Quentin Skinner (1988). See as well the historical scholarship on political ideas by J. G. A. Pocock (1971; 1993). Also see Dario Castiglione and Iain Hampsher-Monk (2001).
69. Q. Skinner (2002: 47).
70. On rhetorical styles, see George Williamson (1951).
71. L. Marcus (1988: 153).
72. *Ibid.* (151).
73. N. Bryson (1992: 31).

7 The theatrical event and its conditions: a primer with twelve cruxes

1. On this debate, besides the essay by R. Vince (1997), see E. Fischer-Lichte (1997): 338–52; 372. And for a full engagement by dozens of scholars with the historical issues, see the five volumes edited by Peter Holland (2004–07).
2. For two recent studies of audience reception, from the perspectives of historical reconstruction and performance analysis, see respectively J. Davis and V. Emeljanow (2001) and J. Tulloch (2005).
3. R. G. Collingwood (1946: 213). For well-measured analyses of Collingwood's philosophy of history, including his argument for reconstructing the inside of an

event, see two books by Louis O. Mink (1969) and (1987). Also see William Dray (1995), which is the most comprehensive study of Collingwood's historiographical ideas. As well, see Dray (1963; 1964; 1966).

4. C. Behan McCullagh (2004: 40).
5. D. Fischer (1970: 15).
6. Besides *A Grammar of Motives*, which appeared in 1945 and was republished in 1962 and 1969, see the key writings listed in Works cited (1959; 1964; 1968).
7. L. Wittgenstein (1953: 108).
8. G. Iggers (1984: 11).
9. P. Munz (1977: 178).
10. Q. Skinner (2002: 47).
11. For a valuable analysis of the distinction between *parole* and *langue*, see Paul Ricoeur. He clarifies, from the perspective of historical study, why we need to understand that "a message is individual, its code is collective" (1976: 3).
12. There are always dangers when we generalize. For instance, in the investigation of intellectual history (e.g., the kinds of studies that appeared regularly in the *Journal of the History of Ideas*), it is tempting to trace the ideas of great thinkers, from Plato forward. History moves from mountain peak to mountain peak, but the daily life in the valleys remains invisible, even irrelevant. Yet despite the tendency of some scholars to limit themselves to the great works as the basis of their historical research, we should not dismiss all of the rich attempts to understand cultural, political, social, and religious ideas of specific times and places But the great ideas must be brought down to earth, as the best work in both microhistory and the Annales school demonstrates.
13. And yet theatre histories of the production, including my own, provide either no answer to these questions or only a partial explanation, usually tied to specific arguments about the individuals involved and the nature of the Ibsen campaign.
14. For a comprehensive presentation of the concept of dialogical thinking, see M. M. Bakhtin (1981). For an analysis of Bakhtin's ideas from the perspective of historical inquiry, see Dominick LaCapra (1983; 1989).
15. See ch. 7 in J. Bratton (2003: 171–200).
16. See J. Roach (1996) and M. Foucault (1977).
17. See the appendix in T. Postlewait (1986) for a full list of Archer's articles, books, translations, and productions for Ibsen.
18. M. Carlson (1989: 3).
19. Perhaps it takes a musicologist to investigate this rich heritage of music on the British and American stages of the nineteenth century. Michael Pisani is writing such a study (University of Iowa Press, forthcoming).
20. There are bibliographical guides that help in the investigation of theatre critics and their journals. On nineteenth-century British theatre, for example, see Tracy C. Davis (1984) and Christopher Kent (1980).
21. Jonathan Spence (1978); Emmanuel Le Roy Ladurie (1978); Robert Darnton (1984).
22. Jim Sharpe (2001).
23. See, for example, Tracy C. Davis (1991), Viv Gardner and Susan Rutherford (1992), Kristina Staub (1992), Ellen Donkin (1995), Tracy C. Davis and Ellen Donkin (1999), Jane Moody (2000), Maggie B. Gale and Viv Gardner (2000), Catherine

Burroughs (2000), Betsy Bolton (2001), and Jacky Bratton (2003). This scholarship focuses on British theatre, primarily London. In similar ways, scholars are reconstructing the histories of women in the theatres of many other countries.

24. Errol Hill (1992), and Krystyn R. Moon (2005). Recent scholarship on both African American theatre and Asian American theatre illustrates, quite well, that no single methodology controls the historical studies. For representative works on African American theatre, see Jennifer Devere Brody (1998), George A. Thompson, Jr. (1999), and Nadine George-Graves (2000). And for representative studies on Asian American performance, see James Moy (1993), Yuko Kurahashi (1999), and Esther Kim Lee (2006). Likewise, a great diversity of scholarship and methodology can also be charted for Latin American, Asian, and African theatre.

25. See Jill Lane (2005) and Edward Ziter (2003).

26. J. Achurch and C. Charrington (1894: 488–89).

27. See Margot Peters (1980).

28. The problems of forgery and plagiarism by historians always haunt historical scholarship, as the infamous case of John Payne Collier, the Shakespearean scholar, demonstrates. For a masterful study of his activities in the archives over several decades, see Arthur Freeman and Jane Ing Freeman (2004).

29. The evasiveness of Archer is a problem I address, in more general terms, in T. Postlewait (1986).

30. The sketches were provided by someone identified as A. J. F.

31. There are several helpful studies on the uses and misuses of visual documents in historical research. For an overview of key issues, see Francis Haskell (1993) and Peter Burke (2001). And for representative studies in theatre history, see John Astington (1997; 1999), Christopher Balme (1997), Marvin Carlson (1990a), Tarnya Cooper (2006), R. A. Foakes (1985; 1993; 2004), J. Richard Green and E. W. Handley (1995), Thomas Heck (1999), Barbara Hodgdon (1996; 2003), M. A. Katritzky (2006), Tadeusz Kowzan (1985), Stephen Orgel (2002), Thomas Postlewait (2009), Joseph Roach (2007), Laurence Senelick (1987; 1997), I. A. Shapiro (1948), Oliver Taplin (1993; 1997), A. D. Trendall (1987; 1989), A. D. Trendall and T. B. L. Webster (1971), T. B. L. Webster (1967; 1978; 1995), Shearer West (1991). Also, on the processes of reading images, see Roland Barthes (1977), John Berger (1972), Jonathan Crary (1990), David Freedberg (1989), E. H. Gombrich (1961; 1978), Chris Jenks (1995), W. J. T. Mitchell (1986; 1994), Christopher Prendergast (2000), Thomas Sebeok (2001), John Tagg (1988).

32. All quotations taken from Yael Zahry-Levo (2008), an excellent study of how theatre historians focus their attention on certain events, adding commentary no matter whether they agree or disagree about the significance of the event.

33. For a revisionist history of Ibsen productions in the 1890s, see Kirsten Shepherd-Barr (1997).

34. See Rosalyn L. Knutson (2001: 1–20).

35. *Ibid.* (13).

36. For representative scholarship on Henslowe, see the select bibliography in R. A. Foakes (2002: x–xii). On Henslowe and his practices, see as well Bernard Beckerman (1971), Carol Chillington Rutter (1999), Neil Carson (1988), Roslyn Lander Knutson (1985; 1991; 2001), Andrew Gurr (1996), Susan E. Krantz (1991), Masayuki Yamagishi (1992), S. P. Cerasano (1985; 1993; 1994; 2004), among other studies.

37. In T. Postlewait (1986), I argue that the spread of his Ibsen translations proved more decisive in the campaign for Ibsen and modern drama than the early productions in London. Tracy C. Davis makes a similar point (1985: 21–38). But as both of us have discovered, measuring this kind of historical "event" (that is, the nature of a reading public) is far more difficult than describing a production that generated a number of theatre reviews. Documents can thus be misleading.

38. See Robert Weimann's valuable analysis (1984: 18–56).

39. A revisionist history of the Ibsen campaign began to emerge in the 1980s. James Woodfield (1984) argued that we should focus on *A Doll' House*. Also, I published a collection of Archer's essays in 1984, and followed this with my study of Archer and the Ibsen campaign in 1986. Likewise, Tracy C. Davis wrote a dissertation on the Ibsen movement in 1985, and followed with articles that helped transform our histories.

40. See, for example, Jane Connor Marcus (1973); Gay Gibson Cima (1978; 1980); Joanne E. Gates (1985; 1994), and Angela V. John (1995). Also, in the 1980s and early 1990s both Tracy C. Davis and I made contributions to the history of the Ibsen campaign, and Peter Whitebrook published his biography of Archer in 1993.

41. Kerry Powell (1997: 167–68).

42. As for Oscar Wilde's support for Robins, Ibsen, and a revolutionary theatre, it is true that Wilde and Robins met soon after she arrived in London. He showed some interest in her growing commitment to Ibsen, but as she herself noted, he did not stand by her when she went forward with Marion Lea to produce *Hedda Galber*. And he was not a factor in the following production of *The Master Builder*. He remained on the sidelines, sympathetic but marginal. And of course he was completely out of the picture by 1895 when his trial occurred. Wilde's most telling contributions to a "theatre of the future" was in the West End theatres, where his plays contributed to the growing partnership between fashionable theatre and the fashion industry. See J. Kaplan and S. Stowell (1994).

43. In an attempt to redress my own narrow focus, I have revised my perspective on the late Victorian and Edwardian theatre. See T. Postlewait (2004a; 2007).

44. Jacob Burckhardt (1979: 57).

45. R. G. Collingwood (1946: 163).

46. O. B. Hardison, Jr (1965).

47. See Thomas Kuhn (1970; 1977); Raymond Williams (1982); and Michel Foucault (1970).

48. On the changing ideas of the idea of change, along with reflections upon ideas of historical time, see the essential writings of Reinhart Koselleck (1985; 2002). As Hayden White states, Koselleck "is one of the most important theorists of history and historiography of the last half-century" (2002: ix).

49. Jacques Le Goff (1992: 117).

50. R. Koselleck (1985: 105).

51. David Carr (1988: 16).

52. Paul Ricoeur (1985: vol. III: 91).

53. See my essay on theatre autobiographies as historical evidence (1989: 248–272).

54. For my narrative in *Prophet of the New Drama*, I set up a major conflict between the new and the old drama, the alternative theatre and the established theatre. Archer and Robins served as hero and heroine, with Shaw as the confederate or helper and

Clement Scott as a representative villain. Today, if I were to rewrite the study, I would be less interested in the adversarial narrative and more attentive to the relationship between the alternative theatre movement and the West End theatre establishment, both of which benefited from the growth of the entertainment industry and a changing demographics on audiences.

55. That is, historical representation attains an organization of events; in Ricoeur's plotted action of threefold mimesis this is done by means of a prefiguration (mimesis-1), configuration (mimesis-2), and refiguration (mimesis-3). For the historian, the representation offers a reference (mimesis-1) and a reflection (mimesis-3), which are negotiated or mediated by an act of creation (mimesis-2). See *Time and Narrative*, vol. I (1984: 52–87) and vol. (1985: 207–74). Ricoeur: "In a word, narrative identity is the poetic resolution of the hermeneutic circle" (1985: vol. III 248).

Works cited

Abbott, H. Potter. 2002. *The Cambridge Introduction to Narrative*. Cambridge: Cambridge University Press.

Abrams, M. H. 1953. *The Mirror and the Lamp: Romantic Theory and the Critical Tradition*. New York: Oxford University Press.

Achurch, Janet and Charles Charrington. 1894. "A Confession of Their Crimes by Janet Achurch and Charles Charrington from the Cell of Inaction to which They Were Condemned in the Latter Half of the Year of Grace, 1893." *New Review* 10 (April): 488–98.

Ackerman, Robert. 1991. *The Myth and Ritual School: J. G. Frazer and the Cambridge Ritualists*. New York: Garland Publishing.

Adams, John Cranford. 1961. *The Globe Playhouse*. 1942; 2nd edn. London: Constable.

Adams, Joseph Quincy. 1917. *Shakespearean Playhouses*. Boston: Houghton Mifflin; reprinted Gloucester, Mass.: Peter Smith, 1960.

Adorno, Theodor. 1997. *Aesthetic Theory*. Trans. Gretel Adorno, Rolf Tiedmann. Minneapolis: University of Minnesota Press.

1992. *Negative Dialectics*. New York: Continuum.

Alpers, Svetlana. 1987. "Style is What You Make it: The Visual Arts Once Again." In *The Concept of Style*. Revised and expanded edn. Ed. Berel Lang. Ithaca, N.Y.: Cornell University Press, 95–118.

Alter, Jean. 1990. *A Sociosemiotic Theory of Theatre*. Philadelphia: University of Pennsylvania Press.

Ankersmit, Frank. 2001. *Historical Representation*. Stanford, Calif.: Stanford University Press.

Appleby, Joyce Oldham, Lynn Avery Hunt, and Margaret C. Jacob. 1994. *Telling the Truth about History*. New York: W. W. Norton.

Archer, Charles. 1931. *William Archer: Life, Works, and Friendships*. New Haven: Yale University Press.

Archer, William. 1923. *The Old Drama and the New*. London: W. Heinemann.

1897. *The Theatrical World of 1896*. London: Walter Scott.

1984. *William Archer on Ibsen: 1889–1919*. Ed. Thomas Postlewait. Westport, Conn.: Greenwood Press.

Archer, William and Harley Granville Barker. 1907. *A National Theatre: Scheme & Estimates*. London: G. Duckworth.

1904. *Scheme & Estimates for a National Theatre*. London: privately printed.

Aristotle. 1991. *Aristotle on Rhetoric, A Theory of Civic Discourse*. Trans. and Introduction by George A. Kennedy. New York: Oxford University Press.

1987. *The Poetics of Aristotle*. Trans. and commentary by Stephen Halliwell. Chapel Hill: University of North Carolina Press.

Arlen, Shelley. 1990. *The Cambridge Ritualists: An Annotated Bibliography of the works by and about Jane Ellen Harrison, Gilbert Murray, Francis M. Cornford, and Arthur Bernard Cook*. Metuchen, N.J.: Scarecrow Press.

Arnaud, Noël. 1974. *Alfred Jarry, d'Ubu roi au Docteur Faustroll*. Paris: La Table Ronde.

Arnott, James Fullarton. 1981. "An Introduction to Theatre Scholarship." *Theatre Quarterly* 39: 29–42.

Arnott, Peter D. 1989. *Public and Performance in the Greek Theater*. London: Routledge.

Aron, Raymond. 1961. *Introduction to the Philosophy of History: An Essay on the Limits of Historical Objectivity*. Revised edn. Trans. George J. Irwin. Boston: Beacon Press.

Ashby, Clifford. 1999. *Classical Greek Theatre: New Views of an Old Subject*. Iowa City: University of Iowa Press.

Astington, John. 1999a. *English Court Theatre 1558–1642*. Cambridge: Cambridge University Press.

  (1997). "ReReading Illustrations of the English Stage." *Shakespeare Survey* 50: 151–70.

  (1999b). "Tarlton and the Sanguine Temperament." *Theatre Notebook* 53.1: 2–7.

Astington, John, ed. 1992. *The Development of Shakespeare's Theatre*. New York: AMS Press.

Auerbach, Erich. 1968. *Mimesis: The Representation of Reality in Western Literature*. Trans. Willard Trask. Princeton, N.J.: Princeton University Press.

Auslander, Philip, ed. 2002–2003. *Performances: Critical Concepts in Literary and Critical Studies*. 4 vols. London: Routledge.

Bachelard, Gaston. 1964. *The Poetics of Space*. Boston: Beacon Press.

Backscheider, Paula. R. 1993. *Spectacular Politics: Theatrical Power and Mass Culture in Early Modern England*. Baltimore: Johns Hopkins University Press.

Bacon, Francis. 2000. *The Advancement of Learning*. *The Oxford Francis Bacon*, vol. IV. Ed., with Introduction, notes, and commentary by Michael Kiernan. Oxford: Clarendon Press.

  1858. *Of the Dignity and Advancement of Learning*. In *The Works of Francis Bacon*. Vol. IV. Ed. James Spedding, Robert Leslie Ellis, and Douglas Denon Heath. London: Longman *et al.*, 275–498.

  1964. "The Refutation of Philosophies." In *The Philosophy of Francis Bacon*. Ed. and trans. Benjamin Farrington. Chicago: University of Chicago Press, 103–33.

Baer, Marc. 1992. *Theatre and Disorder in Late Georgian London*. Oxford: Oxford University Press.

Bailey, Peter. 1987. *Leisure and Class in Victorian England: Rational Recreation and the Contest for Control, 1830–1885*. London: Routledge & Kegan Paul, 1978; 2nd edn. London: Methuen.

Bailey, Peter, ed. 1986. *Music Hall: The Business of Pleasure*. Milton Keynes: Open University Press.

Bain, David. 1977. *Actors and Audience*. New York: Oxford University Press.

Bakhtin, M. M. 1981. *The Dialogic Imagination: Four Essays*. Ed. Michael Holquist. Trans. Caryl Emerson and Michael Holquist. Austin: University of Texas Press.

  1968. *Rabelais and His World*. Cambridge, Mass.: MIT Press.

  1986. *Speech Genres and Other Late Essays*. Ed. Michael Holquist. Trans. Caryl Emerson. Austin: University of Texas Press.

Balme, Christopher. 1997a. "Beyond Style: Typologies of Performance Analysis." *Theatre Research International* 22.1: 24–30.

2008. *The Cambridge Introduction to Theatre Studies*. Cambridge: Cambridge University Press.

1994. "Cultural Anthropology and Theatre Historiography: Notes on a Methodological Reapproachement." *Theatre Survey* 35.1: 33–52.

1999. *Decolonizing the Stage: Theatrical Syncretism and Post-Colonial Drama.* Oxford: Oxford University Press.

1997b. "Interpreting the Pictorial Record: Theatre Iconography and the Referential Dilemma." *Theatre Research International* 22.3: 190–201.

Bann, Stephen. 1984. *The Clothing of Clio: A Study of the Representation of History in Nineteenth-Century Britain and France.* Cambridge: Cambridge University Press.

Barber, C. L. 1959. *Shakespeare's Festive Comedy: A Study of Dramatic Form and Its Relation to Social Custom.* Princeton, N.J.: Princeton University Press.

Barker, Harley Granville. 1930. "The Coming of Ibsen." In *The Eighteen-Eighties.* Ed. Walter de la Mare. Cambridge: Cambridge University Press, 59–96.

Barnes, Philip. 1986. *A Companion to Post-War British Theatre.* Sydney, Australia: Croom Helm.

Barroll, J. Leeds. 1988. "A New History for Shakespeare and His Time." *Shakespeare Quarterly* 39: 441–64.

1991. *Politics, Plague, and Shakespeare's Theatre: The Stuart Years.* Ithaca, N.Y.: Cornell University Press.

1996. "Theatre as Text: The Case of Queen Anna and the Jacobean Court Masque." In *The Elizabethan Theatre XIV.* Ed. A. L. Magnusson and E. E. McGee. Toronto: P. D. Meany, 175–94.

Barroll, J. Leeds, Alexander Leggatt, Richard Hosley, and Alvin Kernan. 1975. *The Revels History of Drama in English: Vol. 3: 1576–1613.* London: Methuen.

Barthes, Roland. 1980. *Camera Lucida: Reflections on Photography.* Trans. Richard Howard. New York: Hill & Wang.

1977. *Image, Music, Text.* Trans. Stephen Heath. New York: Hill & Wang.

1982. "Myth Today." In *A Barthes Reader.* Ed. and Introduction by Susan Sontag. New York: Hill & Wang, 93–149.

1985. *The Responsibility of Forms: Critical Essays on Art, Music, and Representation.* Trans. Richard Howard. New York: Hill and Wang.

Bartholomeusz, Dennis. 1969. *Macbeth and the Players.* Cambridge: Cambridge University Press.

Barzun, Jacques and Henry F. Graff. 1992. *The Modern Research.* 5th edn. New York: Harcourt, Brace, Jovanovich.

Bate, Jonathan. 2001. *The Oxford Illustrated History of Shakespeare on Stage.* Oxford: Oxford University Press.

Bate, W. Jackson. 1970. *The Burden of the Past and the English Poet.* New York: W. W. Norton.

Baudelaire, Charles. 1949. *Selected Critical Studies of Baudelaire.* Ed. D. Parmée. Cambridge: Cambridge University Press.

Bazin, André. 1967, 1971. *What Is Cinema?* Trans. Hugh Gray. 2 vols. Berkeley: University of California Press.

Beard, Charles. 1934. "Written History as an Act of Faith." *American Historical Review* 39 (January): 219–29.

Beaumont, Keith. 1987. *Jarry: Ubu Roi*. London: Grant and Cutler.

Becker, Carl. 1959. "What Are Historical Facts?" In *The Philosophy of History In Our Time*. Ed. Hans Meyerhoff. Garden City, New York: Doubleday Anchor Books, 120–39.

Beckerman, Bernard. 1970. *Dynamics of Drama: Theory and Method of Analysis*. New York: A. Knopf.

    1971. "Philip Henslowe." In *The Theatrical Manager in England and America*. Ed. Joseph Donohue, Jr. Princeton, N.J.: Princeton University Press, 19–62.

    1962. *Shakespeare at the Globe. 1599–1609*. New York: Macmillan.

Bell, Daniel. 1997. "Social Science: An Imperfect Art." In *Sociological Visions*. Ed. Kai Erikson. Lanham, N.J.: Rowman & Littlefield Publishers, 101–22.

Benedikt, Michael. 1966. "Introduction." In *Modern French Theatre*. Ed. M. Benedikt and G. Wellwarth. New York: Dutton, ix–xxxv.

Benedikt, Michael and George Wellwarth, eds. 1966. *Modern French Theatre: The Avant-Garde, Dada, and Surrealism*. Trans. M. Benedikt and G. Wellwarth. New York: Dutton.

Benjamin, Andrew E. 2005. *Walter Benjamin and History*. New York: Continuum.

Benjamin, Walter. 1968. *Illuminations*. New York: Harcourt, Brace, & World.

    1996–2003. *Selected Writings*. 4 vols. Ed. Marcus Paul Bullock, Michael William Jennings, Howard Eiland, Gary Smith, and Paul Mattick. Cambridge, Mass: Harvard University Press.

Bennett, Susan. 1997. *Theatre Audiences*. Rev. edn. New York: Routledge.

    2000. "Theatre History, Historiography and Women's Dramatic Writing." In *Women, Theatre and Performance: New Histories, New Historiographies*. Ed. Maggie B. Gale and Viv Gardner. Manchester: Manchester University Press, 46–59.

Bennett, Tony. 1987. "Texts in History: The Determinations of Readings and Their Texts." In *Post-Structuralism and the Question of History*. Ed. Derek Attridge, Geoff Bennington, and Robert Young. Cambridge: Cambridge University Press, 63–81.

Bentley, G. E. 1941–1968. *The Jacobean and Caroline Stage*. 7 vols. Oxford: Clarendon Press.

    1971. *The Profession of Dramatist in Shakespeare's Time, 1590–1642*. Princeton, N.J.: Princeton University Press.

    1984. *The Profession of Player in Shakespeare's Time, 1590–1642*. Princeton, N.J.: Princeton University Press.

    1961. *Shakespeare: A Biographical Handbook*. New Haven, Conn.: Yale University Press.

Bentley, Michael. 1997. *Companion to Historiography*. New York: Routledge.

    1999. *Modern Historiography: An Introduction*. New York: Routledge.

Berger, John. 1972. *Ways of Seeing*. London: British Broadcasting Corporation; Hasmondsworth, Penguin.

Berlin, Isaiah. 1978. *Selected Writings: Volume 2: Concepts and Categories*. London: Hogarth Press.

Berlioz, Hector. 1969. *The Memoirs of Hector Berlioz*. Ed. and trans. David Cairns. London: Gollancz.

Bernal, Martin. 1987. *Black Athena: the Afroasiatic Roots of Classical Civilization.* New Brunswick, N.J.: Rutgers University Press.

Bernal, Martin and David Chioni Moore. 2001. *Black Athena Writes Back: Martin Bernal Responds to His Critics.* Durham, N.C.: Duke University Press.

Berry, Herbert. 1987. *Shakespeare's Playhouses.* New York: AMS Press.

Bertens, Johannes Willem. 1995. *The Idea of the Postmodern: A History.* New York: Routledge.

Besserman, Lawrence, ed. 1996. *The Challenge of Periodization: Old Paradigms and New Perspectives.* New York: Garland Publishing.

Bevington, David. 1968. *Tudor Drama and Politics: A Critical Approach to Topical Meaning.* Cambridge, Mass.: Harvard University Press.

Bevington, David and Peter Holbrook, eds. 1998. *The Politics of the Stuart Court Masque.* Cambridge: Cambridge University Press.

A Biographical Dictionary of Actors, Actresses, Musicians, Dancers, Managers, & Other Stage Personnel in London, 1660–1800. 1973–1994. 16 vols. Ed. Philip H. Highfill, Kalman A. Burnim, and Edward A. Langhans. Carbondale: Southern Illinois University Press.

Blau, Herbert. 1991. *The Audience.* Baltimore: Johns Hopkins University Press.

1964. *The Impossible Theatre: A Manifesto.* New York: Macmillan.

1982. *Take Up the Bodies: Theater at the Vanishing Point.* Urbana: University of Illinois Press.

Blayney, Peter W. M. 1996. *The First Folio of Shakespeare.* Washington, D.C.: Folger Library, 1991; 2nd edn. New York: W. W. Norton.

1997. "The Publication of Playbooks." In *A New History of Early English Drama.* Eds. John. D. Cox and David Scott Kastan. New York: Columbia University Press, 383–422.

Bloch, Marc. 1953. *The Historian's Craft.* Introduction by Joseph R. Strayer; note by Lucien Febvre; trans. Peter Putnam. New York: Alfred P. Knopf.

Bloom, Harold. 1973. *The Anxiety of Influence.* New York: Oxford University Press.

Boas, George. 1953. "Historical Periods." *Journal of Aesthetics and Art Criticism* 11: 248–54.

Bolt, Rodney. 2004. *History Play: The Lives and Afterlife of Christopher Marlowe.* London: Bloomsbury.

Bolton, Betsy. 2001. *Women, Nationalism and the Romantic Stage: Theatre and Politics in Britain, 1780–1800.* Cambridge: Cambridge University Press.

Booth, Michael. 1991. *Theatre in the Victorian Age.* Cambridge: Cambridge University Press.

1981. *Victorian Spectacular Theatre, 1850–1910.* London: Routledge & Kegan Paul.

Booth, Wayne C., Gregory G. Columb, and Joseph M. Williams. 1995. *The Craft of Research.* Chicago: University of Chicago Press.

Borges, Jorge Luis. 1970. *The Book of Imaginary Beings.* Rev. edn. New York: Avon.

1998. *Collected Fictions.* Trans. Andrew Hurley. New York: Penguin Books.

1968. *Other Inquisitions.* Trans. Ruth L. C. Simmes. New York: Simon and Schuster.

Boswell, James. 1953. *Boswell's Life of Johnson.* Introduction by C. B. Tinker. Ed. R. W. Chapman. Oxford: Oxford University Press.

Bouissac, P. 1985. *Circus and Culture: A Semiotic Approach.* Washington, D.C.: University Press of America.

Bowers, Fredson. 1964. *Bibliography and Textual Criticism*. Oxford: Clarendon Press.
   1978. "Greg's '*Rationale of Copy-Text*' Revisited." *Studies in Bibliography* 31: 90–161.
   1955. *On Editing Shakespeare and Other Elizabethan Dramatists*. Enlarged edn.
      Charlottesville: University of Virginia Press, 1966; original edn: Philadelphia:
      University of Pennsylvania Press.
Bradbrook, Muriel C. 1982–89. *The Collected Papers*. 4 vols. Brighton: Harvester.
Bratton, Jacky. 2003. *New Readings in Theatre History*. Cambridge: Cambridge
      University Press.
Bratton, J. S., ed. 1986. *Music Hall: Performance and Style*. Milton Keynes: Open
      University Press.
Bratton, J. S. *et al.*, eds. 1991. *Acts of Supremacy: The British Empire and the Stage,
      1790–1930*. Manchester: Manchester University Press.
Braudel, Fernand. 1980. *On History*. Trans. Sarah Matthews. Chicago: University of
      Chicago Press.
Breisach, Ernst. 1983. *Historiography: Ancient, Medieval, and Modern*. Chicago:
      University of Chicago Press.
Bremmer, Jan N. 1994. *Greek Religion*. Oxford: Oxford University Press.
Bristol, Michael. 1985. *Carnival and Theatre: Plebeian Culture and the Structure of
      Authority in Renaissance England*. London: Methuen.
   1997. "Theatre and Popular Culture." In *A New History of Early English Drama*. Ed.
      John D. Cox and David Scott Kastan, New York: Columbia University Press,
      231–48.
Brockett, Oscar J. 1982. *History of the Theatre*. 4th edn. Boston: Allyn & Bacon.
Brockett, Oscar J. and Robert R. Findlay. 1973. *Century of Innovation: A History of
      European and American Theater and Drama since 1870*. Englewood Cliffs, N.J.:
      Prentice-Hall.
Brockett, Oscar J., with Franklin Hildy. 2003. *History of the Theatre*. 9th edn. Boston:
      Allyn & Bacon.
Brody, Jennifer Devere. 1998. *Impossible Purities: Blackness, Femininity, and Victorian
      Culture*. Durham, N.C.: Duke University Press.
Brook, Peter. 1968. *The Empty Space*. New York: Atheneum.
Brooks, Douglas A. 2001. *From Playhouse to Printing House: Drama and Authorship in
      Early Modern England*. Cambridge: Cambridge University Press.
   2005. *Printing and Parenting in Early Modern England*. Aldershot: Ashgate.
Brown, Frederick. 1980. *Theatre and Revolution: the Culture of the French Stage*. New
      York: Viking Press.
Bruster, Douglas. 2004. "The Birth of an Industry." In *The Cambridge History of British
      Theatre*. Ed. Jane Milling and Peter Thomson. Cambridge: Cambridge
      University Press, vol. I: 224–41.
   1992. *Drama and the Market in the Age of Shakespeare*. Cambridge: Cambridge
      University Press.
Bryant-Bertail, Sarah. 2000. *Space and Time in Epic Theater: the Brechtian Legacy*.
      Rochester, N.Y.: Camden House.
Bryson, Norman. 1992. "Art in Context." In *Studies in Historical Change*. Ed. Ralph
      Cohen. Charlottesville: University Press of Virginia, 18–42.
Bryson, Norman, Michael Ann Holly, and Keith Moxley, eds. 1991. *Visual Theory:
      Painting and Interpretation*. Cambridge: Polity Press.

Bulwer, John. 1644. *Chirologia, or the Naturall Language of the Hand, composed of the speaking motions and discoursing gestures thereof.* . . . London: Tho. Harper.

Burckhardt, Jacob. 1990. *The Civilization of the Renaissance in Italy.* Introduction by Peter Burke. Trans. S. G. C. Middlemore. Notes by Peter Murray. London: Penguin Books.

    1979. *Reflections on History.* Trans. M. D. Hottinger. Introduction by Gottfried Dietze. Indianapolis: Liberty Classics.

Burke, Kenneth. 1959. *Attitudes Towards History.* 2nd edn. Los Altos: Hermens.

    1968. "Dramatism." In *International Encyclopedia of the Social Sciences.* Ed. David L. Sills. New York: Macmillan Co. & The Free Press, 445–52.

    1969. *A Grammar of Motives.* Berkeley: University of California Press.

    1964. *Perspectives by Incongruity* and *Terms for Order.* Ed. Stanley Edgar Hyman. Bloomington: Indiana University Press.

Burke, Peter. 1998. *The European Renaissance: Centres and Peripheries.* Oxford: Blackwell.

    2001. *Eyewitnessing: The Uses of Images as Historical Evidence.* Ithaca, N.Y.: Cornell University Press.

    1990. *The French Revolution: The Annales School, 1929–1989.* Stanford, Calif.: Stanford University Press.

    2005. *What Is Cultural History?* Cambridge: Polity Press.

Burke, Peter, ed. 2001. *New Perspectives on Historical Writing.* 2nd edn. University Park: Pennsylvania State University Press.

Burkert, Walter. 1987. *Ancient Mystery Cults.* Cambridge, Mass.: Harvard University Press.

    2004. *Babylon, Memphis, Persepolis: Eastern Contexts in Greek Culture.* Cambridge, Mass.: Harvard University Press.

    1985. *Greek Religion.* Cambridge, Mass.: Harvard University Press.

    1992. *The Orientalizing Revolution: Near Eastern Influence on Greek Culture in the Early Archaic Age.* Cambridge, Mass.: Harvard University Press.

Burns, Elizabeth. 1972. *Theatricality: A Study of Convention in Theatre and Social Life.* London: Longman.

Burroughs, Catherine, ed. 2000. *Women in British Romantic Theatres: Drama, Performance and Society 1790–1840.* Cambridge: Cambridge University Press.

Buurman, Peter. 1988. *Wayang Golek: The Entrancing World of Classical Javanese Puppet Theatre.* Oxford: Oxford University Press.

Calinescu, Matei. 1990. *The Five Faces of Modernity: Modernism, Avant-Garde, Decadence, Kitsch, Postmodernism.* Durham, N.C.: Duke University Press.

Calinescu, Matei and Douwe Fokkema, eds. 1987. *Exploring Postmodernism.* Amsterdam: John Benjamins.

Callinicos, Alex. 1988. *Making History: Agency, Structure, and Change in Social Theory.* Cambridge: Polity Press, 1987; Ithaca, N.Y.: Cornell University Press.

Canning, Charlotte. 1993. "Constructing Experience: Theorizing a Feminist Theatre History." *Theatre Journal* 45: 529–40.

    2001. "'I am a Feminist Scholar': The Performative of Feminist History." *Theatre Research International* 26.3: 223–32.

Canning, Charlotte and Thomas Postlewait, eds. 2009. *Representing the Past: Essays in the Historiography of Performance.* Iowa City: University of Iowa Press, forthcoming.

Carlson, Marvin. 1990a. "David's *Oath of the Horatii* as a Theatrical Document." *Theatre History Studies* 10: 15–30.

2001. *The Haunted Stage: The Theatre as Memory Machine.* Ann Arbor: University of Michigan Press.

2004. *Performance: A Critical Introduction.* Revised edn. New York: Routledge.

1989. *Places of Performance: The Semiotics of Theatre Architecture.* Ithaca, N.Y.: Cornell University Press.

2007. "Semiotics and Its Heritage." In *Critical Theory and Performance.* Ed. Janelle Reinelt and Joseph R. Roach. Ann Arbor: University of Michigan Press, 13–25.

1990b. *Theatre Semiotics: Signs of Life.* Bloomington: Indiana University Press.

Carr, David. 1988. *Time, Narrative, and History.* Bloomington: Indiana University Press.

Carrard, Philippe. 1992. *Poetics of the New History: French Historical Discourse from Braudel to Chartier.* Baltimore: Johns Hopkins University Press.

Carrier, David. 1974. *Principles of Art History Writing.* University Park: Pennsylvania State University Press.

Carson, Neil. 1988. *A Companion to Henslowe's Diary.* Cambridge: Cambridge University Press.

Carter, Alexandra, ed. 2004. *Rethinking Dance History: A Reader.* New York: Routledge.

1998. *The Routledge Dance Studies Reader.* New York: Routledge.

Case, Sue-Ellen. 1988. *Feminism and Theatre.* London: Methuen.

1990. *Performing Feminisms: Feminist Critical Theory and Theatre.* Baltimore: Johns Hopkins University Press.

2007. *Performing Science and the Virtual.* New York: Routledge.

1992. "Theory/History/Revolution." In *Critical Theory and Performance.* Ed. Janelle G. Reinelt and Joseph R. Roach. Ann Arbor: University of Michigan Press, 418–29.

Case, Sue-Ellen and Janelle Reinelt, eds. 1991. *The Performance of Power: Theatrical Discourse and Politics.* Iowa City: University of Iowa Press.

Castiglione, Dario and Iain Hampsher-Monk, eds. 2001. *The History of Political Thought in National Context.* Cambridge: Cambridge University Press.

Castro, Tom (pseudonym of Arthur Orton). N.d. *A Universal History of Iniquity.* Buenos Aires: House of Borges.

Cerasano, S. P. 1985a. "The 'Business' of Shareholding, the Fortune Playhouses, and Francis Grace's Will." *Medieval and Renaissance Drama in England* 2: 231–51.

1989. "Competition for the Kings's Men? Alleyn's Blackfriars Venture." *Medieval and Renaissance Drama in England* 4: 173–86.

2004. "Edward Alleyn." *Oxford Dictionary of National Biography.* Oxford: Oxford University Press.

1994. "Edward Alleyn: 1566–1626." In *Edward Alleyn: Elizabethan Actor, Jacobean Gentleman.* Ed. Aileen Reid and Robert Maniura. London: Dulwich Picture Gallery, 11–32.

2006. "The Geography of Henslowe's Diary." *Shakespeare Quarterly* 56.3: 328–353.

1991. "The Master of the Bears in Art and Enterprise." *Medieval and Renaissance Drama in England* 5: 195–209.

1993. "Philip Henslowe, Simon Foreman, and the Theatrical Community of the 1590s." *Shakespeare Quarterly* 44: 145–58.

1985b. "Revising Philip Henslowe's Biography." *Notes and Queries* 230 [new series 32]: 66–72; correction: 230: 506–07.

Chambers, E. K. 1923. *The Elizabethan Stage.* 4 vols. Oxford: Clarendon Press.

1933. *The English Folk Play.* Oxford: Clarendon Press.

1903. *The Medieval Stage.* 2 vols. Oxford: Oxford University Press.

1930. *William Shakespeare: A Study of Facts and Problems.* 2 vols. Oxford: Clarendon Press.

Charney, Maurice, ed. 1988. *"Bad" Shakespeare: Revaluations of the Shakespearean Canon.* Rutherford, N.J.: Fairleigh Dickinson University Press.

Chartier, Roger. 1990. *Cultural History: Between Practices and Representations.* Trans. Lydia G. Cochrane. Ithaca, N.Y.: Cornell University Press.

Chassé, Charles. 1947. *Dans les coulisses de la gloire, D'Ubu-Roi au Douanier Rousseau.* Paris: Nouvelle Revue Critique.

1921. *Sous le masque d'Alfred Jarry (?) Les sources d'Ubu roi.* Paris: H. Floury.

Cheetham, Mark A., Michael Ann Holly, and Keith Moxey, eds. 1998. *The Subjects of Art History: Historical Objects in Contemporary Perspective.* Cambridge: Cambridge University Press.

Chen, Xiaomei. 2002. *Acting the Right Part: Political Theater and Popular Drama in Contemporary China.* Honolulu: University of Hawai'i Press.

Chen, Xiaomei and Claire Sponsler, eds. 2000. *East of West: Crosscultural Performance and the Staging of Difference.* London: Palgrave.

Chillington, Carol Anne. 1979. "Philip Henslowe and His Diary." Ph.D. dissertation, University of Michigan.

Cima, Gay Gibson. 1980. "Elizabeth Robins: The Genesis of an Independent Manageress." *Theatre Survey* 21: 145–63.

1978. "Elizabeth Robins: Ibsen Actress, Manageress." Ph.D. dissertation, Cornell University.

Clark, Barrett H. 1965. *European Theories of the Drama, with a Supplement on the American Drama.* Revised by Henry Popkin. New York: Crown Publishing.

Clark, Elizabeth A. 2004. *History, Theory, Text: Historians and the Linguistic Turn.* Cambridge, Mass.: Harvard University Press.

Clayton, Thomas, ed. 1992. *The Hamlet First Published (Q1, 1603): Origins, Form, Intertextualities.* Newark: University of Delaware Press.

Clifford, James and George E. Marcus, eds. 1986. *Writing Culture: The Poetics and Politics of Ethnography.* Berkeley: University of California Press.

Coletti, Teresa. 1990. "Reading REED: History and the Records of Early English Drama." In *Literary Practice and Social Change in Britain, 1350–1530.* Ed. Lee Patterson. Berkeley: University of California Press, 248–84.

Collingwood, R. G. 1946. *The Idea of History.* London: Oxford University Press.

1993. *The Idea of History.* Revised edn with Lectures 1926–28. Ed. Jan Van Der Dussen. Oxford: Oxford University Press.

Conners, Robert J., Lisa S. Ede, Andrea Lundsford, and Edward P. J. Corbett., eds. 1984. *Essays on Classical Rhetoric and Modern Discourse.* Carbondale: Southern Illinois University Press.

Cook, Ann Jennalie. 1981. *The Privileged Playgoers of Shakespeare's London: 1576–1642.* Princeton, N.J.: Princeton University Press.

Cooper, Tarnya, ed. 2006. *Searching for Shakespeare.* London: National Portrait Gallery; New Haven: Yale University Press.

Corbett, Edward P. J. 1971. *Classical Rhetoric for the Modern Student.* 2nd edn. New York: Oxford University Press.

Cornford, Francis M. 1923. *Greek Religious Thought from Homer to the Age of Alexander.* London: J. M. Dent.

    1968. *The Origin of Attic Comedy.* Gloucester, Mass.: P. Smith.

Cox, John D. and David Scott Kastan, eds. 1997. *A New History of Early English Drama.* New York: Columbia University Press.

Crary, Jonathan. 1990. *Techniques of the Observer: On Vision and Modernity in the Nineteenth Century.* Cambridge, Mass.: MIT Press.

Cremona, Vicky Ann, Peter Eversman, Hans van Maanen, Willmar Sauter, and John Tulloch, eds. 2004. *Theatrical Events: Borders, Dynamics, Frames.* Amsterdam: Rodopi.

Csapo, Eric. 1993. "A Case Study in the Use of Theatre Iconography as Evidence for Ancient Acting." *Antike Kunst* 36: 41–58.

Csapo, Eric and William J. Slater. 1995. *The Context of Ancient Drama.* Ann Arbor: University of Michigan Press.

Culler, Jonathan. 1988. *Framing the Sign: Criticism and Its Institutions.* Oxford: Basil Blackwell.

Dale, A. M. 1969. *Collected Papers.* Ed. T. B. L. Webster and E. G. Turner. London: Cambridge University Press.

Damerval, Gérard. 1984. *Ubu roi: la bombe comique de 1896.* Paris: A. G. Nizet.

D'Amico, Robert. 1989. *Historicism and Knowledge.* New York: Routledge.

Dant, T. and G. Gilloch. 2002. "Pictures of the Past: Benjamin and Barthes on Photography and History." *Communications Abstracts* (Sage Publications) 25.5: 591–750.

Danto, Arthur. 1965. *Analytical Philosophy of History.* Cambridge: Cambridge University Press.

    1985. *Narration and Knowledge.* Expanded edn (of *Analytical Philosophy of History*). New York: Columbia University Press.

Darnton, Robert. 1984. *The Great Cat Massacre and Other Episodes in French Cultural History.* New York: Basic Books.

Davies, Alistair. 1982. *An Annotated Critical Bibliography of Modernism.* Totowa, N.J.: Barnes and Noble.

Davis, Jim and Victor Emeljanow. 2001. *Reflecting the Audience: London Theatregoing: 1840–1880.* Iowa City: University of Iowa Press.

Davis, Natalie Zemon. 1983. *The Return of Martin Guerre.* Cambridge, Mass.: Harvard University Press.

    2006. *Trickster Travels: A Sixteenth-Century Muslim between Worlds.* New York: Hill & Wang.

Davis, Susan G. 1986. *Parades and Power: Street Theatre in Nineteenth-Century Philadelphia.* Philadelphia: Temple University Press.

Davis, Tracy C. 1991. *Actresses as Working Women: Their Social Identity in Victorian Culture.* London: Routledge.

    2002. "Between History and Event: Rehearsing Nuclear War Survival." *The Drama Review:* 11–45.

    2000. *The Economics of the British Stage, 1800–1914.* Cambridge: Cambridge University Press.

    1985. "Ibsen's Victorian Audience." *Essays in Theatre* 4: 21–38.

    1989. "Questions for a Feminist Methodology in Theatre History." In *Interpreting the Theatrical Past.* Ed. Thomas Postlewait and Bruce McConachie. Iowa City: University of Iowa Press, 59–81.

1993. "Reading for Economic History." *Theatre Journal* 45.4: 487–504.

1984. "Theatre Critics in Late Victorian and Edwardian Periodicals: A Supplementary List." *Victorian Periodical Review* 17.4: 158–64.

2007. "What Are Fairies For?" In *The Performing Society: Nineteenth-Century Theatre's History*. Ed. Tracy C. Davis and Peter Holland. Houndsmill, Basingstoke: Palgrave Macmillan, 32–59.

Davis, Tracy C. and Ellen Donkin. 1999. *Women and Playwriting in Nineteenth-century Britain*. Cambridge: Cambridge University Press.

Davis, Tracy C. and Peter Holland, eds. 2007. *The Performing Century: Nineteenth-Century Theatre's History*. Houndsmill, Basingstoke: Palgrave Macmillan.

Davis, Tracy C. and Thomas Postlewait, eds. 2003. *Theatricality*. Cambridge: Cambridge University Press.

Dawson, Anthony and Paul Yachnin. 2001. *The Culture of Playgoing in Shakespeare's England*. Cambridge: Cambridge University Press.

Deak, Frantisek. 1993. *Symbolist Theater: The Formation of an Avant-Garde*. Baltimore: Johns Hopkins University Press.

de Certeau, Michel. 1986. *Heterologies*. Trans. Brian Massumi. Minneapolis: University of Minnesota Press.

1984. *The Practice of Everyday Life*. Trans. Steven Rendall. Berkeley: University of California Press.

1988. *The Writing of History*. Trans. Tom Conley. New York: Columbia University Press.

De Grazia, Margreta. 1991. *Shakespeare Verbatim: The Reproduction of Authenticity and the 1790 Apparatus*. New York: Oxford University Press.

De Marinis, Marco. 1993. *The Semiotics of Performance*. Trans. Aine O'Healy. Bloomington: Indiana University Press.

Dening, Greg. 1996. *Performances*. Chicago: University of Chicago Press.

Dessen, Alan C. 1977. *Elizabethan Drama and the Viewer's Eye*. Chapel Hill: University of North Carolina Press.

1984. *Elizabethan Stage Conventions and Modern Interpreters*. Cambridge: Cambridge University Press.

1996. "Recovering Elizabethan Staging: A Reconsideration of the Evidence." In *Textual and Theatrical Shakespeare: Questions of Evidence*. Ed. Edward Pechter. Iowa City: University of Iowa Press, 44–65.

1995. *Recovering Shakespeare's Theatrical Vocabulary*. Cambridge: Cambridge University Press.

1999. "Stage Directions as Evidence: The Question of Provenance." In *Shakespeare: Text and Theater*. Ed. Lois Potter and Arthur F. Kinney. Newark: University of Delaware Press, 229–47.

Dessen, Alan C. and Leslie Thomson. 1999. *A Dictionary of Stage Directions in English Drama, 1580–1642*. Cambridge: Cambridge University Press.

Diamond, Elin. 1997. *Unmaking Mimesis: Essays on Feminism and Theater*. New York: Routledge.

Diamond, Elin, ed. 1996. *Performance and Cultural Politics*. New York: Routledge.

Dickinson, Emily. 1955. *Poems; Including Variant Readings Critically Compared with All Known Manuscripts*. 3 vols. Cambridge, Mass.: Belknap Press at Harvard University Press.

Dictionary of National Biography. Ed. Leslie Stephens and Sidney Lee. 66 vols. London: Oxford University Press, 1885–1901; reprinted, 21 vols., Oxford: Oxford University Press, 1921–22.

Dillon, Janette. 2006. *The Cambridge Introduction to Early English Theatre*. Cambridge: Cambridge University Press.

1999. "Tiring-house Wall Scenes at the Globe: A Change in Style and Emphasis." *Theatre Notebook* 53: 163–73.

Dils, Ann and Ann Cooper Albright, eds. 2001. *Moving History, Dancing Cultures: A Dance History Reader*. Middleton, Conn.: Wesleyan University Press.

Dodsley, Robert. 1876. *A Select Collection of Old English Plays*. 4th edn. Ed. W. Carew Hazlitt. Vol. XV. London: Reeves and Turner.

Dollimore, Jonathan. 1984. *Radical Tragedy: Religion, Ideology, and Power in the Drama of Shakespeare and His Contemporaries*. Hemel Hempstead: Harvester Wheatsheaf.

Donkin, Ellen. 1995. *Getting into the Act: Women Playwrights in London, 1776–1820*. London: Routledge.

Donohue, Joseph. 2006. *Fantasies of Empire: The Empire Theatre of Varieties, Leicester Square, and the Licensing Controversy of 1894*. Iowa City: University of Iowa Press.

Dray, William H. 1963. "The Historical Explanation of Actions Reconsidered." In *Philosophy of History: A Symposium*. Ed. Sydney Hook. New York, 105–35.

1995. *History as Re-Enactment: R. G. Collingwood's Idea of History*. Oxford: Clarendon Press.

1964. *Philosophy of History*. Englewood Cliffs, N.J.: Prentice-Hall.

Dray, William H., ed. 1966. *Philosophical Analysis and History*. New York: Harper and Row.

Droysen, Johann Gustav. 1893. *Outline of the Principles of History*. Trans. Elisha Benjamin Andrews. Boston: Ginn & Co.

Dryden, John. 1957. *Three Plays*. Ed. George Saintsbury. New York: Hill & Wang.

Dutton, Richard. 1997. "Censorship." In *A New History of Early English Drama*. Ed. John D. Cox and David Scott Kastan. New York: Columbia University Press, 287–304.

2000. *Licensing, Censorship and Authorship in Early Modern England: Buggeswords*. Basingstoke: Palgrave.

1991. *Mastering the Revels: Regulation and Censorship of English Renaissance Drama*. Iowa City: University of Iowa Press.

Dutton, Richard, ed. 2009. *Oxford Handbook on Early Modern Theatre*. Oxford: Oxford University Press.

Duvignaud, Jean. 1972. *The Sociology of Art*. Trans. Timothy Wilson. New York: Harper & Row.

Eagleton, Terry. 1989. "Base and Superstructure in Raymond Williams." In *Raymond Williams: Critical Perspectives*. Ed. Terry Eagleton. Boston: Northeastern University Press, 165–75.

1991. *Ideology: an Introduction*. London: Verso.

1990. *The Ideology of the Aesthetic*. Oxford: Blackwell.

Easterling, P. E. 1997. "A Show for Dionysus." In *The Cambridge Introduction to Greek Tragedy*. Ed. P. E. Easterling. Cambridge: Cambridge University Press, 36–53.

Easterling, P. E., ed. 1997. *The Cambridge Introduction to Greek Tragedy*. Cambridge: Cambridge University Press.

Easterling, Pat and Edith Hall, eds. 2002. *Greek and Roman Actors: Aspects of an Ancient Profession*. Cambridge: Cambridge University Press.

Eco, Umberto. 1977a. "The Influence of Roman Jakobson on the Development of Semiotics." In *Roman Jakobson: Echoes of His Scholarship*. Ed. D. Armstrong and C. H. van Schoonefeld. Lisse: Peter de Riddeer Press, 39–58.

1984. *Semiotics and the Philosophy of Language*. Bloomington: Indiana University Press.

1977b. "Semiotics of Theatrical Performance." *The Drama Review* 21: 107–17.

1976. *A Theory of Semiotics*. Bloomington: Indiana University Press.

Eco, Umberto and Thomas A. Sebeok, eds. 1983. *The Sign of Three: Dupin, Holmes, Peirce*. Bloomington: Indiana University Press.

Egan, Gabriel. 1999. "Reconstruction of the Globe: A Retrospective." *Shakespeare Survey* 52: 1–16.

Elam, Harry and David Krasner, eds. 2001. *African American Performance and Theatre History: A Critical Reader*. Oxford: Oxford University Press.

Elam, Keir. 1980. *The Semiotics of Theatre and Drama*. London: Methuen.

Elias, Norbert. 1983. *The Court Society*. Trans. Edmund Jephcott. New York: Pantheon.

Eliot, T. S. 1951. *Selected Essays*. London: Faber & Faber.

Else, Gerald F. 1965. *The Origins and Early Form of Greek Tragedy*. Cambridge, Mass.: Harvard University Press.

1986. *Plato and Aristotle on Poetry*. Chapel Hill: University of North Carolina Press.

Erikson, Kai, ed. 1997. *Sociological Visions*. Lanham, N.J.: Rowman & Littlefield.

Erin, Williams Hymen. 2005. "Theatrical Terror: *Attendats* and Symbolist Spectacle." *The Comparatist* 29: 101–22.

Erne, Lukas. 2003. *Shakespeare as Literary Dramatist*. Cambridge: Cambridge University Press.

Esslin, Martin. 1987. *The Field of Drama: How the Signs of Drama Create Meaning on Stage and Screen*. London: Methuen.

Eysteinsson, Ástráudur. 1988. *The Concept of Modernism*. Ithaca, N.Y.: Cornell University Press.

Feher, Michael, with Romona Naddeff and Nadia Tazi, eds. 1989. *Fragments for a History of the Human Body*. 3 vols. New York: Rizzoli.

Féral, Josette, ed. 2002. "Theatricality: Special Issue." *Substance: A Review of Theory and Literary Criticism* 31.2 and 3: 2–318.

Fineman, Joel. 1989. "The History of the Anecdote: Fiction and Fiction." In *The New Historicism*. Ed. H. Avam Veeser. New York: Routledge, 49–76.

Fink, Carol. 1989. *Marc Bloch*. Cambridge: Cambridge University Press.

Finkelpearl, Philip J. 1990. *Court and Country Politics in the Plays of Beaumont and Fletcher*. Princeton, N.J.: Princeton University Press.

Finer, W. E. 1997. *The History of Government from the Earliest Times*. Oxford: Oxford University Press.

Finley, M. I. 1975. *The Use and Abuse of History*. New York: Viking Press.

Fischer, David Hackett. 1970. *Historians' Fallacies: Toward a Logic of Historical Thought*. New York: Harper & Row.

Fischer-Lichte, Erika. 1992. *The Semiotics of Theatre*. Trans. Jeremy Gaines and Doris L. Jones. Bloomington: Indiana University Press.

1997. *The Show and Gaze of Theatre: A European Perspective*. Iowa City: University of Iowa Press.

Fitzgerald, Tim and Wendy Millyard. 2000. "Hangings, Doors and Discoveries: Conflicting Evidence or Problematic Assumptions?" *Theatre Notebook* 54: 1–23.

Foakes, R. A. 2004. "Henslowe's Rose/Shakespeare's Globe." In *From Script to Stage in Early Modern England*. Ed. Peter Holland and Stephen Orgel. Basingstoke: Palgrave Macmillan, 11–31.

    1985. *Illustrations of the English Stage 1580–1642*. Stanford, Calif.: Stanford University Press.

    1993. "The Image of the Swan Theatre." In *Spectacle & Image in Renaissance Europe*. Ed. André Lascombes. Leiden: E. J. Brill, 337–59.

Foakes, R. A., ed. 2002. *Henslowe's Diary*. 2nd edn. Cambridge: Cambridge University Press.

Fokkema, Douwe and Hans Bertans, eds. 1986. *Approaching Postmodernism*. Amsterdam: John Benjamins.

Foner, Eric, ed. 1997. *The New American History*. Revised and expanded edn. Philadelphia: Temple University Press.

Foster, Susan Leigh, ed. 1995. *Choreographing History*. Bloomington: Indiana University Press.

    1996. *Corporealities: Dancing, Knowledge, Culture, and Power*. New York: Routledge.

Foucault, Michel. 1977. "Nietzsche, Genealogy, History." In *Language, Counter-Memory, Practice: Selected Essays and Interviews*. Ed. Donald F. Bouchard. Ithaca, N.Y.: Cornell University Press, 139–64.

    1970. *The Order of Things, An Archaeology of the Human Sciences*. New York: Random House.

Fowler, Alastair. 1972. "Periodization and Interart Analogies." *New Literary History* 3.3: 487–509.

Frazer, J. G. *The Golden Bough: A Study in Magic and Religion*. 3rd edn. 9 in 13 vols. New York: Macmillan, 1935–37.

Freedberg, David. 1989. *The Power of Images*. Chicago: University of Chicago Press.

Freeman, Arthur and Janet Ing Freeman. 2004. *John Payne Collier: Scholarship and Forgery in the Nineteenth Century*. 2 vols. New Haven, Conn.: Yale University Press.

Friedman, Susan. 1996. *Marc Bloch: Sociology and Geography: Encountering Changing Disciplines*. Cambridge: Cambridge University Press.

Friedrich, Rainer. 1983. "Drama and Ritual." In *Themes in Drama: Drama and Ritual*. Ed. James Redmond. Cambridge: Cambridge University Press, 159–223.

Frye, Northrop. 1957. *The Anatomy of Criticism: Four Essays*. Princeton, N.J.: Princeton University Press.

Fulbrook, Mary. 2002. *Historical Theory*. London: Routledge.

Gadamer, Hans-Georg. 1997. *Truth and Method*. Second, revised edn. Trans. Joe Weinsheimer and Donald G. Marshall. New York: Continuum.

Gaedertz, Karl Theodor. 1888. *Zur Kenntnis der altenglischen Bühne nebst andern Beiträgen zur Shakespeare-Litteratur*. Bremen: C. Ed. Müller.

Gale, Maggie B. and Viv Gardner, eds. 2000. *Women, Theatre and Performance: New Histories, New Historiographies*. Manchester: Manchester University Press.

Gallagher, Catherine and Stephen Greenblatt. 2000. *Practicing New Historicism*. Chicago: University of Chicago Press.

Gardner, Viv and Susan Rutherford, eds. 1992. *The New Woman and Her Sisters: Feminism and Theatre, 1850–1914*. Ann Arbor: University of Michigan Press.

Gasper, Julia. 1990. *The Dragon and the Dove: The Plays of Thomas Dekker*. Oxford: Oxford University Press.

Gates, Joanne E. 1985. "Elizabeth Robins and the 1891 Production of *Hedda Gabler*." *Modern Drama* 28: 611–19.

1994. *Elizabeth Robins, 1862–1952: Actress, Novelist, Feminist*. Tuscaloosa: University of Alabama Press.

Gay, Peter. 2000. "Do Your Thing." In *Historians and Social Values*. Ed. Joep Leerssen and Ann Rigney. Amsterdam: Amsterdam University Press, 33–44.

Geertz, Clifford. 2000. *Available Light: Anthropological Reflections on Philosophical Topics*. Princeton, N.J.: Princeton University Press.

1973. *The Interpretation of Cultures*. New York: Basic Books.

1983. *Local Knowledge: Further Essays in Interpretive Anthropology*. New York: Basic Books.

Gendrat, Aurélie. 1999. *Alfred Jarry: Ubu roi*. Paris: Bréal.

Gentili, Bruno. 1979. *Theatrical Performances in the Ancient World: Hellenistic and Early Roman Theatre*. Amsterdam: J. C. Gieben.

George, David, ed. 2004. *Coriolanus, 1687–1940*. New York: Continuum.

George-Graves, Nadine. 2000. *The Royalty of Negro Vaudeville: The Whitman Sisters and the Negotiation of Race, Gender, and Class in African-American Theatre, 1900–1940*. New York: St. Martin's Press.

Giddens, Anthony. 1984. *The Constitution of Society*. Cambridge: Polity Press.

1987. *Social Theory and Modern Sociology*. Stanford, Calif.: Stanford University Press.

1993. *Sociology*. Cambridge: Polity Press.

2000. *The Third Way and Its Critics*. Cambridge: Polity Press.

Ginzburg, Carlo. 1994. "Checking the Evidence: The Judge and the Historian." In *Questions of Evidence: Proof, Practice, and Persuasion across the Disciplines*. Ed. James Chandler, Arnold I. Davidson, and Harry Harootunian. Chicago: University of Chicago Press, 290–303; 321–24.

1980. *The Cheese and the Worm: The Cosmos of a Sixteenth-Century Miller*. Trans. Anne and John Tedeschi. Baltimore: Johns Hopkins University Press.

1989. *Clues, Myths, and Historical Method*. Trans. John and Anne Tedeschi. Baltimore: Johns Hopkins University Press.

Gleason, John B. 1981. "The Dutch Humanist Origins of the De Witt Drawing of the Swan Theatre." *Shakespeare Quarterly* 32: 324–28.

2003. "New Questions about the Globe." *Times Literary Supplement*. September 26, 15.

Goethe, Johann Wolfgang von. 1986. "Stages of Man's Mind" [1817]. In *Essays on Art and Literature, Volume 3 of Goethe's Collected Works*. Ed. John Gearey. Trans. Ellen von Nardroff and Ernest H. von Nardroff. Princeton, N.J.: Princeton University Press, 203–05.

Goldberg, Jonathan. 1983. *James I and the Politics of Literature: Jonson, Shakespeare, Donne, and their Contemporaries*. Baltimore: Johns Hopkins University Press.

Goldhill, Simon. 1995. Book review of Richard Seaford's *Reciprocity and Ritual: Homer and Tragedy in the Developing City-State*. *The Classical Review* 45.2: 226–29.

Goldhill, Simon and Robin Osborne, eds. 1999. *Performance Culture and Athenian Democracy*. Cambridge: Cambridge University Press.

Gombrich, E. H. 1961. *Art and Illusion*. Princeton, N.J.: Princeton University Press.

1974. "The Renaissance–Period or Movement?" In *Background to the English Renaissance.* Ed. Arthur G. Dickens *et al.* London: Gray-Mills, 9–30.

1979. "In Search of Cultural History." In *Ideals and Idols: Essays on Values in History and in Art.* Oxford: Phaidon, 24–59; 209–11.

1969. *In Search of Cultural History.* Oxford: Clarendon Press.

1978. *Symbolic Images: Studies in the Art of the Renaissance.* London: Phaidon Press.

Goodman, Nelson. 1968. *Languages of Art: An Approach to a Theory of Symbols.* Indianapolis: Bobbs-Merrill.

1978. *Ways of Worldmaking.* Indianapolis: Hackett Publishing Co.

Goody, Jack. 1997. *Representations and Contradictions: Ambivalence Towards Images, Theatre, Fiction, Relics and Sexuality.* Oxford: Blackwell.

Gottschalk, Louis. 1969. *Understanding History: A Primer of Historical Method.* 2nd edn. New York: Alfred A. Knopf.

ed. 1963. *Generalization in the Writing of History.* Chicago: University of Chicago Press.

Green, J. Richard. 1994. *Theatre in Ancient Greek Society.* London: Routledge.

1999. "Tragedy and the Spectacle of the Mind: Messenger Speeches, Actors, Narrative, and Audience Imagination in Fourth-Century BCE Vase-Painting." In *The Art of Ancient Spectacle.* Ed. B. Bergmann and C. Kondoleon. New Haven, Conn.: Yale University Press, 37–63.

Green, J. Richard and E. W. Handley. 1995. *Images of the Greek Theatre.* London: British Museum Press.

Green, W. A. 1992. "Periodization in European and World History." *Journal of World History* 3.1: 13–53.

Greenblatt, Stephen. 1990. *Learning to Curse.* New York: Routledge.

1980. *Renaissance Self-Fashioning: From More to Shakespeare.* Chicago: University of Chicago Press.

1988. *Shakespearean Negotiations: The Circulation of Social Energy in Renaissance England.* Berkeley: University of California Press.

Greg, W. W. 1931. *Dramatic Documents from the Elizabethan Playhouses.* 2 vols. Oxford: Clarendon Press.

1955a. *The Editorial Problem in Shakespeare: A Survey of the Foundations of the Text.* 2nd edn. Oxford: Clarendon Press.

1955b. *The Shakespeare First Folio: Its Bibliographical and Textual History.* Oxford: Clarendon Press.

1923. *Two Elizabethan Stage Abridgements: The Battle of Alcazar & Orlando Furioso.* London: F. Hall, for the Malone Society at Oxford University Press.

Grossvogel, David. 1958. *Twentieth Century French Drama.* New York: Columbia University Press.

Gurr, Andrew. 2001. "Doors at the Globe: The Gulf between Page and Stage." *Theatre Notebook* 55: 59–71.

2004a. *Playgoing in Shakespeare's London.* 3rd edn. Cambridge: Cambridge University Press.

1992. *The Shakespearean Stage, 1574–1642.* 3rd edn. Cambridge: Cambridge University Press.

2004b. *The Shakespeare Company, 1594–1642.* Cambridge: Cambridge University Press.

1996. *The Shakespearian Playing Companies*. Oxford: Oxford University Press.

1999. "Stage Doors at the Globe." *Theatre Notebook* 53.1: 8–18.

Gurr, Andrew and Mariko Ichikawa. 2000. *Staging in Shakespeare's Theatres*. Oxford: Oxford University Press.

Gurr, Andrew, Ronnie Mulryne, and Margaret Shewring. 1993. *The Design of the Globe*. London: The International Shakespeare Globe Centre.

Gurr, Andrew and John Orrell. 1989. *Rebuilding Shakespeare's Globe*. Foreword by Sam Wanamaker. London: Weidenfeld and Nicolson.

Haack, Susan. 1993. *Evidence and Inquiry: Towards a Reconstruction in Epistemology*. Oxford: Blackwell.

1998. *Manifesto of a Passionate Moderate: Unfashionable Essays*. Chicago: University of Chicago Press.

Hacking, Ian. 1999. *The Social Construction of What?* Cambridge, Mass.: Harvard University Press.

Hadjinicolaou, Nikos. 1978. *Art History and Class Struggle*. Trans. Louise Asmal. London: Pluto Press.

Hall, Edith. 1989. *Inventing the Barbarian: Greek Self-Definition through Tragedy*. Oxford: Oxford University Press.

1997. "The Sociology of Athenian Tragedy." In *The Cambridge Companion to Greek Tragedy*. Ed. P. E. Easterling. Cambridge: Cambridge University Press, 93–126.

Hall, Kim. 1995. *Things of Darkness: Economics of Race and Gender in Early Modern England*. Ithaca, N.Y.: Cornell University Press.

Halleran, Michael R. 1985. *Stagecraft in Euripides*. London: Croom Helm.

Halliwell, Stephen. 2002. *The Aesthetics of Mimesis: Ancient Texts and Modern Problems*. Princeton, N.J.: Princeton University Press.

1986. *Aristotle's Poetics*. Chapel Hill: University of North Carolina Press.

1992. "Epilogue: The *Poetics* and Its Interpreters." In *Essays on Aristotle's Poetics*. Ed. Amélie Oksenberg Rorty. Princeton, N.J.: Princeton University Press, 409–24.

Hamilton, Donna B. 1992. *Shakespeare and the Politics of Protestant England*. Lexington: University of Kentucky Press.

Hamilton, Richard F. 1996. *The Social Misconstruction of Reality: Validity and Verification in the Scholarly Community*. New Haven, Conn.: Yale University Press.

Hanssen, Beatrice. 1998. *Walter Benjamin's Other History: Of Stories, Animals, Human Beings, and Angels*. Berkeley: University of California Press.

Harbage, Alfred. 1941. *Shakespeare's Audience*. New York: Columbia University Press.

Harding, James, ed. 2000. *Contours of the Theatrical Avant-Garde: Performance and Textuality*. Ann Arbor: University of Michigan Press.

Hardison, Jr., O. B. 1965. *Christian Rite and Christian Drama in the Middle Ages: Essays in the Origin and Early History of Modern Drama*. Baltimore: Johns Hopkins University Press.

Harner, James L. 2002. *Literary Research Guide: An Annotated Listing of Reference Sources in English Literary Studies*. 4th edn. New York: Modern Language Association of America Publications.

Harrison, Jane Ellen. 1927. *Themis, A Study of the Social Origins of Greek Religion*. Cleveland, Ohio: World Publishing Co.

Haskell, Francis. 1993. *History and Its Images*. New Haven, Conn.: Yale University Press.

Hattaway, Michael. 1982. *Elizabethan Popular Theatre: Plays in Performance*. London: Routledge & Kegan Paul.

Hauser, Arnold. 1985. *The Philosophy of Art History*. Evanston, Ill.: Northwestern University Press.

Hawthorn, Geoffrey. 1991. *Plausible Worlds: Possibility and Understanding in History and Social Sciences*. Cambridge: Cambridge University Press.

Heck, Thomas F. 1999. *Picturing Performance: the Iconography of the Performing Arts in Concept and Practice. Thomas Heck, with contributions from Robert Erenstein, M. A. Katritsky, Frank Peeters, A. William Smith, Lyckle De Vries*. Rochester, N.Y.: University of Rochester Press.

Hegel, Georg Wilhelm Friedrich. 1975. *Aesthetics: Lectures on Fine Arts*. Trans. T. M. Knox. Oxford: Clarendon Press.

   1902. *Lectures on The Philosophy of History*. Trans. John Sibree. London: G. Bell & Sons.

   1953. *Reason in History: A General Introduction to the Philosophy of History*. Trans. Robert S. Hartman. New York: Liberal Arts Press.

Heinemann, Margot. 1990. "Political Drama." In *The Cambridge Companion to English Renaissance Drama*. Ed. A. R. Braumuller and Michael Hattaway. Cambridge: Cambridge University Press, 161–206.

   1980. *Puritanism and Theatre*. Cambridge: Cambridge University Press.

Hemmings, F. J. W. 1987. "La Claque: une institution contestée." *Revue d'Histoire du Théâtre* 34.3: 297–305.

   1993. *The Theater Industry in Nineteenth-Century France*. Cambridge: Cambridge University Press.

Henrichs, Albert. 1995. "Why Should I Dance?" *Arion* 3: 56–111.

Herder, Johann Gottfried von. 1993. *Against Pure Reason: Writings on Religion, Language, and History*. Ed. and trans. Marcia Bunge. Minneapolis: Fortress Press.

Herodotus. 1996. *The Histories*. Trans. Aubrey de Sélincourt. Revised, with introductory matter and notes by John Marincola. London: Penguin Books.

Hess-Lüttich, Ernest, ed. 1982. *Multimedial Communication. Vol. II: Theatre Semiotics*. Tübingen, Narr.

Highfill, Jr., Philip H., Kalman A. Burnim, and Edward A. Langhams. *A Biographical Dictionary of Actors, Actresses, Musicians, Dancers, Managers, and Other Stage Personnel in London, 1660–1800*. 16 vols. Cardondale: Southern Illinois University Press, 1973–93.

Hildy, Franklin J., ed. 1990. *New Issues in the Reconstruction of Shakespeare's Theatre*. New York: Peter Lang.

Hill, Errol. 1992. *The Jamaican Stage, 1655–1900: Profile of a Colonial Theatre*. Amherst: University of Massachusetts Press.

Hinman, Charlton. 1963. *The Printing and Proof-Reading of the First Folio of Shakespeare*. 2 vols. Oxford: Clarendon Press.

Hitchcock, David and Bart Verheji. 2006. *Arguing the Toulmin Model: New Essays in Argument Analysis and Evaluation*. Dordrecht: Springer.

Hobsbawn, Eric. 1987. *The Age of Empire: 1875–1914*. London: Weidenfeld.

Hobson, Harold. 1978. *French Theatre since 1830*. London: John Calder.

Hodgdon, Barbara. 1996. "'Here Apparent': Photography, History, and the Theatrical Unconscious." In *Textual and Theatrical Shakespeare: Questions of Evidence.* Ed. Edward Pechter. Iowa City: University of Iowa Press, 181–209.

    2003. "Photography, Theater, Mnemonics; or, Thirteen Ways of Looking at a Still." In *Redefining Theatre History – Theorizing Practice.* Ed. W. B. Worthen and Peter Holland. London: Palgrave, 88–119.

Holland, Peter, gen. ed. 2004–07, *Redefining British Theatre History.* 5 vols. Houndsmill, Basingstoke: Palgrave Macmillan.

Holly, Michael Ann. 1984. *Panofsky and the Foundations of Art History.* Ithaca, New York: Cornell University Press.

Hornblower, Simon, ed. 1994. *Greek Historiography.* Oxford: Clarendon Press.

Horovitz, Joseph. 1972. *Law and Logic: A Critical Account of Legal Argument.* New York: Springer-Verlag.

Hosley, Richard. 1975. "The Playhouses." In *The Revels History of Drama in English.* Ed. J. Leeds Barroll, Alexander Leggatt, Richard Hosley, and Alvin Kernan. London: Methuen, vol III: 122–226.

    1964. "The Staging of the Monument Scenes in *Antony and Cleopatra.*" *University of Pennsylvania Library Chronicle* 30: 62–71.

Hotson, Leslie. 1928. *The Commonwealth and Restoration Stage.* Cambridge, Mass.: Harvard University Press.

Howard, Jean E. 1994. *The Stage and Social Struggle in Early Modern England.* New York: Routledge.

Huerta, Jorge. 2000. *Chicano Drama: Performance, Society, and Myth.* Cambridge: Cambridge University Press.

Hugo, Victor. 1906. *Hernani.* Ed. James D. Bruner. New York: American Book Co.

Huizinga, Johan. 1960. "The Task of Cultural History." In *Men and Ideas.* Trans. James S. Holmes and Hans van Marle. London: Eyre and Spottiswoode.

Humboldt, Wilhelm von. 1973. "On the Historian's Task." In Leopold von Ranke. *The Theory and Practice of History.* Ed. with introduction by Georg C. Iggers and Konrad von Moltke. Trans. Wilma A. Iggers and Konrad von Moltke. Indianapolis: Bobbs-Merrill Co., 5–24.

Hume, Robert D. 2002. "The Aims and Limits of Historical Scholarship." *The Review of English Studies,* new series, 53. 211: 399–422.

    1999. *Reconstructing Contexts: The Aims and Principles of Archaeo-Historicism.* Oxford: Clarendon Press.

Ibsen, Henrik. 1889. *A Doll's House.* Trans. William Archer. London: Fischer Unwin. *The Works of Henrik Ibsen.* 1906–12. 12 vols. Ed. and trans. William Archer. London: Heinemann.

Ichikawa, Mariko. 2006. "Were the Doors Open or Closed? The Use of Stage Doors in the Shakespearean Theatre." *Theatre Notebook* 60.1: 5–29.

Iggers, Georg. 1997. *Historiography in the Twentieth Century: From Scientific Objectivity to the Postmodern Challenge.* Hanover, N.H.: University Press of New England/ Wesleyan University Press.

    1984. *New Directions in European Historiography.* Revised edn. Middletown, Conn.: Wesleyan University Press.

Ingram, William. 1992. *The Business of Playing: The Beginnings of the Adult Professional Theater in Elizabethan London.* Ithaca, N.Y.: Cornell University Press.

1999. "The Economics of Playing." In *A Companion to Shakespeare*. Ed. David Scott Kastan. Oxford: Blackwell, 313–27.

Innes, Christopher. 1993. *Avant garde Theatre. 1892–1992*. New York: Routledge.

1981. *Holy Theatre: Ritual and the Avant-Garde*. Cambridge: Cambridge University Press.

Ioppolo, Grace. 2006. *Dramatists and Their Manuscripts in the Age of Shakespeare, Jonson, Middleton, and Heywood*. New York: Routledge.

Irace, Kathleen O. 1994. *Reforming the "Bad" Quartos: Performance and Provenance of Six Shakespearean First Editions*. Newark: University of Delaware Press.

Irving, Laurence. 1952. *Henry Irving: The Actor and the World*. New York: Macmillan.

Jackson, Shannon. 2004. *Professing Performance*. Cambridge: Cambridge University Press.

Jakobson, Roman. 1960. "Linguistics and Poetics." In *Style in Language*. Ed. Thomas A. Sebeok. New York: John Wiley & Sons, 350–77.

1971. *Selected Writings II: Word and Language*. The Hague: Mouton.

James, Henry. 1958. *In the Cage and Other Tales*. Ed. Morton Dauwen Zabel. New York: Doubleday Anchor Books.

1960. *Roderick Hudson*. Introduction by Leon Edel. New York: Harper.

James, William. 1971. *Essays in Radical Empiricism and A Pluralistic Universe*. Ed. Ralph Barton Perry. Introduction by Richard J. Bernstein. New York: E. P. Dutton.

Jamieson, Michael. 1990. "Shakespeare in Performance." In *Shakespeare: A Bibliographical Guide*. New edn. Ed. Stanley Wells. Oxford: Clarendon Press, 37–68.

Jarry, Alfred. 1972a. *Oeuvres complètes*. 3 vols. Ed. Michèl Arrivé. Paris: Gallimard.

1963. *Selected Works*. Ed. Roger Shattuck and Simon Watson Taylor. London: Methuen.

1972b. "Textes relatifs á *Ubu roi*." *Oeuvres completes*. Ed. Michel Arrivé. Paris: Gallimard, vol. I: 399–423.

1962. *Tout Ubu*. Ed. Maurice Saillet. Paris: Librairie Générale Français.

1974. *Tout Ubu: Ubu roi, Ubu cocu, Ubu enchanté. Almanachs du père Ubu, Ubu sur la lutte: avec leurs prolégomènes et paralipomènes*. Paris: Librairie Générale Français.

1978. *Ubu*. Ed. Noël Arnaud. Paris: Gallimard.

1968. *The Ubu Plays*. Ed. and trans. Simon Watson Taylor. New York: Grove Press.

1900. *Ubu roi, Drame en cinq Actes*. Preface de Jean Saltas. Paris: Fasquelle editeurs.

1922. *Ubu roi*. Paris: Charpentier & Fasquelle.

Jasper, Gertrude. 1947. *Adventure in the Theatre: Lugné-Poë and the Théâtre de l'Œuvre to 1899*. New Brunswick, N.J.: Rutgers University Press.

Jenks, Chris, ed. 1995. *Visual Culture*. London: Routledge.

John, Angela V. 1995. *Elizabeth Robins: Staging a Life, 1862–1952*. London: Routledge.

Johnson, Odai. 2006. *Absence and Memory in Colonial American Theatre*. London: Palgrave.

Johnson, Odai and William J. Burling. 2001. *The Colonial American Stage, 1665–1774: A Documentary Calendar*. Madison, Wis.: Fairleigh Dickinson University Press.

Johnston, Sarah Iles. 2007. *Ancient Religions*. Cambridge, Mass.: Belknap Press at Harvard University Press.

2004. *Religions of the Ancient World: A Guide.* Cambridge, Mass.: Belknap Press of Harvard University Press.

1999. *Restless Dead: Encounters between the Living and the Dead in Ancient Greece.* Berkeley: University of California Press.

Johnston, Sarah Iles and Fritz Graf. 2007. *Ritual Texts for the Afterlife: Orpheus and the Bacchic Gold Tablets.* New York: Routledge.

Jopeck, Sylvie. 2007. *Etude sur Alfred Jarry, Ubu roi.* Paris: Ellipses.

Kaimio, Maarit. 1988. *Physical Contact in Greek Tragedy: A Study of Stage Conventions.* Helsinki: Suomaliainen Tiedeakatemia.

Kamps, Ivo, ed. 1991. *Shakespeare Left and Right.* New York: Routledge.

Kantor, Tadeusz. 1993. *A Journey Through Other Spaces: Essays and Manifestoes, 1944–1990.* Ed. and trans. Michal Kobialka. Berkeley: University of California Press.

Kaplan, Joel and Sheila Stowell. 1994. *Theatre and Fashion: Oscar Wilde to the Suffragettes.* Cambridge: Cambridge University Press.

Kastan, David Scott. 1999. *Shakespeare after Theory.* New York: Routledge.

2001. *Shakespeare and the Book.* Cambridge: Cambridge University Press.

Katritzky, M. A. 2006. *The Art of Commedia: A Study in the Commedia dell'Arte 1560–1620, with Special Reference to the Visual Records.* Amsterdam: Rodopi.

Kelley, Donald R. 1998a. *Faces of History: Historical Inquiry from Herodotus to Herder.* New Haven, Conn.: Yale University Press.

2003. *Fortunes of History: Historical Inquiry from Herder to Huizinga.* New Haven, Conn.: Yale University Press.

1998b. "History and the Disciplines: The Reclassification of Knowledge in Early Modern Europe." *The American Historical Review* 103.2: 638–67.

Kelley, Donald. R., ed. 1991. *Versions of History from Antiquity to the Enlightenment.* New Haven, Conn.: Yale University Press.

Kelly, Joan. 1984. *Women, History, Theory: The Essays of Joan Kelly.* Chicago: University of Chicago Press.

Kemp, Anthony. 1991. *The Estrangement of the Past: A Study in the Origins of Modern Historical Consciousness.* New York: Oxford University Press.

Kennedy, Dennis. 2003. "Confessions of an Encyclopedist." In *Theorizing Practice/ Redefining Theatre History.* Ed. W. B. Worthen and Peter Holland. Houndsmill, Basingstoke: Palgrave Macmillan, 30–46.

Kennedy, Dennis, ed. 2003. *The Oxford Encyclopedia of Theatre and Performance.* 2 vols. Oxford: Oxford University Press.

Kent, Christopher. 1980. "Periodical Critics of Drama, Music, & Art, 1830–1914: A Preliminary List." *Victorian Periodical Review* 13: 1 and 2: 31–55.

Kernan, Alvin. 1995. *Shakespeare, the King's Playwright, Theatre in the Stuart Court.* New Haven, Conn.: Yale University Press.

Kiefer, Frederick. 2003. *Shakespeare's Visual Theatre: Staging the Personified Characters.* Cambridge: Cambridge University Press.

King, T. J. 1971. *Shakespearean Staging, 1599–1642.* Cambridge, Mass.: Harvard University Press.

Kinney, Arthur F. 2003. *Shakespeare by Stages: An Historical Introduction.* Oxford: Blackwell.

Kirby, Michael. 1987. *A Formalist Theatre*. Philadelphia: University of Pennsylvania Press.

Knapp, Bettina L. 1988. *The Reign of the Theatrical Director: French Theatre: 1887–1924*. Troy, N.Y.: Whitston Publishing Co.

Knowles, Richard Paul. 2004. *Reading the Material Theatre*. Cambridge: Cambridge University Press.

Knox, Bernard. 1993. *The Oldest Dead White European Males and Other Reflections on the Classics*. New York: W. W. Norton.

1979. *Word and Action: Essays on the Ancient Theater*. Baltimore: Johns Hopkins University Press.

Knutson, Roslyn Lander. 1991a. "The Commercial Significance of Payments for Playtexts in Henslowe's *Diary*, 1597–1603." *Medieval and Renaissance Drama in England* 5: 117–63.

1985. "Henslowe's Diary and the Economics of Play Revision for Revival, 1592–1603." *Theatre Research International* 10.1: 1–18.

2001. *Playing Companies and Commerce in Shakespeare's Time*. Cambridge: Cambridge University Press.

1991b. *The Repertory of Shakespeare's Company 1594–1613*. Fayetteville: University of Arkansas Press.

2002. "Two Playhouses, Both Alike in Dignity." *Shakespeare Studies* 30: 111–17.

Kobialka, Michal, ed. 1999. *Of Borders and Thresholds: Theatre History, Practice, and Theory*. Minneapolis: University of Minnesota Press.

Koselleck, Reinhart. 1985. *Futures Past: On the Semantics of Historical Time*. Trans. Keith Tribe. Cambridge, Mass.: MIT Press.

2002. *The Practice of Conceptual History: Timing History, Spacing Concepts*. Trans. Todd Samuel Presner *et al.* Foreword by Hayden White. Stanford, Calif.: Stanford University Press.

Kostelanetz, Richard. 1993. *Dictionary of the Avant-Garde*. Chicago: Cappella Books/Chicago Review Press.

2000. *A Dictionary of the Avant-Gardes, with Contributions from H. R. Brittain and Others*. New York: Schirmer Books.

Kowzan, Tadeusz. 1968. "The Sign in the Theatre." *Diogenes* 61: 52–80.

1985. "Theatrical Iconography/Iconology: The Iconic Sign and Its Referent." Trans. Scott Walker. *Diogenes* 130.2: 53–70.

Krantz, Susan E. 1991. "Henslowe and Alleyn's Entrepreneurship at Its Best: A Reexamination of the Globe-Fortune Rivalry." *Explorations in Renaissance Culture* 17: 109–24.

Kubler, George. 1962. *The Shape of Time: Remarks on the History of Things*. New Haven, Conn.: Yale University Press.

1987. "Toward a Reductive Theory of Visual Style." In *The Concept of Style*. Revised and expanded ed. Ed. Berel Lang. Ithaca, N.Y.: Cornell University Press, 163–73.

Kuhn, Thomas. 1977. *The Essential Tension: Selected Studies in Scientific Tradition and Change*. Chicago: University of Chicago Press.

1970. *The Structure of Scientific Revolutions*. 2nd edn. Chicago: University of Chicago Press.

Kurahashi, Yuko. 1999. *Asian American Culture on Stage: The History of the East–West Players*. New York: Garland.

LaBelle, Maurice Marc. 1980. *Alfred Jarry: Nihilism and the Theater of the Absurd.* New York: New York University Press.

LaCapra, Dominick. 1985. *History and Criticism.* Ithaca, N.Y.: Cornell University Press.

1983. *Rethinking Intellectual History: Texts, Contexts, Languages.* Ithaca, N.Y.: Cornell University Press.

1989. *Soundings in Critical Theory.* Ithaca, N.Y.: Cornell University Press.

Lane, Jill. 2005. *Blackface Cuba, 1840–1895.* Philadelphia: University of Pennsylvania Press.

Lawrence, William J. 1913. *The Elizabethan Playhouse and Other Studies.* Stratford upon Avon: Shakespeare Head Press.

1927. *The Physical Conditions of the Elizabethan Public Playhouse.* Cambridge, Mass.: Harvard University Press.

Lee, Esther Kim. 2006. *A History of Asian American Theatre.* Cambridge: Cambridge University Press.

LeFebvre, Henri. 1991. *The Production of Space.* Oxford: B. Blackwell.

Leggatt, Alexander. 1992. *Jacobean Public Theatre.* London: Routledge.

Le Goff, Jacques. 1992. *History and Memory.* Trans. Steven Rendall and Elizabeth Clamen. New York: Columbia University Press.

Le Goff, Jacques and Pierre Nora, eds. 1985. *Constructing the Past: Essays in Historical Methodology.* Trans. David Denby *et al.* Cambridge: Cambridge University Press.

Leinwand, Theodore B. 1999. *Theatre, Finance, and Society in Early Modern England.* Cambridge: Cambridge University Press.

Le Roy Ladurie, Emmanuel. 1979. *Carnival in Romans: A People's Uprising at Romans, 1579–1580.* Trans. Mary Feeney. New York: George Braziller.

1984. *The Mind and Method of the Historian.* Trans. Siân Reynolds and Ben Reynolds. Chicago: University of Chicago Press.

1978. *Montaillou: The Promised Land of Error.* Trans. Barbara Bray. New York: George Braziller.

Leunen, Mary-Claire van. 1992. *A Handbook for Scholars.* Revised edn. New York: Oxford University Press.

Lévesque, Jacques-Henry. 1951. *Alfred Jarry.* Paris: Pierre Seghers.

Levi, Giovanni. 2001. "On Microhistory." In *New Perspectives on Historical Writing.* 2nd edn. Ed. Peter Burke. University Park: Pennsylvania State University Press, 97–119.

Levine, Laura. 1994. *Men in Women's Clothes: Anti-theatricality and Effeminization.* Cambridge: Cambridge University Press.

Limon, Jerzy. 1986. *Dangerous Matter: English Drama and Politics in 1623/24.* Cambridge: Cambridge University Press.

Lindenberger, Herbert. 1984. *Opera: The Extravagant Art.* Ithaca, N.Y.: Cornell University Press.

Liu, Alan. 1989. "The Power of Formalism: The New Historicism." *English Literary History* 56: 721–71.

The London Stage, 1660–1800: A Calendar of Plays, Entertainments, and Afterpieces Together with Casts, Box-Receipts, and Contemporary Comment. Compiled from the Playbills, Newspapers, and Theatrical Diaries of the Period. 5 pts. and index in 12 vols. Carbondale: Southern Illinois University Press, 1960–79. Part I:

1660–1700, ed. William Van Lennep; Part II: 1700–1729, ed. Emmett L. Avery; Part III: 1729–1747, ed. Arthur H. Scouten; Part IV: 1747–1776, ed. George Winchester Stone, Jr.; Part V: 1776–1800, ed. Charles Beecher Hogan.

Lotman, Yuri M. 1990. *Universe of the Mind: A Semiotic Theory of Culture.* Trans. Ann Shukman. Introduction by Umberto Eco. Bloomington: Indiana University Press.

Lott, Eric. 1993. *Love and Thief: Blackface Minstrelsy and the American Working Class.* New York: Oxford University Press.

Lublin, Robert L. 2007. " 'An vnder black dubblett signifying a Spanish hart': Costumes and Politics in Middleton's *A Game at Chess.*" *Theatre Survey* 48.2: 247–64.

Forthcoming. *Costuming the Shakespearean Stage: Visual Codes of Representation in Early Modern Theatre and Culture.* Burlington, Vt.: Ashgate.

Lucid, Donald P., ed. 1977. *Soviet Semiotics, An Anthology.* Trans. Donald P. Lucid. Foreword by Thomas A. Sebeok. Baltimore: Johns Hopkins University Press.

Lynch, Jack. 2003. *The Age of Elizabeth in the Age of Johnson.* Cambridge: Cambridge University Press.

McConachie, Bruce. 2003. *American Theater in the Culture of the Cold War.* Iowa City: University of Iowa Press.

2001. "Doing Things with Image Schemas: The Cognitive Turn in Theatre Studies and the Problem of Experience for Historians." *Theatre Journal* 53.4: 569–94.

2007. "Historicizing the Relations of Theatrical Production." In *Critical Theory and Performance.* Revised edn. Ed. J. Reinelt and J. Roach. Ann Arbor: University of Michigan Press, 284–94.

2004. "Narrative Possibilities in U.S. Theatre Histories." In *Writing and Rewriting National Theatre Histories.* Ed. S. E. Wilmer. Iowa City: University of Iowa Press, 127–52.

1985. "Towards a Postpositive Theatre History." *Theatre Journal* 37: 465–86.

McCullagh, C. Behan. 1978. "Colligation and Classification in History." *History and Theory* 17: 267–84.

1984. *Justifying Historical Descriptions.* Cambridge: Cambridge University Press.

2004. *The Logic of History: Putting Postmodernism in Perspective.* New York: Routledge.

1998. *The Truth of History.* New York: Routledge.

McCullough, David E. 1972. *The Great Bridge.* New York: Simon and Schuster.

McGann, Jerome J. 1983. *A Critique of Modern Textual Criticism.* Chicago: University of Chicago Press.

1991. *The Textual Condition.* Princeton, N.J.: Princeton University Press.

McIlwain, James, ed. 1918. *The Political Works of James I.* Cambridge, Mass.: Harvard University Press.

MacIntyre, Jean. 1992. *Costumes and Scripts in the Elizabethan Theatres.* Edmonton: University of Alberta Press.

McKenzie, D. F. 1986. *Bibliography and the Sociology of Texts.* London: British Library.

2002. *Making Meaning: "Printers of the Mind" and Other Essays.* Ed. Peter D. McDonald and Michael F. Suarez, S. J. Amherst: University of Massachusetts Press.

McLeod, Randall. 1982. "The Marriage of Good and Bad Quartos." *Shakespeare Quarterly* 33: 421–32.

McLeod, Randall, ed. 1994. *Crisis in Editing: Texts of the English Renaissance.* New York: AMS Press.

McMillan, Scott. 1972. "Casting for Pembroke's Men: The *Henry VI* Quartos and *The Taming of a Shrew.*" *Shakespeare Quarterly* 23: 141–59.

    1992. "Casting the *Hamlet* Quartos: The Limit of Eleven." In *The Hamlet First Published (Q1, 1603).* Ed. Thomas Clayton. Newark: University of Delaware Press, 179–94.

McMillan, Scott and Sally-Beth MacLean. 1998. *The Queen's Men and their Plays.* Cambridge: Cambridge University Press.

Mackie, J. L. 1967. "Fallacies." In *The Encyclopedia of Philosophy.* 8 vols. Ed. Paul Edwards. New York: Macmillan, vol. III: 175.

Madoff, Steven Hendry. 1997. *Pop Art: A Critical History.* Berkeley: University of California Press.

Maguire, Laurie E. 1999. "The Craft of Printing (1600)." In *A Companion to Shakespeare.* Ed. David Scott Kastan. Oxford: Blackwell, 434–49.

    1996. *Shakespearean Suspect Texts: the "Bad" Quartos and the Their Contexts.* Cambridge: Cambridge University Press.

Maguire, Laurie E. and Thomas L. Berger. 1998. *Textual Formations and Reformations.* Newark: University of Newark Press.

Mali, Joseph. 2003. *Mythistory: The Making of a Modern Historiography.* Chicago: University of Chicago Press.

Mann, Thomas. 1998. *The Oxford Guide to Library Research.* Oxford: Oxford University Press.

Manning, Susan. 2004. *Modern Dance, Negro Dance: Race in Motion.* Minneapolis: University of Minnesota Press.

Marcus, George E. 1988. *Ethnography Through Thick and Thin.* Princeton, N.J.: Princeton University Press.

Marcus, George E. ed. 1999. *Critical Anthropology Now: Unexpected Contexts, Shifting Constituencies, Changing Agendas.* New York: Sar Press.

Marcus, Jane Connor. 1973. "Elizabeth Robins: A Biography." Ph.D. dissertation, Northwestern University.

Marcus, Leah. 1986. *The Politics of Mirth: Jonson, Herrick, Milton, and Marvell, and the Defense of the Old Holiday Pastimes.* Chicago: University of Chicago Press.

    1988. *Puzzling Shakespeare: Local Reading and Its Discontents.* Berkeley: University of California Press.

Marinis, Mario de. 1987. "Dramaturgy of the Spectator." *The Drama Review* 31.2: 100–14.

    1993. *The Semiotics of Performance.* Trans. Aine O'Heally. Bloomington: Indiana University Press.

Marsak, Leonard Mendes. 1970. *The Nature of Historical Inquiry.* New York: Holt, Reinhart, and Winston.

Martin, Peter. 1995. *Edmond Malone, Shakespearean Scholar: A Literary Biography.* Cambridge: Cambridge University Press.

Marx, Karl. 1963. *Eighteenth Brumaire of Louis Bonaparte.* New York: International Publishers.

Matejka, Ladislav and Irwin R. Titunik, eds. 1976. *Semiotics of Art, Prague School Contributions.* Cambridge, Mass.: MIT Press.

Mazer, Cary. 1996. "Historicizing Alan Dessen: Scholarship, Stagecraft, and the 'Shakespeare Revolution'." In *Shakespeare, Theory, and Performance*. Ed. James C. Bulman. New York: Routledge, 149–67.

Megill, Allan, ed. 1994. *Rethinking Objectivity*. Durham, N.C.: Duke University Press.

Meisel, Martin. 1983. *Realizations: Narrative, Pictorial, and Theatrical Arts in Nineteenth-Century England*. Princeton, N.J.: Princeton University Press.

1963. *Shaw and the Nineteenth-century Theater*. Princeton, N.J.: Princeton University Press.

Melberg, Arne. 1995. *Theories of Mimesis*. Cambridge: Cambridge University Press.

Melzer, Annabelle Henkin. 1994. *Dada and Surrealist Performance*. Baltimore: Johns Hopkins University Press.

Meredith, Peter, ed. 1990. *The Passion Play from the N. Town Manuscript*. London: Longman.

Metz, Christian. 1974. *Film Language: A Semiotics of Cinema*. Trans. Michael Taylor. Oxford: Oxford University Press.

1982. *The Imaginary Signifier: Psychoanalysis and Cinema*. Trans. Celia Burton *et al.* Bloomington: Indiana University Press.

Meyerhoff, Hans, ed. 1959. *The Philosophy of History In Our Time: An Anthology*. Garden City, N.Y.: Doubleday & Co..

Middleton, Thomas. 1993. *A Game at Chess*. Ed. T. H. Howard-Hunt. Manchester: Manchester University Press.

Milhous, Judith and Robert D. Hume. 1991. "New Light on English Acting Companies in 1646, 1648 and 1660," *Review of English Studies*, new series 42. 168: 487–509.

1991. *A Register of English Theatrical Documents 1660–1737*. 2 vols. Carbondale: Southern Illinois University Press.

Milling, Jane and Peter Thomson, eds. 2004. *The Cambridge History of British Theatre*. Vol. I. Cambridge: Cambridge University Press.

Mink, Louis O. 1987. *Historical Understanding*. Ed. Brian Fay, Eugene O. Golob, and Richard T. Vann. Ithaca N.Y.: Cornell University Press.

1969. *Mind, History and Dialectic: The Philosophy of R. G. Collingwood*. Bloomington: Indiana University Press.

1971. Review essay of David H. Fisher's *Historians' Fallacies*. *History and Theory* 10: 110–12.

Mitchell, W. J. T. 1986. *Iconology: Images, Text, Ideology*. Chicago: University of Chicago Press.

1994. *Picture Theory: Essays on Verbal and Visual Representations*. Chicago: University of Chicago Press.

Momigliano, Arnaldo D. 1990. *The Classical Foundation of Modern Historiography*. Berkeley: University of California Press.

1977. *Essays in Ancient and Modern Historiography*. Oxford: Blackwell.

1966. *Studies in Historiography*. New York: Harper & Row.

Montaigne, Michel de. 1958. *Essays*. Trans. J. M. Cohen. Harmondsworth: Penguin.

Montrose, Louis. 1992. "New Historicisms." In *Redrawing the Boundaries: The Transformation of English and American Literary Studies*. Ed. Stephen Greenblatt and Giles Gunn. New York: Modern Language Association of America, 392–418.

1989. "Professing the Renaissance: The Poetics and Politics of Culture." In *The New Historicism*. Ed. H. Aram Veeser. New York: Routledge, 15–36.

1996. *The Purpose of Playing: Shakespeare and the Cultural Politics of the Elizabethan Theatre*. Chicago: University of Chicago Press.

Moody, Jane. 2000. *Illegitimate Theatre in London, 1770–1840*. Cambridge: Cambridge University Press.

Moon, Krystyn R. 2005. *Yellowface: Creating the Chinese in American Popular Music and Performance, 1850s to 1920s*. New Brunswick, N.J.: Rutgers University Press.

Moy, James. 1993. *Marginal Sights: Staging the Chinese in America*. Iowa City: University of Iowa Press.

Mukarovsky, Jan. 1978. *Structure, Sign, and Function*. Ed. and trans. John Burbank and Peter Steiner. New Haven, Conn.: Yale University Press.

1977. *The Word and Verbal Art, Selected Essays*. Ed. and trans. John Burbank and Peter Steiner. New Haven, Conn.: Yale University Press.

Mullaney, Stephen. 1988. *The Place of the Stage: License, Play, and Power in Renaissance England*. Chicago: University of Chicago Press.

Mulryne, J. R. and Margaret Shewring, eds. 1997. *Shakespeare's Globe Rebuilt*. Cambridge: Cambridge University Press.

Munz, Peter. 1977. *The Shapes of Time: A New Look at the Philosophy of History*. Middletown, Conn.: Wesleyan University Press.

Murray, Gilbert. 1935. *Five Stages of Greek Religion*. London: Watts.

Nabokov, Vladimir. 1972. *Transparent Things*. Greenwich, Conn.: Fawcett Publications/ McGraw Hill.

Neiiendam, Klaus. 1992. *The Art of Acting in Antiquity: Iconographical Studies in Classical, Hellenistic, and Byzantine Theatre*. Copenhagen: Museum Tusculanum, University of Copenhagen.

Nelson, Robert S. and Richard Shiff, eds. 2003. *Critical Terms for Art History*. 2nd edn. Chicago: University of Chicago Press.

Nisbet, Robert A. 1972. *Social Change*. Oxford: Basil Blackwell.

Norberg-Schulz, Christian. 1971. *Existence, Space, and Architecture*. London: Studio Vista.

Norbrook, David. 1987. "*Macbeth* and the Politics of Historiography." In *Politics of Discourse: The Literature and History of Seventeenth-Century England*. Ed. Kevin Sharpe and Steven N. Zwicker. Berkeley: University of California Press, 78–116.

Norton, Mary Beth, gen. ed. 1995. *The American Historical Association's Guide to Historical Literature*. 2 vols. 3rd edn. New York: Oxford University Press.

Nöth, Winifried. 1990. *Handbook of Semiotics*. Bloomington: Indiana University Press.

Novick, Peter. 1988. *That Noble Dream: the "Objectivity Question" and the American Historical Profession*. Cambridge: Cambridge University Press.

Orgel, Stephen. 2002. *The Authentic Shakespeare and Other Problems of the Early Modern Stage*. New York: Routledge.

1975. *The Illusion of Power: Political Theater in the English Renaissance*. Berkeley: University of California Press.

1996. *Impersonations: The Performance of Gender in Shakespeare's England*. Cambridge: Cambridge University Press.

Orlin, Lena Cowen, ed. 2000. *Material London, ca. 1600*. Philadelphia: University of Pennsylvania Press.

Orrell, John. 1988. *The Human Stage: English Theatre Design, 1567–1640*. Cambridge: Cambridge University Press.

1982. *The Quest for Shakespeare's Globe.* Cambridge: Cambridge University Press.

Oshorne, John. 1981. *A Better Class of People: An Autobiography.* New York: Dutton.

The Oxford Classical Dictionary. 1970 Ed. N. G. L. Hammond and H. H. Scullard. 2nd edn. Oxford: Clarendon Press.

Palmer, Richard E. 1969. *Hermeneutics: Interpretation Theory in Schleiermacher, Dithey, Heideggar, and Gadamer.* Evanston, Ill.: Northwestern University Press.

Panofsky, Erwin. 1960. *Renaissance and Renascences in Western Art.* New York: Harper & Row.

Patterson, Annabel. 1984. *Censorship and Interpretation: The Conditions of Reading and Writing in Early Modern England.* Madison: University of Wisconsin Press.

1989. *Shakespeare and the Popular Voice.* Oxford: Basil Blackwell.

Pavis, Patrice. 1998. *Dictionary of the Theatre: Terms, Concepts, and Analysis.* Toronto: University of Toronto Press.

1982. *Languages of the Stage: Essays in the Semiology of Theatre.* New York: Performing Arts Journal Publication.

1992. *Theatre at the Crossroads of Culture.* Trans. Loren Kruger. New York: Routledge.

Pechter, Edward. 1995. *What Was Shakespeare?: Renaissance Plays and Changing Critical Practice.* Ithaca, N.Y.: Cornell University Press.

Pechter, Edward, ed. 1996. *Textual and Theatrical Shakespeare: Questions of Evidence.* Iowa City: University of Iowa Press.

Peck, Linda Levy. 1990. *Court Patronage and Corruption in Early Stuart England.* Boston: Unwin Hyman.

Peirce, Charles Sanders. 1960. *Collected Papers of Charles Sanders Peirce.* Ed. Charles Hartshorne, Paul Weiss, and Arthur W. Burks. Volume V. Cambridge, Mass.: Harvard University Press.

Pelling, Christopher, ed. 1997. *Greek Tragedy and the Historian.* Oxford: Clarendon Press.

Perkins, David. 1992. *Is Literary History Possible?* Baltimore: Johns Hopkins University Press.

Peters, Margot. 1980. *Bernard Shaw and the Actresses.* New York: Doubleday.

Pickard-Cambridge, A. W. 1927. *Dithyramb, Tragedy, and Comedy.* Oxford: Clarendon Press.

1988. *The Dramatic Festivals of Athens.* Revised by J. Gould and D. M. Lewis. 3rd edn. with supplements and corrections. Oxford: Clarendon Press.

1946. *The Theatre of Dionysus in Athens.* Oxford: Clarendon Press.

Pirandello, Luigi. 1974. *On Humor.* Trans. Antonio Illiano and Daniel P. Testa. Chapel Hill: University of North Carolina Press.

Pladott, Dinnah. 1982. "The Dynamics of the Sign Systems in the Theatre." In *Multimedial Communication: Vol. II: Theatre Semiotics.* Ed. Ernest Hess-Lüttich. Tübingen: Narr, 28–45.

Platter, Thomas. 1937. *Thomas Platter's Travels in England.* Ed. and trans. Clare Williams. London: Jonathan Cape.

Pocock, J. G. A. 1971. *Politics, Language and Time.* New York: Atheneum.

1993. *The Varieties of British Political Thought, 1500–1800.* New York: Cambridge University Press.

Podro, Michael. 1982. *The Critical Historians of Art.* New Haven, Conn.: Yale University Press.

Pollard, A. W. 1920. *Shakespeare's Fight with the Pirates and the Problems of the Transmission of His Texts.* 2nd edn., revised. Cambridge: Cambridge University Press.

    1909. *Shakespeare's Folios and Quartos: A Study in the Bibliography of Shakespeare's Plays, 1594–1685.* London: Methuen.

Popper, Karl. 1969. "A Pluralist Approach to Philosophy of History." In *Roads to Freedom.* Ed. Erich Streissler. London: Routledge & Kegan Paul, 181–200.

Postlewait, Thomas. 1989. "Autobiography and Theatre History." In *Interpreting the Theatrical Past.* Ed. Thomas Postlewait and Bruce McConachie. Iowa City: University of Iowa Press, 248–72.

    2003a. "The Criteria for Evidence: Anecdotes in Shakespearean Biography, 1709–2000." In *Redefining British Theatre History: Practice and Theory.* Ed. Peter Holland and W. B. Worthen. Houndsmill, Basingstoke: Palgrave/Mcmillan, 47–70.

    1988. "The Criteria for Periodization in Theatre History." *Theatre Journal* 40.3: 299–318.

    2009. "Eyewitnesses to History: Visual Evidence for Theatre in Early Modern England." In *Oxford Handbook on Early Modern Theatre.* Ed. Richard Dutton. Oxford: Oxford University Press, 575–606.

    2007a. "George Edwardes and Musical Comedy: The Transformation of London Theatre and Society, 1878–1914." In *The Performing Century: Nineteenth-Century Theatre's History.* Ed. Tracy C. Davis and Peter Holland. Houndsmill, Basingstoke: Palgrave Macmillan, 80–102.

    1991. "Historiography and the Theatrical Event: A Primer with Twelve Cruxes." *Theatre Journal* 43: 157–78.

    1992. "History, Hermeneutics, and Narrativity." In *Critical Theory and Performance.* Ed. Janelle Reinelt and Joseph Roach. Ann Arbor: University of Michigan Press, 356–68.

    2001. "The Idea of the 'Political' in Our Histories of Theatre: Texts, Contexts, Periods, and Problems." *Contemporary Theatre Review* 12: 1–25.

    2004a. "The London Stage: 1895–1918." In *The Cambridge History of British Theatre.* Volume III. Ed. Baz Kershaw. Cambridge: Cambridge University Press, 34–59.

    2004b. "A Matter of Credibility: Constructing Events in Theatre History." In *Theatrical Events – Borders, Dynamics, Frames.* Ed. Vicki Cremona, Willmar Sauter, John Tulloch, and Hans van Maanen. Amsterdam: Rodophi, 33–52.

    1986. *Prophet of the New Drama: William Archer and the Ibsen Campaign.* Westport, Conn.: Greenwood Press.

    2007b. "Theatre Events and their Political Contexts: A Problem in the Writing of Theatre History." In *Critical Theory and Performance.* 2nd edn. Ed. Janelle Reinelt and Joseph Roach. Ann Arbor: University of Michigan Press, 198–222.

    2003b. "Theatricality and Antitheatricality in Renaissance London." In *Theatricality.* Ed. Tracy C. Davis and Thomas Postlewait. Cambridge: Cambridge University Press, 90–126.

    2000. "Writing History Today: A Review Essay." *Theatre Survey* 41.2: 83–106.

Postlewait, Thomas, ed. 1984. *William Archer on Ibsen.* Westport, Conn.: Greenwood Press.

Postlewait, Thomas and Bruce McConachie, eds. 1989. *Interpreting the Theatrical Past: Essays in the Historiography of Performance.* Iowa City: University of Iowa Press.

Powell, Kerry. 1997. *Women and Victorian Theatre.* Cambridge: Cambridge University Press.

Prendergast, Christopher. 2000. *The Triangle of Representation.* New York: Columbia University Press.

Press, Gerald A. 1982. *The Development of the Idea of History in Antiquity.* Kingston and Montreal: McGill-Queen's University Press.

Preziosi, Donald, ed. 1998. *The Art of Art History: A Critical Anthology.* Oxford History of Art. Oxford: Oxford University Press.

Proudfoot, Richard. 2001. *Shakespeare: Text, Stage, & Canon.* London: Thomson Learning.

Putter, Ad. 2006. "Medieval Mindsets." *Times Literary Supplement,* July 7, 7.

Quinn, Michael L. 1990. "Celebrity and the Semiotics of Acting." *New Theatre Quarterly* 6.22: 154–61.

   1995a. "Concepts of Theatricality in Contemporary Art History." *Theatre Research International* 20.2.: 106–13.

   1995b. *The Semiotic Stage: Prague School Theatre Theory.* New York: Peter Lang.

   1991. "*Theaterwissenschaft* in the History of Theatre Study." *Theatre Survey* 32: 123–36.

Quinn, Shelley Fenno. 2005. *Developing Zeami: The Noh Actor's Attunement in Practice.* Honolulu: University of Hawai'i Press.

Rachilde [Marguérite Eymery Vallette]. 1928. *Alfred Jarry; ou, Le Surmâle de lettres.* Paris: B. Grasset.

Ranke, Leopold von. 1973. *The Theory and Practice of History.* Ed. with introduction by Georg C. Iggers and Konrad von Moltke. Trans. Wilma A. Iggers and Konrad von Moltke. Indianapolis: Bobbs-Merrill Co.

Rayner, Alice. 2006. *Ghosts: Death's Double and the Phenomena of Theatre.* Minneapolis: University of Minnesota Press.

Records of Early English Drama. 1979–present. Exec. Ed.: Sally-Beth MacLean; Director: Alexandra F. Johnston. Toronto: University of Toronto Press.

Rees, Joan. 1953. "An Elizabethan Eyewitness of *Antony and Cleopatra.*" *Shakespeare Survey* 6: 91–93.

Rehm, Rush. 1992. *Greek Tragic Theatre.* London: Routledge.

Reinelt, Janelle R. and Joseph Roach, eds. 2007. *Critical Theory and Performance.* Ann Arbor: University of Michigan Press, 1992; new edition.

Renier, Gustaaf J. 1950. *History: Its Purpose and Method.* London: Allen & Unwin.

Richter (Barton), Anne. 1962. *Shakespeare and the Idea of the Play.* London: Chatto & Windus.

Ricoeur, Paul. 1974. *The Conflict of Interpretations: Essays in Hermeneutics.* Ed. Don Ihde. Evanston, Ill.: Northwestern University Press.

   1991a. "Discussion: Ricoeur on Narrative." In *On Paul Ricoeur: Narrative and Interpretation.* Ed. David Wood. New York: Routledge, 179–87.

   1981. *Hermeneutics and the Human Sciences: Essays on Language, Action, and Interpretation.* Ed., trans., and introduction by John B. Thompson. Cambridge: Cambridge University Press/Paris: Editions de la Maison des Sciences de l'Homme.

1965. *History and Truth.* Trans. with introduction by Charles A. Kelbley. Evanston, Ill.: Northwestern University Press.

1976. *Interpretation Theory: Discourse and the Surplus of Meaning.* Fort Worth: Texas Christian University Press.

1991b. "Narrative Identity." In *On Paul Ricoeur: Narrative and Interpretation.* Ed. David Wood. New York: Routledge, 188–99.

1984; 1985; 1988. *Time and Narrative.* 3 vols. Trans. Kathleen McLaughlin and David Pellauer. Chicago: University of Chicago Press.

Ripley, John. 1998. *Coriolanus on Stage in England and America, 1609–1994.* Madison: University of Wisconsin Press.

Ritter, Christina. 2007. "On Hallowed Ground: The Significance of Geographical Location and Architectural Space in the Identities of the Royal Shakespeare Company and Shakespeare's Globe." Ph.D. Dissertation, Ohio State University.

Roach, Joseph. 1996. *Cities of the Dead: Circum-Atlantic Performance.* New York: Columbia University Press.

2007. *It.* Ann Arbor: University of Michigan Press.

1993. *The Player's Passion: Studies in the Science of Acting.* Ann Arbor: University of Michigan Press.

Robins, Elizabeth. 1928. *Ibsen and the Actress.* London: Hogarth Press.

Rokem, Freddie. 2000. *Theatrical Representations of the Past in Contemporary Theatre.* Iowa City: University of Iowa Press.

Rorty, Richard. 2000. "Afterword." In *Historians and Social Values.* Ed. Joep Leerssen and Ann Rigney. Amsterdam: Amsterdam University Press, 197–203.

Rozik, Eli. 1992. *The Language of the Theatre.* Glasgow: Theatre Studies Publications.

2002. *The Roots of Theatre.* Iowa City: University of Iowa Press.

Rutter, Carol Chillington, ed. 1999. *Documents of the Rose Playhouse.* Revised edn. Manchester: Manchester University Press.

Sahlins, Marshall. 2000. *Culture in Practice: Selected Essays.* New York: Zone Books.

Salgado, Gamini. 1975. *Eyewitnesses of Shakespeare, 1590–1890.* New York: Harper & Row.

Sauter, Willmar. 2004. "Introducing the Theatrical Event." In *Theatrical Events: Borders, Dynamics, Frames.* Eds. Vicky Ann Cremona, Peter Eversmann, Hans van Maanen, Willmar Sauter, and John Tulloch. Amsterdam: Rodopi, 1–14.

2000. *The Theatrical Event: Dynamics of Performance and Perception.* Iowa City: University of Iowa Press.

Sauter, Willmar, ed. 1990. *Nordic Theatre Studies: Yearbook for Theatre Research in Scandinavia.* Special Issue on "New Directions in Theatre Research." Copenhagen: Munksgaard.

Schama, Simon. 1991. *Dead Certainties (Unwarranted Speculations).* New York: Random House/Vintage Books.

Schechner, Richard. 1985. *Between Theatre and Anthropology.* Philadelphia: University of Pennsylvania Press.

2002. *Performance Studies: An Introduction.* New York: Routledge.

Schlegel, A. W. 1846. *Lectures on Dramatic Art and Literature* (1809–11). Revised edn. Ed. A. J. W. Morrison. Trans. John Black. London: Bohn.

Schoenbaum, S. 1991. *Shakespeare's Lives.* New edn. Oxford: Clarendon Press.

Schorske, Carl E. 1990. "History and Study of Culture." *New Literary History* 21.2: 407–20.

Schumacher, Claude. 1984. *Alfred Jarry and Guillaume Apollinaire.* Houndsmills, Basingstoke: Macmillan.

Schwartz, Vanessa R. 2001. "Walter Benjamin for Historians." *The American Historical Review* 106.53: 1721–41.

Scott, Clement W. 1899. *The Drama of Yesterday & To-day.* 2 vols. London: Macmillan.

Scott, Joan Wallach. 1988. *Gender and the Politics of History.* New York: Columbia University Press.

Seaford, Richard. 1994. *Reciprocity and Ritual: Homer and Tragedy in the Developing City-State.* Oxford: Oxford University Press.

Sebeok, Thomas A. 1981. *The Play of Musement.* Bloomington: Indiana University Press.

1991. *A Sign Is Just A Sign.* Bloomington: Indiana University Press.

2001. *Signs: An Introduction to Semiotics.* 2nd edn. Toronto: University of Toronto Press.

Senelick, Laurence. 1997. "Early Photographic Attempts to Record Performance Sequence." *Theatre Research International* 22.3: 255–64.

1987. "Melodramatic Gesture in *Carte-de-Visite* Photographs." *The Theatre*: 5–13.

Senelick, Laurence, ed. 1992. *Gender in Performance: The Presentation of Difference in the Performing Arts.* Hanover, N.H.: University Press of New England.

Shafer, Robert Jones, edn. 1980. *A Guide to Historical Method.* 3rd edn. Homewood, Illinois: The Dorsey Press.

Shakespeare, William. 1998. *Antony and Cleopatra.* Ed. Richard Madelaine. Cambridge: Cambridge University Press.

1980. *The Complete Works of Shakespeare.* Ed. David Bevington. New York: Longman.

1994. *A Midsummer Night's Dream.* Ed. Peter Holland. Oxford: Oxford University Press.

1623. *Mr. William Shakespeares Comedies, Histories, & Tragedies.* Ed. John Heminges and Henry Condell. London: Printed by Isaac Jaggard and Ed. Blount.

1974. *The Riverside Shakespeare.* Ed. G. Blakemore Evans *et al.* Boston: Houghton Mifflin Co..

Shapiro, I. A. 1948. "The Bankside Theatres: Early Engravings." *Shakespeare Survey* 1: 25–37.

Shapiro, James. 2005. *A Year in the Life of William Shakespeare, 1599.* New York: HarperCollins.

Sharpe, Jim. 2001. "History from Below." In *New Perspectives on Historical Writing.* 2nd edn. Ed. Peter Burke. University Park: Pennsylvania State University Press, 25–42.

Sharpe, Kevin. 1987. *Criticism and Compliment: The Politics of Literature in the England of Charles I.* Cambridge: Cambridge University Press.

Shattuck, Roger. 1968. *The Banquet Years: The Origins of the Avant-Garde in France, 1885 to World War I.* Revised edn. New York: Random House/Vintage.

Shaw, Bernard. 1965. *Collected Letters: 1874–1897.* Ed. Dan H. Laurence. Vol. I. New York: Dodd, Mead.

1991. "A Play by Henrik Ibsen in London." In *Bernard Shaw: The Drama Observed.* 4 vols. Ed. Bernard F. Dukore. University Park: Pennsylvania State University Press, vol. I: 106–07.

1891. *The Quintessence of Ibsenism.* London: Walter Scott.

Shepherd-Barr, Kirsten. 1977. *Ibsen and Early Modernist Theatre, 1890–1900.* Westport, Conn.: Greenwood Press.

Silk, M. S., ed. 1995. *Tragedy and the Tragic: Greek Theatre and Beyond.* Oxford: Oxford University Press.

Silk, M. S. and J. P. Stern. 1981. *Nietzsche on Tragedy.* Cambridge: Cambridge University Press.

Simon, Erika. 1982. *The Ancient Theatre.* 2nd edn. Trans. C. E. Vafopoulou-Richardson. New York: Methuen.

1983. *Festivals of Attica: An Archaeological Commentary.* Madison: University of Wisconsin Press.

Singleton, Brian. 2003. "Alfred Jarry." In *The Oxford Encyclopedia of Theatre and Performance.* Ed. Dennis Kennedy. Oxford: Oxford University Press, vol. I: 642.

Skinner, Quentin. 1978. *The Foundations of Modern Political Thought.* 2 vols. Cambridge: Cambridge University Press.

1988. "A Reply to My Critics." In *Meaning and Context: Quentin Skinner and His Critics.* Ed. and introduction by James Tully. Princeton, N.J.: Princeton University Press, 231–288.

2002. *Visions of Politics: Volume One: Regarding Method.* Cambridge: Cambridge University Press.

Sloan, Kim, ed. 2003. *The Enlightenment.* London: British Museum.

Smith, Bonnie G. 1998. *The Gender of History: Men, Women, and Historical Practice.* Cambridge, Mass.: Harvard University Press.

Smith, Bruce R. 1999. *The Acoustic World of Early Modern England Attending to the O-Factor.* Chicago: University of Chicago Press.

Sohmer, Steve. 1999. *Shakespeare's Mystery Play: The Opening of the Globe Theatre 1599.* Manchester: Manchester University Press.

Sonesson, Göran. 1989. *Pictorial Concepts: Inquiries into the Semiotic Heritage and Its Relevance for the Analysis of the Visual World.* Lund: Lund University Press.

Sontag, Susan. 1977. *On Photography.* New York: Farrar, Straus and Giroux.

Sourvinou-Inwood, Christiane. 2003. *Tragedy and Athenian Religion.* Lanham, Md.: Lexington Books.

Southern, Richard. 1961. *The Seven Ages of Theatre.* New York: Hill & Wang.

Southgate, Beverley. 1996. *History: What and Why? Ancient, Modern and Postmodern Perspectives.* New York: Routledge.

Spence, Jonathan D. 1978. *The Death of Woman Wang.* New York: Viking Press.

1984. *The Memory Palace of Matteo Ricci.* New York: Viking Penguin.

Sprinchorn, Evert. 1992. "An Intermediate Level in the Elizabethan Theatre." *Theatre Notebook* 46: 73–94.

Stallybrass, Peter and Ann Rosalind Jones. 2000. *Renaissance Clothing and the Materials of Memory.* Cambridge: Cambridge University Press.

Stalnaker, Robert C. 1967. "Events, Periods, and Institutions in Historians' Language." *History and Theory* 6: 159–79.

Stanford, Michael. 1994. *A Companion to the Study of History.* Oxford: Blackwell.

1998. *An Introduction to the Philosophy of History.* Oxford: Blackwell.

1986. *The Nature of Historical Knowledge.* Oxford: Blackwell.

States, Bert O. 1985. *Great Reckonings in Little Rooms*. Berkeley: University of California Press.

2007. "The Phenomenological Attitude." In *Critical Theory and Performance*. Ed. Janelle Reinelt and Joseph R. Roach. Ann Arbor: University of Michigan Press, 26–36.

Staub, Kristina. 1992. *Sexual Suspects: Eighteenth-Century Players and Sexual Ideology*. Princeton, N.J.: Princeton University Press.

Steinberg, Michael. 1996. *Walter Benjamin and the Demands of History*. Ithaca, N.Y.: Cornell University Press.

Stern, Fritz, ed. 1972. *The Varieties of History: From Voltaire to the Present*. Revised edn. New York: Random House/Vintage.

Stern, Tiffany. 2001. "Behind the Arras: The Prompter's Place in the Shakespearean Theatre." *Theatre Notebook* 55: 110–18.

2004. "Re-patching the Play." In *From Script to Stage in Early Modern England*. Ed. Peter Holland and Stephen Orgel. New York: Palgrave Macmillan, 151–80.

Stevens, Wallace. 1961. *The Collected Poems of Wallace Stevens*. New York: A. Knopf.

1957. *Opus Posthumous*. New York: A. Knopf.

Stow, John. 1912. *Survey of London*. London: J. M. Dent.

Strindberg, August. 1965. *Miss Julie*. Ed. Henry Popkin. Trans. Elizabeth Sprigge. New York: Avon Books.

Styan, J. L. 1981. *Modern Drama in Theory and Practice*. 3 vols. Cambridge: Cambridge University Press.

Summers, David. 2003. "Representation." In *Critical Terms for Art History*. 2nd edn. Ed. Robert S. Nelson and Richard Shiff. Chicago: University of Chicago Press, 5–20.

Tagg, John. 1988. *The Burden of Representation: Essays on Photographs and Histories*. London: Macmillan.

Tanselle, G. Thomas. 1989. *A Rationale for Textual Criticism*. Philadelphia: University of Pennsylvania Press.

1987. *Textual Criticism since Greg: A Chronicle, 1950–1983*. Charlottesville: University Press of Virginia.

Taplin, Oliver. 1993. *Comic Angels and Other Approaches to Greek Drama through Vase-Painting*. Oxford: Oxford University Press.

1978. *Greek Tragedy in Action*. Berkeley: University of California Press.

1997. "The Pictorial Record." In *The Cambridge Companion to Greek Tragedy*. Ed. P. E. Easterling. Cambridge: Cambridge University Press, 69–92.

2008. *Pots and Plays: Interactions between Tragedy and Greek Vase-Painting of the Fourth Century BC*. Los Angeles: J. Paul Getty Museum.

1977. *The Stagecraft of Aeschylus*. Oxford: Oxford University Press.

Taruskin, Richard. 1993. "Of Kings and Divas: Opera, Politics, and the French Boom." *The New Republic*, December 13, 31–44.

Taylor, Diana. 2003. *The Archive and the Repertoire: Performing Cultural Memory in the Americas*. Durham, N.C.: Duke University Press.

1997. *Disappearing Acts: Spectacles of Gender and Nationalism in Argentina's Dirty War*. Durham, N.C.: Duke University Press.

Taylor, Gary and Michael Warren, eds. 1983. *The Division of the Kingdom: Shakespeare's Two Versions of King Lear*. Oxford: Clarendon Press.

Taylor, Simon Watson. 1968. "Introduction." In *The Ubu Plays*. Ed. and trans. Simon Watson Taylor. New York: Grove Press, 9–16.

Teague, Frances N. 1991. *Shakespeare's Speaking Properties*. Lewisburg, Pa.: Bucknell University Press.

Terrasse, Claude. 1898. *Marche des polonais: extraite d'Ubu roi, d'Alfred Jarry, pour piano*. Paris: Mercure de Paris.

The Theatre, a monthly review and magazine. London, January 1880–December 1894. Editors: Clement Scott (1880–90); Bernard Capes (1890–92); Bernard Capes and Charles Eglington (1892–93); Charles Eglington (1892–94).

Thomas, Rosalind. 1989. *Oral Tradition and Written Records in Classical Athens*. Cambridge: Cambridge University Press.

Thompson, Ann and Gordon McMullan, eds. 2003. *Editing Shakespeare: Essays in Honour of Richard Proudfoot*. London: Arden Shakespeare.

Thompson, George A., Jr. 1999. *A Documentary History of the African Theatre*. Evanston, Ill: Northwestern University Press.

Thompson, Leslie. 1989. "*Antony and Cleopatra*, Act 4, Scene 16: 'A Heavy Sight'." *Shakespeare Survey* 41: 77–90.

Thomson, Peter. 1992a. *Shakespeare's Professional Career*. Cambridge: Cambridge University Press.

1992b. *Shakespeare's Theatre*. 2nd edn. New York: Routledge.

2000. "The True Physiognomy of a Man: Richard Tarlton and His Legend." In *Shakespeare and His Contemporaries in Performance*. Ed. Edward Esche. Brookfield, Vt.: Ashgate, 191–210.

Tilly, Charles. 2006. *Why? What Happens When People Give Reasons . . . And Why?* Princeton, N.J.: Princeton University Press.

Tillyard, E. M. W. 1943. *The Elizabethan World Picture*. London: Macmillan.

Tosh, John. 1991. *The Pursuit of History: Aims, Methods, and New Directions in the Study of Modern History*. 2nd edn. London: Longman.

Toulmin, Stephen Edelston. 1958. *The Uses of Argument*. Cambridge: Cambridge University Press.

Toulmin, Stephen and June Goodfield. 1972. *The Discovery of Time*. Chicago: University of Chicago Press.

Trendall, A. D. 1987. *The Red Figure Vases of Paestum*. Rome: British School at Rome.

1989. *The Red Figure Vases of South Italy and Sicily: A Handbook*. London: Thames & Hudson.

Trendall, A. D. and T. B. L. Webster. 1971. *Illustrations of Greek Drama*. London: Phaidon.

Trompf, G. W. 1979. *The Idea of Historical Recurrence in Western Thought, From Antiquity to the Reformation*. Berkeley: University of California Press.

Tulloch, John. 2005. *Shakespeare and Chekhov in Production*. Iowa City: University of Iowa Press.

Tully, James, ed. 1988. *Meaning and Context: Quentin Skinner and His Critics*. Princeton, N.J.: Princeton University Press.

Urkowitz, Steven. 1980. *Shakespeare's Revision of King Lear*. Princeton, N.J.: Princeton University Press.

Van Gogh, Vincent. 2007. *Vincent Van Gogh – Painted with Words: The Letters to Emile Bernard*. Ed. Leo Jansen, Hans Juijten, and Nienke Bakker. New York: Rizzoli/ Morgan Library and Musuem/Amsterdam: Van Gogh Museum.

Vansina, Jan. 1985. *Oral Tradition in History*. Madison: University of Wisconsin Press.

Veeser, H. Aram, ed., 1989. *The New Historicism*. New York: Routledge.

Vernant, Jean-Pierre and Pierre Vidal-Naquet, eds. 1988. *Myth and Tragedy in Ancient Greece*. Cambridge: Cambridge University Press.

Veyne, Paul. 1984. *Writing History: Essay on Epistemology*. Trans. Mina Moore-Rinvolucri. Middletown, Conn.: Wesleyan University Press.

Vickers, Brian. 1993. *Appropriating Shakespeare: Contemporary Critical Quarrels*. New Haven, Conn.: Yale University Press.

　1973. *Towards Greek Tragedy*. London: Longman.

Vidal-Naquet, Pierre. 1997. "The Place and Status of Foreigners in Athenian Tragedy." In *Greek Tragedy and the Historian*. Ed. Christopher Pelling. Oxford: Clarendon Press, 109–19.

Vince, R. W. 1984a. *Ancient and Medieval Theatre: A Historiographical Handbook*. Westport, Conn.: Greenwood Press.

　1983. "Comparative Theatre Historiography." *Essays in Theatre* 1: 64–72.

　1997. "Industry or Mere Accident: The Making of a Theatrical Event." *Journal of Theatre and Drama* 3: 103–13.

　1988. *Neoclassical Theatre: A Historiographical Handbook*. Westport, Conn.: Greenwood Press.

　1984b. *Renaissance Theatre: A Historiographical Handbook*. Westport, Conn.: Greenwood Press.

　1989. "Theatre History as an Academic Discipline." In *Interpreting the Theatrical Past: Studies in the Historiography of Performance*. Ed. Thomas Postlewait and Bruce McConachie. Iowa City: University of Iowa Press, 1–18.

Voltaire (François Marie Arouet). 1759. *An Essay on Universal History, the Manners, and Spirit of Nations*. 2nd edn, revised by the author. London: J. Nourse.

Wallace, Charles W. 1969. *The First London Theatre: Materials for a History*. New York: B. Blom.

Walton, J. Michael. 1984. *The Greek Sense of Theatre*. New York: Methuen.

　1980. *Greek Theatre Practices*. Westport, Conn.: Greenwood Press.

Warburg, Aby. 1995. *Images from the Region of the Pueblo Indians of North America*. Trans. Michael P. Steinberg. Ithaca, N.Y.: Cornell University Press.

　1999. *The Renewal of Pagan Antiquity: Contributions to the History of the European Renaissance*. Los Angeles: Getty Research Institute for the History of Art and the Humanities.

Webster, T. B. L. 1970. *Greek Theatre Production*. 2nd edn. London: Methuen.

　1995. *Monuments Illustrating New Comedy*. 2 vols. 3rd edn., revised and enlarged by J. R. Green and A. Seeberg. London: Institute of Classical Studies.

　1978. *Monuments Illustrating Old and Middle Comedy*. 2nd, enlarged edition by J. R. Green. London: Institute of Classical Studies.

　1967. *Monuments Illustrating Tragedy and Satyr Play*. 2nd edn. London: Institute of Classical Studies.

Weimann, Robert. 2000. *Author's Pen and Actor's Voice: Playing and Writing in Shakespeare's Theatre*. Cambridge: Cambridge University Press.

　1978. *Shakespeare and the Popular Tradition in the Theatre*. Ed. Robert Schwartz. Baltimore: Johns Hopkins University Press.

1984. *Structure and Society in Literary History, Studies in the History and Theory of Historical Criticism.* Expanded edn. Baltimore: Johns Hopkins University Press.

Weiner, Albert B. 1961. "Elizabethan Interior and Aloft Scenes: A Speculative Essay." *Theatre Survey* 2: 15–34.

Wells, Stanley, ed. 1990. *Shakespeare: A Bibliographical Guide.* New edn. Oxford: Clarendon Press.

Wells, Stanley and Gary Taylor, with John Jowett and William Montgomery. 1997. *William Shakespeare: A Textual Companion.* Reprinted with corrections, New York: W. W. Norton.

Wellwarth, George. 1971. *The Theatre of Protest and Paradox.* New York: New York University Press.

Werstine, Paul. 1982. *Cases and Compositors in the Shakespeare First Folio Comedies.* Charlottesville: University of Virginia Press.

1999. "A Century of 'Bad' Shakespeare Quartos." *Shakespeare Quarterly* 50: 310–33.

1997. "Plays in Manuscript." In *A New History of Early English Drama.* Ed. John D. Cox and David Scott Kastan. New York: Columbia University Press, 481–98.

1995. "Shakespeare." In *Scholarly Editing: A Guide to Research.* Ed. D. C. Greetham. New York: Modern Language Association, 253–82.

West, M. L. 1992. *Ancient Greek Music.* Oxford: Oxford University Press.

West, Shearer. 1991. *The Image of the Actor: Verbal and Visual Representations in the Age of Garrick and Kemble.* London: Pinter.

West, William N. 2002. *Theatres and Encyclopedias in Early Modern Europe.* Cambridge: Cambridge University Press.

White, Hayden. 1987. *The Content of the Form: Narrative Discourse and Historical Representation.* Baltimore: Johns Hopkins University Press.

2002. "Foreword." In Reinhart Kosseleck. *The Practice of Conceptual History.* Trans. Todd Samuel Presuer *et al.* Stanford, Calif.: Standford University Press, ix–xiv.

1973. *Metahistory, The Historical Imagination in Nineteenth-Century Europe.* Baltimore: Johns Hopkins University Press.

1978. *Tropics of Discourse: Essays in Cultural Criticism.* Baltimore: Johns Hopkins University Press.

Whitebrook, Peter. 1993. *William Archer: A Biography.* London: Methuen.

Wickham, Glynne. 1959–1981 *Early English Stages, 1300–1660.* 3 vols. in 4. London: Routledge & Kegan Paul.

Wickham, Glynne, Herbert Berry, and William Ingram, eds. 2000. *English Professional Theatre, 1530–1660; Theatre in Europe: A Documentary History.* Cambridge: Cambridge University Press.

Wikander, Matthew H. 2002. *Fangs of Malice: Hypocrisy, Sincerity, & Acting.* Iowa City: University of Iowa Press.

Wiles, David. 2000. *Greek Theatre Performance: An Introduction.* Cambridge: Cambridge University Press.

1991. *The Masks of Menander.* Cambridge: Cambridge University Press.

1987. *Shakespeare's Clown: Actor and Text in the Elizabethan Playhouse.* Cambridge: Cambridge University Press.

2003. *A Short History of Western Performance Space.* Cambridge: Cambridge University Press.

1997. *Tragedy in Athens.* Cambridge: Cambridge University Press.

Wiles, Timothy J. 1980. *The Theater Event.* Chicago: University of Chicago Press.

Williams, Gary Jay. 1997. *Our Moonlight Revels: A Midsummer Night's Dream in the Theatre.* Iowa City: University of Iowa Press.

Williams, George Walton. 1985. *The Craft of Printing and the Publication of Shakespeare's Works.* Washington, D.C.: Folger Shakespeare Library.

Williams, Raymond. 1981. *Culture.* London: Fontana.

1977. *Marxism and Literature.* Oxford: Oxford University Press.

1989a. *The Politics of Modernism: Against the New Conformists.* Ed. and introduction by Tony Pinkney. London: Verso.

1980. *Problems in Materialism and Culture: Selected Essays.* London: Verso.

1982. *The Sociology of Culture.* New York: Schocken Books.

1989b. "The Uses of Cultural Theory." In *The Politics of Modernism: Against the New Conformists.* Ed. and introduction by Tony Pinkney. London: Verso, 163–76.

Williams, Tennessee. 1958. *Cat on a Hot Tin Roof.* New York: Dramatist Play Service.

Williamson, George. 1951. *The Senecan Amble: A Study in Prose from Bacon to Collier.* Chicago: University of Chicago Press.

Wilmer, S. E., ed. 2004. *Writing and Rewriting National Theatre Histories.* Iowa City: University of Iowa Press.

Wilmeth, Don B. and Christopher Bigsby, eds. 1999. *The Cambridge History of American Theatre.* 3 vols. Cambridge: Cambridge University Press.

Wilson, Peter. 1999. *The Athenian Institution of the Khoregia: The Chorus, the City, and the Stage.* Cambridge: Cambridge University Press.

Winchester, Simon. 2003. *Krakatoa: the Day the World Exploded, August 27, 1883.* New York: HarperCollins.

Winkler, J. J. and F. Zeitlin, eds. 1990. *Nothing to do with Dionysos? Athenian Drama in its Social Context.* Princeton, N.J.: Princeton University Press.

Wise, Jennifer. 1998. *Dionysus Writes: The Invention of Theatre in Ancient Greece.* Ithaca, N.Y.: Cornell University Press.

Witham, Barry. 2007. "Percy Hammond and the Fable of the Scottish Play." *New England Theatre Journal* 18: 1–12.

Wittgenstein, Ludwig. 1953. *Philosophical Investigation.* Trans. G. E. M. Anscombe. New York: Macmillan Co..

Wolff, Janet. 1983. *Aesthetics and the Sociology of Art.* London: George Allen & Unwin.

1981. *The Social Production of Art.* London: Macmillan.

Wölfflin, Heinrich. 1953. *Classic Art: An Introduction to the Italian Renaissance.* Trans. Peter and Linda Murray. London: Phaidon Press.

1932. *Principles of Art History.* Trans. Marie Donald Mackie Hottinger. New York: Dover.

1967. *Renaissance and Baroque.* Trans. Kathrin Simon. Introduction by Peter Murray. Ithaca, N.Y.: Cornell University Press.

Wood, David, ed. 1991. *On Paul Ricoeur: Narrative and Interpretation.* New York: Routledge.

Woodfield, James. 1984. *English Theatre in Transition, 1881–1914.* London: Croom Helm; Totowa, N.J.: Barnes & Noble.

Woodruff, Paul. 1992. "Aristotle on Mimesis." In *Essays on Aristotle's Poetics.* Ed. Amélie Oksenberg Rorty. Princeton, N.J.: Princeton University Press, 73–96.

Worthen, W. B. and Peter Holland, eds. 2003. *Theorizing Practice: Redefining Theatre History*. Houndsmill, Basingstoke: Palgrave Macmillan.

Wright, Georg Henrik von. 1971. *Explanation and Understanding*. Ithaca, N.Y.: Cornell University Press.

1983. *Practical Reason: Philosophical Papers, Volume 1*. Oxford: B. Blackwell.

Wright, James. 1876. *Historia Histrionica*. In *A Select Collection of Old English Plays*, originally published by Robert Dodsley in 1774. 4th edn. ed. W. Carew Hazlitt. Vol. XV. London: Reeves and Turner.

Yamagishi, Masayuki, ed. 1992. *The Henslowe Papers Supplement: the Theatre Papers*. Kyoto, Japan: Apollon-Sha.

Yeats, William Butler 1938a. *The Autobiography of William Butler Yeats*. New York: Macmillan Co.

1938b. *A Vision*. New York: Macmillan Co.

Zahry-Levo, Yael. 2008. *The Making of Theatrical Reputations: Studies from the Modern London Theatre*. Iowa City: University of Iowa Press.

Zarrilli, Philip B., Bruce McConachie, Gary Jay Williams, and Carol Sorgenfrei. 2006. *Theatre Histories: An Introduction*. New York: Routledge.

Ziter, Edward. 2003. *The Orient on the Victorian Stage*. Cambridge: Cambridge University Press.

Index

Johnston, Alexandra F. 93
Jonson, Ben 38, 199

Kabuki theatre 18
Kastan, David Scott 274 (note 17)
Kazan, Elia 60
Kelley, Donald R. 5
Kelly, Joan 166, 172
Kennedy, Dennis 95
Kernan, Alvin 202–3
King, T. J. 50
King's Men 33, 35, 204
Kirby, Michael 63
Knox, Bernard 152
Knutson, Rosalyn 251–2
Koselleck, Reinhart 10, 144, 260
Kostelanetz, Richard 9, 63
Kott, Jan 48
Kubler, George 187
Kuhn, Thomas 188, 259

LaBelle, Maurice Marc 69
Le Goff, Jacques 175, 195, 241, 260
Le Roy Ladurie, Emmanuel 109, 175, 241
Lessing, Gotthold Ephraim 163
Lévesque, Jacques-Henry 70
Lillo, George 211
   The London Merchant 211
Lindenberger, Herbert 171
localization 214, 220
locus 30–5, 53
Lord of Misrule 205–6
Lotman, Yuri 148
Louis XIV, king of France 160
Lugné-Poe, Aurélien-Marie 61, 66, 71, 72, 75–6, 79

McConachie, Bruce 8, 169
McCullagh, C. Behan 74, 228
McCullough, David 106
MacLean, Sally-Beth 51, 93
McMillan, Scott 51
Mackie, J. L. 253
Mallarmé, Stephane 83
Malone, Edmond 40, 57, 58, 252
Marcus, Jane 254
Marcus, Leah 205, 219–20

Marlowe, Christopher 31, 199, 258, 260, 261–2, 293 (note 10)
   Edward II 199
   Tamburlaine 31
Marx, Eleanor 235, 244
Marxism 11, 21, 100, 110, 161, 166–7, 181, 207–9, 211, 221
Master of the Revels 204
Meisel, Martin 16
Melzer, Annabelle 66, 76–7
Menander 158
Mendès, Catulle 74, 76
mentalité 100, 116, 174–5, 219
microhistory 9–10, 98, 146, 214, 230
Middleton, Thomas 214
   A Game at Chess 214
Mielziner, Jo 60
Milhous, Judith 94
Milton, John 160
mimesis, see representation
Mink, Louis 98–9, 106, 115, 175, 191, 260
modernism in the theatre 63–6, 69–70, 78, 79–81, 278 (note 11) (*see also* avant-garde theatre)
Momigliano, A. M. 1
Montaigne, Michel de 1, 24, 201
Montrose, Louis 207–9
Moon, Krystyn R. 241
Mukarovsky, Jan 41
Munz, Peter 114, 228, 230
Murray, Gilbert 152
Nabokov, Vladimir 239

narrative (historical) 4, 7, 9–10, 61–85, 98, 101–2, 259–65, 266, 267, 298 (note 54) (*see also* representation)
New Historicism 21, 206–10
Nietzsche, Friedrich 152, 160
Nisbet, Robert A. 107
Norberg-Schulz, Christian 46
Norbrook, David 201
Novick, Peter 2

objectivity 4, 6–7, 114, 263, 266 (*see also* documentary scholarship, witness, positivism)
O'Neill, Eugene 18

Cambridge Introductions to...

AUTHORS

TOPICS